AMERICA
BECOMES
URBAN

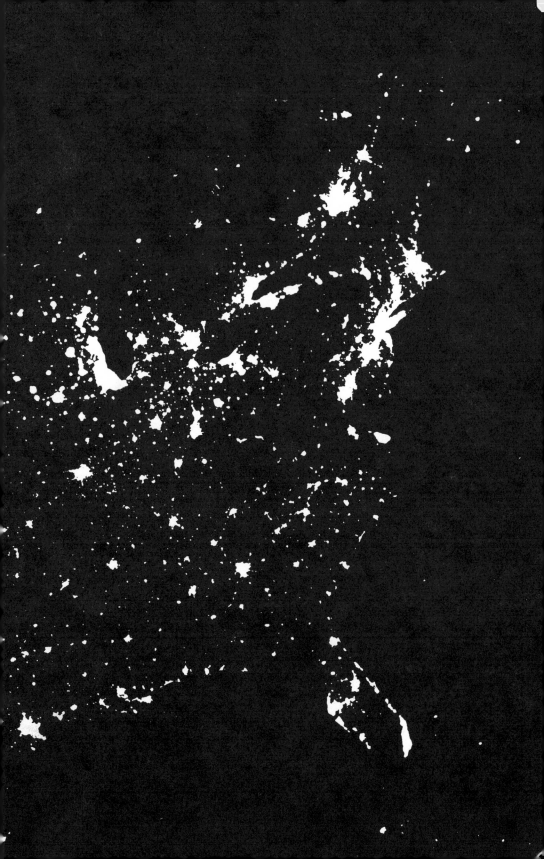

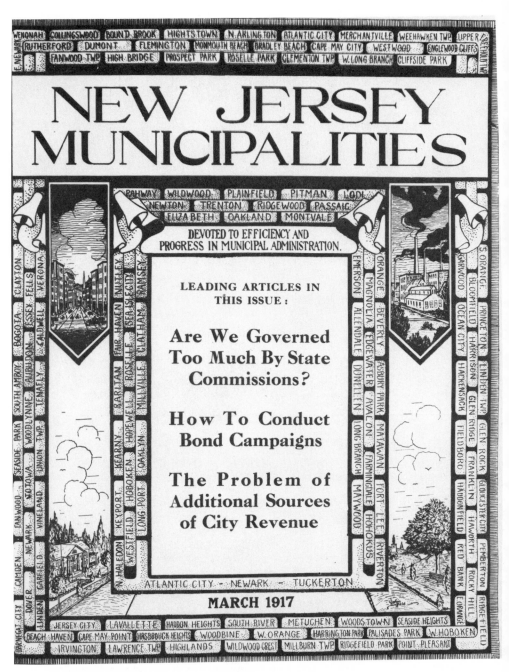

NEW JERSEY MUNICIPALITIES

DEVOTED TO EFFICIENCY AND
PROGRESS IN MUNICIPAL ADMINISTRATION.

LEADING ARTICLES IN
THIS ISSUE:

Are We Governed Too Much By State Commissions?

How To Conduct Bond Campaigns

The Problem of Additional Sources of City Revenue

ATLANTIC CITY - NEWARK - TUCKERTON

MARCH 1917

Municipal Magazines: *New Jersey Municipalities,* 1917.
The elegant art deco graphics of such magazines gave verve to the seemingly dull and faceless organizational machinery of cities. By communicating with one another, city professionals rationalized and made invisible
many of the necessary operations of city governments.

AMERICA BECOMES URBAN
The Development of U.S. Cities & Towns 1780~1980

Eric H. Monkkonen

University of California Press
Berkeley · Los Angeles · London

University of California Press
Berkeley and Los Angeles, California

University of California Press, Ltd.
London, England

Copyright © 1988 by The Regents of the University of California

Library of Congress Cataloging in Publication Data

First Paperback Printing 1990

Monkkonen, Eric H., 1942–
    America becomes urban: the development of U.S. cities and towns,
1780–1980 / Eric H. Monkkonen.
        p.   cm.
    Bibliography: p.
    Includes index.
    ISBN 0-520-06972-2 (alk. paper)
    1. Cities and towns—United States—History.   2. Municipal
government—United States—History.   3. Municipal services—United
States—History.   I. Title.
HT123.M63   1988
307.7′6′0973—dc19

Printed in the United States of America

1 2 3 4 5 6 7 8 9

Satellite Photo: USA at Night, Fall, 1985.
This dramatic composite photograph of the United States at night captures the location and nature of the current urban pattern. In it we can see the relatively fine web of cities east of the Mississippi, the intense coastal urbanization of the Florida peninsula, and the contrasting western pattern of enormous metropolitan concentration and little infill. The presence of Florida and the West make the whole image differ sharply from that of Europe, where, an economic historian has observed, a similar photo taken today would identify "the urban cores of two and even five centuries ago."

Source: Produced from U.S. Air Force Defense Meteorological Satellite Program film transparencies archived for the National Geophysical Data Center at the University of Colorado, Cooperative Institute for Research in Environmental Sciences, National Snow and Ice Data Center. Quotation from George Grantham, "Tracing Europe's Cities: Ideal Types versus Social Process in the History of Europe's Urban Growth," *Historical Methods*, 20 (Spring 1987), 90.

The history of American cities, though striking and instructive, has been short.

—James Bryce, *The American Commonwealth*

Contents

Preface

The American city: we think of the Manhattan skyline, of Chicago curving along the shore of Lake Michigan, or of the Golden Gate Bridge arcing into San Francisco. Or, if we think historically, we might envision steerage passengers, crowded shopping streets and fetid tenements, leafy boulevards and Victorian mansions. This book captures a different American city, a city epitomized by suburbs and freeways as well as high-rise downtowns. This city, the unglamourous place where most Americans through history have lived, is not the ideal city and does not even represent necessarily the kind of place where people should live. This city, where nearly all Americans today do live—sprawling, diffuse, varied—began in the nineteenth century. It is characterized by its nonvisible foundation, a political center around which its citizens have built the physical and institutional bases of modern transportation, welfare, and education.

The United States has two major kinds of government: territorial and corporate. Territorial governments include counties and states. Cities, on the other hand, have corporate governments, and their territorial bounds are not rigidly set. As corporate legal creatures, American cities are more akin to the business corporation than to other governmental entities. Corporations are purely legal entities, constitutionally protected "persons." A form of the private corporation, cities are "public" corporations and as such cannot quite do everything their commercial counterparts can, illogical as that may sound. But these limitations are not nearly as important to urban history and development as the similarities are. Just as a visual metaphor for the private corporation is difficult to fix, so is the visual metaphor of the city. For a city can "look" like Manhattan's skyline, or like some stakes driven into the prairie, or like Chicago in 1835. One reason we cling to images of Manhattan, Chicago, and San Francisco is that such images have clean edges, definite boundaries. Who could paint the edge of a city away from the waterfront? Yet anyone who has driven through the outskirts of an American city knows that the actual edge of a city is impossible to grasp in any kind of image. Is the edge where the billboards begin? Where the traffic gets denser? Where truck farms yield to auto wrecking yards? The visual metaphor just cannot be fixed. Thus the legally precise but physically elusive notion of a corporation helps define the city far better than any one image of a skyline.

From their corporate status cities derive a surprising array of powers. They can borrow and lend, build and destroy, expand and contract, appear and disappear. They can act to change things, including themselves. They are not inevitable physical manifestations of vague economic and social and geographical forces, but creatures—in law, "persons"—endowed by legislation with the power to act. The Constitution leaves much power to the states, and the states in turn leave much to local government. It is hard to consider the historical meaning of so many small loci of power, so when we think of political history, we inevitably think of national rather than local history. Yet, until the changes wrought by the New Deal and World War II, local governments handled almost all of the welfare, education, infrastructural building (bridges, sewers, wharves, streets) and regulation in the United States. Physically diffuse, the power of U.S. cities pervades the lives of their residents. We may think today that state or federal governments somehow hold cities in political thrall, but this thought in part arises because institutions, rational and bureaucratic, hide city power. Because they work as well as they do, we do not see them. Most people think of their relationship to government through income taxes, military service, perhaps Social Security. But local governments have determined the kinds of streets and sidewalks we travel on, the sizes and shapes of houses and apartments, their construction standards, the location and number of schools that educate our children, and the nature of the organizations that provide public safety. In a sense, the success of cities is that we do not have to know very much about them as corporate, political entities. That we take for granted the local bureaucracies that con-

Chicago, 1835.
This bucolic scene collects the geopolitical elements of a new city: con-
fluence of transportation routes and modes, a place to transfer goods, and
modest physical infrastructure, and the presence of the U.S. government
protecting market transactions. The businesses that have already begun
suggest commerce and information—is the flag flying over a post office?
But this only became a real city because of something unseen; its legal
status, which allowed it to act like a person.

Source: Keystone-Mast Collection, California Museum of Photography, University
of California, Riverside.

trol the details of everything from building construction to recreation center programs is a tribute to the hard-fought organization building of the past century and a half.

The history of our cities is, then, the history of how they came to their corporate status, what they have done with this status, and how they have shaped themselves. Our cities are what we have made them. They will be what we make them. Not everyone shares evenly in the power to shape and make them, and this is a part of the story. Also, a large part of the story must include those fuzzy blotches of light on the ground that air travelers see at night—the thousands of small and medium-sized cities and towns. It must leave a place for the auto wrecking yards that compete with tract housing developments for the suburban frontiers of twentieth-century urban settlement. The history of U.S. cities must show what makes them American, what underlies their diversity, and why they share more with the business corporation than they do with their historical, Old World, predecessors. And finally, the history of the U.S. city must show that along with the images of Manhattan's skyline, Chicago's shoreline, and San Francisco's bridges, the suburban tract carries in it a spirit that has characterized the New World city, even in the colonial period. All of these jumbled and contrasting images are the U.S. city, and none alone captures adequately the physical, cultural, and economic variety that their corporate identities have undergirded. They move, change, grow, decay, succeed, and fail, just as the American city itself.

Acknowledgments

I wish to thank first the dozens of librarians and archivists who searched their collections for my often difficult requests; especially but not only the University Research Library (University of California, Los Angeles), the Minnesota Historical Society, and the Wisconsin Historical Society. The Academic Senate of the University of California, Los Angeles, has supported various aspects of the research reported here for the past several years, as has in part a Fellowship from the National Endowment for the Humanities. Matthew Lee dug out materials for this project over a three year period, and more recently Sheila O'Hare has been an able and inventive research assistant. I have had the unusual privilege of working closely with the editors and production artist for the University of California Press and know that the book is the better for this support: Stanley Holwitz has born with my enthusiasms for nearly a decade, Shirley Warren has kept the whole book together, David Lunn has responded to my visual questions, and Kate Edgar entered into the spirit of the manuscript with her supportive copy editing.

Without the generosity of mind of several of my friends and colleagues, this book would have been far less coherent. The text has benefited from the generosity of several people who gave it their serious readings and subtle criticisms: in particular, I wish to thank Joyce Appleby, J. Nicholas Entrikin, and Terrence McDonald (who helped me rethink two previous versions), all of whom read earlier forms of the book manuscript in its entirety and who I hope would see in this book all their challenges met. For reading portions of the book and for helping me with specific arguments and conceptual points, I thank my wife, Judith Monkkonen, Jon H. Butler, Kenneth T. Jackson, Clifford Clark, Jack R. Pole, David H.

Fisher, Pat Thane, Scott L. Bottles, Richard Bessel, and an unusually detailed and thoughtful anonymous outside reader for the University of California Press. For the original challenge to think about the issues raised here, I wish to acknowledge dozens of honors students, Giorgio Buccellati, and especially Stanley Wolpert, who invented and then bequeathed to me a course on the city in world history.

E. H. M.

Introduction

The United States has become one of the world's most urban nations, but strangely, it has a rural sense of its own history. Because it lacked a single dominating, capital city in the beginning and because it still lacks urban primacy today—no one Tokyo, no Paris, no London, no Moscow—it continues to conceal its urbanness from itself. At the end of the nineteenth century, James Bryce, a Scottish visitor, was so struck by this absence that he devoted a whole chapter of *The American Commonwealth* to "The Absence of a Capital." "The United States," he observed, "are the only great country in the world which has no capital." Explaining what a capital city meant to a nation, he discussed the benefits of the "heaping together in such a place of these various elements of power, the conjunction of the forces of rank, wealth, knowledge, intellect." This missing urban element troubled Bryce greatly, for it accounted for the diffuse, genial plainness of the country. He finally concluded that the loss of a capital city's advantages exceeded the gain afforded by the widespread distribution of its cultural and economic virtues throughout many cities. He hoped, but with little conviction, that "local independence" might in return produce future benefits.[1]

As a consequence, the United States is urban but not urbane. I wish to amend this partial, rural self-understanding through a study that implicitly addresses the history of U.S. cities from a world historical context. This history is about U.S. cities; thus it compares indirectly. It is designed to account for the American side of the differences between cities of Western Europe and the United States which are so apparent in the late twentieth century but which had their roots in much earlier events. In so doing it deliberately bridges several different research traditions, incorporating and building on "old" and "new," political and social, urban histories. A deliberate awareness of the city's long history and the rather short history of the United States makes apparent how the cities we live in are much closer in kind to those of a century ago than they are to virtually all the rest of cities in history. We are at once a more urban nation and a nation with a different kind of "urban" than we sometimes realize.

This book falls between the comprehensive textbook and the more substantively focused scholarly monograph. In spirit, though not content, it owes much to the late nineteenth-century American social scientist, Adna F. Weber. It builds upon the specialized work produced by urban historians in the past two decades. The notes indicate, if only slightly, the depth, complexity, and specialization of this corpus, which has been accessible mainly to subspecialists. There are clusters of historians specializing in urban pavements, urban finance, urban reform, urban women, urban blacks, urban crime, urban mobility (written by both geographers and social historians), urban government, urban education, and urban society. And, of course, many individual cities—notably Boston, Philadelphia, New York, San Francisco, Los Angeles, and Milwaukee—have dozens of specialists. Los Angeles alone has a thick reference book of nothing but bibliographic citations to books and articles about its history. In addition to these varied specialist literatures, a rich lode of individual city biographies—a branch of local history which began in the late nineteenth century and still thrives—blesses the historian of the American city. These individual city stories contain a wealth of narrative detail and of visual evidence, and often convey a highly personalized, visceral sense of a city's past. The genre has recently been raised to a new literary status by novelist William Kennedy's *O Albany!*, which deliberately exploits the form to convey a sense of time and place for one "improbable city" (an adjective used, not surprisingly, for many American cities).[2]

Historians have much primary information about our cities. The details, images, visceral evidence, social analyses, pile up like the pages of a nineteenth-century statistical compendium. For example, the stereo photos archived at the California Museum of Photography in Riverside literally allow us to see the late nineteenth-century city in three dimensions. For example, one can position oneself on the top of a four-story building, and look down on early turn-of-the-century Asheville, North Carolina, seeing the downtown with stunning precision. But the information we have about our cities becomes cacophonous unless we know how to order it. This book is a guide to help organize the details of the city, from buildings to bread lines, freeways to flophouses. It suggests how to go about making the present intelligible in terms of the past, and suggests those aspects of our cities about which we should wonder. It also expresses my own appreciation of the way in which the social foundations of our cities require constant human energy and effort; that they require our constant action. This is an assessment well understood by policy activists. In 1895, Frederick H. Wines, an active reformer and prison official, in a fight to maintain the presence of the Illinois State Board of Charities, which oversaw county poorhouses, jails, and similar institutions, wrote, "Eternal vigilance is the price, not only of liberty, but of everything else worth having or preserving."[3]

In the post–World War II era, most urban observers have grown accustomed to analyzing our cities in a peculiarly passive context, envisioning them not as historically, and therefore humanly, determined, but as passive creations of vague "forces," in particular the forces of technological and economic determinism. It is important, therefore, to keep in mind that human action has been the principal force shaping our cities. When we hide our actions from ourselves—when we invent, finance, build, and make viable railroads, for instance, and then embed the railroad in our thinking as a causal rather than a caused urban feature—we create for ourselves the strange notion that we have come to where we are by some "natural" process unrelated to human history. History is about human actions, about contingencies, unexpected consequences, unplanned chains of events, and ungrasped opportunities. But when we are still in the midst of a dramatic historical process, that thought process that allows us to see things as technologically determined, as macrohuman, comforts us by deception.[4]

A central historical precondition underlies the larger course of American urban history: timing. Richard Hofstadter emphasized this aspect of American development, reminding us that the United States was "the first post-feudal nation, the first nation in the world to be formed and to grow from its earliest days under the influence of Protestantism, nationalism, and modern capitalist enterprise."[5] This aspect of historical timing meant that by the nineteenth century, when United States city formation began in earnest, cities began building under the protective aegis of the nation state, which in its grasp for political power assumed the cost and management of the military. Cities were freed to be more than fortified, mercantile warehouses, to design themselves as service oriented, debt financed, growth (and therefore capital) promoting, economic (not social) centers.

In both structure and form the modern American city was born in the nineteenth century, a century of dramatic transformation on practically every front. The temptation to the retrospective analyst is to see the city as a passive respondent to other larger changes, rather than an initiator of change. From the functionalist point of view, the urban promoters, politicians, and citizens, inventing and implementing the urban institutions that actually accomplished these goals, seemed to be responding to needs. And all too often historians have readily acquiesced to this causal analysis. Consider, for instance, the deceptively simple statement that "cities created modern proactive police in response to the threat of rising crime." This statement raises two questions. First, without the police to gather data systematically, how could one have known that crime was rising? Second, why should the city have responded at all? "Response" is an inappropriate word, for in fact the city acted, perhaps rationalizing its actions with the passive verbal construction of responses. The city's acceptance of responsibility for problems within its purview constituted a historically significant act worthy of our careful attention.

Cities could have chosen to ignore sewage, crime, unschooled children, and slow transportation by simply tolerating higher disease rates, offense rates, illiteracy rates, and traffic tangles. That there is indeed wide variation in tolerance between cities today illustrates that no "natural" level generating a response to problems exists. Instead, beginning in the mid-nineteenth century, cities chose to intervene aggressively in the local economic setting, intentionally creating what they hoped would be ideal environments for economic growth. By these actions individual villages, towns, and cities attempted to amplify their existing locational or economic advantages. Success, defined as population growth, increased the wealth of all real property owners. A conservative Milwaukee newspaper observed in 1887 that it was the city's "paramount duty . . . that she grow just as rapidly as circumstances aided by increasing vim and push and good judgment will permit."[6] The capital returns from simple population growth justified expansive policies for local residents. And the consequences of growth integrated the disparate activities of nineteenth-century local governments.

Because U.S. cities took their corporate status from that of commercial, profit-oriented corporations, they were able to act with few limitations other than their politicians' imaginations. The new, powerful, corporate borrowing privileges of the mid-nineteenth century set the political preconditions with which any incorporated municipality might create or seize economic advantages in unprecedented ways. Not until after the Civil War did local governments experience formal limitations on their financial activities. Their corporate status provided them the basis for both the minimal, regulatory city and the maximal, promotional, service providing city, allowing them intentionally to create the optimal environment for economic growth and population expansion. Unintentionally, these city-provided services have become the basis of our modern expectation that cities will protect us from crime, keep public behavior orderly, and cushion or protect citizens from threats to their health and welfare, both social and physical. These formal urban organizations made possible the orderly expansion of cities filled with strangers, conflicting ethnic and racial groups, and highly fluid and mobile populations.

Three Eras of American City Growth

The basic chronology of U.S. cities has three parts:

First, the premodern era, which came to a close in the period 1790–1830, retained a deep similarity to and continuity with European cities. Containing about 5 percent or less of any region's population, cities functioned as commercial and political centers. Although both the population and the number of cities had begun to expand, this era was quiescent compared with the explosive century that followed.

Second, the century-long period of local economic and population growth from 1830 to 1930 saw a dynamic and historically unprecedented expansion of cities—in absolute size, in proportion of the total population, and in number. Prior to this century, cities had been much more responsive agents. But during this phase, cities began to work out their new mode of providing services, acting positively in local affairs, and doing so as competitive entrepreneurs. Local governments financed two transportation revolutions, in railroads and hard surfaced roads. Demographically, European migration fueled a substantial portion of this expansion. When this ended prior to World War I, rural migration took up the slack, only to cease during the Great Depression, which abruptly terminated the era. The individualistic local underwriting of growth ended unpredictably and, equally as unpredictably, a reluctant federal government stepped in to support the end of a century of urban growth.

Finally, post-Depression cities made the innovations of the previous century permanent and somewhat invisible, by creating bureaucracies to accomplish the new services. New federal government actions during the Depression helped dissipate intense local concerns about cities. The subsequent federal period of American cities had its organizational basis laid during the Depression and World War II, and continued until the mid-1970s. Demographic change in this period continued to be as important as it had been earlier, with the very form of the residential city consciously reorganized around the burgeoning nuclear families of the baby boomers. Intracity finance of transportation continued the transportation revolution begun by cities in the late nineteenth century with hard surfaced roads. Thousands of intensely local governments built new, competing small cities on the fringes of older ones, continuing the expansion and significance of small- and medium-sized cities, cities all too often ignored by urban analysts.[7] The result has been the decentralized metropolis. Since the mid-1970s, the proportion of the population living outside of cities has stabilized, and change now occurs within and between cities and regions. Metropolitan spread continues, following the network of hard surfaced roads.

A Century and a Half of Growth and Its Influence on Thinking about Cities

A deep shift in the role of the city undergirded this three-phased demographic and organizational expansion. In 1790, the city was a passive, regulatory, noninstitutionalized, and voluntary organization, described in detail in chapters two and four. By the Depression, the U.S. city had been transformed into a very different, nearly opposite, model, actively providing a range of services; it is described in chapter nine. In its firmly established, modern mode, this new city foreshadowed the federal programs of the New Deal. Detroit, for instance, responded to unemployment by instituting its own extensive relief programs. But because the long swing of the city's growth came to an abrupt halt during the Depression, it could not successfully finance its programs. Across the country, expected increases in property values failed to materialize. Weeds grew in lots platted on these expectations. The crisis triggered massive tax defaults, temporarily undermining local government revenues. Thus the Depression closed an era of city building, both physically and organizationally, which set the limits to our contemporary urban world.

The benefits of simple population growth made a range of policy outcomes seem successful. Without the economic consequences of rising property values for generation after generation, local governments would not have been quite so able to combine conservative taxation with generous indebtedness policies and get the same benefits. These economic prospects loosened up otherwise cautious property owners, who knew that increases in land value compensated for the costs of city expansion. For instance, a letter written by a leading Milwaukee capitalist in 1857 explicitly made the connections between population growth and wealth:

> But there is another mode of investment capital here that is very profitable. Our city has grown up within 20 years from an entire wilderness—it now has a population of about 40,000 souls. You readily see how rapidly all real estate must be increasing in value. Many fine fortunes are made simply by the purchase of real estate which after a year or two may be sold for perhaps double its cost. The constant immigration, the construction of our system of railroads, and the rapid improvement of our farming lands around us all assure us that this increase in the value of real estate will continue for a great number of years.[8]

We have articulated much of our understanding of American cities within the context of nearly continuous population growth, the cessation of which usually brings local disaster. In the past century and a half the United States has changed from almost purely rural to almost purely urban, a process now virtually completed. New growth cannot be transitional in the same fundamental way. As a consequence, we have not come to grips with the historical departure our cities have made from their medieval predecessors, nor, subsequently, have we learned how to conceptualize this new kind of urban world. I come to these fundamental changes and intellectual problems from my own research, interest in urban history, which derives from both professional specialization, in particular the study of crime and police, and from a deeper need for self-understanding. I need to know why life in late twentieth-century urban America is the way it is in order to understand my own personal circumstances. This, for me, is what history is for: to gain in self-understanding through social understanding. And the understanding of society must come through history, both to describe what now is and to analyze simultaneously the salient features of how it got that way.

Much of this book is a sketch. It cannot pretend to be comprehensive. Thousands and thousands of pages have been written on the urban working class, on ethnic groups, on women, on racial groups, on politics, on disorder, and on a host of other fascinating details that have gone into the diverse past of everyday urban life. As in a pencil sketch, a line suffices for a whole, white space a background. The sketches and their frames are there only to guide the reader's imagination. The notes are there both to establish my own claims and to guide the curious to further reading.

1 ☆ Writing About Cities

A fresh rethinking of the history of American cities requires a brief excursion into the well-tilled intellectual landscape of urban thinkers and urban historians. Why have the most fundamental aspects of American urbanization—population growth, suburban expansion, growth of midsize and small cities, and the transformation of the city to an aggressive, service providing entity—been analyzed so little? To answer this question, we have to discuss critically three very different bodies of research and writing that have influenced our conceptions of U.S. urban history. The first is the best known to the general reader and is characterized by the work of Lewis Mumford and Jane Jacobs. I have labeled it the humanist critique of the modern city. The second body of literature is from specialized social scientists who have been analyzing the American city in great detail since the end of the nineteenth century. The most influential in this little-known group is Adna Ferrin Weber. I call this school of thought the statistical approach. And the third body of literature became a sensation among historians in the late 1960s, when it was known as the "new urban history." The names most prominently associated with the new urban history are Stephan Thernstrom and Sam Bass Warner, Jr.

Each of these three bodies of literature has made positive contributions to the way we think about cities, but each has serious weaknesses. Mumford and Jacobs, for instance, present overviews of the city that are both comprehensible and convincing. But with their persuasively crafted polemics, they present idealized views that distort any clear understanding of the much more complex historical reality. The statistical specialists, for their part, added a valuable concern for accuracy and logical consistency to the study of urban history, but because their approach precluded sweeping statements or grand visions, they have principally addressed one another. And the "new urban history" has almost faded now from the professional scene, its legacy of intense analyses of thousands of individuals having established a literature concerned with what seem like rather small issues. The result: urban history, like the American city itself, has been left centerless. This chapter discusses each of these three major currents of thought in order to clarify the problems and strengths inherent in any modern analysis of the U.S. city. For we cannot study our past without understanding the traditions within which we conduct that study.

The Humanist Critique: Lewis Mumford

Lewis Mumford wrote *The Culture of Cities* in 1938 to advocate a particular kind of urban planning. Strongly influenced by the teachings of the Scottish city planner Patrick Geddes, Mumford divided urban history into three major, technologically determined eras: the medieval city (the "eotechnic age"), the industrial city (the "paleotechnic age"), and the future (the "biotechnic age"), or what some commentators now call the "post-industrial" city. In Mumford's view, the medieval city was good because while it reflected some planning, this was an organic planning that had unfolded naturally. Like the medieval city, New England towns and villages and most of New York State around 1850 also met this ideal: an "integrated regional life . . . [with] a multitude of settlements, no one of which, outside New York, achieved a disproportionate size." The evils of the paleotechnic age, embodied in the industrial city, resulted either from a lack of planning or inhumane planning—straight lines, blank facades, lack of sunlight. The promise of a bright urban future in the biotechnic age would be in natural planning, on a human scale. Frank Lloyd Wright's writings best elaborated on the idea of organic planning, "using the machine but not dominated by it." Mumford loosely related urban form to social, political, and economic history, equating fascist brutality with the ugliness of straight lines, monumental scale, and insensitivity to nature.[1]

Mumford's work continues to appeal to readers, perhaps because of his authoritative style, best exemplified in the bibliography to *The Culture of Cities*, an impressive collection of some 700 titles in English, German, Italian, and French, annotated with comments and judgments which suggest authority and scholarship: "unimportant," "essential," "invaluable," "fundamental," and the like. A careful reading of his bibliographic annotations, however, brings into question many of his judgments. His citing of Thoreau's *Walden* and *Cape Cod* as "fundamental classics in regionalism" hints that the bibliography was aimed at listing books that were in fashion rather than those that might help readers learn about cities. If Mumford had read it and liked it, it was important. Moreover, the bibliography reveals an essentially aesthetic view of the past: Dickens's *Hard Times* presented the "classic picture of the paleotechnic town," dark, filthy, and ugly. Mumford dismisses the only scholarly history of the American city then published, Arthur M. Schlesinger's five-year-old *The Rise of the City: 1878–1898*. Of this first serious example of modern urban historical scholarship, now considered a classic, Mumford wrote, "as usual with historians of the passing generation, without a grasp of the city as organic whole." At the time he wrote this, Mumford was forty-two years old, Schlesinger forty-nine.[2]

Mumford's history, and his analysis of the present, consisted of a series of aesthetic judgments. The "massing" of industries made them ugly, but a factory where the blankets were bleached and shrunk in "the open air of a charming countryside" earned Mumford's approval. Should the changing urban world be judged by its conformance to our contemporary aesthetic standards, much less to the standards of one individual? Mumford, for instance, dismissed not only Le Corbusier but also Charles Eastlake, "whose dreadful incised decoration left its scar on both wood and stone": in a very direct way Mumford attached his values to the Arts and Crafts movement. He castigated the British Victorian city as "a junkheap of discarded styles . . . the solidification of chaos." By refusing to admit any standard other than his own, Mumford became ahistorical. Robert Venturi and Denise Scott Brown have shown how much the nature of the urban aesthetic continues to change: Victorian clutter, Eastlake-style decoration, and now even Las Vegas kitsch can fade in and out of style. By claiming the aesthetic territory he did, Mumford precluded any sense of historical change or analysis, save that of what charmed him and what did not. This gave his work a dual appeal; first his confidence and authoritative dicta comforted their readers. Second, although (unlike Mumford) we now favor Victoriana, much of what Mumford liked has continued to appeal to twentieth-century observers—medieval cities or their elegant remains, the architecture of Frank Lloyd Wright, wilderness conservation and urban greenbelts. Yet an examination of the pictures in Mumford's book also should give one pause: the large apartment blocks of which he so approved, and showed in aerial photographs, seem now to be little different from the monumental fascist architecture he so despised. Mumford's aesthetic insisted on a sculptural sense of mass housing, on buildings designed to look planned, but at the same time, not too regular or too square.[3]

Mumford idealized the small town and walled city; spreading metropolitan areas of the United States in the nineteenth and twentieth century, in his words, "stretch over the countryside in an amorphous blob." Thus he emphasized the importance of the visual, and anathematized cities without sharply demarcated visual boundaries. This he made clear in his discussion of worker housing in industrial cities: even if Manchester, New Hampshire, and midwestern industrial towns were better than most, "the improvement was but one of degree: the *type* had definitely changed for the worse."[4] He didn't care whether there was running water or indoor plumbing or adequate living space; his main concern was how they looked. This aggressive intrusion of his aesthetic bias into an essentially nonaesthetic judgment also subtly reinforced a historical error in Mumford's argument: for industrial workers, the proper housing comparison should have been with rural cottage housing, in which almost all medieval workers lived, not with the rare few who dwelt in the medieval city.

These aesthetic standards caused Mumford to reject visionary plans like those of Frank Lloyd Wright. Mumford adored Wright's organic architecture for the detached home, but felt that he went too far in his idealized plan of an automobile suburb, Broadacre City, which was too square and too spread out for Mumford's visual sense. Mumford's definition of chaos, of what did not cohere visually, was a highly personal one. The architectural critic Reyner Banham's *Los Angeles: The Architecture of the Four Ecologies* provides a belated but much needed visual and aesthetic counterargument to Mumford. Through the eyes of its residents, Banham shows how an architectural critic can visualize and make order out of the chaotic sprawl of Los Angeles. Like Venturi and Brown, Banham makes it clear that the formal aesthetic of urban sprawl has lagged behind its popular understanding. "Disorder," "sprawl," and visual "chaos" are not objective descriptions; they represent instead the reactions of one rather narrow sensibility to the North American city.

By presenting his reactions as historically objective, Mumford managed to create simultaneously an ahistorical past and an equally unrealistic planning goal. His version of the past takes the physical object to be the social and psychological actuality. Mumford claimed that by holding the remaining "hollow shells" of medieval cities "quietly to one's ear, as with a seashell, that one can catch in the ensuing pause the dim roar of the old life that was once lived, with dramatic conviction and solemn purpose, within its walls." On closer examination, his metaphor seems as inappropriate as it is erroneous: if the seashell is the physical shell of the medieval city, then the slimy and silent mollusk inside would be the appropriate analogy to city life. The metaphor's ahistoricity is demonstrated in its description of nineteenth-century cities as chaotic: their inhabitants in all probability found an order in them just as freeway commuters find an order in late twentieth-century southern California.[5]

Mumford disliked the modern city, mass production, and machines in general. While this is an understandable aesthetic position, it virtually disqualifies his analysis of the past and of planning options. Nothing exemplifies this better than one of Mumford's modern "good" examples, the planned garden city of Radburn, New Jersey. The brainchild and "most visible product of one of the most innovative planning groups in American history"—that is, Mumford, Henry Wright, Sr., Benton MacKaye, Clarence Stein, and Stuart Chase—Radburn was built in the 1930s and it remains a charming, attractive, and desirable place to live. But Radburn's population in 1980 was only 3,000 people, and it did not have the status of an incorporated town. Had there been 501 fewer people, it would not even have met the formal census definition of urban! The model it did provide was for the small suburban housing developments and shopping malls (it had one of the first) which are so much a part of the decentralized, automobile- and freeway-dependent metropolis that Mumford hated. From the beginning, in 1929, Radburn's residents moved there, as one recently told a historian, because "being out of the city was what appealed to us at the time. . . . My wife was pregnant and we wanted to start a family in that kind of environment rather than in the city streets."[6]

Since Mumford sympathizes neither with urban sprawl nor the automobile, it is not surprising that he has often used Los Angeles as an example of the "anti-city." Predictably, he blamed the automobile for destroying the central city, and asserted that the abandonment of the railroad and promotion of the automobile was a great planning error of the twenties and thirties. Yet as chapter seven makes apparent, popularization of the automobile was not induced by planners at all, but the result of an innovation pushed to the fore by ordinary people who used it to expand the variety and distance of personal travel, not merely as a substitute for other forms of mass transit. Mumford, by distorting the reasons for the spread of the automobile, urged a forced return to fixed rail transit. Just as he hated the ugly furniture produced for mass consumption in the Victorian era, so he hated the form of city opted for by masses of ordinary families.[7]

Why did Mumford concentrate on buildings rather than the city itself as sources for his historical sense, on seashells rather than sea? Ask anyone who has been a tourist. Much of what we know as tourists, as visitors with limited time, ability, and knowledge, focuses on the physical city. Because of this necessary limitation, it is all too easy to make what might be called the architectural fallacy: to read economy, politics, and society through buildings. An ordinary stance for a tourist, this is a very poor way to understand history and an even poorer way to plan the future. Because we can grasp buildings, and imagine how to shape them, we seize that aspect of urban life in intellectual desperation. Just as it seemed to nineteenth-century reformers that the proper prison architecture would reform criminals, so it seems that we could make cities better places by simply making them more attractive. And we make superficial efforts to understand cities through the same apparatus. But buildings and their inhabitants are often wildly out of sync. Some ghettos of Los Angeles look like pleasant suburbs, while the desirable Park LaBrea apartments in the same city look like 1930s public housing. In their basic shape and to the unwary, luxury apartment towers in New York look just like awful high-rise housing projects. Renovated nineteenth-century warehouses make elegant inner city housing throughout the older cities of the United States. In Britain many castle keeps have been trans-

Public Housing: Pruitt-Igoe, St. Louis, 1974.

Hailed as exemplary high taste brought to the poor for efficient public housing, designed by an impressive team that included the famous architect, Minoro Yamasaki, the high-rise Pruitt-Igoe towers soon became the symbol for modern urban ills. Less than twenty-five years after construction, most of this housing project for the urban poor was abandoned, destroyed, and labeled an architectural and planning disaster, with the design of the buildings, in particular their high rise modernism, being most implicated. Critics blamed modern design aesthetics for the social and physical problems such buildings sometimes contained. Yet the original caption to the portion of this photo that appeared in the newspaper observed succinctly, "Because there was no maintenance fund, Pruitt-Igoe's broken windows let in wintry air, freezing and bursting the pipes, leading to the project's downfall."

Source: *St. Louis Post Dispatch* (August 25, 1974), 27.

formed from homes for kings to prisons to art museums, all the while looking much the same. Mumford ignored this point when he showed Fifth Avenue apartment buildings in New York and compared them implicitly to the dark, small, and nasty back-to-back houses of Leeds and Bradford.[8]

The Humanist Critique: Jane Jacobs

In his 1962 essay, "Megalopolis as Anti-City," Mumford reiterated and made explicit the reason he had originally connected the city with the essence of human culture: "the city once spontaneously generated . . . dynamic ideas"; it was the generator of human intellectual progress. The anti-city, therefore, was the cultural equivalent of "a nuclear catastrophe." The city, as Mumford defined it, was more than the sum of its parts, it was the growth center of human culture. Presumably at this point he parted with Thoreau. But he joined with his premier successor as city spokesperson, Jane Jacobs, whose book, *The Death and Life of Great American Cities*, has provoked as much recent urban discourse as Mumford's many books did somewhat earlier.[9]

Jacobs at first glance seems to be everything Mumford was not: she rips apart the garden city notion, castigates Mumford and others like him as antiurban, and reasserts the value of the great city. But her work is no less ahistorical; it depends on a special definition of urban and relies on a physical analog to social and economic relations. And most important in the context of this book, her work profits not at all from academic urban research. To present a firm course of policy, must one project a distorted vision of history? Must one see the past as concluded and assume that knowledge about it is equally conclusive? In Jacobs's view, the past is not so much an arena in which to conduct research and investigate human action, as a museum of completed and completely understood action. Thus it furnishes static, closed-case studies, like Mumford's seashells, rather than an opportunity to conduct living case studies. And the historian, in this view, is akin to the custodian of a small, regional museum, polishing the cabinets and keeping the exhibitions in easily viewed order. Jacobs, however, does not draw her authority from the past as Mumford does. Instead she employs a different rhetorical device: present reality. Do not, she tells the reader, look for illustrations in her book; instead, "the

Private Housing: Park LaBrea, Los Angeles, 1987.
Designed in the same era and modernist spirit as Pruitt-Igoe, these similar looking buildings house very different kinds of people in very different kinds of neighborhoods. But the building types do not create the neighborhoods. The visual comparison with the Park LaBrea apartments is instructive, for Park LaBrea's simple concrete facades could be accused of creating a barren, dehumanizing environment. But high rents, elegant grounds maintenance, and uncrowded apartments continue to make these buildings attractive to renters.

Source: photo by author; for discussion of the continuing attractiveness of Park LaBrea, see *Los Angeles Times* (April 2, 1987), II:1.

scenes that illustrate this book are all about us . . . look closely at real cities.[10]

Like a religious revivalist, Jacobs tells us that the kingdom of heaven—Greenwich Village, 1950s style—is nigh, and to enter it we only need follow her four-step process to salvation. First, get the right residential density. Second, get the right mix of land use. Third, get the right angles and lengths to city blocks. And fourth, get a good mix of building types and ages. Like most utopian pictures, hers is attractive, and because entry seems less difficult than to Mumford's, which virtually required starting anew, it is easy to understand her popular appeal. Her ideal also shares another characteristic with Mumford's seemingly opposite kind of place: just as his occurred in medieval Europe, hers occurs near the center of the oldest, largest, and best-off American cities. Her diverse, vital, lively, artistic urban community requires the protective existence of a major city surrounding and supporting it. Jacobs makes clear that her vision includes only "great cities," and that by great she means large as well as important. These cities include New York, Chicago, Boston, Washington, Philadelphia, San Francisco and, apparently, no others. As the next chapter demonstrates, such a formulation leaves out most urban Americans, who have never resided in the "great cities."[11]

Jacobs contrasts her vision of exciting public life, urban diversity, small shops, children playing, and vibrant nightlife with the dull sameness of boringly bourgeois suburbs or urban residential areas. Sameness, suburbs, middle-class residential areas, and large public housing tracts comprise her main targets.

One of the major pitfalls in the "great city" viewpoint is that it defines urban in a way that excludes the mundane reality of most U.S. cities and towns. It is concerned with the tip of the iceberg, not the iceberg. For example, Jacobs joins Mumford in rejecting or ignoring inconvenient counterexamples, those thousands of cities which do not look like cities "should." Los Angeles, whether one likes it or not, must be considered a major U.S. city, yet it enters Jacobs's book only as a source of superficial and stereotypical bad examples, while San Francisco supplies her with good ones. The South and the West do not otherwise enter her New York–centered arguments at all. Yet no doubt urban planners have paid far more attention to Jacobs than the millions who continued their suburban exodus as she wrote. Although she vehemently argues against urban planning for its mistakes, she continues to share with Mumford the basic assumption that cities are essentially dense physical agglomerations of multiuse buildings and inherently plannable. "Cities," she states flatly, "are thoroughly physical places."[12] This seriously misleading assumption, which underlies the Mumford and Jacobs approach, is implicitly antihumanist, for humans are thoroughly physical creatures but much of what they think and do is not accessible to a purely physical analysis. To understand society and its history by studying the human body would be a foolish enterprise, yet that is precisely what Jacobs and Mumford do.

At least one major historian has been influenced by Jacobs: Richard Sennett, who has taken up her role as urbane New York City promoter. For instance, in his book *Families Against the City*, Sennett fueled the anti-suburban debate by demonstrating that family suburbs were worse than boring, that they actually crippled their residents when it came to coping with the complexity of modern urban life. Focusing on an unnamed suburb of Chicago at the turn of the century, Sennett's book, based on research in the manuscript of the 1880 census, purported to show that families retreated inward, that sons of successful fathers slipped down the occupational scale because of their overprotected youthful lives, and that by escaping urban complexity, the families had succumbed to even worse urban evils, economic failure in particular. Since the publication of this book in 1970, Sennett has become a major New York intellectual figure, addressing in subsequent books such issues as the question of the civic-spirited "public man," of urban creativity. In general he has carried on Jane Jacobs's promotion of the Greenwich Village lifestyle. From both the message is the same: be different, be creative, be diverse, be just like us. Sennett's historical work has been rejected by some historians as riddled with hopeless methodological flaws and poorly analyzed data, but nevertheless it is appreciated as a brilliant polemic.[13]

An American Tradition: The Statistical Approach

The present situation of U.S. cities can be better understood by reading those historians who have a long, technically demanding tradition that bridges local history, law, and the social sciences. By the end of the nineteenth century, a solid beginning to the scholarly investigation of the American city had been established.

Among these early historians, Adna F. Weber, Richard T. Ely, and Carroll D. Wright contributed monographs or sponsored survey research which is still useful. Others have followed in their historical approach. None has been as self-publicizing as Mumford, nor have they been as confidently prescriptive as Jacobs. But caution is not always a vice. In the case of a subject as diverse, complex, and unfinished as the modern American city, it would be all too easy to show how lucky we are that flamboyant prescriptions have largely been ignored.

The end of the nineteenth century saw the real flowering of systematic urban scholarship. The scholars in this generation included, notably, reform-minded social scientists who believed that the primary vehicle for social reform was information, and that once the systematic basis for a social science had been created, all right-minded people would agree on the course of action. To this end they compiled masses of statistics in works which began the explosion of data gathering which has continued through the twentieth century.[14]

The next data collecting breakthrough came during the Great Depression, when nearly overwhelming fiscal crises mobilized probing and systematic empirical research. Again the motivation was to address massive economic and social problems through statistical knowledge, though without the earlier optimism that with numerical knowledge would come the obvious course of reform action. Some of the scholars of this generation, Arthur M. Hillhouse, Paul Betters, Bessie L. Pierce, and Arthur M. Schlesinger, produced the foundations of what should have been a continuing scholarly literature. But in the aftermath of World War II, their work went unheralded, partly because prosperity masked continuing urban problems. The baby-boom generation seemed unique, and many in it may have felt that previous decades had no relevant guidelines to offer. War, growth, and prosperity created a demographically and economically distinct era. A clean intellectual break with the earliest years occurred. Consequently, promising research agendas from the Depression era fell apart as quickly as the poor-quality paper on which the original studies had been printed. How could analyses framed two decades earlier, in the grimmest years ever faced by the United States, apply to the breathtaking new world of the 1950s?

The statistical approach to understanding the city, dedicated as it was to exact information and critical analysis of sources, expanded knowledge but limited the chronological scope of understanding the past. Post–World War II scholarship slighted the Depression era, partly because the data did not seem consistent with postwar data. New questions created new data for which no prewar concomitant existed. The vast expansion after 1945 in federal government data gathering and publication unintentionally encouraged research that concentrated primarily on the postwar era. Consequently, the most methodologically advanced work was not only ahistorical but it was based on the data from a few decades at most. The enormous difficulty of constructing any analysis that can cross the data boundaries of the war years means that research which does so cannot take advantage of modern theory and statistical methods, while conversely, any consistent data spanning the break will be so limited that the consistency may defeat all gains. Ironically, any research which does accept the historically artificial but empirically real boundaries of World War II is doomed to be built on an extraordinary era in American history. We are almost forced to see the Depression and World War II as periods of transformation, because during those years our information base was expanded so dramatically. A considerable part of the literature of social science is thus temporally bounded by unconsidered and essentially accidental data limitations.

One may construct a measure of the growth and consequent boundedness inherent in the statistical approach to the city from the Time Period Index to the *Historical Statistics of the United States*. This index lists, by subject, the time at which new data series were initiated. Not all series are equally meaningful, and occasionally one subject series simply replaces an earlier one. The total population of the United States, for instance, is probably more important to know than the population of places between 1,000 and 2,500 persons. The former we know from 1790; the latter from 1890. Moreover, some series were constructed by researchers long after the fact: many price series which stretch back to the mid-nineteenth century were painstakingly constructed by economists only recently. Nevertheless, the Time Period Index gives a reasonable, if imperfect, sense of the rate of expansion of information over the past two centuries.

The graph of new population data series in figure 6 demonstrates the three primary expansion phases in this most elemental aspect of official statistics. The first burst of activity, in the 1790s, reflects the initial establishment of the census to count white males in order to determine congressional representation for each state. The second burst, in the 1890s, represents the activity of the great nineteenth-century social data collectors, in particular the efforts of Francis Amasa Walker and Carroll D. Wright, both great campaigners for and administrators of expanding federal data collection efforts from 1870 to 1910. But this was not just the role of a few individuals, for the last decade of the century saw the flowering of the American side of an international social statistics movement, with which Adna Weber and Richard Ely were also prominently associated.[15] And the most recent burst, in the 1940s, represents the postwar refinement of census data collection. That so many of these most elemental series were added in two bursts, illustrates the limitations on any easily performed, consistent, and national historical data analysis. For as much as each new series may represent a conceptually significant refinement, it also represents another door to the past which is unlikely ever to be opened. The more finely tuned our understanding of the postwar era, the less probable any bridging of the longer span.

Given the trend toward practically more of everything in the United States since 1790, the growth in statistical information is not surprising. But the bursts are of substantive interest. We may turn from the actual number of statistical series added every decade to the proportional amount added beyond what might have been expected: that is, the expansion over and above the longer trend. This is done by looking at the residuals (the difference between the actual and predicted value) of a regression predicting the natural log (which transforms the actual number into a value that shows proportional rather than absolute size) of the total series for all subjects added every decade. In other words, the residual values show how much any one decade differs from the long linear trend.

This residual analysis adds some interesting insights to the actual numbers. First, it shows the initial dramatic burst of data from the census.[16] And then it highlights the continuous, aggressive expansion of data from 1900 through the 1940s. Data from the 1940s, which came to publication in the 1950 census, had the largest absolute expansion. And the 1940s is also the twentieth century decade that takes the prize for the largest expansion beyond what might have been expected. The exceptional data expansion of the

TABLE 1

THE PEAK OF MAJOR NEW SOURCES OF INFORMATION BY CENSUS DECADE,
1790–1960

Year	Burst of New Subjects
1790	Population
1800	–
1810	–
1820	–
1830	–
1840	–
1850	–
1860	–
1870	–
1880	–
1890	–
1900	Government, Labor
1910	Housing, Minerals, Agriculture
1920	Migration, Services, Income, Forests, Transportation
1930	Energy, Prices
1940	Vital, Social, Land, International Commerce, Communications, Business, Manufacturing, Consumer Activity, Productivity, Finance
1950	–
1960	–

NOTE: This table is determined by the year with the highest count in each subject, unadjusted for trend.

SOURCE: Bureau of the Census, *Historical Statistics of the United States, Colonial Times to 1970* (Washington, D.C.: Government Printing Office, 1975), A-4–A-9.

first half of the twentieth century represents the flowering of modern data-oriented social science, the result of seventy years of statistical work. This expansion has also provided a kind of natural limit to social inquiry, for the questions can only go forward from the first point of data collection. Each decade, as the statistical approach gained in power, it also became more ahistorical, ironically strengthening the humanist critics' interpretive bite.

Riding both the trend toward more information and the secondary crest of exceptional expansion, the post–World War II census additions, while not as unexpectedly large as those published in 1910, still reflected the most additional data of any census. In addition, as shown in table 1, with ten new statistical categories— vital, social, land, international commerce, communications, business, manufacturing, consumer activity, productivity, and finance—more new series were added in the 1940s than in any other decade.

One-fourth of all historical data series began in the postwar era, over half since the 1920s. And as each new series of data tends to represent newly formulated conceptions about society, so also each new series cuts off another avenue of social inquiry by creating a discontinuity in the data. Virtually by definition, the most advanced social research must be ahistorical. And research that tries to consider history must be periodized by the exigencies of data collection, rather than by the nature of the subject.

The precision ushered in with Adna F. Weber's *The Growth of Cities* has continued to create retrospective gaps and to make the sweeping and imprecise work of Mumford and Jacobs seem much more satisfying. As new research questions have been asked, they have often been able to be answered only for more recent periods, the unintended consequence of which has been to periodize or foreshorten our statistical views of the American city. The culmination of such foreshortening may be seen in such policy oriented work as comes out of the Brookings Institution, an organization with the highest social scientific standards. A recent publication, *Urban Decline and the Future of American Cities*, exhibits almost no knowledge of the relevant historical research, and in spite of a few graphs with pre–World War II data, focuses all too much on the post-1960 and even post-1970 period. And even when the authors do glance at historical work on urban crime, work which suggests that poverty does not in itself account for other urban social problems, and which therefore raises subtle problems for urban policy advice, they continue to make policy recommendations that disregard past experience.[17]

The New Urban History and City Biography

The 1960s saw a flowering of university-based historical research accompanied by both substantive and methodological breakthroughs. And of all the "new" histories that were launched in the 1960s, the "new urban history" probably flew the highest. It promised to use the statistical approach's tradition of exact work and detailed, replicable analyses to ask empirical and social historical questions about the American city. The work ignored the humanist critics as well as pioneers like Adna F. Weber. More specifically, the new urban historians rebelled against urban biography, creating a divide between two kinds of urban history. Each of these two different modes of thinking and writing embodies a particular way of grounding description, understanding, and explanation in concreteness and empirical particularity. One comprehensively tells the "story" of a single city, while the other analyzes thematic subjects, its geographical coverage ranging from a small section of a single large city to many small cities. These two modes—the new urban history and the city biography—illustrate the analytic difficulty that modern urban societies pose for historical understanding.

The new urban history and city biography, while satisfying in themselves, show no conscious or developed relationship to each other. Neither asks nor answers questions posed by the other. In certain ways this is fitting, for many urban observers, not only historians, are struck by the fragmented nature of the modern city. So, too, the historical research itself seems fragmented and lacking in a sense of self-awareness, of unified purpose, of historical continuity and discontinuity. Thus the concept of "fragmentation" offers an interesting insight into those who employ it, for as much as it may reflect urban disorder and chaos, it may equally suggest that the observer has failed to see order and cohesiveness, lacking the necessary perceptual conditioning to unify a set of observations.[18]

Beginning in the late thirties, the earlier form of urban history—urban biography—treated an individual city as an anthropomorphic entity with a unique personality, working out its individual destiny. This genre is best exemplified by Constance M. Green's work on Holyoke, Massachusetts, Bessie L. Pierce's on Chicago, Blake McKelvey's on Rochester, and Bayrd Still's on Milwaukee. Like individual biographies, these studies balanced the city's unique personality with larger external forces. For example, Pierce depicts Chicago as a brash newcomer to the Midwest in the 1870s, competing for business and commercial dominance with stodgy and slightly inept St. Louis. Filled with useful information, these urban biographies represent traditional historical methods at their best and are vast improvements over the hundreds of local city and county histories written during the last two decades of the nineteenth century. But these urban biographical styles tended to compress important archival research into the conceptual framework provided by the chronology of an individual city. Some have recently become even more specialized, narrating the history of one ethnic group or organization in a single city, telling, for example, the story of Italians in Tampa, Florida. Alternatively, some urbanists have taken this narrative mode and selectively applied it to a particular topic across several cities.[19]

The new urban history mode of urban writing implicitly conceptualizes the city as an arbitrary container of some socioeconomic activity, a social "process." The nature of the container, the city, merits no more attention than the theater design would in a play's script. This new urban history deliberately ignores most unique aspects of a particular city, which provides no more than a concrete, almost accidental case study site or historical laboratory. The most notable work of the new urban historians studies social mobility, examining the economic and occupational mobility of ordinary people in the nineteenth century. When historians and reviewers familiar with the more traditional urban biography discussed this somewhat acontextual history, they inevitably complained that the new urban history told them nothing about the particular city, only about social processes. Representing perhaps an extreme case, my own first book focused on Columbus, Ohio, solely because it met all my previously stipulated requirements for a case study site. Thus this mid-Ohio city, although very interesting in its own right, simply represented the urbanization and industrialization process, just as Cleveland or Brooklyn might well have done.[20]

Although the new urban history flew the highest, it also came down the quickest, apparently having covered little actual distance. Within a scant four years after the field's most prominent scholar, Stephan Thernstrom, had coined the term, he disavowed it in a way which probably insured the subject's renown. He essentially claimed that it was neither new nor urban nor history. If Thernstrom's *Poverty and Progress* in 1964 was the finest substantive example of the new urban history, his *Other Bostonians* in 1973 may be seen as the last well-known example of the genre. Although several fine monographs in this mode appeared in the following decade, they were based on research begun when the new urban history was at the peak or even still ascending its brilliant but brief parabola; and few or none were started after the mid-seventies. Each subsequent monograph raised the level of research intensity, and theoretical and technical sophistication so that the most recent examples, for instance Olivier Zunz's massive study of Detroit, represented enormous research efforts. What is perhaps most remarkable and telling about the field is that few of the historians most closely associated with the new urban history have yet published a second monograph, a delay partly explained by the enormous research requirements of this kind of history. Thus, in a very important sense, the exemplars of the movement have become exemplars of its demise.[21]

Where Did the New Urban History Go Wrong?

Where did such a promising movement go? There has been, after all, continued activity in other forms of "new" history. The new economic history is firmly established, with its own journals, and the list of subjects earning its scrutiny has expanded as new economic history moves through a rather careful research agenda. While the new political history has not become quite as entrenched, either as a method or as a subject, it and its practitioners continue to be active and visible. And the new rural history has proved to be a lively field, and has moved comfortably into an established journal, *Agricultural History*.[22]

First, a brief description of what the new urban history was. Because the field has generated its own extensive historiographic essays, this description need not be burdened with extensive exemplification. The new urban history started out by asking, "Was it easier to get ahead in the past?" and ended up asking, "Where did all those people go?" Its historians found that it was relatively hard to get ahead in the past and that Americans have always been a geographically mobile lot with something like half of any city moving on within a decade.[23] These empirical discoveries came from the detailed analysis of large samples drawn from census manuscripts, representing generalizations based on thousands of ordinary urban dwellers.

These two findings are quite important and have ramifications throughout the American past. Given the imprecise work of Mumford and Jacobs, these early results gave a thrilling sense of the power inherent in numbers. And as contrasted with the statistical approach's exclusive attention to aggregated information, the new urban history illuminated genuine individuals in their social contexts. But as many who teach urban history quickly discovered in their lectures, a little mobility goes a long way. A course in the new urban history which stuck to its essence—mobility tables filled with "climbers and skidders," exact analysis of the relationship of job descriptions and occupational status, the details of father-son occupational change, "intergenerational skill transfer," all in myriad cities, from Newburyport to Atlanta to Omaha to Roseburg, Oregon—became as stupefying in its detail as it was lacking in any arguments that could be transferred to other history courses.

The new urban history was in fact highly research oriented, possibly the reason for its favor among graduate students during the years when graduate enrollments in history were at their highest. But as a research oriented subject, the new urban history had two possible developmental paths to follow, and it did not take either. The first and most obvious was to make the methodology more subtle in order to overcome the interpretive problems created by hundreds of tables, which authors wearily referred to as "mounds of computer output." Such in fact has occurred in sociological mobility studies, where advanced statistical and mathematical techniques continue to try to attack the problems inherent in the tabular analysis and percents so favored by the new urban history. That the data analyzed by the new urban history are amenable to more sophisticated analysis has been recently demonstrated in two reanalyses of Thernstrom's data.[24]

The second path, also a path not taken, would have been to pursue the implications of the new urban history's research findings, that it was hard to get ahead and that people moved a lot. These simplified observations raise many questions. What does the concept of community designate when only a handful of people remain over any long period of time? How does a stratified but mobile society differ from a stratified but immobile one? What difference did this make to Americans? How did this differ from various other nations, and therefore for immigrants from these nations? Did the high mobility create a national identity in politics, or did movers quickly pick up local political culture? What difference did mobility make to organizational activity: did it give stayers an automatic advantage or did organizations adjust to a fluid membership?[25] A comparison with mobility research in Britain suggests that American mobility research was not, in fact, properly housed in history departments. In Britain, vigorous research on mobility is being carried forward by geographers, not historians. For geographers, the study of residential mobility is particularly important as it resolves several important theoretical questions relating to migration fields and spatial concentration. Occupational mobility is less important for this research, to be sure, except as it impinges on residential mobility. In any case, for the geographer, analysis of migration has been important for over a century, and British geographers have followed a research path that shows the genuine promise inherent in mobility research.[26]

Instead of following these obvious leads, mobility studies in the United States caved in to criticism, criticism that should have sharpened the researchers, not terrified them. These critiques argued forcefully that occupational mobility did not matter, for as a question and research agenda it violated historical sensibility. Rather than asking what happened, the new urban history should have been asking, what did the actors want to happen and did that happen? The critics claimed that the seeming objectivity of mobility studies actually forced twentieth-century academic careerist values onto the past. One scholar, Herbert Gutman, quoted Sartre to sum up this critical perspective: history is not about what people did but about what they did with what they had. Others argued that in defining those who had increased pay over their careers as "successful," the researchers were imposing their own values on the past. They argued for a radical relativism, where each actor would be comprehended in his or her own cultural sphere. The argument paralleled that made by ethnohistorians, who made similar demands on the writers of Indian history. Rather than defend these charges of cultural imperialism, the new urban historians disbanded. The timing of this criticism appears in retrospect to have been perfect, as the field was already in disarray. The new urban historians had had enough intellectual self-doubt that their critics were able to counter their arguments permanently, if prematurely.[27]

The sum of the critical attack was to condemn occupational mobility studies because they implied that an Irish laborer who stayed a laborer all of his life was not "successful." Because the study did not ask what he considered life success to mean, it was to be junked. This critique threw out the baby with the bathwater, and the great pity is that the baby's parents stood by and watched passively. The subtlest mobility monographs to be published, including those by Kathleen N. Conzen and Clyde Griffen and Sally Griffen, had been in press prior to the angry critical outburst of the late seventies. No subsequent studies of occupational mobility have been published in the United States, other than the two recent methodological articles reanalyzing Thernstrom's data.[28] Like a river flowing into a delta, one can trace the impact of the original new urban history into many rivulets, and could even argue that these many areas carry on the traditions of the new urban history. Social historians Olivier Zunz and Suzanne Lebsock, for instance, ask quite different questions, but with a research methodology that flows directly out of the new urban history—census and other lists of names, wealth and occupational variables, a single city focus, an interpretive dependence on quantitative evidence.[29] But the hope that a new kind of history of American cities would be written has faded.

Neither the humanist critique, the statistical approach, nor the new urban history has provided a lasting, dominant analytic paradigm. But from each approach we can take something. From the humanist critics, we can learn to define the concept of city broadly, encompassing the medieval walled corporate entity and the suburban village. From the statisticians, we can take seriously the need to use large numerical overviews. And from the new urban historians, we can learn to look for the impact of urban structures on individuals.

2 ☆ The Premodern Heritage

Compared with their European and British counterparts, American cities retain far fewer characteristics to identify them with the very earliest cities. In fundamental ways urban Americans live in a New World. Modern U.S. cities, both in their pasts and in their prospects, have a dual relationship to the ancient city. On the one hand, they build, change, and evolve in seeming contradiction to and ignorance of all ancient traditions, taking as their models only one another. On the other hand, until as recently as the early eighteenth century, they had at least one foot anchored in the ancient past.

As social and spatial forms, cities have had a continuous 5,000-year history. That is, for the past 5,000 years there have been cities, even though no single city has been in continuous existence for that long. Damascus, with the longest history as a city, is some 4,000 years old. Millennia of human experience with cities has made their physical forms, their social traditions, and the conceptual framework in which we comprehend them all an essential part of our culture. Most people "know" and have "known" what cities are.

A long evolving growth in the understanding and imagery of cities has been disrupted and challenged in the past 300 years. John Winthrop used the then easily visualized metaphor of a "city upon a hill" in his famous sermon to the early Massachusetts Bay colonizers to give them a clear model of their enterprise. His metaphor is not quite so clear to us in the twentieth century, but for Winthrop's listeners, it evoked an image stretching back thousands of years before Christianity. If he had said "castle upon a hill," our instant image would be close to what he meant, for he evoked a walled, defended city, busy and wealthy with trade, dominating transport routes and the surrounding agricultural lands and villages. The rise of the nation-state and industrial capitalism have transformed the urban landscape, so that virtually all the cities we know today differ radically from their historical predecessors. This is one reason Lewis Mumford could position the medieval city as a critical counterpoint to the modern city. Yet the way we think about cities is grounded in a history extending back well beyond the lifetimes of our own New World cities. To clearly see the city in its new forms, we must understand it in the context of the distant past. The very old and the very new must be held up together in order to build our historical concept of the city.

The Classic City

Social scientists have termed the simultaneous emergence of the city and writing, around 3000 B.C. in what is now Syria, the "urban revolution." This revolution was facilitated by two elements necessary to ensure a regular and permanent urban form. The first, a self-sustaining and self-conscious bureaucracy, represented and effectively implemented the power of the state. And the second, writing, enabled the encoding and transmitting of state power both across space and through time. Writing, of course, was most effective when generalized and exported at the least to the geographic perimeters of a city's influence. Without its writing system a city could not transmit orders effectively, remember transactions, establish or enforce distant property relationships. The state, a regular and organized system of finance and defense, had to inhere within the city walls, and the actual walls formed an important part of the state's working system. Without its walls, a city could not protect its inhabitants, its economic base, or its power to extract taxes. These two prerequisites for urban life, a state and writing, in turn fostered those activities we more usually associate with city life—religious leadership, intellectual advancement, commerce, warehousing, industrial or craft processing of varied bulk materials, and specialization in a broad range of human endeavors.[1]

The city represented privilege and power, even for its poorest and most powerless inhabitants. Until the rise of the nation-state, rural peoples always lived with an element of danger, whether from attack by bands of robbers, invading armies, or members of the local military. Additionally, the vagaries of weather, of crop failure, and of natural disaster always threatened. Rural life never had the variety, complexity, and richness represented by city life. In contrast, the most menial inhabitants of a city shared its military protection, enjoyed the benefits of an economic life more predictable than that on the outside, and participated at least marginally in the city's rich and varied life. The image of the rural took on the positive aspects so familiar to us only as cities became the dwelling places for the masses in the eighteenth century. Thus, in the western world, from 3000 B.C. until about 250 years ago, city dwellers constituted an elite class.

Once achieving its urban locus, state power could attain a high level of permanence and stability, which in turn enabled the state to exact taxes regularly on the surrounding countryside. We often imagine that cities emerged naturally as agricultural productivity increased and liberated a proportion of the population to join the urban workforce. However, recent research has established that a level of agricultural productivity high enough to support a non-agricultural, urban population had been present for a long period before the urban revolution. In fact, the best evidence hints that even preagricultural hunting and gathering societies have the physical potential to produce food surpluses. The technology of food production did not in itself create the capacity for city growth. Rather, political organizations enabled and encouraged technologies to support non–food producers—city dwellers. The urban revolution brought about for the first time an efficient means of levying taxes. City-based political organizations extracted surpluses from food producers, rather than allowing them to produce less and have leisure time.[2]

The urban revolution created permanent cities, and it also gave them their basic look. Walls were a fundamental and distinctive feature of the city, as necessary as people. Visually distinct from the surrounding countryside, walled cities looked like spread-out castles, which in fact they were. Massive stone walls and embankments made them defendable, and a limited number of entry gates ensured that relatively few officials could control and tax those entering or leaving the city. Because the cost of building and maintaining walls was enormous, city officials limited their circumference: hence city areas tended to be compact. Walled cities

/ 33

persisted as the major form of urban settlement until about the sixteenth century. That the appearance of cities changed so little in almost 4,500 years testifies to their efficient design and functionality. That it has proved so volatile in the modern era testifies to the city's new and multiple functions.

The Rise of the Nation-State

It may be argued that there have been no more than two dramatically different kinds of cities: the first, which incorporate the apparatus of the state, and the second, which do not. The physical shape, political structure, and economy of the first type of city cannot be separated from its nature as the state: centralized, rationalized, and regularized political power. About four centuries ago, the state began to escape from its urban base, leaving behind the modern city and changing forever the nature of both. Nothing symbolizes this split better than the palaces of the two Western monarchs who also began the political construction of the modern nation-state. Louis XIV built his palace, Versailles, near but not in Paris; similarly Henry VIII located his Hampton Court Palace near, but not in, London. In a sense, these two monarchs recognized the need to "capture" and appropriate the political and military power of the city.

This dissociation of the state from the city slowly beginning in the sixteenth century marked a significant dividing point in world urban history. Customarily the rise of the nation-state from the seventeenth to the nineteenth century is cast in the conceptual framework of politics and economics. But it may be more useful here to regard the growth of the nation-state as both freeing the city from its limiting burdens of statehood, and at the same time subjugating it to a state with often separate and conflicting interests and goals. A particularly liberating influence, for instance, was the greater flexibility cities gained once they no longer had to be large enough to support a permanent military. The only precedent for this had been almost 2,000 years earlier, when the Roman Empire had allowed secondary, specialized cities to develop, but the decline of the empire left such cities vulnerable. The rise of the nation-state achieved similar results: small cities, specialized cities, undefended cities could thrive. They invested their limited resources elsewhere than in costly walls. Nonhistorians like Mumford often link the rise of the modern city to the industrial revolution, even though historians of that revolution stress its rural nature; this erroneous thinking occurs because all these broad changes did have many interrelationships and because city history is almost never considered in the political context of the nation-state.[3]

This dichotomous world urban history has a demographic and economic analog. When cities embodied the state they probably never held more than 3 to 5 percent of the total population of their geographic region. When the state and the city separated, the proportion of people dwelling in cities began its drift upward. And although cities retained their power as centers of economic activity, particularly commerce, factories and industrial enterprises began to appear in the countryside, near sources of water power. Industry never had quite the same powerful ties to urban centers as commerce did, and an uneasy relationship between the two existed from the time of the earliest factories up to the present, when automobile manufacturers are more likely to build new factories near small towns than near large, "industrial" cities.

In other words, until the transition that had begun by in the seventeenth century and still continues in some regions of the world, fewer than one person in twenty had ever experienced urban life. It has been pointed out that the preurbanized world was one where few people ever even saw a crowd of strangers, much less lived in proximity to them. Today, in contrast, the number of people who experience solitude, or spend their lives in small communities where everyone knows each other, has diminished to tiny proportion. In some parts of the United States, the ratio of rural to urban dwellers has almost completely reversed the long-standing and ancient norms, so that in New Jersey and California, only one person in ten lives outside of a city. And 17 million people, a population not reached by England until the middle of the nineteenth century, live in the metropolitan region clustered around New York City.[4]

The Colonial Fringes

In the seventeenth century the North American colonies made their modest urban start, just at the moment when what might be termed the second urban revolution had begun. Like the first revolution nearly five thousand years earlier, the second had a political basis, one that used and encouraged technological change to create new urban forms, which in turn organized and perpetuated new forms of state. In the nation-state, the city finally became the primary residential site for most of the population, and agriculture became an industry like any other. In a sense, the city itself became a part of the technological and economic apparatus during the second urban revolution.

In any economic system not based purely on subsistence agriculture, the city has built-in advantages for many economic activities. It has economies of scale—the lowered costs of economic activities which can occur when performed on a large scale—and economies of agglomeration—savings which are made possible when economic activities take place near one another. For instance, a cluster of several or many waterpowered mills fosters specialists in waterwheel technology. Likewise, shipmakers who have access to nearby moneylenders can more easily finance new ventures than those who do not. City-based economies of scale and agglomeration encourage an exponential increase in communication and creativity. In nineteenth-century America, inventors clustered in medium-sized cities; Yankee ingenuity apparently did not find rural places as fertile as urban ones.[5] In the new kind of cities, change became the constant, so that urban forms, institutions, and populations reorganized quickly and sometimes unpredictably. Recently, for instance, the rise of "doughnut" cities in the northeastern United States—cities with abandoned inner cores—has reversed all prior expectations of urban shape; rarely before would one have found the city center abandoned.

American colonists began building their cities at a time in world history when it was possible to break sharply with the past, helping to assure that premodern forms of urbanization would not occur. Had the colonization occurred, say, in the thirteenth century, the resulting cities might have taken settlement forms more like medieval British country towns. But to the extent that the state and city were still intertwined in the seventeenth century, London, Paris, and Amsterdam asserted their metropolitan dominance over the colonies. Consequently, the premodern model of city growth never made a lasting imprint upon North America. And because the conquest and colonization of the North American continent occurred as an aspect of the creation of European nation-states, the colonies grew under the protective wing of major empires in a kind of stateless limbo, a rare circumstance. Within a few decades, the Constitution, although written to ensure a nation-state with decentralized power and to protect a land of farms and villages, nevertheless provided for the expansion of a highly urban nation. Jefferson's often cited antipathy to cities as "sores on the body politic" came out of this vision of a nation-state independent of cities. And when, by the mid-nineteenth century, urban entrepreneurs could avail themselves of the military and economic protection of a new nation-state, they did so with unprecedented gusto, quickly building a system of cities on a new basis.[6]

In fact, much as they might have desired otherwise, Europeans colonizing the New World could only partially replicate the world they had left behind. Their failure to reproduce their former urban environment exactly encouraged change and forced innovation. These deviations from tradition were to become important, even though up through the nineteenth century American cities would appear to be no more than inadequate imitations of the "real things." To cultures incapable of understanding the new forms of cities under construction, the innovations could be interpreted only as chaos and confusion. Almost from the outset the New World cities differed from the traditional city, which made them difficult for Euro-Americans to comprehend or analyze.[7]

Colonial City Form

Colonial cities did have to attend to self-defense. Most important, they had to have militias, entailing the election of a drummer "to doe all Common service in drumming for the Town on Trayning dayes and watches." Not until the constitutional government of the United States was established did they lose this responsibility. But colonial cities avoided the customary city wall systems that required costly capital outlays in the Old World. Certainly New Amsterdam had its famous wooden palisade, which gave the world a Wall Street. But this wall resembled more the temporary stockade of a military outpost than the full-blown walled cities its Dutch settlers had known. Eighteenth-century St. Louis, which the French fortified in 1780 with a ditch, wooden palisade, and stone gates, had some of the appearance of a walled city, but the wall quickly disappeared when the city began to act

SECTION (M) THROUGH THE DEFENCES OF YORK, S.W. OF TOWER 19

After Jeffrey Radley, 1969-70

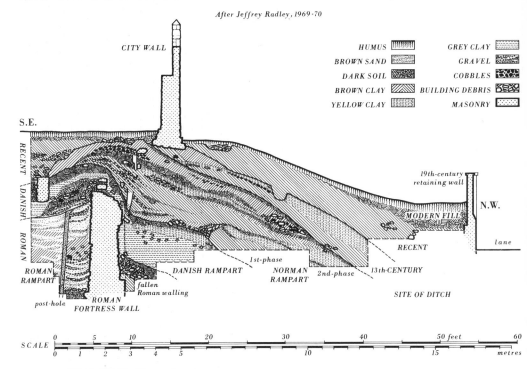

York Wall, Cross Section.
York's impressive wall, in this cross-section, reveals a succession of fortifications since Roman times. The diagram of York's wall suggests just how costly and formidable the medieval city wall actually was. It is no wonder that they stood long after they were no longer needed, even though their surfacing stone was valuable and thus often hauled away for other building purposes.

Source: Royal Commission on Historical Monuments, *An Inventory of the Historical Monuments in the City of York*, vol. 2, The Defenses (London: RCHM, 1972), 114.

York Wall Today
A tourist attraction in contemporary York, this photograph suggests the wall's monumental presence in a medieval city.

Source: Royal Commission on Historical Monuments, *An Inventory of the Historical Monuments in the City of York*, vol. 2, The Defenses (London: RCHM, 1972), pl. 41.

an entrepôt rather than as a fortified trading post on the hostile edge of the French empire. Using deliberately loose criteria, one geographer has identified a total of eleven settlements in the United States that had some form of fortification, but after the most generous allowances he concludes that the lack of influence of walls "may be a characteristic feature of cities in the United States."[8] Certainly no American city invested in the enormous capital infrastructure represented by the massive and sophisticated wall systems of British and European cities.

Max Weber in *The City* argued that the rise of the modern city helped foster a spirit of capitalistic individualism. With this flourishing came a concurrent decline in the distinctive cultures of individual cities and of individual identities tied to these cultures.[9] The liberation of the city from the demanding requirements of defense and autonomous statehood made possible a new and far less responsible role for the individual in the fabric of urban life. American cities epitomized this tendency. Throughout the colonial period cities decreased their demands on the individual as citizen and urban resident and created a laissez-faire economic and social environment. Dubbed "privatism" by Sam Bass Warner, this spirit made cities the stages on which individuals and interest groups pursued their own private goals.[10] The new freedom from the responsibilities of statehood thus affected the individual within the city as well as the city itself. One result of this increased individual freedom was an inconsistency and irregularity in the appearance of cities.

The absence of traditional city forms made colonial American cities seem ugly, chaotic, and scattered to European visitors. Colonial cities did not even have names for their streets. In addition to their confusingly unconventional appearance, these New World cities were probably even smellier and dirtier than their British counterparts. Poor urban families raised pigs, which wandered the streets. Though prohibited by ordinance by the end of the eighteenth century, at least in Providence and New York City, pigs foraged freely well into the mid-nineteenth century. They thrived on the garbage, and on the animal and human excrement in the streets. In order to promenade, the elites of Boston and New York created special parks in the mid-eighteenth century, where railings excluded the omnipresent pigs, horses, and oxen.[11]

Excepting those few cities that had temporary walls, American

Thaxted Guild Hall, fifteenth century

The Thaxted Guild Hall was used as a market and town hall for this small, unfortified market town. Market buildings such as the Thaxted Guild Hall make an appropriate emblem of the city's political and economic functions. Guilds and other groups of the city's governing bodies met in the upper rooms, markets could be held in the open areas, and often the buildings contained a jail.

Source: Royal Commission on Historical Monuments, *An Inventory of the Historical Monuments in Essex* (London: RCHM, 1966), 1:313.

cities did not even have proper boundaries demarcating their edges.[12] Ultimately, though, their very formlessness heralded a new era. Try as they might, they could not repeat British or European models. Even though their own image of what a "real" city should look and act like derived from English antecedents, colonial cities had to struggle to maintain even the barest of appearances. At the Newport Town meeting in 1712 it was argued that: "It is a universal and orderly custom for all towns and places throughout the world when grown to Some considerable maturity by Some general order to name the Streets, lanes, and alleys thereof."[13] The city had unnamed streets and to muster support for naming them, it had to appeal to its citizens' sense of world order and propriety. Neither reason nor tradition alone sufficed.

Colonial urban America's most important contribution to future urban development was, in a literal but quite important sense, negative. When the United States expanded in the nineteenth century, it had no ancient patterns of urban political dominance to stifle change and growth. Of the early cities, New York and Boston retained much of their preeminence, but neither retained exclusive rights typical of British and Continental cities. Neither had trade monopolies. Neither had extensive property rights beyond its boundaries. Dissenters of any kind could simply move elsewhere—and they did. Intracity trade competition reflected the cities' lack of broad chartered powers. Just as New England towns could not prevent political splits from turning into literal fragmentation, with dissidents forming new towns, New Yorkers in the early nineteenth century could not stop the upstart new city of Brooklyn.

Even when tradition was consciously followed, modifications created new forms in the colonies. Early city government often took strange turns. One case in point is the justly famous town meeting, which evolved from Boston's government in the 1630s. This new, potentially democratic form of local government derived from congregational church governance. Both mimicked local church and government in England, where the church vestrymen had administered much of the local law, and where the church governance had represented the village oligarchy. The transformation in the New World came from the rejection of the church hierarchy. The basic form of government remained, but the power now rested in the hands of all church members. Thus tradition, when combined with some slight variation in the composition of the local church, could create a city government quite unexpected in form.[14]

New World Urban Patterns

Colonial cities did exhibit a systematic pattern of dispersal, of spatial arrangement with respect to one another, but they showed no signs of the remarkable urban transformation that would take place west of the Mississippi in the nineteenth century. In the colonial period there were small but functionally important cities with a scattering of smaller places: an unpredictable array of settlements preceded the predictable hierarchical ordering of village, town, city, and metropolis that would come to characterize the nineteenth century.

Five important urban centers existed in the colonies by the early eighteenth century, each dominating its coastal region. These cities supported no carefully articulated network of smaller places: they tended to engross all possible urban activities. Until about 1820, for instance, Philadelphia's "preponderance hindered the growth of other towns." Only those backcountry areas separated by land (rather than by navigable waterways) escaped the pull of the big city and developed urban functions.[15] On or near the coast, Boston, Newport, New York, Philadelphia, and Charleston often had closer ties to London than to one another. Each linked their agricultural hinterland with London merchants and markets rather than forming a single American network. During the colonial period, each city's commercial and transshipping facilities reflected the individual character of the people and agriculture it served. From Puritan Boston to the somewhat more tolerant Newport, from Dutch New York to Quaker Philadelphia and Anglican Charleston, each city served as an undifferentiated service center, concentrating legal, mercantile, and shipping services and colonial wealth in a seaport entrepôt.

These colonial cities did not form a coherent hierarchy. As the geographer Walter Christaller proposes, one expects a mature urban network to form a set of interlocked hexagons, where urban centers of diminishing size, complexity and hinterland array themselves like a honeycomb around one another.[16] In such a system one would expect to find differentiated services at each level of urban settlement, with the urban network itself promoting opportunities for singular economic specialization. In the colonies, the economic specialization of nineteenth-century factory towns like Lowell, Massachusetts, for instance, was nowhere to be seen, with the exception, perhaps, of a fishing port like Nantucket. Nor, while there were some smaller cities, like Nantucket or Salem, did the colonial cities conform to the spatial and power relationships that would order nineteenth-century urban geography.

Modern geographers conceptualize cities as being systematically related to one another within a spatial network of social and economic ties. Cities, in this view, exist in mutual interdependence, exerting as much, or more, influence on one another as they do on the surrounding hinterlands. This systematic perspective of regional geographers apprehends whole regions of cities and towns as aggregates of actors, radically dissociated from the immediate countryside. "The most immediate part of the environment of any city is other cities," Brian Berry asserted in the early 1960s. The questions such geographers address, not surprisingly, have been mainly oriented toward nonhistorical problems and explanations, testing, for instance, various hypotheses explaining urban hinterland formation or relating central communications dominance to the advantages of central urban locations.[17] In some ways this approach resembles the urban biographies writ large, for the notion of a city as one actor in a regular system of actors is indeed anthropomorphic. By looking at cities as aggregates of actors we can build a systematic, descriptive account of the development and change in the larger urban system, though it should be clear that such a historical description makes no claims to scientific status, unlike regional science, which studies the economic geography of cities and regional city systems.

Within this systematic geographical framework the two basic modes of urban history may be incorporated: the new urban history, with more comparative and structural concepts, and urban biography, with its greater emphasis on unique locales and site characteristics. For instance, contemporaries made much of the rivalry between St. Louis and Chicago in the 1850s and 1860s. The major western city of the 1840s and 1850s, St. Louis nonetheless lost in the growth contest to what at first seemed like an upstart, Chicago. Both grew astonishingly. The population of St. Louis leapt from 16,469 in 1840 to 310,864 in 1870; that of Chicago exploded from 4,470 to 298,977 in the same decades. St. Louisans correctly read the growth rates as portents of Chicago's bigger, hence brighter, future. By the turn of the century, Chicago had expanded almost six times, to 1.7 million people. St. Louis had not quite doubled, to somewhat under 600,000, and it was already lamenting its failure to become the population center it had aspired to be. This decline continued and by 1980, the city's population had actually decreased to 453,000, though its metropolitan area was home to 2.3 million. But although they competed for railroads, immigrants, and business, Chicago and St. Louis also needed one another. In the long run, Chicago's port and market benefited St. Louis, even though St. Louis no longer occupied its preeminent frontier position. Both cities grew together, mutually benefiting each other through the flourishing network of smaller cities and farms, tied by equally thriving water and rail transport, which grew between them. Both needed smaller cities, towns, villages. And even the most rural dwellers and farmers needed the cities. One study, for instance, has shown how the farmers surrounding mid-nineteenth century Madison, Wisconsin, choose to settle nearer rather than farther from town.[18]

Schematized by German geographers in the late nineteenth and early twentieth century, the notion of urban networks has considerable relevance in helping us explore the dynamics of American urban expansion. Yet some of the more rigid theorizing of these geographers and location theorists lacks any historical sense and displays little relationship to reality.[19] Sometimes the models seem more prescriptive than descriptive, but they can nonetheless aid in historical understanding. A model that stipulates how cities *should* have been located, what size they *should* have attained given their location, and what their economic functions *should* have been, gives us some context in which to place the cityscapes that actually unfolded. The concept of networks does not so much attempt to explain, but rather to highlight and describe critical shifts in the structure of the city world, especially the kaleidoscopic urban changes of the nineteenth century.

There are two basic kinds of urban network. The first is not so much a network as a one-city system, with a primate city that dominates a region usurping all major urban activities and leaving an atrophied network of villages. Nineteenth-century Paris, for instance, contained the major financial, commercial, cultural, and political enterprises in France, and was the largest single place of manufacture. It had a population of over a million people in 1850, five times greater than that of Marseilles, the next largest city. London, ever an anomaly, dominated Britain and indeed much of the world in the eighteenth and nineteenth centuries. Although it never contained the heavy industrial and factory enterprises that we associate with many cities in the United States, its financial and mercantile services made it the center of the Western economic sphere. Primacy is not just characteristic of London and Paris: certain third-world cities today loom in disproportionate size and importance over all other cities. Mexico City, for example, had a population in 1980 of almost 15 million, six times greater than that of Mexico's second largest city, Guadalajara. In contrast, New York in 1983 was only slightly more than twice as large as Los Angeles, the second largest city in the United States. And none of the three largest U.S. cities—New York, Chicago, and Los Angeles—is a predominant political center, as true primate cities are. While Americans are often aware of the dominance of big cities, they have not experienced the almost complete dominion of a true primate center, which draws politics, economics, culture, and population disproportionately to one place.[20]

Metropolis, City, Town, and Village

The second basic network, the fully developed urban network, in contrast to the primate city's dominating position, contains four functionally distinct kinds of cities and villages, all spatially, socially, and economically interrelated. The network centers on the metropolis, which by virtue of its central location has communication and transportation advantages over other cities. New York City, for example, had developed communication advantages over other coastal cities by the late eighteenth century, even when Philadelphia was still much larger. This superiority meant that information moved more quickly to and from New York than to cities often much closer to the source, whether abroad or within the United States. New York maintained this critically important commercial advantage into the nineteenth century. In 1817, for instance, it took information almost 25 percent longer to travel between New Orleans and Charleston than between New Orleans and New York.[21] By the middle of the nineteenth century New York's commercial dominance was clearly established, but the communications advantages with which the city began marked it as a place of critical metropolitan importance.

In addition to its communications advantages, in an urban network the metropolis attracts any activity that is best carried out in a single location, whether the activity is military, political, religious, social, intellectual, or economic. The resulting growth gives the metropolis economies of scale and agglomeration. Therefore, economic activities that are more efficient on a large scale do best in metropolitan markets. Perhaps more important, the unique advantages of proximity mean that economic specialization and interaction can take place more readily in a metropolitan environment. The merchants' coffeehouses of eighteenth-century New York, for instance, epitomized these metropolitan advantages. In them merchants found shipping information, met potential trading partners and customers, and exchanged essential commercial information. By the mid-eighteenth century, New York City had a range of mercantile services that served shipping and attracted further business through specialized partnerships.[22]

Next in functional rank below the metropolis comes the city, symbolically mapped by geographers at the six points of a large hexagon around the metropolis. In a nation-state it is easy enough to imagine these cities as regional economic and political centers. The city has many specialized functions, lacking only those central activities which must be singular, a Wall Street, for instance. The city still offers economies of agglomeration and scale, though it cannot support the wide range of very specialized services in the metropolis. Thus it may have some specialized services equivalent to or even superior to the metropolis—medicine perhaps—but it lacks other specialized activities—international trading, for instance. Unlike the metropolis, which has an influence on the whole urban system, perhaps even a large portion of the world, the city has a more limited range of influence, extending only to that of the next city in the hexagon. This is why the city cannot have singular specialization as the metropolis does, for it lacks the complete communications and direct relationships necessary to have comprehensive and effective coverage.

Each city is surrounded by towns, again mapped as the points of smaller hexagons. The range of services and degree of specialization of each town reflect its even more limited hinterland, and hence more limited population. Towns may have some economies of scale, but fewer economies of agglomeration. One expects them to have few specialized services, though a town may exist only to support a specialized economic activity—a mining town, for instance. A town may do some simple processing of raw materials, but more complex processing goes to the city. Even the new factories being built away from heavily industrialized regions in the 1980s—the Honda factory near Marysville, Ohio, for instance—are essentially just assembly plants.

Finally, arrayed around the towns are villages, places that provide only basic goods and services. They may have almost no economies of scale, and supply only simple marketing, perhaps some legal services, and schooling. They serve a limited area with a range of very basic services.

If we imagine the activities of a mid-nineteenth-century Ohio farmer, we can illustrate the functions of this four-tiered urban hierarchy. Probably weekly the farmer would have gone by wagon to the nearest village for short-term supplies, perhaps market news, or to attend church. The village was a good place to talk with other farmers and get political news. There might also have been a secondary school and a doctor. Probably he would have hauled his crops by wagon to the village to sell them, for by mid-century it was quite likely there would have been a railroad spur or a small canal, and grain elevator.

Monthly, perhaps, the farmer and his family might have gone to the nearest town in order to buy bulk supplies, more specialized equipment, clothing, and household items. The town probably had a flour mill and a brewery. Certainly the town's merchants would have also supplied the village businesses, and the town might well have been a center for legal and political services. Perhaps it would have been the county seat, with the court house.

The farmer may have visited the nearest city only once a year. But the city's influence would have been pervasive, for it wholesaled to all the towns and villages, trained medical and legal specialists, had central exchanges for the sale of agricultural produce, processed agriculture products, manufactured agricultural implements and furniture sold in the towns, and performed a host of specialized economic activities.

Probably the farmer would never have gone to the metropolis, far-away New York in the early part of the century, Chicago in the latter part. But many of his children might well have migrated there, traveling first to the nearby town, then the city, and finally Chicago, in search of jobs. And the city and town merchants certainly made trips to the metropolis. More important, their economic activities were filtered through the metropolitan center. Credit for major loans, for instance, often depended on metropolitan bankers and credit-rating services. And the agricultural goods, processed in the city or in the towns, often traveled to distant customers via the merchandising and shipping of metropolitan concerns, which produced the ships, directed the railroads, and coordinated the distant sales arrangements.

Thus, although the metropolis may have been invisible to the farmer, the urban network's influence pervaded both rural and urban life. Often its influence was manifested in antagonistic attitudes, people in rural places critical of the city's moral corruption and artificiality, and urbanites cynical about their simple country cousins. But these contrasts simply articulated aspects of the urban network which penetrated both rural and urban life, influencing occupational and residential choices and providing the very fabric of national economic life.

By the mid-nineteenth century, what is known to geographers as the rank-size rule obtained.[23] This rule predicts that in a large region, there will be one large city, several medium-sized cities, many smaller ones, and a plethora of villages, so that as the cities decrease in size ranking they become more numerous. Rank-size ordering stands in contrast to the distribution within a primate city system, in which one large city dominates and there are just a handful of smaller cities or villages. Instead, rank-size describes the honeycomb distribution typical of the four-tiered urban network— metropolis, city, town, and village—that established itself in the New World.

Colonial Cities: Between the City-State and the Nation-State

The strange urban network of the colonial era was neither a portent of things to come nor a remnant of the feudal old world. It remained a unique and relatively static order which lasted about 150 years. In his pioneering study of the five major colonial cities, Carl Bridenbaugh tended to lump them together. In so doing, he unintentionally highlighted an aspect of colonial urbanization that

TABLE 2
RANK SIZE DISTRIBUTION OF MAJOR COLONIAL CITIES

City	*1690* Population
Boston	7,000
Philadelphia	4,000
New York	3,900
Newport	2,600
Charleston	1,100

1790 Population	Cumulative number of cities	
25,000 +	2	(Philadelphia, New York)
10,000–24,999	5	(Boston, Charleston, Baltimore)
5,000– 9,999	10/12	(Salem, Newport, Providence, Marblehead, Middletown)
2,500– 4,999	21/24	(Portsmouth, New Haven, Savannah, Hartford, Lancaster, Richmond, Albany, New Bedford, Norfolk, Alexandria, Annapolis)

SOURCE: Evarts B. Greene and Virginia D. Harrington, *American Population Before the Federal Census of 1790* (Gloucester, Mass.: 1966, 1932); Bureau of the Census, *Historical Statistics of the United States, Colonial Times to 1970* (Washington, D.C.: Government Printing Office, 1975), series A 43–56, p. 11, gives figures after the slashes, I can not identify the three additional cities. But they probably mean Richmond and Queens for 5,000 to 9,999, Taunton for 2,500 to 4,999; Bureau of the Census, *Compendium of the Eleventh Census: 1890, Pt. 1 Population* (Washington, D.C.: Government Printing Office, 1892), table 4A, 434–437; Jacob Price, "Economic Function and the Growth of American Port Towns in the Eighteenth Century," *Perspectives in American History* 8 (1974), 176–177.

symbolized its transitional nature, its temporal location between the millennia of the city-state and the coming era of the nation-state. Charleston in the south, Philadelphia in the middle, and New York, Newport, and Boston to the north all displayed social, economic, and locational similarities of theoretical importance, similarities that slowly disappeared in the late eighteenth century and early nineteenth (see table 2).

In each city, a commercial class dominated affairs. This class defined itself in relationship to the metropolis of London and to a larger world of commercial centers. In its very name, one of Boston's two major seventeenth-century coffee houses for merchants, the London Coffee House, identified itself with the metropolitan center of mercantilism. And into the early nineteenth century, the merchants of New York were an aggressively international group, both hosting their agents, "commercial exiles," and sending them out to a far-flung commercial world.[24] In the colonial era, the notion of an American urban hierarchy, of one city dominating the others, of competition between them for more business, never matched that which emerged later. So long as London and European cities dominated world trade, each American port related directly to transatlantic cities rather than to other U.S. cities.

In the colonial period, interurban specialization reflected little more than regional agricultural differences, from lumber and livestock in the North to tobacco and rice in the South. This suggests that uniquely urban economies had not yet begun to affect American city development. That is, given the economic advantages automatically accruing to cities because of their size (yielding economies of scale) and the combination of different activities (yielding economies of agglomeration) we would expect cities with initial advantages of size or location—New York or Philadelphia, for instance—to have begun early on to specialize and thus to have offered economic advantages over other colonial cities, even over distant London. This eventually did occur, but not until the end of the eighteenth century, when New York had begun to achieve its significant communications advantage over Philadelphia.[25]

That it took over a century for this specialization to develop suggests how different the colonial American cities were in their very nature from the New World cities of the nineteenth century. Truly the products of a time of major historical transition, colonial cities were the far-flung outposts of an empire which had as its center an ancient walled city—London—and which exercised primate dominance, though it no longer resembled a city-state, but rather a nation-state. Nothing makes this more evident than the lack of a single primate city at the beginning of the eighteenth century, or the communications dominance which New York achieved while still smaller than Philadelphia. England's colonial outposts in North America would eventually recreate the nation-state, but for U.S. cities there would be an enduring difference: the walls, traditions, and primacy of London would never take root in the North American urban scene.[26]

When one looks within colonial cities, their somewhat anomalous transitional status becomes even more evident, for they lacked the powerful guilds of English cities, but had not yet developed various newer modes of organizing power. In fact, in many ways they resembled English villages in their governance. No American city ever had the independence of cities with ancient charters, like London. The charters of many British cities, deriving from the early Middle Ages, gave them independence from state interference which lasted well into the period of the nation-state, though in somewhat diminished form as urban expansion occurred outside the old corporate boundaries.

London, and other chartered British cities, derived independence from their corporate status, which provided members of the corporation—the mayor, council members and various guilds—with highly concentrated power. By the eighteenth century London's corporate holdings and power expanded for miles around the chartered City. The powers of the City, itself only a mile square, extended well beyond the bounds of the old city walls, compounding the problems of governance, provision of services, and power. By the early nineteenth century, the Corporation of the City of London regulated Thames shipping for eighty miles, collected coal duties over a radius of twelve miles, and monopolized market rights over a seven-mile area. It vigorously protected these privileges, frustrating the governance of the metropolitan area, which extended for miles beyond the medieval city.[27]

American colonial cities, however, were able to act much more independently than many of the newer English manufacturing cities, which, like Manchester and Birmingham, lacked ancient charters and therefore had subordinate legal and political status. Their lack of any meaningful self-government contrasted dramatically with a London or Liverpool's independence. In the nineteenth century, the manufacturing elites of England's industrial cities had to struggle to achieve some political autonomy in order to accomplish the most modest aspects of urban governance. For instance, legislation in the 1830s authorizing English cities to create their own police forces affected neither Birmingham nor Manchester, where old manorial authorities resisted local efforts to create modern police forces.[28]

The powers of ancient charters, exerting significant constraints on nineteenth-century urban settlements, never seriously frustrated American cities. One might say, as historians used to say of the colonies themselves, that colonial American cities developed under conditions of benign neglect, for the political relationship of importance was between individual colonies and London. In colonial America, agricultural land defined wealth and status. Those who achieved urban wealth, like Boston merchant Thomas Hutchinson or the merchants of Salem and Charles Town, used their wealth to buy land, the "real" wealth of the colonies.[29] Their image of a proper city still looked back to the medieval city or to a world metropolis like London, to their formal pomp and visual displays of power in processions, costume, and legal jurisdiction—things that were clearly lacking in colonial cities.

Small places like Boston or New York were neither powerful enough to threaten the independent power of the colonial legislatures nor economically central enough to be seen as something special. Yet even in the seventeenth and eighteenth centuries they actually were quite special, more so than the English provincial capitals with which their size and economic functions compare.[30] In retrospect it easy enough to see New York's natural economic advantages: its central coastal location, its year-round deep water harbor, and the Hudson River tapping a rich hinterland.[31] To see New York this way comes easily now because we no longer consider the east coast of North America as the trading fringe of a world centered in London, Amsterdam, or Paris. But in the seventeenth century, New York was, like Boston and other colonial cities, a colony planted on the edge of the wilderness, on the extreme edge of the world, underrated and ignored.[32] Today, the only comparable human colonizations would be those in Antarctica or perhaps those proposed for the moon.

The Legacy of Colonial Cities

For twentieth-century urban America, the colonial period's major political and legal significance can be termed negative. The actual foundations of colonial cities did not provide models or even guides for what was to come, even though the colonists tried to reproduce their legal and political heritage. But, in their failure to reproduce European precedents, they provided a legal and political tabula rasa. The modern U.S. city does not have a linear, direct, or mechanical relationship to its colonial predecessors. But underlying conceptions that ended up making a significant difference to nineteenth- and twentieth-century urban development can be traced back to the colonial era. These legal and political ideas preceded even the barest hint of the modern city, demonstrating one of the themes of this book, that the foundations of modern U.S. cities were created unintentionally. These legal foundations were not conceived with the intention of buttressing the entrepreneurial cities of the nineteenth century or the bureaucratized entities of the twentieth century. Rather, they were conceived by a society in the cultural and intellectual center but on the physical fringe of Europe. The ancient city's heritage simply could not have very much impact in the New World.

When nineteenth-century Americans celebrated their escape from the feudal grip of Europe, they unwittingly celebrated the foundation of twentieth-century urban sprawl.[33] Colonial cities differed from their European predecessors physically as well as legally. The tiny and fragile settlements that were to become the seaports of the muscular New World two centuries later never had more than wooden palisades and ditches. The wood quickly rotted away and the ditches filled with rubble. No American city saw real defenses, twenty feet thick at the base, faced with smooth, finished stones, carefully engineered gatehouses, all fastidiously designed to resist sieges. Lacking such impenetrable boundaries, they had from the beginning a powerful influence countervailing the traditional city's power to control its own internal shape. This influence, land with no physical barriers, ensured that the city's outer limits were unfixed, receding, and therefore unpredictable. Only the center, a geometric concept, could be considered fixed.

It had not been uncommon for walled cities of the ancient and medieval world to spill over, in the sense that people lived and worked outside of the walls. Residential and economic development that was functionally urban also occurred outside of city walls. But those people on the outside did not share the same urban benefits as the privileged inner inhabitants of the city. They lacked political and economic power, holding no hope of ever becoming members of the city corporation. Politically, economically, and practically this aspect of city life stayed extra-urban and truly marginal until the late eighteenth century.[34] Walls put a definable edge on the city, which limited its horizontal expansion and flexibility much more than American cities were ever to experience. That those people who threw up shacks or shops outside the walls were defined as extra-urban suggests the rather precise limits to a walled city.

Flexible boundaries created new and unforeseen opportunities for American cities. As is evident in the colonial land grants that specified vague western boundaries, edges did not make as much sense in the New World as they did in the Old. Apparently cities could expand indefinitely, as did the colonial land grants and the individual land grants made by towns. Often when New England villages suffered divisive political splits, one faction simply moved away, founding a new village within a day's walk from the old one. Only capital and population limited the exploitation of the seemingly endless resource, land. And because traditional city walls represented an enormous capital investment, their absence freed capital for other uses. Most important, without defined and limited edges, American cities lost a critical constraint affecting their planning, the absolute need for control which walls had imposed. The external boundary of a city wall and location of gates had required cities to make explicit locational decisions; unwalled cities no longer faced such decisions. The absence of walls also removed what had been a major factor influencing locational choices of various kinds that had been made in reference to the edges rather than the center of the city. The center of a city, an abstract geometric concept, even when anchored by a green, a city hall, or some other physical marker, conveys little sense of location compared, say, to an imposing stone gateway tower on the edge. In an unwalled city locational factors, beginning with distance and anything else that might be defined as an amenity, became all-important in determining value, access, and choice. This contrasts dramatically with walled cities, for within their walls, virtually all locations were good.

The lack of walls had a new impact on urban land value. In a walled city, or a city begun as one, land at the fringe, beyond the wall, had marginal value because it was beyond the scope of the city's direct protective power. The value provided by the city's economic, political, social, and military functions overwhelmed the value of its land as space. Within the walls economic transactions were secure, as were warehouses and personal property. Once inside the walls, land closer to the city center did not have inherently greater value for urban uses, nor did it preclude residential use. If we construct rent density gradients for two hypothetical cities, walled and unwalled (fig. 1), we can see that the walled city has a flat, sharply stepped curve compared to the concave decline in rents away from the center of the unwalled city. But land outside the city walls lost its urban utility, and its value as pure space was modest, probably little more than agricultural or village land. One might liken the difference to that of owning an automobile in a place with roads and a place without.

Colonial American cities began with new, unpredictable, and considerably less visible constraints than their European and British predecessors. Because state and military apparatuses were not tied to any particular urban locale, city locations had changing economic values. In a place with mutable boundaries the center defines utility and value, for the center alone is permanent. But no one had ever conceived of urban land utility this way before. Therefore, New World cities began with a subtle but highly significant difference. They did not, and still do not, look like Old World cities: they were not so compact; land use was less mixed. This difference would not be conceptualized for at least two more centuries, continually frustrating the contemporary understanding of the new cities. Older cities that had started out in walled form could tear down the walls, but predominating patterns of land use and attitudes toward urban space had already been solidly established. Similarly, the practical city government control of space had been well established, so that change and expansion could build along conscious, rational, and preexisting principles. To begin *de novo*, in a world where one of the most important limits no longer obtained, was and continues to be a difficult chore. To write free verse in an age raised on the sonnet posed a challenge of incomprehensible dimensions.

Although Old World city walls contained and constrained, their massive physical presence also gave clear witness to the concept of the city. By contrast, the more confusing urban form is one where there are no edges, where abstract principles derived from transportation costs and "frictions," that is, invisible impediments due to fragmented land ownership and control, from time to the center, primarily determine utility and hence value. It is this form of the city which so perturbs Jane Jacobs. And the dominance of the American city center has had an impact on the way geographers and historians have defined city growth eras. For example, the most widely accepted periodization of American urban development has been made on the basis of transportation eras and the effects of transportation on city design and location.[35] From the seventeenth

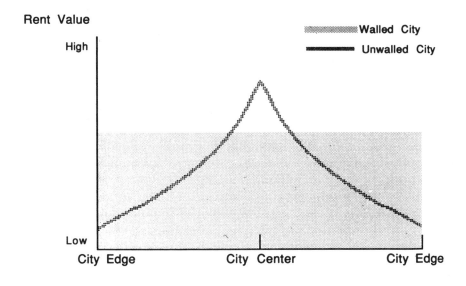

Figure 1. Hypothetical Land Rent Values for Walled and Unwalled Cities

century on, American urban dwellers constructed their cities with the knowledge that there was always more space on the edges, making caution and control irrational. The amount of space for an activity could be balanced rationally against travel time to the center, with access to other goods and services also entering the equation. Should the government decide to exercise a very costly control over locational or building decisions, one could always move farther away, if necessary beyond the political scope of the particular city. Even today, the American visitor to Britain or Europe cannot help but be struck by the comparative differences in the edges of cities. American cities have no sharp demarcation between them and the surrounding countryside, but exhibit instead a slow decrease in housing density, an increase in auto wrecking yards and other space consuming enterprises, and in land used neither for farming nor for purely urban purposes. European and British cities cease clearly, often abruptly, and agricultural land usage begins immediately. Although in the late twentieth century planning boards firmly retain and reinforce this sharp differentiation, it is as ancient as the city itself.

Ultimately, in the United States, the freedom from a city space restricted by walls introduced a new tyranny, that of the center. Powerful though often invisible, the center added many new complexities and problems to cities. The center could move, for instance, as a peninsular city like Boston expanded asymmetrically. The buildings, streets, water supply, and sewers, if any, could become inadequate to the changing demands imposed on the center by growth at the periphery. The center would therefore often appear to be problematic: inner city decay became one of the prominent urban problems by the 1960s. And so the tyranny of the center has become masked in our century by its apparent status as the passive victim of changes beyond its control. This paradoxical nature of the unbounded city is most obvious in the "doughnut" cities of the 1970s and 1980s, with their all-but-abandoned city centers.

Nevertheless, the center remains a battered but still dominant tyrant in the twentieth century. We have come to accept its dominance as the one "natural" point in the city and to see the walls of the ancient city as artificially confining. That land utility and therefore value should decline as distance from the center increases has become an axiom of urban economics.[36] The center's dominance also meant that the edges of the city took on particular material characteristics analogous to this economic law. The cross-sectional profile of a nineteenth-century city looks like a tent, supported in the middle by the American invention, the skyscraper (usually dated to William Le Baron Jenney's 1885 Home Insurance Building in Chicago), in contrast to the boater hat shape of the medieval city. Only an expansionist development of peripheral land for low-density usage made much economic sense. The most picturesque suburban edges upwind of urban smoke went to high-cost, low-density housing, as wealthy residents could expect to have the time to commute to the center. Individual buffers of land around each house provided the best control over neighbors. For these reasons, suburbanization, mostly of the wealthy, began very early in the nineteenth century, even before horse-drawn street railways made commuting simple.

The Edge of Town

On the other, less desirable, edges of cities, noisome and polluting economic activities (slaughterhouses, for instance) and poor people found space for small enclaves. Intentionally or not, all these activities on the edge of town existed beyond the control of the city government. In a new country, the simplicity of low-density, outward expansion preempted any rigorous physical planning. Some planning historians identify the cause of these planning failures as the primacy of private profit, a decline from "community enterprise."[37] But planning was almost universally derived from old patterns in Europe, which had been created under the tremendous constraints of preexisting property rights and physical structures like walls. In the colonies, grand schemes on paper were destined to fail, as these constraints simply did not exist. While American cities were to gain many very important advantages over their European predecessors, they began with this persistent, invisible, planning disadvantage that masqueraded as a natural freedom.

More important than the sheer presence of residences and economic activities beyond the city's political boundaries was their subtle, continuous, and pervasive pressure in helping urban activities to escape from any city control which became costly, inconvenient, or coercive. One could simply move beyond the reach of city government, while still benefiting from its nearby presence. This had been impossible in the walled city era, when all of a city's economic, military, and political attractions had been contained within its walls. Land beyond the city boundaries had a unique allure in the New World, offering proximity to the city's economic and locational advantages, but freedom from its obligations. Even rural New England towns, which retained a great deal of nominal power over the distribution of large tracts of agricultural land, saw their central power slip away because of this allure.[38] Free from the costly burdens of protection and control born by their predecessor city-states, American cities at the same time competed with their own very boundlessness to gain control over their internal shape and destiny. What American cities had that made them unique was the power to grow, to compete with one another as economic units.[39] U.S. cities lacked the political autonomy of ancient British cities on the one hand. Yet, on the other, they had more power than the new industrial cities of late eighteenth- and early nineteenth-century Britain. Their circumstances have in this way been complex and consistent over the course of three and a half centuries, expansion and growth defining the appropriate model for a city to follow. American cities could intentionally make themselves denser, bigger, richer, and taller, but they could not control their appearance.

Early nineteenth-century residential suburbs symbolized the attraction of the edge. Suburbs as elite residential locations are unique products of the modern era of unwalled cities. Through almost two centuries of colonial expansion, the elite had often chosen to live in the cities. But at the very moment that cities began to expand at the end of the eighteenth century, to take more than their traditional 5 percent of the population, those few who could afford to, began to move out, building themselves large rural estates.[40] Cities were a necessary evil to which the elite accommodated themselves: whenever their negative aspects began to overshadow their positive aspects, those who could afford to withdrew to suburbs, retaining access to urban power but rejecting the cities themselves.

Colonial Urban Society

New England towns often escaped the complex fate of growth, expansion, and central decay. The social conditions and economic costs of their success are illuminating.[41] These compact towns, which are rewarding to visit in the late twentieth century, contain artful arrangements of square and meeting house, with residential housing casually but closely interspersed. Their abrupt separation from the fields beyond was recognized and commercially exploited as a planning and esthetic delight as early as the mid-nineteenth century.[42] Many towns made successful transitions from farming villages to wealthy suburban villages in this period, luring wealthy urban residents. Why didn't these towns suffer the fate of cities, expanding into the suburbs and letting their centers decay?

The classic New England town began in fact as a farming center. The primary factor of the farmers' production, arable land, ringed the town and provided the first economic impediment to residential expansion. Town statutes discouraged or forbade living away, so that farmers tended to live in the town and walk to their fields, which were often scattered rather than contiguous. Expansion of the town would have meant a longer distance to walk to the fields. Moreover, the fields were economically vital to the townspeople, so that unlike a city, the edge of town was not the

J. JACOB ASTOR'S FORMER RESIDENCE 88TH ST. NEAR EAST RIVER.
House in which Washington Irving wrote his Astoria.

Astor's Suburban Home, New York, 1802.
While wealthy people lived near the center of early nineteenth-century cities, the notion of a suburban dwelling had already become fashionable. John Jacob Astor's home embodies the suburban virtues—near the country, the land not used for productive agricultural purposes, yet also close to the city's economic, political, and social attractions. By the middle of the nineteenth century, this estate was venerable enough to be considered a historic monument.

Source: Photo Library, Museum of the City of New York.

end of the townspeople's activities, but rather a continuation of them. Finally, the agricultural production that supported the town also limited its population. The town had to be relatively self-sufficient in food production, which meant in turn that its population could grow no larger than the fields allowed.

Several New England town studies have established that by the third generation of settlement, younger sons and daughters had to leave in order for their older siblings to retain enough land to survive. Population pressure grew to crisis proportions by the 1690s, and the idyllic stability of the town was achieved only at the cost of social repression, economic tension, and out-migration of sons and daughters. Town constables "warned out" transient paupers, community coming at the cost of conformity. The towns literally traded growth for stability. Today, when we visit these towns we marvel at their beauty, proportions, and tranquility, unable to imagine the family stress and severity required to produce such enduring stability. The departure of many brought community for few.[43]

As the seaport cities grew bigger they retained their differences from older European cities and from one another. Unlike the classic New England villages, they contained heterogeneous populations and were vulnerable to economic fluctuations. Wars precipitated social crises of varying dimensions in the three major colonial cities. Boston, for instance, particularly suffered from the loss of many men during King George's War (1744-1748), leaving for a time three married women to every seven widowed. Consequently, Boston's almshouse filled, while in Philadelphia only a handful of persons received relief in either the almshouse or in their own homes. In all the major colonial cities in the eighteenth century, population growth brought increased numbers of poor people. Philadelphia, Boston, and New York built almshouses for the destitute, rather than continue paying other poor people to board the sick and destitute.[44]

Within these port cities, elite groups established themselves and grew entrenched in their power, in parallel with an equally well-established and traditional laboring class. City governments attended to political and economic functions which mirrored, on a larger scale, those of village and town governments: regulating markets, selecting menders of fences, and passively operating within traditional categories.[45] These major cities served as important communications centers, their small but critical urban masses playing a major role in bringing on the Revolution. Throughout the late eighteenth century, the coastal cities provided the all-important sites of national governmental growth.

Even the minute, swampy, and crude city of early nineteenth-century Washington, D.C., provided a critical communications nexus.[46] The elected officials and tiny staff of the early federal government considered their tenure in the city temporary, and few took up permanent residence there. Instead they stayed in boardinghouses, and these boardinghouses quickly acquired importance because they provided a communications basis for government personnel, an otherwise disparate group from all over the country. Thus a city which on the surface served as little more than a camp began to exert a central power in the young republic.

Colonial Cities and the Economy

The most important urban development of the late eighteenth century, however, was not to be found in the role cities played in the political affairs of nation building. Rather, their crucial role was to be leaders in promoting and shaping economic growth. A seemingly minor aspect of the federal government's late eighteenth-century move to Washington provides a clue. In an attempt to drum up land sales in the rural District of Columbia and to encourage residential settlement as a more seemly alternative to the transitory habit of boarding, the government sponsored a land auction. In 1793 George Washington led a procession with two brass bands and Masons in full costume across the Tiber to a barbecue and land auction at which he purchased the first four lots of the new capital's undeveloped swampland.[47] Even this bit of sales promotion failed to spark the desired land sales in the District, which remained an uncouth, muddy, and sparsely populated embarrassment throughout most of the early nineteenth century. But self-promotion, boosterism, and a constant attention to the economic main chance soon came to characterize the young nation's cities.

Most eighteenth-century cities had made no attempts to promote themselves, for they saw themselves as regulatory entities, controlling access to urban privileges. They had "police" powers of control within their boundaries. Like princely rulers, they could watch over their inhabitants' economic as well as social behavior,

though cities in the Massachusetts Bay Colony tended to emphasize the social over the economic. In the seventeenth and eighteenth centuries, to become a full urban citizen, a "freeman of the
city," was to ascend to privileged status. To practice most urban
trades, in all the colonies but Massachusetts, one had to purchase
freemanship, a fee that assured the city revenue and control over
trades. (Massachusetts Bay Colony cities had to collect taxes to
augment their lack of revenues from markets and fees.) Freemen
also ran the city governments, making them resemble something
like twentieth-century chambers of commerce. In Boston, so often
an exception, the town meeting made decisions, thus basing the
franchise on property ownership rather than freemanship.

Power and its ruling elites—religious, military, and economic—were essentially one; modern scholarship emphasizes the
unitary nature of colonial elites, linked and intertwined by personal and family relationships. Michel Foucault's investigations of
state power have evoked a notion of precapitalist princely power
that commanded absolutely: the monarchy emphasized its power
in confrontation with individuals. But modern bureaucratic power,
he argues, has become a faceless, nameless, and pervasive presence,
constantly defining and observing the individual's life course from
birth to death.[48] Though artfully constructed, Foucault's dichotomy
bears little descriptive resemblance to either the modern or the
colonial city. Limited by the colonial governments, local governments never had the absolute power they might have wished for.
Contemporary local government in the United States, while pervasive, has not sought to permeate the individual's life. Perhaps
this has occurred on the state and national level, where most transitions in life are registered or regulated, from birth to marriage
through retirement and death. But just as the city was never the
locus of princely power in the United States, it is not now the locus
of bureaucratic power. Thus Foucault's metaphor helps us think
about the way confrontational power and bureaucratic power differ,
more than it helps us describe the differing kinds of city. Moreover,
his model helps us consider how colonial city governments essentially reacted to a defined range of events and situations. The nature of the reaction took the shape of state power confronting an
individual's actions: for instance, a shop owner built out onto the
public road, and the town officers ordered him to remove the
building.

The significant exception to a reactive stance came in the market, where medieval traditions held sway into the nineteenth century. The market, the traditional center of the city for thousands of years, epitomized in a most literal way the political, economic, and social nature of a city. Historians consider the Greek city-state's *agora* representative of an aesthetic and political pinnacle of the urban market, for in the agora the city transacted its politics, created vital trade centers, and debated intellectual issues. The functions epitomized by the agora continued in European markets after the fall of Rome, through the Middle Ages, and arrived in North America with Western European colonization. Colonial city governments vigorously exercised their economic powers, setting prices and wages as only the federal government occasionally undertakes in the twentieth century. Except for Boston, they maintained and supervised the marketplaces, setting and enforcing standards of quality, for instance, as well as prices.

City governments literally owned their marketplaces. A physical locus, whether an open place or a building, had to exist for the city to regulate prices. The city minimally maintained the place, protected it if need be, and exerted complete control over trading privileges. It often extended its market control and ownership to other commercial facilities, such as docks and warehouses. The market brought agricultural produce to urban customers, it dispersed urban manufactures to rural customers, and it served as the central place of communication to a broad public. In it the city role of policing public behavior saw daily exercise, and in it the urban economies of scale and agglomeration worked at their most basic levels.[49] The market, although symbolizing the city's economic functions, was no longer a literal requirement for a rich and complex urban economy, but rather an ancient form within which to organize and regulate that economy. Marketless Boston, which mandated door-to-door trading, made this clear, though one wonders if the lack of the market did not in some ways work against economies of scale; one thing was clear—the lack of a market was highly inconvenient for both buyers and sellers.

Not only did the marketplace capture the city's ancient symbolic aspects but its careful regulation and its privileged and protected economic activities highlighted the politics of the trading economy. It was a simple and visible political economy. To be awarded the privilege of trading in the market, stall holders paid the city fees. If they violated the rules of the market, sold underweight bread, for instance, they paid fines or lost their trading privilege. In 1686 the Albany Mayor's court confiscated a nonfreeman trader's wampum and deer skins, exacting a fine for trading in violation of the city's monopoly over both the participants and places approved for Indian trade. Philadelphia imprisoned a nonfreeman who set up as a butcher in 1718. New York explicitly made exceptions as an indirect means of providing welfare, for instance giving nonfree Widow Robinson in 1708 the privilege of following "any Lawful Trade or Employment within this Corporation for better Obtaining a livelihood for her and her family."[50]

The demise of city market regulation in favor of free trade began between 1800 and 1830. In an analysis of city statutes and ordinances, Jon C. Teaford has traced the replacement of the responsive city with what he calls the late eighteenth-century "expansion of municipal purpose." Until as late as 1821 New York City had set the price of bread, and not until 1829 did the first butcher break away from the city-mandated market sales stall and set up a private shop. These changes all involved state legislative and city battles over the inviolability of the city charters and, as with the expansion of the franchise, the city corporations gave up each element of their old regulatory power only with a struggle. Yet the same legislatures that took away the privileges of the old charters gave the cities a far greater power, the power to gain revenue from taxes.[51] Thus an apparent loss of power proved in the long run to be the creation of a new power.

Thus early American cities were pale imitations of those in the Old World. The premodern or colonial era selectively retained certain deep similarities and continuities with ancient cities from the time of their first emergence around 3000 B.C. Containing about 5 percent or less of a region's population, these cities functioned as commercial and political centers. By the time Europeans colonized America, Europe's cities were no longer city-states, for the nation-state had taken over their military and political functions; but European and British cities retained many of the formal assets and liabilities of their medieval predecessors. The new American urban network built rather slowly for about two hundred years, yet it did so with increasing independence from old forms. Whether they wanted to or not, the colonists could not replicate the cities

The Columbus, Ohio, Market, circa 1850.
Compare this structure with its medieval predecessor the Thaxted Guild
Hall. The ground floor can be opened to admit movement of goods, while
the upper rooms have diminished in size and functional importance, as
the city now has a separate building for governmental offices. But the
exaggerated scale introduced by the artist suggests a sense of size and
power similar to that conveyed by Thaxted's Guild Hall. Columbus erected
its first market building in 1814. It was so quickly and poorly constructed
that the town council declared it a nuisance after three years and ordered
another built. This picture shows yet another market, at least the city's
third.

Source: from Jacob H. Studer, *Columbus, Ohio, Its History, Resources and Progress*
(Columbus: Jacob H. Studer, 1873), 45.

of the Old World. Explosive, crude, vigorous, and innovative in their failed imitations, by the late eighteenth and early nineteenth century U.S. cities began to produce truly new urban environments.

3 ☆ Growth Begins

Since its founding, the United States has changed from a rural to an urban nation. The most important city, New York, probably contained fewer than 22,000 people at the time of the Revolution. And only one person in twenty lived in a place with a population greater than 2,500—a size even then hardly considered urban. The course of the nineteenth century saw the North American landscape literally transformed by urbanization. But so, for that matter, was most of the Western world: compared to Britain, for instance, the United States has always been less urban. Thus while urbanization represents a dramatic change, it would have been far more remarkable for the United States to have stayed rural. As early as 1872 political leaders recognized implicitly that the city had become the main mode of existence, when they made Yellowstone the country's first national park, setting an early precedent for preserving uncultivated, nonurban areas for future, urban generations. The urban transformation of the United States is mainly remarkable in that it constructed so many new cities, while in Britain the process was much more one of expanding preexisting places.[1] In concentrating on a quantitative understanding, this chapter exemplifies the statistical approach to cities, updated with a healthy dose of recent attitudes and techniques. Just how much we can learn from simple numbers arrayed through time? Quite a bit—perhaps more than one has any right to expect.

The Changing Proportion of Population Living in Cities

Let us begin by examining figure 2, which shows the percentage of the total population living in places with more than

2,500 people and in places larger than 100,000. The smaller value has long been considered the lowest threshold of what could be called a city: though arguably too small, it is a useful definition in its consistency, since it has now been applied by the various data gathering agencies of the U.S. government for almost two centuries. The larger value of 100,000 probably corresponds more to our contemporary sense of what constitutes a "real city," a minimally sized metropolis. The threshold value for the population characterizing a city, or village, or metropolis, is an elusive, perhaps shifting, and certainly much vexed question. It is therefore important to stress that such definitions are most useful in sketching large pictures of the world of cities, using sharp lines to suggest fuzzy concepts.[2]

After a slight initial urban expansion at the beginning of the nineteenth century, the urban population stayed relatively stable until about 1830, when it began a century-long burst of continuous expansion until 1930. The damper of the Great Depression proved to be the precursor of a general decline in urbanization's pace, so that it now appears that the demographic aspect of the urban transition—the creation of a largely urban populace—has been completed. One may therefore read figure 2 as delineating three urban eras: the first up to 1830, the second that of a century of expansion ending with the Depression, and the third, a period of relative stability.

The plot of the percentage of population in cities over 100,000 suggests that this three-phase process of urbanization was even more distinct for larger, metropolitan populations. In the first phase, up to 1830, there were no cities over 100,000. The second phase, lasting a century, saw the metropolitan population climb steadily to somewhat over one-fourth of the total population. And since 1930 this metropolitan population has remained steady or even declined slightly.

Some additional numbers, not shown on the graph, fill out the picture. The percentage of the population living in cities over a million highlights the process that has fostered the growth of middle-sized cities and small metropolises. In 1880, only 3.4 percent of the population lived in cities over a million. This percentage peaked in 1930 at 13.3 percent, and then it began a steady and consistent decline to 7.7 percent in 1980, a proportion lower than that at the beginning of the twentieth century.

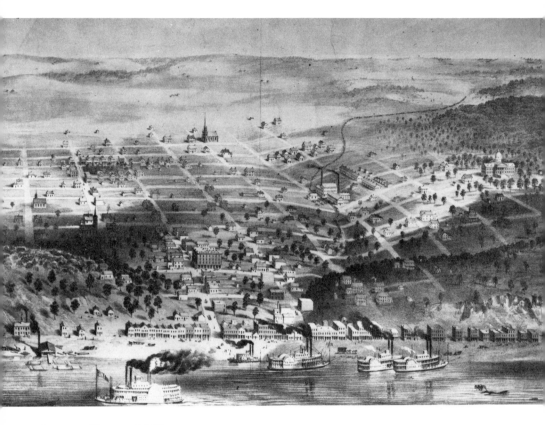

Sumner, Kansas, 1857.
This view is an artist's speculative vision, a crudely drawn sketch conforming only to the grandiose plans of city building entrepreneurs; only a few of these buildings were ever built. The blowing smoke tells us it was a windy day in the artist's mind: but such was the bustle of this town-to-be that a steamboat on the river doubled the speed of the wind, giving a Daliesque vision of smoke blowing both ways in the foreground. Today there are nine Sumners in the United States, but this is not one.

Source: Kansas State Historical Society.

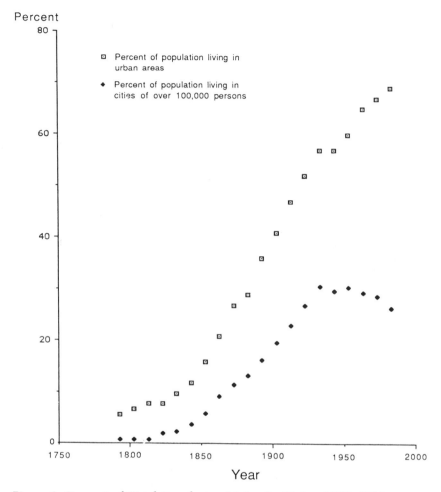

Figure 2. Percent of Total Population Living In Cities, 1790–1980

Source: calculated from Bureau of the Census, *Historical Statistics of the United States, Colonial Times to 1970* (Washington, D.C.: GPO, 1975), 11–12, and *Statistical Abstract of the United States: National Data Book and Guide to Sources, 1982–83* (Washington, D.C.: GPO, 1982), 21.

If we look at farm families as the obverse of urban families, a parallel divergence has occurred in the past fifty years. In 1930, when about 50 percent of the total population lived in places over 2,500, about 30 percent of the population lived on farms, leaving 20 percent in small villages and rural nonfarm residences. This has changed dramatically and steadily, so that only about 3 percent of the 1980 population lived on farms, whereas 23 percent were other nonurban residents, a net increase of rural nonfarmers since the 1930 census.[3]

And very recently, this half-century-old trend away from the extreme of farm living has also emerged at the most metropolitan end of the population. The proportion of people living in the giant metropolitan areas—the seven cities with populations over three million—has declined by half a percent between 1970 and 1980. This latter shift, though slight, has caused considerable excitement and unease among urbanists. Some have termed the drop a new trend, one quickly labeled "counterurbanization" by Brian Berry. Clearly the trend is not new, but a half-century old, having begun in the Depression years, but masked until recently by data that focus on the standard metropolitan statistical area (SMSA), as well as by the baby boom, postwar prosperity, and rural migration from the South to large cities.[4] Whatever the future holds, it is fair to say that the century between 1830 and 1930 saw the most dramatic shift in creating modern urban America, and that the post-Depression era is one of sorting out and a drift toward moderation, toward the mean. Fewer people live in rural isolation; fewer in mass anonymity.

The Changing Number of Cities

Compare with this population shift the changing number of city units displayed in figures 3 and 4. These graphs show clearly the relative stability in the total number of city governments until the second phase of urbanization in 1830, followed by virtually continuous and rapid expansion. A continued expansion in number of city units has accompanied the post-Depression phase, mostly in the smaller city category (fig. 3), which accounts for the stability and decline in metropolitan populations. Thus while urbanization, defined as the movement of population from rural places, may have reached stasis, the process of city building begun in the mid-nineteenth century continues today. As a direct consequence, there are more than five times as many city governments per capita today than in 1790. This indicates that in essence the urbanization process in the United States has consisted of two related but quite different movements, one demographic and the other political.

Cities over 2,500
  Population

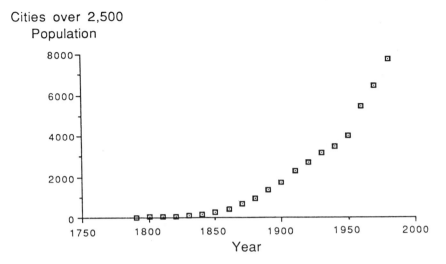

Figure 3. Total Number of Cities over 2,500, 1790–1980

Source: Bureau of the Census, *Historical Statistics of the United States, Colonial Times to 1970* (Washington D.C.: Government Printing Office, 1975), 11, and *Statistical Abstract of the United States: National Data Book and Guide to Sources, 1982–83* (Washington, D.C.: Government Printing Office, 1982), 21.

More people live in vastly more cities. The age of the big city is over, but the age of cities continues with greater vigor than ever.

Figures 3 and 4, like figure 2, convey an immediate visual sense of the changing pace of what was an ordinary yet also extraordinary process. It was ordinary in that other nations were experiencing a similar or even greater residential relocation of people, but it was extraordinary in that no other built so many completely new cities. In Europe at the beginning of the nineteenth century, about 13 percent of the population lived in cities over 5,000 persons; for the United States the figure was only 3.4 percent. More specifically, comparing populations living in cities of over 10,000, in 1800 the United States was less urban than every European nation but Poland. However, ninety years later, only England and Wales, Scotland, the Netherlands, Belgium, and by a scant 0.4 percent, Germany, led the United States. And even more important, the United States made this transition by building physically and politically new cities. Of the 390 European cities with populations over 100,000 in 1979, 176 or 45 percent were "new" in the sense that they had had fewer than 10,000 persons in 1800. In sharp con-

Cities over 100,000
Population

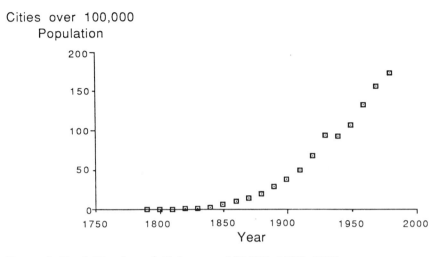

Figure 4. Total Number of Cities over 100,000, 1790–1980

Source: Bureau of the Census, *Historical Statistics of the United States, Colonial Times to 1970* (Washington D.C.: Government Printing Office, 1975), 11, and *Statistical Abstract of the United States: National Data Book and Guide to Sources, 1982–83* (Washington, D.C.: Government Printing Office, 1982), 21.

trast, out of the 153 U.S. cities greater than 100,000 in 1970, only three had had over 10,000 in 1800 and only 23 had existed at all.[5]

Changes within the Urban System

This political and population process has entailed a subtler impact than the three graphs suggest, for the actual relationship of cities to one another changed as the whole system grew explosively. In contrast to Britain and Europe, the U.S. city system never developed a single, disproportionately large, dominant metropolis. But within the more dispersed network of smaller cities, towns, and villages, growth and expansion did not cause an endless replication of the early city patterns. The changing numbers of city units again furnish the basis for an index to this change, as in figures 3 and 4. However, by graphing the proportions of city sizes, as in figure 5, we can see the hints of change. Although the meaning of absolute city size may be impossibly elusive, most urbanists would probably agree that there are size thresholds associated with different city characteristics. For the purpose of clarity, a popula-

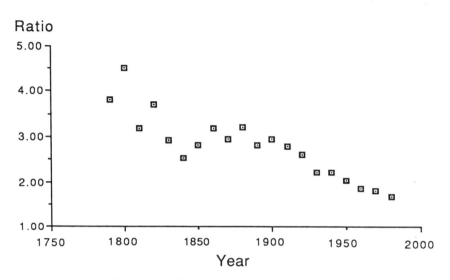

Figure 5. Ratio of Number of Cities under 9,999 to those over 10,000

Source: calculated from Bureau of the Census, *Historical Statistics of the United States, Colonial Times to 1970* (Washington, D.C.: Government Printing Office, 1975), 11, and *Statistical Abstract of the United States: National Data Book and Guide to Sources, 1982–83* (Washington, D.C.: Government Printing Office, 1982), 21.

tion of 10,000 is used here as the criterion for separating major and minor cities. No doubt this is imperfect, either including or excluding the wrong cities, but it does serve as a comprehensible index to the size hierarchy of cities. Figure 5 plots the ratio of the number of small cities—places below 9,999 but above 2,500—to all cities with a population greater than 10,000.

The plot of this changing ratio shows that the number of very small cities relative to medium and large ones has rapidly decreased since 1800. Whereas in 1800 there were over four times as many small as large cities, by 1980 this ratio had fallen to only one-third its former size. The United States, it seems, is more and more becoming a nation of medium and large cities. (If we change the criterion, using the ratio of cities over and under 5,000, this downward decline did not begin until 1880; conversely, if the ratio is raised to cities over and under 25,000, there is a parallel decline from 1800 on.) This change is instructive, for it demonstrates that, in the United States, developed urban networks consist of proportionally more medium and large than small places. And, of course, as they grow, the number of small places always tends to be moving into larger size categories. For the past two centuries the number of U.S. cities over 10,000 has grown 23 percent faster than those under 9,999.[6]

Throughout the seventeenth and much of the eighteenth century, the American colonies had no metropolis on their continent. Colonial American cities made up a minor part of an English urban network that tended toward primacy because of London's domination. By 1700 London had become the largest city in Western Europe, dominating the world's capitalist economy.[7] The English urban network, although containing cities of each functional type, had a metropolis of far greater power and size than theory would have predicted. For both historic and economic reasons the second rank of cities under London was relatively weak and small, as was the third tier of towns. The major American colonial cities functioned as towns through much of the seventeenth century, then began to take on more citylike activities during the eighteenth century. London, however, remained the metropolis. As economic independence slowly followed political independence, the United States escaped from a network based on metropolitan dominance. As the periphery of an urban network whose central functions were usurped by London, the American colonies had developed many small cities and towns. When liberated from London's dominance, they formed part of a network with more dispersed power and less primacy than in the original system.

The Effect of Primacy

At the beginning of the eighteenth century, while London's population was half a million, the rest of Britain boasted seven much smaller cities with between 10,000 and 20,000 people, perhaps 22 with 5,000 to 10,000, and then at least 600 towns and villages with populations less than 5,000. In other words, there were about as many people in London as in all the other cities, towns, and villages in Britain. Lopping off the overpowering metropolis of London creates a distribution of cities closer to that predicted by geographic theory and more comparable to North America. Of course, a world without a London would be provincial, dull, and decentralized—as colonial America was. When this urban American world did begin to expand dramatically a century later, it was already decentralized and more evenly distributed. For its metropolis, it still looked to London, which continued through the mid-nineteenth century to act as a source of specialization, innovation, and of other services that only a metropolis could provide.

The urban benefits of being born on a colonial margin to a primate metropolis like London could have been reaped only by a nation on the verge of expanding into the era of steam and rail transport. That is, the existing model provided a flexible and powerful base for a new kind of urban growth because of a happenstance in historical timing. What might appear from a bird's-eye view to have been a natural expansion of cities across the North American continent was in fact a phenomenon born of timing and a decline in the significance of the primate metropolis. As chapter two has shown, the traditional city had had functional primacy, whether in ancient Syria, first-century Rome or seventeenth-century London. But on the North American fringe, a new model of city arrangement grew, its growth overshadowed at first by the sensational growth and urban spectacle of London.

Comparing the relationships of metropolitan populations, of other cities and towns in the urban system, and of rural areas, in England and the United States yields a measured sense of the different urban system developing in America. Simple population statistics reflect London's dominance over other English cities at the beginning of the nineteenth century. In 1800, 34 percent of the English population lived in cities and towns, as opposed to 6 percent in the United States. Of all the English urban population, 27 percent lived in London, a proportion that rose to 31 percent by 1820. By contrast, in the same period New York contained 18 percent of the American urban populace. And in 1890, when the U.S. urban population reached a proportion comparable to England's ninety years earlier, New York's share of urban dwellers had fallen to a mere 7 percent. Thus, the American urban network began the nineteenth century with no truly dominant metropolis, and ended the century with its major center even less dominant. As the twentieth century began, more than 16 percent of England's total population lived in London, a proportion that continued to increase. In the United States, however, only 4 percent of the total population lived in New York, a figure that continued to decline through the twentieth century.[8]

Although London was preeminent, England's new cities were

important, for they made up the bulk of the mid-nineteenth century manufacturing belt. Urban expansion in the United States was tied to national growth: moreover, locally promoted canal and railroad investment facilitated this national and urban expansion by forging water and rail connections. On the one hand, the peculiar advantage of rail transit over canals was, for the cities, that it allowed them even more flexibility, tapping hinterlands with great ease. On the other hand, the speed and relatively low cost of the railroad meant that established manufacturing cities could increase the size of their marketing regions, so the resulting competitive advantage shifted away from small manufacturing centers toward larger ones. In a detailed study of Ohio and Indiana, Edward Muller has shown how although the coming of the railroad indeed boosted the fortunes of some towns and quenched those of others, a surprising "inertia" afflicted most. That is, the new transportation technology affected established town hierarchies only slightly.[9]

By the 1830s, rail transit had made its powerful and flexible features well known. Although the major metropolises of the east coast had been established well before rail transport, they were all capable of deepening and concentrating their hinterlands with rails. Thus the railroad tended to either reinforce existing patterns of urban settlement and location or, in the plains and far West, affect only new cities. The noisy and smoky symbol of nineteenth-century technology did not so much dramatically alter the urban world as it accelerated the transformation already taking place.

Although five of the ten largest U.S. cities in 1984 had been well established prior to the coming of the railroad, most of the national urban network was built during the era of rail transportation. One may use the 153 American cities that had populations greater than 100,000 in 1970 to index the mature urban network. This choice makes only the modest assumption that no more than a handful of the cities will shift out of this group in the next decades. Of this group, which might be designated the major cities of the United States, fully 75 percent had been established after 1840—or alternatively, 65 percent after 1850—when the railroad had become an established technology. (Only 9 percent was added after 1910, the earliest date one could call the age of the automobile.) Table 3 illustrates wide regional differences in the dates of founding of these major cities. But it is important to note that even on the Atlantic seaboard, what one might think of as the

TABLE 3

DATES OF FOUNDING, MAJOR U.S. CITIES, BY REGION[a]

Year	West	Plains/Mountains	Midwest	East
1960 +	2			
+			1	
+				
+	1		1	
+	1		1	
+	2		1	1
1900 +		1	2	1
+	8	3	2	3
+	2	6	1	2
+	4		1	3
+	4	5	10	3
1850 +	3	3	14	4
+			6	8
+			6	2
+			2	
+			3	3
1800 +			2	4
+			1	
+				
+				
+				3
+				
+				
+				1
1700 +				1
+				1
+				
+				1
+				7
+				2
+				
1620 +				

| | West | Plains/Mountains | Midwest | East |

[a]Plotted above are the 148 U.S. cities that reached populations of over 100,000 in 1970. The four columns correspond to regions of the country, running west to east as on a map. The numbers plotted are the numbers of cities in each region at the decade during which the city first appeared in the census with any population. The median decades for city founding by region are: East = 1830–40; Midwest = 1840–50; Plains and Mountains = 1880–90; West = 1880–90.

SOURCE: Bureau of the Census, *1970 Census of the Population: Characteristics of the Population,* V. 1, Pt. 1, Sect. 1 (Washington, D.C.: Government Printing Office, 1973), 116–119.

colonial urban system, half of the 53 cities were established after 1840, suggesting strong postrailroad elements even in the original colonies. In the Midwest, of course, even more cities, about 80 percent, were platted in the era of railroads. And with a handful of exceptions, all cities west of the Mississippi were established after the railroad.

Thus, as almost all the urban United States west of the Appalachians was constructed in the nineteenth century, city builders could make locational decisions based on the known advantages and requirements of rail transit. Cities like Denver, for instance, located on a high plain with no water transport, were unimaginable before efficient rail transport, and cities originally expecting to boost their trade advantages with canals could quickly change to railroads when they proved advantageous. A famous historical debate over the cost advantages of rail versus canal transport has demonstrated the problematic aspect of the profitability of one transport system over another, but in the context of the American urban system the question is moot.[10]

In retrospect it may appear that the transport technologies themselves determined urban locations and building forms.[11] But the process was one of mutual reinforcement, and it would be as incorrect to say that city settlement patterns caused the success of rail transport as to say that rail transport caused a particular city settlement pattern. Railroads, and later hard surface roads, came to predominate partly because the urban settlement patterns of the nation had been made with conscious expectations of the new transport. In the mid-nineteenth century, aggressive railroad entrepreneurs and city officials both recognized this. Cities often sold bonds specifically to underwrite railroad expansion, sometimes for laying track to the town, sometimes for building a terminus, and sometimes for general financial assistance to a fledgling railroad company. Cities took these risks because the railroad's arrival, a terminus for its convenient stopping, and its general success almost guaranteed the city's future economic expansion and subsequent ability to repay the bonded debt. Of course, railroad entrepreneurs recognized the local importance of their routes and building plans, and they courted cities, subtly arranging bidding contests among them.[12]

The Phased Expansion of the Urban System

Table 3 also shows again the three-phased urbanization of the United States. Its lower portion sketches the colonial urban world, the middle band the expansive nineteenth-century world, and the upper reaches the relatively stable twentieth century. Although city building moved westward along with the center of population, table 3 demonstrates how the east coast also stayed quite busy in its city building, and how twentieth-century southwestern urbanization represents a smooth shift and gradual tendency rather than the abrupt departure it is sometimes seen as.

Throughout the nineteenth century, both technology and topography considerably influenced the imaginary map represented by table 3. In the colonial phase, only water and wagon roads connected the urban world. Mountain ridges provided virtually uncrossable natural barriers, and the federal government's cautious refusal to fund transportation—despite the bold arguments advanced by Secretary of the Treasury Albert Gallatin in 1808, and later supported by John C. Calhoun—had the effect of frustrating urban expansion in the trans-Appalachian west.[13] The nineteenth-century expansion shown on our imaginary map must be interpreted in light of the introduction of railroads, which though slow, primitive, and only a few years old, were already affecting both actual and expected transportation patterns. And the post–Civil War period must be understood as representing a truly booming urban landscape, with capital, immigrants, and transnational railroads making the entrepreneur's wildest dreams come true.

The second mapping addition that imagination must supply is that of the ever-changing urban interstices, the hamlets, villages, towns, and small cities both growing and declining between the larger cities plotted in table 3. In the purely agricultural sections of the country, these places varied in their dispersal with the productivity of the land, the technology of transport, and the size of the land holdings. East of the Mississippi, a dense network of small towns functioned as market centers. West of the Mississippi, the network stretched much more thinly, the number of towns, farms, and amount of rainfall all declining together until reaching the barrier of the Rockies.

There is some evidence that hints at great fluidity in the urban network on the level of the very small village, places under 2,500 that escaped enumeration by falling under the Bureau of the Census' definition of urban. New Hampshire, for instance, experienced rural depopulation and loss of villages in the eighteenth century, perhaps because of the relative infertility of the land and the availability of better agricultural land farther to the west. But even the newly settled land farther west went through a similar cycle of the birth and decline of very small towns. One study, of the towns around Syracuse, New York, in the first decades of the nineteenth century, delineates the process that first sprinkled the countryside with tiny new towns, then within a span of two or three decades winnowed out some and boosted others. These villages were never very stable, though perhaps they were bucolic. A similar pattern appeared in early nineteenth-century Ohio, where the growth in larger places, those over 2,500, also masked a decline in the small villages and hamlets. The rise and fall of small industries and changes in transportation, including wagon roads, meant that shrinkage was a common as growth for these smallest components of the expanding urban network. In addition to small places that dwindled, other towns failed to thrive and stagnated. As canals diminished some of the importance of natural river routes, and railroads in turn replaced canals as the major form of transportation, many towns also experienced changes in commercial and manufacturing importance owing to location.[14]

Necessary, Sufficient, and Contingent Reasons for Growth and Decline

Members of the local elite often congratulated themselves loudly when their cities grew, considering local growth to be a result of their unique entrepreneurial abilities. Yet local entrepreneurship interacted subtly with overall population growth, changes in transport, and the growth of manufacturing, leaving a turbulent urban world where there must have been many disappointed town dwellers and promoters. Not that urban promoters were ignorant of their location in relationship to hinterland resources, transportation, and other cities, but in the nineteenth century, with the whole system building out of what often seemed to be little more than hope and hype, exaggeration and self-deception were rife. Hence, promoters of the port of Duluth, a cold, desolate place located on infertile land at the margins of what is still wilderness, could confidently publish a "fact-filled" pamphlet that described the city as being in the center of a transportation network connecting not only to St. Paul, Chicago, and New York but also to Paris, London, and Calcutta. Historians, too, have often looked at entrepreneurship as a significant factor in growth, neglecting the necessary (if not sufficient in themselves) locational and network influences. Only in very obvious cases has the role of extrinsic factors been brought into the historical analysis. In the rivalry between Houston and Galveston, for instance, it is clear that Houston only forged ahead when a 1900 hurricane wiped out 15 percent of Galveston's population.[15]

Other equally invisible factors influenced the mapped networks of cities across the continent. Extractive industries, particularly western mining, often created urban centers the population sizes of which agriculture and manufacturing alone would not have predicted. Denver, for instance, provided important urban services to a ranching and farming hinterland, which, when combined with mining on the eastern slope of the Rockies, explains its explosive appearance and growth in the 1870s in a region too dry for unirrigated agriculture. The city grew from nothing in 1850 to a modest 4,000 during the sixties and seventies, suddenly bursting to 35,000 in 1880 and then tripling to over 106,000 by 1890.[16] Most growth statistics for nineteenth-century U.S. cities are very high, but the cities that showed comparable growth usually had more locational advantages than Denver. Few landlocked and arid nineteenth-century cities can match its growth. Historians often point to Chicago, with its port and rich agricultural hinterland, as the outstanding growth center of the late nineteenth century, but impressive as Chicago's story is, it is not nearly so unexpected as Denver's. Location theory thus alerts us to the need for additional information to understand cities like these.

The model of urban networks, then, must be considerably modified to correspond with the historical reality of the nineteenth-century United States. These modifications help to both uncover the unexpected and define the expected; in doing so, they also reveal the regular processes that create a history.

An almost fluid urban expansion encompassed both growth and shrinkage while the network of cities, towns, and villages stretched thinly over arid regions, with concentrations of mineral resources distorting its symmetry. In the Southwest, the Spanish and Mexican tradition of large ranches, succeeded by the massive landholdings of capital- and land-intensive agricultural concerns, almost proscribed the tiny hamlets and villages that were the norm east of the Mississippi.[17] In California, the Spanish mission system explicitly anticipated an urban settlement pattern, with the two major metropolises, San Francisco and Los Angeles, one a fort, the other a civil settlement, planned as urban centers long before growth was a realistic expectation.

Consequently, soon after they began to experience population expansion, the southwestern states became proportionally far more urbanized than our impressions of cowboys and Indians might have predicted. California, for instance, reached the 50 percent urban point in about 1885, when the United States as a whole was only about 32 percent urban. Or, to take an extreme case, Arizona remained a relatively unpopulated state until the 1950s. In 1940 it had a population of only 500,000, about 33 percent urban. But in the next twenty years its population shot up to 1,302,000, of which 75 percent was urban. This quantitative index can be easily misread, however, for by bifurcating the world into urban and rural, it ignores the hamlets, the places under 2,500 people, which dotted much of the eastern United States. Thus much of the population that census statistics classified as rural actually lived in tiny hamlets: while one hesitates to call the residents of these places "urban," they certainly had lives that were far less rural than the farmers and farm laborers of the Southwest.[18]

Continuing Urban Transformations

Urbanization continues to transform the settlement patterns of the United States in the twentieth century. These transformations also completely invert our image of what the United States looks like. The new urban world can best be represented by the 1980 ranking of states and regions by percent of urban population, using places larger than 2,500 as the definition of urban. The West has become the most urbanized region, with 84 percent of its populace in cities, as opposed to 74 percent in the Northeast, 70 percent in the North Central states, and 67 percent in the South. Only one state, California, now has over 90 percent of its population in urban areas, and it had already reached this remarkably high level in the 1960s. Using the more inclusive measure of the standard metropolitan statistical area (SMSA), California had reached an astonishing 95 percent proportion in 1980. It might be argued that these proportions are the result of defining urban too inclusively. But even with tightening the definition considerably, to SMSAs over one million, the pattern remains. Over 18 million Californians, 78 percent, live in such places, compared to 13 million New Yorkers, less than 72 percent. In 1980, eleven states had populations that were over 80 percent urban: Rhode Island, New York, New Jersey, Illinois, Maryland, Florida, Colorado, Arizona, Utah, Nevada, and Hawaii. Texas almost squeaked into this category, at 79.6 percent urban.[19] It will take a long time for us to readjust our perceptions of what makes a city before this reordered urban world can be fully understood and accepted.

Using numbers and graphs, this chapter has outlined the building and peopling of the urban United States. It has necessarily and deliberately simplified a complex, effervescent, and sometimes unpredictable world, a world which has in two centuries become something more amazing than the most fantastic imagination could have foreseen. Even a hundred years ago, Edward Bellamy's *Looking Backwards, 2000–1887*, a futuristic novel set in the year 2000, failed to comprehend the magnitude or direction of change that still continues to reshape late twentieth-century urban America.

The rural and urban populations of the United States have begun to approach a complete reversal in proportions from those of the eighteenth century. People live in metropolitan complexes vastly larger than they did two hundred years ago, yet these places lack the population density, the urban feel, of the smaller late eighteenth-century cities. In fact, as the nation has urbanized, the very essence of urban has changed. This is most typified by the sprawling cities of California, our most urban state, where the low-rise openness defies the most sophisticated sense of what is urban.

Paralleling the ascendancy of what some might call the nonurban cities of California has been a trend since the nineteenth century toward a proliferation of more small and medium-sized cities. The list of cities with a population greater than 100,000 in 1980 runs to over 150, including places that few Americans could accurately map, even by state. How many can locate Concord (not Massachusetts!), Garland, Irving, Lakewood, Livonia, Sterling

Heights, or Warren? All these are cities larger than Phoenix was in the 1940s.

It is little wonder that this urbanization process has encouraged commentaries that toss about superlatives as rapidly as the cities grow. Yet it is important to remember that the United States has been a part of an urbanizing world. For comparison, visualize the widely reproduced, speculative graph by David Clark plotting the growth of the world's urban population.[20] It shows 5,000 years of a flat line at less than 5 percent urban, with a sudden almost vertical spike representing the past 200 years of urban growth. The world graph makes a convincing argument about the genuine transformation wrought by urbanization. In this larger context the transformation of the United States seems modest, but only because the time scale has been expanded. Like the U.S. graph, the world graph can be seen as the record of three phased, rapid transformations. In phase one, no visible urbanization took place; in phase two, the rural population achieved its present level while the urban proportion began its rapid increase. And in the third phase, since about 1930, the rural population has held steady, with virtually all population growth taking place in the separate urban world. With only slightly altered timing and scale differences, California can be seen as a paradigm of the larger process. Entering the United States in 1850 as an almost purely agricultural place, its rural population grew until about 1940, then stabilized. However, its urban world changed in an entirely different way, increasing from the 1850s, but accelerating after the turn of the century and again after World War II.

These graphs encourage prediction, something that historians simultaneously abhor and consider frivolous. Our business, after all, is the past, and when we demand the most critical evaluation of what has already happened, it is hard for us to accept what has *not* happened, or the discussion of it, as being properly empirical. But, to the extent that such predictions can be reliable, it appears that the relative stability of the rural populations will in fact be maintained, while urban expansion, the only really variable population figure, will continue to reflect total population growth, thus varying in its proportions but probably stabilizing throughout the United States at a level somewhat lower than California's, say at 80 to 85 percent. This is then a very cautious prediction, that what has historically been a volatile and changing aspect of our history will continue to be so. In other words, the rural parts of the two graphs will continue their historical stability, while the urban portions, so far having shown only wild expansion, will vary, for the most part expanding, of course, but on occasion even contracting.

4 ☆ The Emerging Service City: Fighting Fire and Crime

Proliferation and growth are only portions of the story of nineteenth-century urban change. Cities also changed internally during this period, as evidenced by their changing roles in government, war, social control, law, and fire fighting. In 1790 cities were passive, limited in scope, and organizationally simple. By the end of the Civil War the foundation for more complex, aggressive, and highly bureaucratized cities had been laid. And the post-1870 era saw many of these latent capacities made manifest. This periodization of internal urban change does not parallel exactly the periods of overall urban growth portrayed in the previous chapter, for although the internal and external changes were related, they were not yoked in a direct or mechanical fashion.

Emergent Urban Complexity

In the long transition from city-states to states filled with cities, the city's formal role has been restricted, because it no longer functions as a self-defended military enclave. The notion of maintaining the city's defenses would sound outlandish in a contemporary city council meeting. However, for the most part, even within their older formal functions, cities do far more than they used to. While they still administer welfare, for instance, the scope of welfare, its detailed complexity, has grown vastly. Everything from job training programs to specialized kinds of care has replaced or supplemented direct in-kind or cash payments to individuals. Vast industrial enterprises supply water and drain cities. Solid waste management specialists have replaced pigs and night soil haulers. Financial officers design complex strategies for city investments. City engineers map subsurface geological structures. The formal legal functions of the city may be fewer, but the nature of these functions has become dramatically more specialized, complex, and sophisticated.

Colonial cities employed formal procedures inherited from medieval cities and towns. Only Massachusetts cities did not imitate their predecessors directly, in part because the colony itself was a chartered company and was not empowered to grant city charters. The cities and towns of Massachusetts were not closed corporations, as were, for instance, New York and Philadelphia. In contrast with most major colonial cities, consequently, Boston transacted its business in town meetings until it became a chartered city in 1822.[1]

The model of city government with which we are familiar today reverses the power relationship of colonial city and inhabitant. To begin with, virtually all of a modern city's inhabitants are its citizens, even though they do not share its services equally. There is no such thing as "freemanship"; even the concept is difficult to fathom today. The city's lordly power has been dissolved. Moreover, the city government explicitly claims that it "serves" its inhabitants, a claim that would have been equally incomprehensible to the colonists. In the last quarter of the twentieth century, we have become so accustomed to city services that we no longer are aware that they exist. But in the nineteenth century, as the transition occurred, the contrast between a regulatory and a service oriented city government was often made starkly clear.

Modern cities are not only more organizationally complex than the concept of "service" predicates but also contain widely differing cultural groups, yielding varied and complex urban societies. In traditional societies, individuals shared enough central cultural conceptions to create and maintain an operating vision of order. Individuals knew what was expected in their public behavior and in turn what to expect from others. Public interactions among strangers or persons not well known had predictable qualities and ranges, and even deviant or conflictual behavior conformed to certain norms. For city life such structured expectations were an important social control mechanism. But in the period between 1790 and 1870, new cities, new governmental organizations, and new social groups fractured the old rules.

American cities had more unpredictable and volatile social

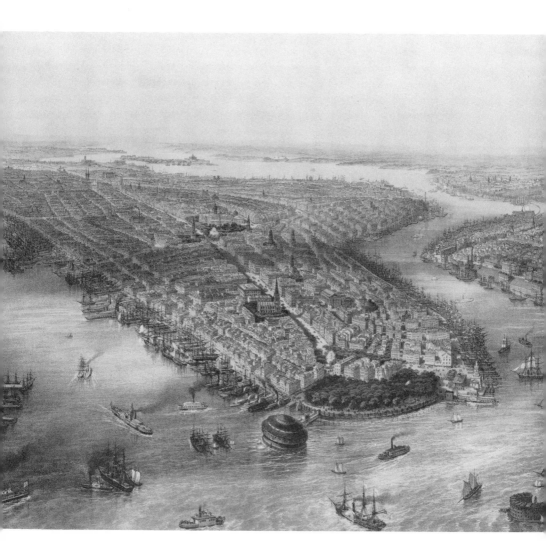

New York City, 1855.
In this finely detailed view, New York looks like a modern metropolis, yet
it did not yet have a professional fire department and its formal police
department was less than a decade old.

bases than their Old World and colonial predecessors. By virtue of their rate of growth, to which was added an influx of immigrants from different nations, from different rural areas, and from different religious and economic backgrounds, U.S. cities simply did not have the personal networks that anchored more established communities. The recurrent idea that cities lacking in public conventions and a common culture are prone to explosive upheavals underlies our view of frontier violence. Popular conceptions of frontier cities in the West have usually allowed for high degrees of violence, simply in recognition of the more unpredictable nature of a society made up of strangers.

Nineteenth-century urban developments specifically facilitated new environments designed to tolerate complex, nonsharing cultures; American cities made what could have been social chaos at least minimally functional. Formal organizations to provide public safety created cities where multiple cultures and classes could coexist or even conflict, without cooperation or shared cultures. This process could encompass individualism, but equally it could encompass tribalism of wildly different ethnic and racial groups. It occurred independently of the rise of individualism or capitalism and was not a teleological process. However, it provided a fertile ground for the burgeoning capitalist system, helping make American cities engines of economic expansion. A formal organizational structure meant that, in activity after activity, professionals replaced volunteers. And voluntary organizations, from unions to churches to chambers of commerce to temperance groups, learned to expect transiency and rapid membership turnover. A mobile people created a stable society.

Rampant individualism and plural, nonsharing cultures can coexist and function only when each culture is willing to adapt and change or where the environment specifically accommodates culturally divergent groups. The latter can be accomplished by replacing social structures carried in each individual's head with formally and externally enforced ones. This argument does not invoke the standard notions of *gemeinschaft* and *gesellschaft*, of traditional face-to-face communities contrasted with modern mass societies. It simply asserts that without shared cultural and behavioral norms, a formal organization of some sort is required to produce a smoothly working social entity like a city. Without the proper organizational forms, the setting for irreconcilable cultural conflict exists, as for instance in Beirut in the 1980s.

From Regulation to Service Government

In the transition to the modern urban nation, therefore, city government has changed its role radically. Its essentially responsive, regulatory nature has disappeared. The city government that emerged from the late nineteenth and early twentieth century emphasizes active service, not passive regulation. This assertion may come as a shock to someone constructing a new building, who has to file for dozens of permits and go through multiple inspections. But modern city regulations are in fact significant services, laying out the best-known modes of construction, of planning, and of achieving physical urban goals. It is a service to all city highrise users, for instance, to have fire-resistant structures. The cooperation between industry and the city rulemakers is all too often ignored by some commentators, who somehow envision city rulemakers in conflict with good practice or private interests. As a recent analysis of the real estate industry makes abundantly clear, the very nature of twentieth-century infrastructural city services has derived from the efforts of private developers, not the other way around.[2] Thus the word "service," its implications contrasting vividly with the old image of city government, has become the appropriate term with which to label modern city government activities.

When they created fire departments, public health boards, or police departments, American cities did something bold and innovative. Even when they were not the first to establish such services, the individual city governments took risky stances against tradition, inertia, and the municipal budget, for new services entailed new expenditures and therefore required far greater revenues. One historian, Jonathan Prude, has shown how in early nineteenth-century Massachusetts even such an innocuous town issue as public responsibility for road building was in fact a troublesome and unresolved political question. In the case Prude analyzes, mill owner Samuel Slater worked from 1816 to 1830 to make roads more convenient to his textile mills. As Slater promoted the building of local turnpikes and invested heavily in them, he tried to get town and county governments to build new roads and change the courses of existing ones. His requests were quite often resisted, not so much for their obvious self-servingness, but because they would require local governments to initiate long-term capital intensive, enterprises. Americans had long used "natural" roads and any improvements necessitated costly governmental action.[3] In fact, the first half of the nineteenth century saw many subsidies granted to canals and railroads, but it was not until the last decade of the nineteenth-century that heavy governmental investment in hard surfaced roads became commonplace. Yet, within forty years, city council minutes recorded almost weekly their massive expansions of street networks.

All these actions taken by nineteenth-century city governments have come only in retrospect to seem like "natural responses" to local needs. And nowhere was this more true than for social control. Of course, the changes were neither sudden nor dramatic for the nation as a whole. They had begun brewing in the eighteenth century. For instance, one historian has analyzed city ordinances in Albany and New York City to show how between 1707 and 1773 public safety issues pertained to a rising percentage—from about 10 percent to about 30 percent—of all ordinances. Arguably, these eighteenth-century ordinances may have been responsive rather than regulatory, but clearly they also intimated the nature of things to come.[4]

There have been three related yet independent components to the history of urban public safety. One is the actual growth, in numbers as well as in organizational complexity and structure, of the various safety organizations, beginning around the middle of the nineteenth century. Another is the change in levels and kinds of threats to public safety, from crimes of violence to accidents and fires. And a third, which developed as an unintended consequence of the first two, was the new and pervasive assumption that government has an obligation to provide safety.

This analytic scheme explicitly diverges from the pervasive social control thesis, which argues that changes and reforms aimed at the public welfare actually masked mechanisms that were intended to control ethnic groups, the working class, or other potentially disruptive social groups. Social reforms, proponents of the social control perspective argue, simply hid increases in oppression by the elite. For instance, one historian has argued forcefully that capitalists created the police purely to control the potentially rebellious working class, while another has argued that in late nineteenth-century Chicago, reformers who wanted to control immigrants' children designed a juvenile justice system for this purpose alone.[5] Although these interpretations sound farfetched when stated so bluntly, the social control perspective does underscore an important if not essential aspect of nineteenth-century social reform: reformers had complex and not always totally benevolent motivations. Even though public safety organizations in cities directly controlled some aspects of social behavior and were very often class or ethnically biased, their purposes, functions, and actual roles were far more subtle and important than the social control thesis implies.[6]

City Services and Urban Problems

Fear of Crime

In the course of American history the fear of predatory violence has migrated from the country to the city. And not without reason, as anyone who has arrived in the center of a large U.S. city on a late-night bus, walked outside the depot and experienced the sense of danger poised there can testify. Three hundred years ago, European colonists experienced similar feelings when they left the protection of their towns for the woods. In his famous sermon, "Sinners in the Hands of an Angry God," Jonathan Edwards terrified his parishioners with images of the wilderness, of Indians lurking in ambush. The intent of these images was to awaken his flock to the dangers of eternal damnation, for he knew their latent fears of personal and spiritual violence when outside of the protection of the town. By the late twentieth century, the wilderness itself has become a place needing protection; it represents a source of deep peace, a place for spiritual renewal. Today, ministers take their congregations there to discover God. If they wished to terrify their parishioners, they would use the image of the inner city terror, of muggers, of subways.

The reasons for this modern fear of city crime are at once simple and complex. Simple because most people, including both predators (no longer visualized as Indians or wild animals) and their victims, have moved to the city. Thus crime, while causally unrelated to the city, is an urban problem simply by virtue of its location. Complex because the nature of criminal offenses and the crime control system have both changed dramatically. Crimes of personal violence—homicides and various kinds of assaults—have declined, while crimes against personal property—theft and assorted types of fraud—have risen. The crime control system, once largely funded by its users, hapless victims and convicted felons, has become an autonomous set of highly visible organizations run by the state.

For nearly two centuries urbanization has transformed the American landscape so continuously and rapidly that no one can escape noticing and being affected by the physical aspects of the change. As a consequence, we tend to attribute all sorts of phenomena to the city, simply because they are located in the city. Pollution, crime, physical decay, and mental illness have all at one time or another been seen as the result of urbanization. The supposed urban cause of each problem has several reasonable-sounding explanations. Aggregation, population density, diseconomies of scale, and other theoretical arguments have been brought forward to account for these phenomena. Aggregation—the massing of so many dissimilar social groups—seems to be the wellspring of conflict. Density creates anomie, by crowding millions of strangers together. Diseconomies of scale cause waste, creating heat and smog concentrations which accelerate photochemical pollution. However, social theorists no longer unequivocally accept the urban origins of all of these urban problems.[7]

The city does not necessarily cause the problems, even though it provides the location for them. Strikingly, the empirical evidence, though imperfect, suggests that the social consequences of urbanization do not in themselves cause crime. Growing cities turned neither their inhabitants nor their newcomers into criminals, but they did make painfully visible social problems that up to then had been seen only on a small scale in a world of scattered villages and towns. Indeed, newspaper articles in the mid-nineteenth century speculated that urbanization caused crime in part because the writers were ignorant of higher rural crime rates. One particularly strong and carefully supported argument posits that nineteenth-century cities actually "civilized" people, making them less homicidal and violent. Research on Philadelphia shows that over the last half of the nineteenth century, Philadelphians not only murdered each other less but learned to deal better with the technologies of city life, dying less often in accidents.[8] Even if the causal mechanisms remain unclear, the evidence assembled by some historians suggests that until approximately World War II, crime and violence in the Western world had been on the decline, not on the rise.[9] Rather than presenting the modern world as a place progressively plagued with more criminal violence, most evidence suggests a cautiously optimistic evaluation, a long, slow decrease in recorded levels of violence since at least the Middle Ages. And in the United States alone, violence and possibly theft declined from the mid-nineteenth century to the 1930s, and perhaps until even more recently.

The prosecution and punishment of criminal behavior have also changed, along with the rates of different types of offense. In the seventeenth century, offenses against morality and God appeared to dominate the courts, combined with a solid proportion of felony crimes which we still punish—theft, homicide, assault, and the like. It is difficult to compare crime trends from the seventeenth century to the twentieth century, if for no other reason than that the relatively homogenous population represented in the colonies was soon replaced by an ethnically and racially diverse one. However, crimes of personal violence, for instance, seem to have declined since the late eighteenth century. Given the rapid increase in movable property, it might also be the case that crimes against property saw a decrease, relative to the amount of movable property available to be stolen. And economic crimes, those involving fraudulent manipulation of fiscal instruments in the burgeoning money economy, have clearly increased.

None of these trends should be taken to mean that crime has lessened as an urban problem. It may in fact be just the opposite: that the decline in crime has made it seem more open to control, hence less a continous social presence and more problematic. This would provide strong motivation to emphasize and augment the various formal mechanisms of crime control, thus continuing to reduce the incidence of crime. However, given our present state of knowledge about the effectiveness of crime control, it is premature to make absolute claims that changes in the system have directly affected crime rates. Thus we can really only draw cautious and conditional inferences about crime and what makes it increase or decrease.

While per capita rates of crime are important for comparative purposes, whether across time or between places, our day-to-day perceptions are another matter.[10] Ordinarily, in the twentieth century we report social phenomena per capita of some broad population at risk: yet we often fear crime because of its absolute numbers, not because of the per capita amount in some geographical area. From the urban point of view, crime is a problem because it exists: the causal explanations and appropriate measurement techniques are problems only to the historians, and not to those people whom they study.

Moreover, the question of why and when societies take organized action against crime is perhaps unanswerable. Does tolerance of crime decrease when control technologies become more effective? When norms and expectations change? With an increase in spendable social wealth, crime control being something of a luxury social good? Or might a decreasing tolerance for crime be simply a by-product of the evolving expectation that social organizations can and should deal with various disorderly behaviors?

It is important, here as elsewhere, to avoid taking the category of "problem" for granted. The identification of something as a "problem" is in itself an important action which in turn may be causally related to the ability to deal with the problem. Equally important, if not more so, is the second step, for a group to decide to confront the "problem." Crime, for instance, has probably always been considered a problem, but it becomes analytically interesting when a group—in this case, the city government—decides it has both the ability and the obligation to act to solve the problem. The way a city approaches crime can tell us much about the relationship of politics to organizations to action.

The New Police

Unlike fire fighting, police systems in big cities have always depended on more than volunteer efforts. In fact, the constable and watch system was based on a combination of user fees, forced labor, and direct taxes. In the Middle Ages, the constable served as a court officer, performing a variety of services, all for fees. The services ranged from making arrests to serving warrants to holding prisoners and producing witnesses. The constables often organized the night watch, made up of men who donated a few nights a year to patrol their community. By the early eighteenth century in some American cities, city government paid for the watch, though formally the paid watchmen were substitutes for volunteers, and revenues to pay them were raised through fines levied on those who did not show up for watch duty. By tradition the watch patrolled only in the dark, from sundown to sunup. The constables, in theory, at least, responded to complaints, usually in the day. By the 1820s Boston's constables patrolled regular daytime routes, consistently earning fees that amounted to salaries by arresting drunks and other petty offenders.[11]

The reform of London's Metropolitan Police in 1829 introduced the basic elements of a new police: they were to be regularly paid, organized in a hierarchical fashion with uniforms, and responsible to the executive rather than the judicial arm of government. Parliament soon created police for all of England and Wales. In the 1830s and 1840s city government reformers in Boston, New York, and Philadelphia urged that the constable and watch system be replaced by one modeled after London's Metropolitan Police. Arguing that the new police would be more efficient, would seek out and deter crime, and would provide a more controllable force, the reformers pressured city governments for two decades before the transition was complete. At first most cities created separate day and night police, a cumbersome organizational structure that formalized the established daytime constabulary and somewhat upgraded the night watch, while still preserving the medieval distinction between the day and night organizations. From these two separate organizations, cities then moved toward a unified day and night police. With this unification, cities created a quasi-military organization form, complete with uniforms, regular patrol beats, and bureaucratic rules and norms. Symbolized by the uniform, the new police owed their allegiance and regular salaries to the city. They no longer responded solely to citizen complaints but actively sought out unreported criminal offenses and prevented other offenses. Prevention, rather than pure reponse to offenses already accomplished, was to be the character of the new police.

Americans copied the visible features of London's Metropolitan Police, but made a significant and uniquely American modification. From their first establishment in New York City in the 1850s, police forces in the United States were created at the local level and on local initiative. American police then, were creatures of municipal government, while London and all other British police reported, finally, to the Home Office. Thus the United States laid the foundations for what would become the most decentralized form of uniformed civil police in the world.

No single conflict or conflagration accounts for the spread of the uniformed police across nineteenth-century urban America. Each city had different individual and immediate reasons for creating its police force, from beer riots in St. Louis to business concerns about labor unrest in Buffalo to elite New Yorkers' fear of street crime.[12] Whatever the momentary reason, the deeper, underlying pressures had little to do with rising crime or class or ethnic conflict. Instead the formally structured and uniformed police were an early step in the creation of the new service providing city government. The transformation of an ancient and theoretically passive urban service to an active one was dramatic, though it was probably not recognized as such at the time. The change was dramatic only in retrospect, when the new police actually began performing their multiple services. Then, in the context of a changing urban government that had begun providing more and more services, services increasingly thought of as services, the police became an important part of the late nineteenth-century city.

The new police officers themselves, those who actually provided the first city services that were available to all, often did not like the new service oriented government. The creation of new police forces out of the traditional constable and night watches in the 1840s and 1850s caused an unanticipated stir within police departments. None of the city governments intended to create an organization that would provide a broad range of social services. They simply wanted to prevent crime in the latest manner, as was done in London. But they did, in fact, end up unintentionally inventing a service organization. The police officers themselves recognized this before anyone else in city government. When Philadelphia reorganized and modernized its police in 1855–1856, for instance, it demanded that they wear uniforms. Police officers vigorously resisted; many quit, others went home and took off their uniforms as soon as they had left the station for patrol, and all protested that they would not wear "servants' livery."[13]

The first U.S. cities that modernized and uniformed their police ran into similar protests. Police officers refused to see themselves as servants, or their role as one of serving. The uniforms made the police servants in two ways. First, of course, they looked a bit like traditional servants' livery. Second, their visible presence on the city streets made them servants to the requests of all, and they could no longer hide behind their anonymous citizen's clothing. Ironically then, today, though it may seem as though the police provide less service than in the nineteenth century, some cities, like Los Angeles, emblazed the motto on their police cars, "To Protect and to Serve." No matter how well or poorly the motto may reflect reality, it does signify the modern conception of the role of city government, a role developed only as recently as the last century.

As nineteenth-century cities became more active agents, their formal organizations of social control reflected the larger process. By definition, the traditional constable and watch form of policing responded only after a crime had been committed. The new police had as their mission the prevention and detection of crime. The difference is subtle but significant: the change, one from response to action. Not only did the new police symbolize urban change but they also partly enabled the transition from cities with common cultural bonds to those without. The creation of public order was a high priority for emerging, growing cities, particularly for their promoters.

The growth of formal urban crime control organizations completed a slow and deep transition in criminal justice which had been occurring throughout the Western world. This involved the demise of a loose criminal justice system that emphasized individual wrongs and retributions, and its replacement by one in which the state assumed responsibility for justice and crime prevention in a more general sense. This new attention to crime control required a dramatic reevaluation of criminal behavior and its control, moving both from the periphery to the center of social thought and action. Consequently, the history of crime and crime control takes us to a central juncture in modern history. From the history of society and social organizations we learn about crime and crime control; from crime and crime control we learn about the city.

Many of the earliest and most important services provided by the nineteenth-century city found their first organizational home in crime control organizations, especially the police. Indeed, the range of specific activities the police engaged in so multiplied and ramified that it must often have seemed that their least important activity was crime control. But almost as quickly as specific police services multiplied, city governments or voluntary, semipublic agencies stripped them away, creating new, permanent, and specialized bureaucracies to take over and professionalize each service. Jobs that the police had originated on a regular basis in the 1850s and 1860s and that devolved to specialists by the turn of the century included a wide range of activities, from health and boiler inspections to the detection and protection of abused children.

All too often historians have tried to account for the creation of the uniformed urban police with the crisis model, which looks for some criminal event or set of events to explain when and why cities suddenly invested scarce fiscal resources in policing. The underlying form of this argument is purely mechanical and ahistorical. It asserts that when some problem increases beyond a limit of tolerability, then a reaction occurs. But political action, which was required to create uniform police, does not operate like the laws of mechanics, and all too often problems which should by all reason demand political action result instead in inaction, sometimes in political extinction. Even if there had been crime waves in nineteenth-century American cities which prompted the creation of police departments, or fire outbreaks which prompted the creation of fire departments, we still have not explained these innovations. Why, after all, should any organization try to solve anew an age-old problem? For a crisis to precipitate action therefore requires a potential actor; the concept of passive response is not enough. Close examination of the political battles—often decades long—involved in creating fire departments, police departments, or public health departments shows that contrary to what many historians have claimed, there was nothing at all inevitable about these services.

In my study of the police in the United States, I asked what seemed at first simple questions, such as: when were the modern police created? what did they do? and how have they changed? Just finding a way to date the police turned out to be a highly ambiguous task. For several reasons, I settled on the dates when cities first uniformed their forces as an index. These dates show the timing of the spread of the police throughout the network of U.S. cities. They emphasize that the innovation occurred slowly, for it was not a simple or obviously necessary change for cities to make. Such organizations, entirely ordinary today, took considerable creative political effort. Each city that undertook this effort had to disband old organizations, fire some personnel, hire new personnel, make complex and uncertain decisions about budgeting, about responsibility, and myriad other concrete problems. In enactment and in content these decisions were political, highly visible, and controversial.

Punishment Moves from the City to the Country

As the locale and mode of crime control shifted, so did the locale and mode of the penitentiary. In the first decades of the nineteenth century Americans developed two somewhat different, internationally famous penitentiary models. The first was the Walnut Street Jail or Philadelphia system; the second was the Auburn system in New York State. Both demanded that their inmates maintain total silence, labor at productive work daily, and read the Bible in heavy doses. The Auburn system allowed the prisoners to work silently in groups, while the Philadelphia system enforced complete physical isolation. Hence they were often referred to as the silent system and the separate system. Both assumed that an inherent and universal moral sense, if given the opportunity to exercise itself, would convince the offender of the wrongfulness of his criminal offense. Solitude provided reflective opportunity, and when the prisoner found himself "alone, in view of his crime, he [would learn] to hate it." Subsequent remorse would ensure that when released, the offender would never again turn to evil.[14] Penitentiaries in the United States, mostly built in the nineteenth century, allowed them to come close to realizing European ideals of the time. Reformers came from Europe to observe these two penitentiaries, not quite aware that the notion of imprisonment with the intent to rehabilitate the prisoner was not a uniquely American invention.

It was an urban one, however. The birth of the urban prison occurred as the growth of nation-states slowly pacified the countryside, and it became less and less feasible to banish offenders to the social wilderness beyond the city walls.[15] First in Amsterdam, later in London, and finally in colonial America, city authorities created urban workhouses in the hopes of changing the basic personality and behavior of criminal offenders. Although called by names other than "penitentiary"—one of Philadelphia's prisons was the "Bettering House," for instance—the distinguishing feature of these places was that they emphasized reformation over retribution. In the late 1700s, Philadelphia Quakers expanded the concept of such centuries—old and often forgotten institutions to include the Christian notion of penitence and change from within. With Quakers' contribution of silence, the Walnut Street Prison appeared to be a new invention. Such a novel program, embodying the hopes of eighteenth-century Enlightenment philosophy in a new nation, was a subject made to order for discourse by foreign visitors like de Tocqueville. For visitors, such institutions provided models on which to project contemporary European visions of the potential for social and human change.

As late as the eighteenth century, the penitentary seemed a quintessentially urban institution. The two best-known American prisons, famous for introducing solitary confinement as the means of inducing offenders' pentience, were located in the two largest cities, Newgate (1791) in New York City and the Walnut Street Jail (1790) in Philadelphia. Yet as they became the subject of public attention and the recipients of larger sums of government money, prisons quickly shed their urban origins and moved to the country, or at least away from the major seaboard centers.

There were two primary reasons for this move. First, under the Constitution, state governments had jurisdiction over felony offenses, bearing the costs of their prosecution and punishment. When governments with felony crime responsibilities had had urban locations, as they did from the fifteenth through the eighteenth centuries, then pentientiaries could be located near or in the centers of formal state power, in cities. But after the American Revolution and the growth of the federal system, cities no longer represented the locus of political power. And when state governments began investing heavily in penitentiaries, the logic that had once linked government, punishment, and the city no longer obtained in a literal sense.

Second, after penitentiaries were no longer city institutions, state investment in their building and operating became an important form of political patronage. There was no locational imperative in their setting, and the jobs and other patronage they provided were, therefore, to be manipulated for political purposes. Most often states made the penitentiary a part of central state government, building it right in the capital. But not always. Like other state institutions, penitentiaries could be located to pay political debts, win friends, and reinforce partisan power. In the last half of the nineteenth century, when rural voters still represented more political power than urban voters, a penitentiary in a small city, an agricultural center, or county seat, earned more votes than did one in a city. So by midcentury, most state penitentiaries were built near small cities or in rural areas, moving farther away from urban centers.[16]

Consequently, the penitentiary seems today like an institution anything but urban in its origins or nature. Certainly, for most of its subsequent history, this has been the case. But it is accurate to say that penitentiaries, just as much as police, began as urban institutions.

Fire Fighting

The histories of nineteenth-century urban police and fire departments resemble one another in significant ways. Both institutions began the century as voluntary organizations with ancient pedigrees and histories. Since the early middle ages, the Anglo-American world had demanded that citizens "volunteer" to serve on the night watch, to be ready to join the *posse comitatus* whenever a felon was on the loose, and to keep some sort of weapon and firefighting bucket ready for use. City governments had begun to intervene by the late sixteenth century in England, hiring "substitutes" for the constable and watch system, and in eighteenth-century America by providing stationhouses, hoses, carts, and other equipment for fire companies. The fines levied upon those unwilling to serve in these voluntary safety organizations were simply a means of taxation to raise revenue for paid substitutes.

Cautious and fiscally conservative city officials and voters struggled for years to convince themselves and one another of the worthiness of establishing the earliest police and fire departments. Such innovations represented unprecedented and costly categories of fixed annual expenditures for local governments: something no politician could afford to treat casually. The resistance to regularized police and fire departments makes it clear that there was nothing very natural about these new organizational forms. Constables and other traditional police officers resisted the new police because their uniforms made them more directly and easily supervised, cutting in on the entrepreneurial aspect of the old police. And "volunteer" fire departments were in some cases virtual private clubs whose "costly houses, beautiful apparatus and extravagant furniture and supplies" the city furnished. They elected their chiefs, who then drew large city salaries, and who aggressively resisted any attempts at outside control by the city council. Their hold over the city was more powerful than the police, for they could refuse to fight fires. If anything, then, the new police and fire departments were unnatural developments, requiring some twenty years of struggle to create in Boston, New York, and Philadelphia. They were in fact early aspects of the new service governments that emerged more fully in the twentieth century: their creation and institutional solidification represent a series of dramatic political initiatives rather than passive responses.[17]

In his colorful account of Philadelphia's fire companies, Bruce Laurie stresses how by the 1830s, the formerly sedate volunteer fire-fighting groups had become rallying points for ethnic and neighborhood youth gangs. On some occasions, established gangs took over the fire companies: the Killers took over the Moyamensing Hose Company, for instance. And in at least one case, the split also subsumed the working-class issue of temperance: the Bouncers infiltrated the membership of the Weccacoe Hose Company, whose former members then reconstituted themselves as a temperate fire company, the Weccacoe Engine Company. Thus the fire companies both contained and promoted gang violence, channeling it at some times toward competitive fire fighting and at others just toward fighting. New York's firehouse conflicts show that in keeping the fire-fighting companies "voluntary," considerable resources were put in the hands of fierce groups of young men. In 1852, for instance, four major conflicts erupted, involving five different companies, during which several people were "dreadfully injured by the stones, brick-bats, & c., which were hurled at them." Or, on July 13, 1860, the *New York Times*, p. 8, could calmly print the following item:

> Dennis Ryan, a member of Engine Company No. 21, died at the New-York Hospital on Wednesday night, in consequence of the injuries he received on the evening of the 3d inst., during the progress of the firemen's riot opposite French's Hotel. The combatants on the occasion referred to were the members of Ryan's

company and those of Engine Company No. 13, between whom
a grudge has long existed. . . . Deceased was 21 years of age. . . .

And one historian has made the explicitly functionalist argument that in Philadelphia, it was not until fire-fighting technology changed and steam engines became the new and very costly
mode of fighting fires that the city began to worry about the fire
gangs. The new technology, which required considerable capital
outlay by the city and a degree of expertise to operate, forced the
creation of a new professional organization in 1871.[18]
As intuitively appealing as this account is, it would be more
accurate to see the costly new technology and higher levels of expertise required as a political means of substituting fire-fighting
technology for firemen. At this time, steam pumps were not superior to hand pumps either in height or distance (although no one
considered volume), but steam did not require so many husky
young volunteers. The political struggle over steam versus hand
pumps in New York, for instance, centered on the issue of who
controlled the streets, the city government or the fire departments.
In a special comparison test of hand versus steam in 1855, Northern Liberty's hand-powered engine (known as "Old Hay-Wagon,"
or "Man-Killer") outpumped a steam engine 200 feet to 185 feet.
Yet the New York city council, a year later, specified two self pro-
pelled steam engines at $17,000. Nonetheless, it took another nine
years before they managed to eliminate the volunteers. In New
York, the final blow to the volunteers came from the city's merchants and property holders, spearheaded by a committee of fire
insurance underwriters, who provided the additional political pressure needed to achieve stricter building codes and fire-fighting
capabilities.[19]
Thus fire became the target of governmental concern. Previously the realm of voluntary organizations and private subscription
fire-fighting companies, this age-old threat to crowded cities may
have been greater in the cities built of wood and steel in the United
States than in those built of stone in Europe. The conditional *may*
should emphasized here, for there is no way to adequately measure
the relative risks of seventeenth-century and nineteenth-century
cities. Perhaps more difficult to explain than the suddenness with
which fire-fighting became systematically controlled, is the long
period in which U.S. cities tolerated haphazard techniques. In analyzing this problem, the notion of a regulatory versus a promotional

city proves useful. The regulatory city could insist on rules within which a voluntary organization could operate, but only the promotional city could provide a safe business and social environment in its effort to attract capital and people. The increased scope of urban public goods incorporated what had been an individual and personal liability. Cities invested in fire fighting just as they subsidized railroads and other forms of private enterprise. They used their debt issuing privileges to fund the new capital requirements that technology-intensive fire departments posed. This also relieved individuals of the costly burdens of fire protection, for in fact fire was an economic risk which any growth promoting city would have been wise to control. Just as medieval city walls protected the merchant's warehouses against destructive armies, nineteenth-century fire departments protected a wide range of economic activities in the city. The service aided downtown property owners (suburban property was not nearly so threatened by the spread of fire). Because the capital cost of fire fighting provided an important investment opportunity for the private money market, city governments neatly mediated between two private sectors, downtown property owners and investors. City government had created a public good which seemed logical and natural, and which virtually as soon as it existed became an essential component of modern urban life.

The City as a Source of New Ideas for Government Activities

The transition of the penitentiary from a city-administered institution to one overseen by state government, often located in a rural place or on the suburban fringe of a city, foreshadowed a subsequent pattern in urban service organizations. These umbrella organizations served a variety of purposes, and in so doing they often fostered other special-purpose organizations which then stripped away some of the umbrella organization's functions. Thus it may appear that the ongoing umbrella organization has become more specialized, when in fact the creation of other, narrower groups has reduced it to a specialized role, at least until it takes on new general duties. This is a subtle but important distinction. It suggests that we should not consider all regularly administered city services throughout the nineteenth and twentieth centuries as tending toward more fragmentation and specialization. Instead, we should regard them as general service organizations that unconsciously provided experimental testing grounds for the trial of new services.[20]

This distinction is particularly important in the case of the urban police. They all too easily appear as a crime-fighting organization frustrated and distracted by peripheral service duties. The police, as their name implies, in fact provided a practical model of the new urban service government. Derived from the Greek *polis*, meaning city or city polity, the term *police* by the early nineteenth century referred to the legal power of the state to regulate a broad range of activities within its boundaries. Police power meant the equivalent of political housekeeping. In the post–civil War era, American legal theorists began to develop a narrower definition of police power, tying the concept more closely to the city and social control.

The new police performed a wide variety of functions, the more legitimate of which devolved to specialized city services as the century waned.[21] They inspected various sources of public health nuisances, like open sewers or faulty boilers, looked for lost children, sometimes illegally controlled voting, took in the indigent and homeless, controlled roaming animals. Their other, less regular jobs varied from city to city. Often their assignments were done for the simple reason that there was no other around-the-clock, readily available government representative. The police represented a unique tool of government administration, one that attracted tasks no government had previously considered doing. Lost children, for instance, had previously been a private problem; parents, neighbors, and relatives had had to search for them as best they could.

Throughout the nineteenth century many tasks at first allocated to the police became the mandates of other, newly specialized branches of local government. The police originally did many of these jobs because of the strategic communication advantages provided by their organizational mode. The state of communication within cities in the early nineteenth century was chaotic.[22] Even sending a simple message across New York City could take longer than communicating with another city. Most cities lacked an accessible and centralized communications hierarchy of any kind. Only the daily newspapers served as a forum for common intelligence. The police, with their centralized, hierarchical structure and their easily identified uniforms, unexpectedly provided a new form of urban communication. Coupled with their regular patrol, their organizational structure provided a new urban mode of service: integrated, accessible, regular, and free.

Thus, from the first continuously uniformed police introduced in New York City in 1856 to their relatively quick spread across the country to smaller and farther-flung cities, innovation followed upon innovation. Even in regard to criminal prosecutions, police provide a major change, making the arrest and prosecution of offenders an activity based not on fees paid by individual victims, but a public service funded by city government. Urban crime control at once became a public good, like streets. Unlike streets, the police spawned other specialized services which in turn also became public goods, like sewage control, boiler inspection, and animal control.

The national crisis of the Civil War came at a time when cities were busy expanding their services, feeling their ways to new modes of government. The war did not undo any of the internal changes described in this chapter, but the heavy fiscal burden that it imposed on local governments ensured that further changes had to be compatible with low taxes and a restricted budget. Because the nineteenth-century cities could finance much of their new activities on the expectations of expanding future incomes, they had little to worry about except growing. While the complete range of city services would continue to develop in the period between 1870 and 1930, the conceptual and practical foundations were well established before 1870. Important details had to be worked out, but the new form of a service city had begun.

5 ☆ From Closed Corporation to Electoral Democracy

It is unclear whether or not cities are "natural" creatures, that is, phenomena that would have arisen in any historical, social, political, and economic context. Our current inability to understand enormous third world cities suggests that their very sprawling and explosive growth is a phenomenon independent of factors traditionally considered by urban historians; this kind of growth therefore seems "natural," unstoppable. But more likely, we use the concept of "natural" to avoid trying to understand the complex phenomena that contribute to urban growth. Either way, it is clear that American cities are definitely not "natural": from their beginnings they have been creatures dependent on legal tradition, on enabling legislation, and on judicial interpretation of legislation.

The City Corporation

In the late eighteenth and early nineteenth century, incorporation was a legal device used by legislatures to encourage and protect large capital investment ventures that benefited the public good. City charters, although not issued for the purpose of protecting capital accumulation, had been legislated in such a spirit, along with other such corporate ventures as toll bridges and roads, and various public enterprises. The corporate charter protected investors by limiting liability to the amount invested, and guaranteeing investors a handsome return on their investment through monopolies. One might invest in a bridge company, for instance, knowing that the bridge would have a monopoly on tolls over the river in perpetuity. The public benefited from such a monopoly, because the charter created the capital fund with which to build the bridge in the first place. In a sense the public traded the toll monopoly for no bridge at all. Thus the corporate charter was a positive legislative tool for the public good.

In the early nineteenth century, with a series of Supreme Court decisions and the mobilization of increasing amounts of capital, the nature of the corporate charter began to shift. By 1840, the charter was no longer a special privilege granted to do public good, but a license to increase private capital. The Supreme Court interpreted the Constitution as giving corporations the status of persons. Their regional character disappeared when the Court decided, in *Bank of Augusta v. Earle* (1839), that the principle of comity—in international law, the assumption that one nation respects another's laws—applied within the United States. In practice, this meant that a corporation chartered in one state could act as a legal person in another state. Within the span of half a century, an ancient and seldom used legal device had been turned into a powerful tool for economic action.

Although both Philadelphia and New York City had corporate charters in the eighteenth century, the city corporations were superficial imitations of their powerful English models. Prior to the Revolution, for instance, Philadelphia's city corporation seems to have restricted its activities to hosting visiting dignitaries and supervising the markets, fairs, and wharves. The corporation apparently acted as no more than an exclusive city club: certainly it did not foreshadow the aggressive cities of a century later. And it was a moribund club whose aldermen held their positions for life, with only rare resignations. Often the aldermen paid for city costs out of their own pockets, emphasizing both the lack of an effective tax levy, and the extent to which the city corporation truly represented an elite club whose commercial interests were identical with those of the city.[1]

Who Ran the City?

The extension of the franchise to adult white males in the first two decades of the nineteenth century, prior to the midcentury explosion of towns and cities and their peopling with immigrants, ensured local political participation. Within a few decades after its extension, the all-white male franchise unseated the local elite from city governments.[2] Almost certainly, the elite would have

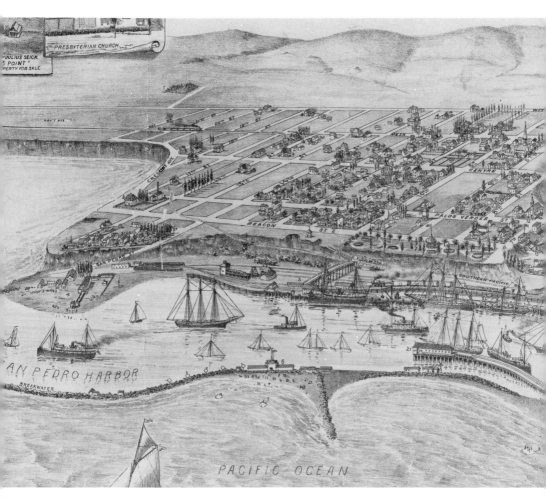

San Pedro, California, 1893.
This small village was soon to become a major urban port. On the left is
the dirt embankment where a half century earlier Richard Henry Dana
had camped. Already a terminus for a rail line to Los Angeles (in the foreground), within two decades after this view, Los Angeles had annexed the
town in order to make it the city's harbor.

Source: Seaver Center for Western History Research, Museum of Natural History,
Los Angeles.

been less generous with the franchise had they envisioned the ensuing decline of their own power and the rise of working-class and immigrant voters. Its extension in older cities like New York and Philadelphia, with their prerevolutionary charters establishing freemanship as a prerequisite to political participation, required state intervention; the city corporations argued that their ancient charters protected their essentially closed membership. Protected though the corporations were, their privileges contradicted the principles of democracy, and their "ancient" status reeked of aristocratic privilege. Moreover, these closed city councils combined legislative, judicial, and executive functions in one body, as anomalous in the constitutional era as restricted corporation membership. By the early nineteenth century state legislators began simply abolishing the old charters, establishing new ones on more democratic and constitutional principles. The possibility that such legislation might open the floodgates to democratic action seemed real indeed. By the late 1820s New York City saw the Workingmen's party challenging (though ultimately losing to) established political parties. It has been argued that in the early part of the nineteenth century, working-class politics and near victories had more impact than in the latter part of the century, when immigrant political machines gave voting power to the poor, but squandered this power to support the urban status quo.[3]

Who held positions of power matters for several reasons. First, if only one social group holds power, other groups are denied the opportunity to govern, whether or not the eventual policy outcomes are similar. Similarly, if a single group governs and it consistently favors its own members above others, then its dominance is unjust. However, the social analysis of urban political power is subtle because of the difficulty in separating intention and outcome. As the American city has taken its various unprecedented forms, the power elite have often found it difficult or even impossible to establish the most self-serving policy directions. When an agenda cannot be comprehensibly established, power can appear to be divided, for its directions are.

The ties of class and status to local political power were more clearly visible in eighteenth-century New England towns, where one historian, Edward M. Cook, Jr., has analyzed the nature of elections to town offices. Two important points emerge from his research. First, local prominence made a specific difference in the age at which people were elected selectmen, the usual entry-level position in town politics. Prominent people were elected on average seven years earlier than the nonprominent. Second, in the larger cities, such as Boston and Salem, there was less father-to-son continuity in office than in smaller places. There, membership in the elite was determined by wealth, not family: "Major offices in cities went overwhelmingly to the current merchant princes and to the leaders of popular political factions, many of whom were recent immigrants or newly risen to prominence." In a sense, Cook's research establishes both the presence of elites in politics, and their differing natures in city and farm village. The villages had multigenerational elites compared with the cities, but both voted for elite members with greater alacrity than they did for the nonelite.[4]

Immigration and Politics

Urban political shifts synchronized the broader shift from regulation to service in city government. Similarly, the changing electoral politics of U.S. cities had an interlocking social, political, and economic basis. The first and most obvious reason for this transfer of political power is demographic. The white male franchise had been extended prior to the first heavy waves of immigration from the British Isles in the late 1840s. Successive waves of immigrants quickly transformed the ethnic base of voters from native-born whites to a complex ethnic mix. As shown in table 4, many cities quickly gained immigrant populations of poor, Irish Catholics and a broad range of Germans by midcentury. Given the intense and active hostility of the native-born and immigrant Protestants toward the Irish, and the linguistic separation of the Germans, their distinct, oppositional voting came as no surprise. Many voting studies have documented the power of this "ethno-cultural" voting throughout the nineteenth century, with splits often coming not over substantive issues but developing simply as ethnic opposition.[5]

The relatively small stakes involved in municipal elections only partially explains the apparent lack of elite resistance to the immigrant accession to political power. Until about the 1890s, all city voters could agree on one thing, that the role of government had to be fiscally limited. Working-class voters in particular wanted a limited and inexpensive government, often opposing such things

TABLE 4

PERCENT FOREIGN-BORN FOR SELECTED CITIES, 1900 AND 1920

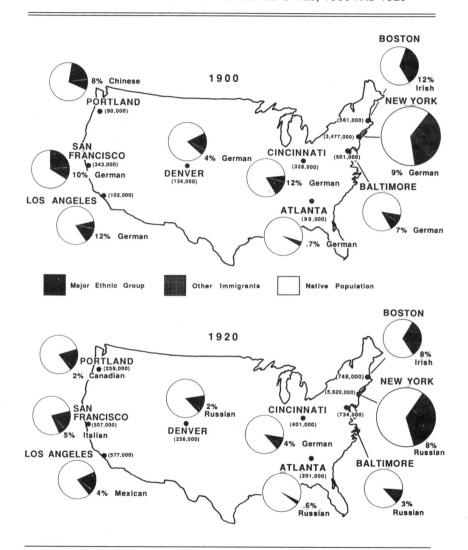

SOURCE: Bureau of the Census, *Population 1920*, Vol. II (Washington, D.C.: Government Printing Office, 1922), table 12, 729–733; Bureau of the Census, *Compendium of the Eleventh Census: 1890*, Pt. II (Washington, D.C.: Government Printing Office, 1894), table 2, 604–611.

as city-run employment bureaus.[6] Moreover, local commercial and new industrial elites had expanded their bases of economic operations on a regional scale by the second half of the century, so that their fortunes were no longer inextricable from those of the city. Their loss of local power simply did not have the economic consequences it might have had earlier, nor did the notion of responsibility for local affairs carry such weight as it had. As long as the elite did not want the role of government to expand considerably, city politics could remain factional but not substantive. Additionally, in new communities springing up to the west of the established colonial cities and towns, if the elite had rigidly refused to yield political power, the already badly fragmented social structures would have split even further, hindering whole towns in their search for new immigrants and capital.

Usually such issues were not explicitly articulated, but in the case of Scranton, Pennsylvania, we do get a sense of the trade-offs involved. The elite of Scranton were boldly presented with competing class interests when they decided to incorporate a large area around the town in order to support their own economic expansion. Scranton was a relatively new city; its iron and coal entrepreneurs had come from outside the region. Their competitive world spread far beyond the bounds of their day-to-day operations, and their acquisitiveness far exceeded its dependence on local power and prestige. They knew the incorporation would bring the town's working-class Irish voters into numerical dominance: the trade-off was the town's enhanced economic power to aid industry versus a loss in elite political power. In choosing the former, those in power decided to "endure the ills we have [rather] than to fly to others we know not of."[7] They choose Irish politicians and expanded fiscal power for the city over a political status quo that carried with it the threat of economic stagnation.

The Dahl Model of Urban Political Sequences

Thus, as political constituencies changed in cities, so did those who governed. Based on New Haven, Connecticut, political scientist Robert A. Dahl has established a schematic, four-period model of American urban political change, which integrates policy, politicians, and changing political constituencies and structure, looking at who occupied different slots rather than at what they did. Like many models, this one does not fit all cities (San Francisco is a notable exception), and it has the further weakness of making political changes seem to be autonomic responses to an economic imperative. But it does serve as a useful starting point in thinking about those who governed. In Dahl's model city, governments evolved from early domination by "patrician elites" to ones run by immigrants and bosses, who in turn were followed by reformers, and finally by modern professional politicians, often "ex-plebes," that is, of working class origins.[8] This change in politicians and their constituencies has often paralleled the shift in urban government's role from regulation to service. The two have not occurred in lockstep, nor have the four eras of urban government first delineated by Dahl proven to be as precisely clear in reality as they have in theory. Cities have varied greatly, and not all bosses were the cigar-smoking Irishmen so often caricatured by reformers. But Dahl's model of a sequence of urban political leadership does capture some of the broader trends of succeeding political styles and groups of political constituencies.

The Dahl model works to summarize the mayoral history of New York City. Vignettes of four different New York City mayors exemplify his simplified, four-period description of the sequence of American urban political development. From the colonial period until the Civil War era, a city government dominated by patricians yielded almost imperceptibly to one led by a commercial elite. Cornelius Van Wyck Lawrence, mayor of New York from 1834 until 1837, typifies this first, transitional era. His mother was of an old, wealthy Dutch family, his father from a not-quite-so-old but wealthy English family. Raised on the family estate in Flushing, Lawrence prospered as a New York City merchant and ran for office at the age of forty-three, a Jacksonian Democrat. After three terms as mayor, he returned to business, becoming a bank president.

Following the Civil War, with large influxes of immigrants into the city, there was a shift to government by large, often corrupt, political machines. Often these were run by bosses who were immigrants themselves, or who catered to the immigrants who usurped power from the old elite. As the elite lost power and abandoned interest in local politics, they either returned to the business of amassing wealth or went on to regional or national politics. William M. Tweed, born in 1823, joined Tammany in 1859 and quickly became a major power broker in New York City's Democratic machine, until his criminal trial in 1873. Probably the best-known boss of the nineteenth century, Tweed never actually held the mayor's office. He was not an immigrant, having been born in New York City. He was not even clearly ethnic, though he was probably of Scottish descent. Nor was he from the impoverished working class; his artisan father made and sold chairs.[9] More typical of this second period was Thomas Coman, born in Ireland in 1836, who became a Tammany Hall mayor briefly when he was thirty-two, and remained an alderman until the downfall of the Tweed Ring in 1872. Prior to his political career, he had been a newspaper reporter and worked in the post office, where he had been accused though not convicted of embezzlement.

Dahl's third period of urban political development falls into the early twentieth century, when native born, middle-class reformers defeated the machines, ousted the corrupt bosses, and ended their illegal control of voters and the ballot box. Seth Low, mayor for one term, 1902-1903, typified the reform era. Born to an old and wealthy Yankee family in Brooklyn, he became president of Columbia University in 1889. He ran for mayor at the age of fifty, as a candidate of the Citizen's Union, and during his year as mayor he tried to apply rational principles of modern management to the corrupt city government.

The fourth and current era of city politics began in the Depression decade, and saw the rise of a new, professional politician. Robert Wagner, mayor from 1954 to 1965, exemplifies this era. The son of a U.S. senator, Wagner went directly from law school into a lifelong political career, becoming mayor at the age of forty-four.[10]

Loosely defined, these four periods in New York City's political history also reflect the city's changing economy. The first phase reminds us of its function as a commercial entrepôt, its commercial elite blending comfortably with landholders, separation between commerce and landed wealth never acquiring quite the distinctive force it had in England. This era of commercial dominance disappeared as industry moved from the countryside into the city in the first decades of the nineteenth century. The owners of industry never entered local politics to the extent that earlier businessmen did, partly because their political interests were better represented on a state and national level. The extension of the franchise and the peopling of cities with immigrants to run the factories precluded any easy political dominance except by the party machines, and this second era thus reflects the industrial growth of the city. Finally, the third and fourth phases of urban politics represent the submergence of immigrant voters, an assertion of middle-class and professional control, and the solidification of the emergent service city. In short, the political phases of New York represent the commercial, industrial, and postindustrial city economies.

If we take St. Louis as another example, and look at its mayors from 1822 to the mid-1960s, the following years (with slight interruptions) had mayors who were native born Protestants with nonworking-class, nonpolitical career backgrounds: 1822-1842, 1854-1864, 1902-1925, 1933-1943. These years sketch in the early patrician elite period, their loss of personal dominance in the late nineteenth century, their return to power in the progressive era, and finally the post–World War II growth of a new breed of professional politician.

Southern Cities

Just as the model of urban political sequences articulated above does not describe the precise political processes in different cities, it is also somewhat geocentric, for it ignores southern cities altogether. Thus it must be modified even further. Southern cities developed somewhat differently from their northeastern counterparts, and must therefore be contrasted carefully. In the South, only a handful of cities went through a period that had anything resembling northern industrial growth and immigration. Even these cities—Richmond, Birmingham, Memphis, and perhaps New Orleans—tended to have immigrants or industry, but never the intense combination of both so common in northern cities large and small. Table 4, which displays some regional cities and their proportions of foreign-born inhabitants, emphasizes the native born character of southern cities.

In part because they had resisted enfranchising black voters, or had disenfranchised them, southern cities never really experienced as powerfully the three factors that had underwritten political machines—immigration, industrialization, and the widespread franchise. Consequently the political sequence in southern cities was less likely to include the political machines, dependent as they were on immigrant votes. There were some southern political machines, which easily matched those in the North for corruption, but they did not need to mobilize immigrant voters. Memphis's Boss Crump, for instance, ran an effective political machine for over thirty years, from 1909 to 1915 and 1927 to 1954. Crump's twentieth-century machine carefully cultivated commercial interests and personal ties rather than immigrant loyalties, as it purchased votes.[11]

Most southern cities remained in the earlier phase of dominance by either commercial leaders or wealthy landowners well into the mid-twentieth century. Urbanist Blaine A. Brownell has termed this the "commercial-civic elite," maintaining that the apex of its "unquestioned" political power came in the 1920s. But this pattern has persisted in some cities up to the present. In some southern cities, even the business elite had difficulty attaining power. In Charleston, for instance, wealthy planters had slightly more political power than did people with commercial interests. In a study comparing Charleston and Boston in the early nineteenth century, William H. Pease and Jane H. Pease explicitly draw this contrast, showing how by the mid-nineteenth century the internal political structure of Charleston remained a "web spun of personal ties; Boston's was one increasingly of institutional linkages."[12] Thus the familiar stereotype of the impersonal, business-like, Yankee city and the personal, paternalistic, and less commercial southern city had some basis in reality.

Local Politics and Industry

How cities were governed is a much more particular question than describing who held office. One study of Scranton and Wilkes-Barre contrasts the nineteenth-century economic and political leadership of these two neighboring Pennsylvania coal and steel towns. It shows how the older city, Wilkes-Barre, which had grown first as a farming and market center in the late eighteenth century, remained in the political stranglehold of a family-dominated elite throughout the nineteenth century. The town's leaders used their considerable political skill in manipulating the state government to restrict the opportunities of outsiders and of other, competing towns such as Scranton. Between 1820 and 1840 Wilkes-Barre's elite had made a quick and profitable transition from agriculture to coal exporting, but once engaged in a profitable enterprise, its caution and defensiveness put an end to further entrepreneurship. In addition, the town's leaders protected their political hegemony by refusing to expand its boundaries, for fear of incorporating the votes of immigrants living outside the city limits.

Scranton, in contrast, was settled by a diverse group of outside capitalists in order to develop it as an industrial city. They used the city government to expand their opportunities, incorporating in 1866, five years earlier than Wilkes-Barre, and aggressively expanding the city boundaries to promote their own mining and foundery ventures. As one consequence of this boundary expansion, in 1866, Irish immigrants took over the city's political machinery. The most notable mayor came in 1880 with the election of Terrence V. Powderly, national president of the Knights of Labor. Yet the city's economic elite consciously choose this democratic "ill" over restricted economic expansion.[13]

Thus Wilkes-Barre exemplified a city where family, political, and economic power, and the daily running of the city government, were all integrated. There was one elite, its interests coterminous with the economy and the polity. Consequently, Wilkes-Barre remained in the first stage of urban governance, one that had characterized colonial cities and that persisted for varying periods into the nineteenth century. In Wilkes-Barre the commercial elite, though it became an industrial elite, still behaved in the manner it had established at the beginning of the nineteenth century. Scranton, however, represented a city where the industrial leaders abandoned political hegemony, albeit unwillingly, in favor of economic advantage, thus becoming an archetypal industrial city of the late nineteenth century.

Urban Diversity and Political Sequences

Few cities had their political history so purely determined by their economic heritage as these two Pennsylvania towns. For instance, one analysis of nineteenth-century San Francisco politics emphasizes the enormous constraints on the political actions of officeholders. The fiscal conservatism of the voters profoundly shaped politicians' options, whether they represented highly politicized working-class constituencies or more elite interest groups. City policy had much less margin for variation than we might now imagine, so that bosses and reformers did not do things all that differently. This example provides an important counterbalance to what might be called a personalistic understanding of city politics, for it shows how legislative limits, budgetary rules, and the voters' concern about their personal tax burdens operated powerfully to restrict the actual behavior of city officials.[14]

The four-act drama of urban political succession—with the bosses and reformers clashing in the climactic third act, and with professionals and, lurking in the background, the federal government, marching onstage for the final act—encompasses most major cities in the United States, although it requires substantial modification for the South. It is an incomplete scenario for all U.S. cities, however, because for every New York or Omaha, there were many more small places. Although individually these small places may seem insignificant to larger issues in American urban history, their net importance has actually been greater than is usually recognized, for they enhanced agriculture, fed the larger cities, and helped build a rich network of transportation and manufacturing throughout the country. In addition, these smaller places were repositories of entrepreneurial activity, often translated into sheer local boosterism. This booster spirit manifested itself in economic activity as well as political. In fact, so entrepreneurially aggressive were smaller urban places that their inhabitants sent in far more inventions to be patented than did either farmers or big-city folk. The numerical importance of smaller cities and towns to political history may be illustrated by comparing the total population of the major cities selected for analysis in the *Biographical Dictionary of American Mayors* with the remaining cities in the United States. The fifteen cities documented only accounted for about one-third of those living in towns and cities with populations greater than 2,500.[15] Even if one looks at cities above 25,000 persons in 1900, well over 40 percent of the urban population lived in smaller cities.

Arguably, the importance of the largest cities has been greater even when inventions and political changes came from small towns. Both the city manager and the commission forms of government, for instance, originated in smaller places, although big-city usage legitimized the innovations. But the histories of the small places have often differed significantly from those of the larger ones, and these separate stories are important in their own right. Henry Binford's history of Boston's antebellum suburbs, for instance, establishes how their relationship to growth changed qualitatively in the 1850s. Previously, the towns had conceived of themselves as politically and economically separate places, exploiting the nearby city as a resource: their character changed decidedly with population growth resulting from Boston's metropolitan influence. The earlier vision, Binford calls the "New Model," one that emphasized "small enterprise and scattered residential settlement" as well as "simple, cheap, municipal corporations." But in the second half of the nineteenth century, the conception of suburban city changed to one of middle-class, commuter homes. The literal growth of the central city and suburbs, then, had changed their understanding of growth.[16]

Introducing the political histories of smaller cities and towns to an urban history of the United States might at first appear to pose a difficult question: to the extent that there has been a political progression from commercial elites to professional politicians, how much has this been a function of urban growth? Some historians have argued that the transition from patrician government was simply a function of the urbanization process.[17] If there were natural stages of political change, then might not smaller cities and towns simply represent the earlier stages? Conversely, if the political transitions discussed in this chapter represented a historical process across all but the South, what reasons are there to predict that smaller places would not have experienced corresponding development? For instance, why not expect that Watertown, Wisconsin, with its 6,400 people in 1870, would have gone from elite to machine to progressive to professional politicians in the past century and a half?

One obvious fact about the government of smaller cities and towns stands out: their size and subsequent scope of government put an effective, if historically flexible, upper limit on the number of full-time, paid politicians they could support. This in turn inhibited the development of machine politics, of professional reformers, and of twentieth-century career politicians. The tendency of the smaller towns and villages should have been toward a maintenance of the status quo, not out of any natural conservatism but out of demographically and fiscally limited opportunities for change. Even if the political development of small towns and cities had moved in lockstep with larger cities, the consequences would have been far more limited and less visible.

Smaller cities and towns had a second difference that made

them more likely to appear conservative and resistant to political change. By the last decades of the nineteenth century, larger, more central cities experienced a regional and national extension of their economies.[18] Inefficient local industries died out when transportation made competition and specialization more powerful. The successful local industrialists operated in an expanding world whose fortunes were visibly tied to other cities, other regions, and even other nations. Their economic affairs no longer mirrored the fate of their city. The control of local government no longer mattered to their businesses as it had in the early part of the century. This spatial broadening and overlaying of the economic base affected everyone in the economy, but smaller cities and towns continued to retain more of the old unity of business and city interests.

Booster Politics

By 1890, what was good for New York City was no longer necessarily good for J. P. Morgan, while what was good for Watertown, Wisconsin, was quite often still good for its bankers, newspapers, and wage earners—and vice versa. The governments and businesses of smaller places seemed provincial because they were: local events meant more to them than purely local events did to the big cities. George Babbitt boosted Zenith because his business depended on it. Economic circumstances denied blasé metropolitan sophistication to small cities and towns, so that when Sinclair Lewis wrote of life in small towns and cities in the early twentieth century, he could caricature the local greed and shameless self-promotion. Efforts by local businessmen to boost a city through the chamber of commerce simply were neither so all-pervasive nor so necessary in larger places. But residents of new cities recognized along with Chicago that: "to induce immigrants to come here and settle the vacant lands . . . to control and center here the trade and travel of the West . . . to induce capitalists to make investments here in works of public and private improvement, are, all of them, objects worthy of the best exertion of her citizens."[19]

Local boosters often had even less credibility than traveling snake-oil salesmen. The hypocrisy inherent in making claims about a city's advantages purely to achieve personal profit forced many small-town officials and business leaders into positions which by the early twentieth century seemed anomalous. The economic fates of the biggest cities were no longer so easily affected, and once in place the network of U.S. cities became relatively stable. Boosterism of the most egregious kind lost its effectiveness. That the major cities of the early twentieth century could scorn such shameless behavior simply demonstrated their own short memories, for they had promoted themselves similarly in the previous century.

Not every small city had an ethos dominated by promotional histrionics. Many were dominated by factional splits and conflicts which left no one energy for self-promotion. Small industrial cities such as Scranton, or Homestead, Pennsylvania, or Troy, New York, housed heavy industries that drew immigrant workers, who dominated local politics.[20] In Scranton, in the decades after the Civil War, the patrician and commercial leaders grudgingly accepted the power of the Irish, working class. In Troy, the iron workers fought a constant battle to retain the political power that they had gained in the immediate post–Civil War period. The predominance of working-class voters within Troy's boundaries forced the city's conservatives to unite with county activists. Together they attempted to dilute working-class electoral impact by broadening control of the police to the county level. The county would then be able to order the police to side with factory owners rather than workers during strikes. In Homestead, with only 25,000 people, a corrupt political machine depended on graft from vice. Carnegie's steel mills, located just over the city boundaries, operated in a national economy, so that local politics remained relatively unimportant to the company's business. When the infamous strike of 1892 occurred, the Carnegie Steel Company turned immediately to a private, nonlocal army, the Pinkerton National Detective Agency, rather than trust any local police forces.

The fates of these three small cities suggest that whenever ethnic voters predominated, one could expect, logically enough, to find ethnic politicians. But machines were not necessary correlates of ethnic voters in these smaller cities, perhaps because their small size meant a less fragmented political environment than in large cities. Small city elites did not always gracefully acquiesce to ethnic predominance. In Watertown, a vicious split over the city debt in the mid-1870s set the local economic elite in opposition to German and Irish ethnics for over two decades. Conducting bilingual meetings, the Irish and Germans managed to dominate the town's unofficial government by coalition and to regularly send a representative to the state legislature. The split stifled town government and extended to the state legislature, where factional representation continued. This factionalism also weakened the town's economic growth, or at least so thought the upper classes.

That local conflict might inhibit a town's economic growth by frightening away entrepreneurs, immigrants, and investors did not escape the notice of the small cities springing up throughout the West. Historians have long observed that the desperate nature of local boosterism sprang from the realization that only through unity could a town and its inhabitants prosper. Political historian Allan Bogue has argued that the lack of any real community in the new towns made political conflict and fragmentation endemic.[21] Don H. Doyle's detailed study of Jacksonville, Illinois, supports Bogue's thesis. Doyle shows how the town had potentially irreversible splits: its Southerners and Northerners conflicted, often violently, first over slavery and then the Civil War; its native-born and its ethnics—Germans, Portuguese, Irish, and blacks—disagreed over issues ranging from temperance to housing; religious disagreements caused constant friction among the town's dozens of denominations; the town aristocracy despised the fighting and drinking class that gathered in the square on weekends, a rough underbelly to the decorous Victorian veneer. Yet the desperate spirit of boosterism managed to put a smile on these potentially deadly conflicts. Everyone in Jacksonville knew that their economic future depended on outdoing neighboring Springfield in the competition to attract business, new inhabitants, and legislative largess. Of necessity then, the "ethos of boosterism equated social unity with progress."[22]

Economic promise was incentive enough to overcome or at least ignore otherwise irreparable schisms. In a sense, the newer small cities and towns of the nineteenth century had to live with internal conflict. Because real property ownership was possible for even the working poor, the prospects of population growth and thus increase in property values united a fragmented but expanding society. The elite had to tolerate ethnic political participation. Ethnic groups had to tolerate one another. In Jacksonville, the temperance movement occasionally gained enough power to make the town dry: the Irish and Germans reluctantly then held separate, wet, Fourth of July celebrations outside the town. When the town was wet, proper teetotalers avoided the town center on weekends. Each faction was unwilling to give up the prospect of economic growth to fight for its own successful dominance of the other factions. Tolerance paid.

In towns and cities where economic prospects appeared poor, where boosterism's seed did not sprout, the impetus to tolerate conflict was not so strong. Such was often the case in the urban South, where failure to achieve the West's economic and demographic growth undermined the credibility of urban boosters.[23] The image a community gave to investors did not really matter where there were no investors and little hope for economic and demographic growth. Those in power sometimes resorted to violence to keep it. In Wilmington, North Carolina, in 1898, for example, local whites burned the offices of a black newspaper after its editor wrote in favor of political equality. Local whites then threatened black politicians with death if they did not immediately abdicate their elected positions. The Democrats used the opportunity provided by statewide outrage over the editorial as a pretext to expel the Republican and Populist government of the city.[24]

Throughout the nineteenth and early twentieth century, the major economic resource of the South was a staple crop agricultural system remarkable for its economic independence from nearby cities. While cotton left the South through urban entrepôts like Mobile and New Orleans, its transshipping did not create mercantile or manufacturing opportunities. Cotton did not support the dense network of cities, towns, villages, and economic activities that wheat and corn did in Illinois, for instance. In place of agricultural service towns, the post–Civil War South saw the oppressive emergence of the general store. Antithetical to the small town or city, the general store resisted all economies of scale and agglomeration, charged usurious fees for credit, and blocked more creative forms of economic activity. Two historians, in fact, argue that the general store provided a major force for retarding the economic growth of the South during the post–Civil War era.[25]

The Interrelationship of Federal, State, and Local Governments

A truism in need of revision is that larger, constitutional governments, in particular those of the states, hold American city governments hostage. Constitutional theorists in the late nineteenth century affirmed the dependent position of city governments. In addition, some dramatic partisan confrontations between state and city governments seem to have confirmed the theory, which conceptualized state government as granting only conditional governing power to cities, liable to revocation at any moment. Combine with this the notion that city governments have recently become passive dependents on federal aid, and one has the present popular vision of the abject status of city government.

The work of three scholars in particular provides strong grounds for revising this legal and constitutional picture. First, in a book primarily focusing on federal-state relations, Daniel J. Elazar demonstrates how from early in the nineteenth century, federal-state relations were cooperative and supportive, not separate and independent. In one chapter devoted to city-federal relationships, he points out how during the first half of the nineteenth century, the federal government aided cities in conscious, crucial, and varied ways. These particularly included the dredging of harbors and rivers, either conducted or supervised by the Army Engineers, actions explicitly authorized by the Constitution and detailed by the Rivers and Harbors Act of 1826. For instance, in the 1850s, the city of Richmond purchased a steam dredge which it then leased back to the Army, a lease which paid for the dredge. And the Army supervised the whole dredging operation. Elazar shows how most harbor and river projects were initiated and supervised by the Army, with cities funding costs of completion. Even earlier, in the 1820s, Norfolk had been an investor in the federal-state building of the Dismal Swamp Canal. And the Chesapeake and Ohio Canal, another federal-state venture, had over 25 percent of its stock purchased by the cities of Alexandria, Georgetown, and Washington alone. In the case of Minnesota, Elazar estimates the relative contributions made to railroads in the nineteenth century by federal, state, and local governments: of the $66 million total, the federal government conveyed land valued at $60 million, but the state and local governments contributed the most cash, about $3 million each. From very early on, the three levels of government worked together, committing cash, land, and expertise in cooperative ventures.[26]

Intergovernmental cooperation, not conflict, also characterized city-state relationships. Hendrik Hartog has shown how the early nineteenth-century charters of New York City, which on the surface appeared to lessen city power, actually pointed it in the direction of the modern service city. And Jon C. Teaford makes the crucial point that legislation affecting cities relied on expert evaluation, which was most likely to be supplied by the cities themselves. Standing committees on legislation affecting cities needed city representatives, and much of the rural-urban legislative conflict had to be rhetorical, as no one understood the ramifications of technical legislation other than the city representatives. In an identical development at the level of state government, Elazar cites several examples of governors and legislators affirming the separation of state and federal powers at the same time that they accepted and managed various forms of federal aid. The point that comes across consistently is that local urban government was not the passive victim of the whims of rural legislators, but did pretty much as it wished.[27]

Less clear is the perceived importance of local government. In a challenging article based on an analysis of Cleveland newspapers for the middle six decades of the nineteenth century, Samuel Kernell argues that local government diminished in its share of public discourse in the early decades of the century. Analyzed from another perspective, his data show that all forms of government earned more public discussion in that period, and that it was only in proportion to national political news that local political news diminished. And in fact, local news occupied more newspaper space than state political news for the years from 1860 to the end of the survey data, 1876. Given the argument of this chapter, that by the 1870s the foundation for the service-oriented city had become established, one can only wish that it were possible to extend Kernell's analysis three decades further. It seems quite likely that the service model of city government would have become less newsworthy and less visible as it became more successfully entrenched and silently bureaucratized.[28]

6 ☆ Paying for the Service City

In the late twentieth century, children learn about state level taxes when they buy toys and pay sales tax. Teenagers with their first jobs discover the federal government through Social Security taxes. Ironically, the government bureaucracies closest to our daily lives—schools, police, and fire—we discover last, if at all, when we buy property. In my own case, I didn't directly pay property taxes until I bought my second house, for the finance arrangement for my first house had included the payment of taxes through the bank that held the mortgage. Of course, my landlord and my parents knew the reality of property tax, but I was well into my adult life before I paid them directly. Probably most people are more acutely aware of sales and income tax in their own daily lives than of property tax, and thus are more concerned about what happens at state legislatures and in Washington, D.C., than they are about the nearby city hall. We are perceptually farthest from that government which is closest.

City Budgets and Revenues

In studying cities and their social processes an elemental question helps us to describe and understand how and why they look and act the way they do. Where do they get their money, and where do they spend it? The city's various social, spatial, and economic structures both create and facilitate nongovernmental economic activity, but its budget represents an actual cash outlay. Prior to the Depression, local property taxes were the most visible form of taxation. The relatively short psychological distance from its major source of revenue, individual property owners, made a city's budget a sensitive sociopolitical barometer. Because budgeting decisions were, and to a lesser extent still are, an annual political event and tax collection is either annual or semiannual, the city's revenues and expenditures are almost always in the public eye.[1] The complex political process that determines the final budget may not be of any interest to taxpayers, but the outcome is. Political careers may rise and fall on the budget's revenues and expenditures, for it represents a fairly concrete and highly visible outcome of a governmental process.

In an important but skewed sense, the city budget may be taken as an operational definition of the city's priorities. Every year the city budget shows what resources most deserve funding. The skew in the definition of priorities by budget alone comes from noncash subsidies—those created by regulation of locational choices, by city-granted monopolies, and by the basic urban economies of scale and agglomeration. Most visible in the colonial cities, these indirect aspects of the city fisc resulted from economic opportunities granted by the city to private entrepreneurs or property owners. And in return for the granting of a franchise, some entrepreneurs might have taken over a specific city service—maintaining a street, for instance. Some economists would argue that in addition to these factors, governmental spending occurs in those sectors where the free rider problem inhibits capital investment. Schooling, public safety, and streets cannot easily be financed and operated by tolls on the users, for their real benefits extend to the whole society. For the actual users to support these services by fees would burden them unfairly, so governmental expenditures solve the free rider problem by distributing the costs over the whole population. Therefore, taking the budget as a reflection of priorities works only in a very narrow sense, for it actually represents priorities that are exercised either inefficiently or not at all by private initiative. The budget is, therefore, at the minimum, a definition of what may be considered the city's public goods, those activities that benefit all.[2]

Almost seventy years ago, Joseph Schumpeter argued that the budget and the process that created it would provide future scholars a central focus for social and political analysis. Perhaps because of the budget's complexity, perhaps because other topics in social science proved more tantalizing, or perhaps because the budget is in fact such an imperfect and skewed point of entry, it is only recently

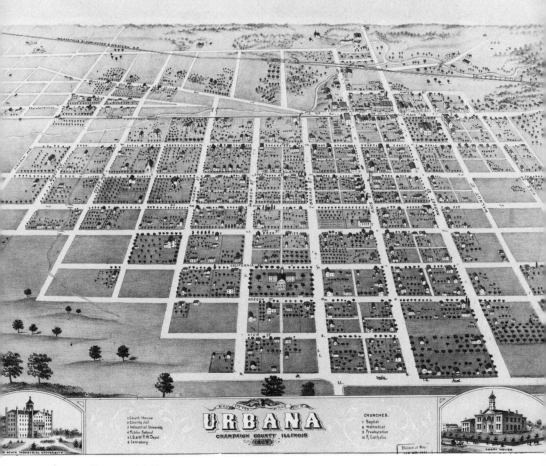

Urbana, Illinois, 1869.
A small Midwestern city: note the empty lots and platted streets determining speculative value and shaping the city investment directions. Unlike Sumner, Kansas, Urbana was not pure speculative smoke, and it
prospered.

Source: Geography and Map Division, Library of Congress.

that historians and social scientists have begun to attend to Schumpeter's argument.[3]

American city revenues derive from a mix of taxes (usually on real property), license and user fees, fines, and occasionally sales of real property. Property taxes dominated this income mix until the early twentieth century, when nonlocal revenues, especially from the federal government, begin to form a portion of the city budget. Although the transition away from almost complete reliance on property taxes was gradual, it accelerated with the Depression in the 1930s. One particular aspect of the crisis, unemployment, helped trigger the conscious turn to the federal government for aid. Cities had traditionally cared for their poor, but never had the poor been so numerous. While debt load and the bank holiday may have been the underlying causes and precipitators of default, cities had borne the great brunt of welfare to the unemployed for the first three years of the Depression. By 1933 they had exhausted their resources: more important, they saw themselves as handling a national problem. Unlike debt that financed local capital expansion, welfare benefits went to all in need. In a classic problem that has plagued American cities since the colonial era, the responsibility for the welfare of urban residents fell upon city government, but by 1930, the separation of political boundary from economic region had become so obvious as to send mayors to the federal government. All other governmental entities were seen as too geographically limited to accept the responsibility for a much larger problem. The relationship to the federal government began to be perceived by urban politicians as the critical political and economic relationship.[4] Among a broad range of requests, the cities sought federal legislation to help them reorganize and refund debt to avoid default, but the modest legislation that did get enacted was overturned by the Supreme Court within three years.[5]

National figures for the proportion of all city taxes which came from property taxes do not exist, but for analyzing the trend since the Depression, the combined state and local government figure stands as a reasonable substitute. Between 1932 and 1934, the property tax percentage of receipts for state and local governments fell dramatically, from 60 percent to 45 percent. Even the latter figure seemed high by the 1980s, when property tax contributed less than 20 percent of the total revenue.[6]

These figures would be considerably higher, perhaps as much as 50 percent, for municipalities alone, because the addition of state figures, which rely far less on property taxes, dilutes the real property tax base of cities. For instance, the average percentage of revenue coming from property tax for all municipalities in Illinois in 1962 was just under 45 percent, which contrasts with a nation-wide state and local average of 32 percent. The range of contribution of real property tax in Illinois municipalities in 1962 was also quite broad, some cities taking as much as 62 percent of their revenue from property taxes, others as little as 28 percent. Chicago itself struck the mean at 43 percent. Thus, while the trend away from reliance upon property tax revenues is clear, its absolute level depends on the unit of government examined and varies from city to city.[7]

One might expect that increased revenues from the federal government have accounted for this relative decline in the importance of property tax, particularly after the New Deal's shift in power from the local to the federal level. Although this does not in itself account entirely for the move away from complete reliance on property tax, there has been a dramatic increase in federal and state aid to cities. Again, the most dramatic shift came in 1932–1934, when the federal contribution moved from 2 percent to almost 20 percent, a proportion that fell back to 10 percent by the start of World War II. But the federal contribution to local government revenue has not begun to assume as large a share as property taxes once did. The two did reach parity for state and local government combined in 1975, but again, because states rely less upon property tax revenues than cities, this parity has not yet arrived at the municipal level.

In Illinois, by 1962 the contribution of property tax to the total municipal revenue had fallen to about 43 percent, but all other governmental revenues contributed only slightly more than 12 percent of municipal budgets. And the decade of the 1980s began with property tax contributing 40 percent, state and federal aid 38 percent.[8] There is a clear correlation between the decline in property tax and the rise of intergovernmental revenue, that is city revenue from state or federal government. But intergovernmental revenue does not yet constitute a net replacement.

The degree to which there is a substitution does imply a slow loss of local attention to the city budget, simply because its tie to local and direct revenue from property taxes has been considerably loosened. If the experience of California's widely discussed "tax revolt" and its constitutional limitation of property taxes is any portent, the irony of the revolt may be an acceleration of the decrease in importance of property taxes, with a concomitant increase in nonlocal revenues and decrease in local control of local government.[9] As it stands, the twentieth century draws to a close with property tax remaining an important part of the revenue structure of cities. But, unlike a century ago, it is now only one of several important revenue sources.

In the regulatory era of city government, from the seventeenth to the early nineteenth century, expenditures went for streets, maintenance of markets, docks, and warehouses, and aid to the poor. As the service city began to take shape, city expenditures became more varied and complex. By the mid-nineteenth century, modest amounts of support began to go to fire and police, schools, transportation, water and sewers, public health, the administrative mechanism of the government itself, various forms of welfare, libraries, and occasionally public utilities. As budgets increased in complexity, they also increased in amount. An exact per capita measure may be impossible to construct, but there is no question that since at least 1840, government expenditures on the local, state, and federal levels have increased.[10] Yet, for cities, there has always been an important lid on expenditures, for their charters stipulate that city expenditures must equal revenues, and since revenues are limited by tax rates set by state governments, revenues have de facto state-imposed ceilings.

The Civil War and Local Finance

Just as the fledgling service governments began to act, the Civil War intervened, raising taxes even higher. The war assured that nation's political unification, cementing the social and economic changes of the first half of the century. In the late 1830s, the Supreme Court case *Bank of Augusta v. Earle* ensured the foundations of interstate corporate mobility, and illustrated the intimate linkage between mobile capital and the developing urban network. The case decided the issue of whether or not a corporation chartered by one state's legislature (Georgia and also Louisiana) could borrow and lend in another (Alabama). The Georgia lender was a bank; the Louisiana one a railroad.[11] The defaulter, Joseph Earle, in order to avoid paying his debt, made the plausible claim that legislation by one state, including acts of incorporation, could not carry into another state. His action set off other local defaults, including one on a debt made by the Bank of the United States in Philadelphia. But the whole legal and theoretical issue involving capital and its corporate form had its actual location in an urban network, tying banks, cities, and individual entrepreneurs together with the transportation medium of the railroad. The case literally swept across the three major port cities on the Gulf of Mexico, suggesting the fine webs of commerce tying these cities together. All the principals in the case were urban, either corporations or individuals, from Joseph Earle in Mobile, to the Bank of Augusta, Georgia, to the New Orleans and Carrollton Railroad Company. The Supreme Court found against Earle and in favor of chartered corporations acting across state boundaries. Of course, since colonial times, the new urban networks had largely disregarded state boundaries. *Bank of Augusta v. Earle*, however, ensured the dispersion of political-economic action across state lines.

Data collected in 1888 by Richard T. Ely indicate the impact of the Civil War on local taxes in Massachusetts and New York. Plotted in note 12, they suggest the following scenario: local antebellum tax revenues had been climbing very slowly for decades. The war virtually doubled them. Cities, towns, and counties paid for many war-related things, mainly those having to do with welfare of local people affected by the war, including relief and draft bounties. (By the end of the war, New York City paid bounties as high as $1,000, virtually three years' salary. Such a price for going off to war must have been very attractive. So too the incentive to desert and reenlist under another name.) And thereafter local taxes continued their climb, but from a new, higher plateau and at a steeper rate. Of course, cities and towns grew too, and their level of increase also steepened after the Civil War. However, the tax slope increased more sharply than the population growth slope. And obviously, the tax leap during the war had nothing to do with population growth. In the North, at least, the Civil War solidified a new type of local government, firmly anchoring the service city in place.[12]

The question of the war's fiscal impact on local government is yet to be resolved. Two different studies of three small Massachusetts cities suggest that the high local cost of the war introduced new levels of spending, with the discovery that government could spend considerably more than it had. But it is equally possible that this new level of spending gave local taxpayers incentive to reduce spending once war debts had been paid off. Rather than demonstrating new possibilities, debt showed its vulnerability. An analysis of local debt, without considering revenue, suggests that just five years after the war's end, southern towns had comparatively greater debt loads than northern ones. But, as the case of Watertown, Wisconsin, discussed later in this chapter demonstrates, local debt has to be analyzed over time. We need to know the purposes to which debt was put. Did it promote growth or resolve crises? Did it pay for the war or build an infrastructure? And in building for the future, was it effectively spent or not?[13]

Local Debt and Borrowing

For cities with growth rates as steep as those in the nineteenth-century United States, taxes adequate to finance high-quality, service-intensive capital expansion could never have been raised on existing real property. The newer cities in the mid-nineteenth century literally built themselves from nothing. For the newest cities, the capital for construction of buildings, streets, water systems, and sewerage could hardly have been derived from taxes, as there was only the expectation and hope of growth. For all cities, population either lagged behind or just kept up with infrastructural growth, and a high tax on the existing inhabitants would have deterred new arrivals and investors. In new cities, subscription appeals for city construction, though numerous (particularly in the 1830s), had little success, given a general local capital shortage anywhere urban growth took place away from the eastern seaboard.[14] Cities therefore financed their growth by issuing debt, usually in the form of bonds marketed to investors in major eastern cities or in Europe.

Since ancient times, cities had used their corporate charter privileges to borrow money, but American cities have been unique in the degree to which they have depended on borrowing in the money market, and in their consequent competition with private debt instruments.[15] Very carefully drawn legal distinctions between public and private corporations appeared in the nineteenth century, coinciding with the development of an active market in the bonds issued by public corporations. Ironically then, as judicial decisions insisted on the subservience of city corporations to states, municipal debt became an important part of the private money market.

In Britain, by contrast, nineteenth-century cities did occasionally borrow money, but about one-third of their borrowing was specifically directed by such national legislation as the Public Health and Artisans Dwellings Acts, which enabled them to borrow through the Board of Public Works Loan Commissioners of the Treasury, rather than in the private market. All local borrowing had to be authorized by special acts to go through the Treasury, or if in the private market, it had to be conducted for purposes similar to those authorized by the Board of Public Works Loan Commissioners. The Municipal Corporations Act of 1835 limited total local borrowing to no more than "two year's rateable value of the district," that is, no more than twice the annual total local property tax.

No American state constitutions set debt or tax ceilings until after 1870. As late as 1881, cities in twenty-three states had no constitutional debt limits, though some of them could no longer invest in private corporations, especially railroads. When states began to limit debts, they typically set them at a proportion of the assessed value of real property, usually 5 percent. For instance, Illinois, a leader in limitation, did not set local debt ceilings until 1870, when they were set at 5 percent of the real property value. In the 1920s, constitutional amendments raised Chicago's ceiling to 7 percent. Across the states, debt ceilings varied from 3 percent to 7 percent. Of the fifteen that were set by state constitutional restrictions or the three states where legislatures were authorized to set limits, all were based on a proportion of assessed property value. This, of course, made the actual amount of the debt highly flexible at the will of the city assessors. This means that in two ways, nominal limits and assessments, the U.S. debt limitation was substantially more generous than Britain's, perhaps by a factor of ten.[16]

The implied British principle was that specific prior authority had to be established before securing loans, whereas in the United States most state legislatures and constitutions gave carte blanche for borrowing purposes. State legislatures restricted borrowing only when excesses appeared to be causing default crises. Thus, in the late 1870s, the recession seemed to have caused defaults on city bonds supporting railroads, and several states banned the lending of city debt to railroads.

A statistical analysis comparing the effect of debt limitation state by state shows that such limits were paper tigers, contrary to the impression given by some historians, who see them as putting "severe limitations" on a city, locking its "fiscal options into a rigid mold." The stepwise regression analysis reported in note 17 estimates the relationship of debt limitation, state age, the actual number of cities, and the number of cities per capita. Most relevant, the state-mandated limitations had no measurable impact. Nor did the number of cities in a state. Instead, the net city debt was mainly determined by the age of a state (older states had somewhat less debt than younger ones), the region (the North had greater per capita debt), and the number of cities per capita. What is most interesting from this point of view, is that the number of cities per capita rather than the number of city dwellers had such a powerful effect on debt. Given two states of equal urban population and age, the one with the greater number of smaller cities would have had the greater debt. By implication, the closer the local government to its voters, the more debt the government was willing to issue. It is possible that in smaller cities, where they were close to city government, property owners were more likely to see debt as an opportunity and a public good while their big-city counterparts were less likely to be so supportive.[17]

The British policy on local debt significantly contrasted with the broad general rules governing city debt in the United States. In Britain the national government sanctioned borrowing for specified sets of projects, from harbors to jails. All other local borrowing needed a special parliamentary act. This contrast is important, for it foreshadowed liberal and conservative theories of corporate regulation in the nineteenth century. By the liberal theory, corporations had the right to act as they wished; they would be regulated by civil and criminal law, or by special legislation if need be. The conservative theory allowed corporations to do only that which they were specifically chartered to do; new or different activities required legislative charter amendments. The British operated under the conservative theory of corporations, while American cities (and business corporations) operated under the liberal theory.

In the 1880s British reformers expressed concern about the

amount and increase in local indebtedness, most of it urban, which had risen from 80 million to 137 million pounds between 1870 and 1880. This compares to a much higher per capita local debt in the United States, which increased only a few dollars in per capita figures but increased substantially in its total. At an exchange rate of about $4.90 per pound, the U.S. debt was $13 higher per capita in 1870, perhaps $14 higher in 1880.[18]

Most of the total government debt in the nineteenth century was issued by local, not state or federal, government. Illinois, for instance, in 1869, had a state debt of $6.3 million, a county debt of $8.5 million, and the enormous debt of cities and towns of $39.8 million. Across the Atlantic, municipal borrowing remained much more slight and uncoordinated; in Glasgow, for instance, each city department borrowed independently in 1886. More typical, when Leeds wished to build an elegant city hall at midcentury, city officials first tried to raise money by subscription. Failing this attempt, they built the hall with a loan from the national government, one eventually repaid from the property taxes and profits from the municipal water system. The caution of the council in borrowing was overcome only by its shame at the city's downtown appearance when compared to neighboring Bradford. As only about 5 percent of those eligible to vote for city council members were working class voters, there is no way of judging the popular appeal of debt financing for civic building. However, the effective exclusive of the British working class from home ownership suggests that it would not have been in its interest to support any expansion of local government.[19]

Entrepreneurial Competition, Local Debt, and Boosterism

Such schemes could only work in cities which already had enough property to tax. Rapidly growing American cities could not finance infrastructural development out of their current revenues because they were building for a short-term but quickly expanding population. A city of 10,000, making do with a city hall built for a village of 1,000, had to finance the building of a new hall for a city of 20,000. The fortunes of individuals, cities, and the new services cities provided often became inextricably tied, so that the speculative sale of land, business shares, and city bonds themselves could determine a new city's future. And although George Washington may not have been able to sell land in the District of Columbia, real estate developers, city officials, and speculators followed his precedent time and time again in subsequent land sales. From the very early decades of the nineteenth century on, a shameless hucksterism accompanied the explosion of new cities in the nineteenth century. It accelerated throughout the century, so that by the 1870s, empty stretches of land across the Midwest and West were touted as the new Rome, Athens, or Paris. In spite of uncountable false starts, heavy competition, and severe attrition, there are still eight Romes, fifteen Athenses, fourteen Parises, twenty-two Manchesters, twenty Oxfords, fourteen Cambridges, and seventeen Londons or New Londons in the United States![20]

This bubbly spirit of urban boosterism fronted a very serious enterprise. It also masked a unique moment in urban history, a moment when thousands of entrepreneurs seized opportunities to build a whole new system of cities on a basis never before tried. The new basis included unprecedented demographic growth and an expansion of a capitalist economic system underwritten and boosted rather than restricted by government.[21] State constitutions ensured that any group of people so petitioning could gain articles of incorporation as a village, town, or city. General incorporation legislation for businesses did not become widespread until the late nineteenth century, which meant that each new business seeking the privileges of incorporation had to have special legislation introduced in a state's legislature. Prior to the middle of the century, such incorporation was often difficult and expensive.[22] The privileges of incorporation are critical to capital enterprises, for they lower the costs of capital by protecting investors with limited liability. By granting virtually any settlement the privileges of a corporate charter, state legislatures created a spectacular opportunity for a new form of entrepreneurship, the city (or village or town) as economic actor. From the investor's perspective, particularly in the early nineteenth century, the money lent to growing cities was almost uniquely protected. Thus the carnival of land sales provided a facade for the business of capital expansion across the continent.

For instance, Morgan County, Illinois, made Jacksonville its county seat in return for a large land donation from investors in the as-yet-unbuilt city in 1825. During the nineteenth century the county constructed two courthouses. The first was raised in 1832, when the city had about 2,000 people and the county about 14,000.

The second courthouse came in 1869, when the city had grown to just over 9,000 and the surrounding county to about 27,500. To expect either a city or county to finance a structure for a population doubling or quadrupling every three decades was clearly unfeasible. Only debt, issued with the not unreasonable expectation that future growth would ease its repayment, made sense in an urban system increasingly wedded to a service government.

City building by entrepreneurship meant that services formerly provided by volunteers had to be regularized in advance, since there was no community on which to call. Hence, slowly, emerging urban services replaced the individual citizen volunteer. Thus, by the end of the nineteenth century, activities formerly accomplished as an obligation of all urban citizens had become a part of city government. And intercity communication about the techniques of accomplishing these tasks had resulted in the creation of national professional societies. Urban residents no longer actually performed these tasks; instead, they indirectly contracted for services through property taxes. Monetized and rationalized, traditional relationships of obligation and responsibility between city and citizen became contractual.[23]

With their powerful borrowing potential, these new cities burst upon the economic and demographic scene of the Western world, competing with other capital enterprises for loans and providing relatively secure investment opportunities. Even when the capital did not go directly to build streets and schools in brand-new towns and cities, it often went into the businesses that the new towns in turn aided and supported with large local subsidies, from manufacturing firms to the burgeoning railroads.

Cities then, faced a double fiscal burden, simultaneously financing a new infrastructure and the increasing expenditures associated with their transformation from regulators to public servants. These two local shifts took place within a context of increasing state and federal government expenditures.[24] The increases, occurring both in per capita terms and as a proportion of the gross national product, meant that cities competed with more powerful and unified governmental units as well as with one another for revenues.

And compete American cities did, issuing debt for a stunning multiplicity of projects, ranging from the mundane building of street and schools, to revenue-generating docks and bridges, to straight cash aid to lure capitalists to invest in local projects. We know most about those projects that failed, for the failure to repay debt led to lawsuits and publicity. In 1870, the Census Bureau began to collect information on amounts of indebtedness, although it was not until 1902 that this became systematic. One can only crudely estimate local debt for 1870, 1880, and 1890, for not only was the reporting irregular but the census did not record the population of those places answering questionnaires concerning indebtedness. To add further complication, sometimes places reported subscribed but still-unissued debt, and at other times they subtracted the assets in sinking funds (that is, funds legally designated for the repayment of specified debts) from the indebtedness figures.

The figures, however, suggest a local debt that grew absolutely but declined in per capita terms from 1870. In 1870, counties had contracted debts for a total of $187.5 million, cities and towns for a total of $328.2 million. The per capita county debt was about $4.86, the local debt about $39.6. By 1880 the per capita county debt figures had fallen to $2.50, and they fell again to $2.30 by 1890. It is unclear whether this decline was actual or an artifact of different reporting methods. Nevertheless, the total county debt rose substantially between these decades, from $124.1 million to $145.0 million. Local debt rose to $701.9 million in 1880 and $761.2 million in 1890; this represented a slight per capita decline. As the twentieth century opened, the overall indebtedness and revenues of local governments (excluding state governments) were 50 percent greater than that of the federal government. By the watershed era of the Great Depression, this relationship had begun to reverse. World War II began the era we now consider typically twentieth-century, with the federal government's debt and revenue overwhelming state and local government debt by a ratio of five to one. This dramatic reversal of federal and local fiscal stances reflects the importance of local government at the beginning of the twentieth century, when, for instance, virtually all welfare and educational expenditures were local.[25]

What Got Taxed?

Taxes on real property were the easiest for governments to collect, for they were liens on immobile property rather than on mobile individuals. Yet their simplicity from this point of view belies their complexity from any other perspective. The eighteenth-century corporate charter of New York City, for instance, made no allowance for any city tax levies. Those few taxes that were collected by the city had to have special enabling legislation from the colonial government. New York City depended on its property to earn its revenues. In addition, by carefully attaching requirements to its grants of valuable land, particularly waterfront lands, the city avoided capital expenditures. With the grants of waterfront lots extending 400 feet into the river, the city required that the owner build wharves and connecting waterfront streets.[26] In essence the city transformed its own property into private collateral in order to foster private capital investment in a public good.

By the mid-nineteenth century, New York City would use a different strategy. With its charter of 1830—like that of every other city, now guaranteeing a right to tax private property—the tax-generating aspect of the private property within the city's boundaries became collateral on its debt. In this period, the budget expenditure record included debt principal and interest payments and served as an excellent indicator of the city's financial activities. For the eighteenth century, however, the city's revenues and expenditures simply do not reflect the city's effective fiscal power. By selling its waterfront land with undeveloped earning potential, it created an opportunity for private capital, the direct earnings of which it shared with the new owners. In addition, the city levied indirect taxes for the use of these waterlots by requiring the owners to build and maintain contiguous streets and various public slips. The city accounts, however, show only the direct revenues, not the private expenditures on wharf construction, slip dredging, or street construction and maintenance. Through regulation and careful control of its own property, the city could underwrite a vital aspect of its economic growth without any visible revenue or expenditure.[27]

In the nineteenth century, the terms *municipal* and *city* took on different technical meanings. They denoted virtually identical agencies in the popular mind, and so they do today to most people. In public law, however, the term *municipal* specifically denoted any governmental unit to which the state had delegated power. Therefore municipal governments could include cities as well as many other forms of state-created government. (This is why municipal bonds in the late twentieth century fund a range of projects, only some of which are urban, including everything from straightforward city improvements to sprawling nuclear utility networks.) In the eighteenth century, a city like New York was not in fact a municipal corporation, for its charter gave it power independent of the colonial government.[28]

The introduction of separate school and irrigation districts in the late nineteenth century transformed the mid-nineteenth century legal definition of municipal government from a category containing one kind of instance—cities—to one with a bewildering variety of instances. The growth of special districts, ostensibly in order to overcome the inefficient boundary limitations posed by cities, was probably a way for county and state level politicians to circumscribe the power of ethnic political machines and at the same time escape the increasing limits that state legislatures had begun to place on cities in the aftermath of defaults during the depressions of the 1870s and 1890s.

As a result, an overlay of city government, and various functionally specialized districts—most notably school districts and water districts—comprise the typical twentieth-century city's governing body. These special districts each have a fund whose revenues come from property and other taxes, fees, and intergovernmental transfers. Consequently, to find a city that has a government contiguous with other special districts may no longer be possible in the United States. Figure 6 demonstrates, in a simplified form, the reason for this historical complexity. Note that here the word *historical* has a double meaning, suggesting as it does that the complexity itself has risen for historical reasons, as new accretions of special political districts overlaid older ones, and also that the complexity frustrates historical generalization on a scale large enough to have meaning.[29]

Each unit in this complex of modern municipal government may issue debt to finance its capital construction, whether for schools, water and sewerage systems, or roads. For the first seventy years or so of the nineteenth century, unitary governmental units issued debt, collected taxes, and spent money. But as the service government expanded, so did its organizational specialization.

A study of mid-twentieth-century Illinois, for instance, illustrates that only in the case of two types of special district, roads and schools, did the number shrink between 1940 and 1962. The

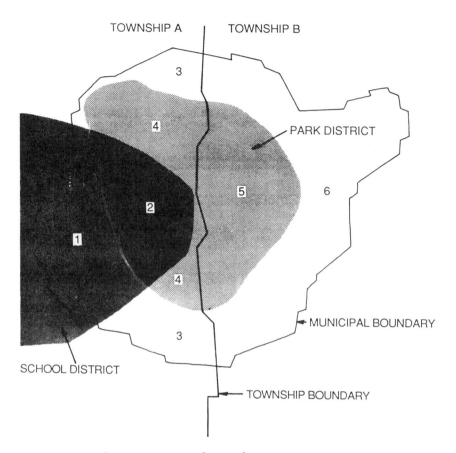

TOWNSHIP A   TOWNSHIP B

3

4

PARK DISTRICT

5   6

2

1

4

MUNICIPAL BOUNDARY

3

SCHOOL DISTRICT

TOWNSHIP BOUNDARY

Figure 6. Overlapping Municipal Boundaries
    This diagram shows six different government units—excluding state, federal, and other units such as flood control districts—which overlap in what might seem like a homogeneous area.

Source: Glen W. Fisher and Robert P. Fairbanks, *Illinois Municipal Finance: A Financial and Economic Analysis* (Urbana: University of Illinois Press, 1968), 82.

number of school districts across the United States diminished through consolidation during this period, the consequence of a centralization and reform movement which had begun much earlier, in the Progressive era. The number of school districts in the nation fell from over 127,000 in the early 1930s to 115,000 in 1942 to 35,000 in 1962 and under 15,000 in 1982.[30] In Illinois, though, all other special districts proliferated, including actual municipalities, fire, park, and sanitary districts, so that by 1962, the state had 1,251 city governments and 5,221 other governmental units. The mean number of governmental overlays—that is, governments having jurisdiction over any one location—increased from 6.9 in 1940 to 9.0 by 1962.[31]

The Politics of Local Finance: The Watertown Railway Bond Issue

The Watertown, Wisconsin, ordeal over debt and debt payment illustrates in a microcosm several aspects of nineteenth-century urban finance. A small city struggling to capture the potential economic benefits of its proximity to Madison, Watertown epitomized mid-nineteenth-century tensions and hopes. Although it was an extreme case, lasting nearly four decades and unresolved even by a Supreme Court decision, the dynamics of the local struggle illustrate features of town finance, debt, and default that figured in small and large cities across the United States. Its heavy debt load, its persistent creditors, and its complex social, economic, and political structure evoked a complete range of local responses to an urban fiscal crisis. Moreover, the town's default on debt repayment highlighted the sense in which default was and still is a political action.

In 1856 the Wisconsin legislature authorized the issuance of $400,000 of railroad aid bonds by the city of Watertown.[32] These bonds were divided between two fledgling railroad companies; apparently the railroads were to pay both principal and interest payments. Such an arrangement was in effect a collateralization, the city's credit underwriting the railroads' capitalization. The panic of 1857 caused one of the railroads to virtually collapse, and the lessees of the company sold the city's bonds in Boston for 32.5 percent of their face value. The other railroad traded its stock to the city for the bonds. But the $200,000 owed to the Milwaukee & St. Paul Railroad brought the city neither railroad nor capital improvements, and one historian of this debt claims "its crushing weight stayed its growth, paralyzed its industries."[33] By 1870 the city debt plus interest equaled one-half of the city's assessed property value.

Although one might doubt that Watertown's destined greatness had been foiled by this debt, the debt became a major public and political issue. In 1867 townspeople met and discussed various schemes to deal with it, from buying up the discounted debt to "foolish speeches" in favor of repudiation.[34] By 1868 the city had discovered a clever solution to its problem. It began over two decades of governing without government, without those persons in its government upon whom a lawsuit could be served. The city business was always accomplished prior to the first council meeting, which formally consisted of a handing in of all signed business and resignations to the city clerk. A Board of Street Commissioners made all council-like decisions. For instance, in 1874, the Board's regular order of business included such jobs as paying various city employees and spending money from the fifth ward "poor fund" for medical assistance to a poor woman. Two years later, at its regular meeting the Board planned the upcoming Fourth of July celebration, arranging prizes, processions, and stipulating that school children would sing national songs.[35]

Thus, as courts awarded first one judgment and then another against the city, creditors found no one upon whom to serve papers. In 1872 the state legislature passed a bill making it impossible to seize private property to satisfy municipal creditors, effectively protecting the city's property owners from the seizure and sale of their property. The *Watertown Republican* (March 6, 1872) alleged that the city's debt had been issued irresponsibly by the propertyless, "by a rabble of railroad laborers thrown out of employment on a road that had stopped." These unpropertied workers encumbered the honest property owners, including, of course, "every widow and orphan" who would gladly pay a real debt, but would refuse "to satisfy the avarice of the men . . . who have combined to use the wealth they wrung from the sweat and blood of the farmers of Wisconsin [referring to the great mortgage scandals of the 1850s], to buy these Railroad bonds against cities, towns, counties, and villages, at a small fraction of their par value, in order to build their fortunes upon the ruin of so many." Having blamed the debt on irresponsible and transient workers, the essay shifted to threaten a revolution of decent townspeople if the greedy speculators persisted in attempting to collect the debt.

Five of the town's "prominent and influential citizens" (including two former mayors) awoke one summer morning in 1872 to find miniature wooden coffins on their doorsteps, in an incident reminiscent of the Captain Swing riots forty years earlier in England. A letter within each coffin urged: "In this bury all your Railway Bonds and your villainy with it." One month later the prorepudiation forces formed an organization of working-class homeowners, the Union League, which was to play an influential role in city politics for the next two decades.[36]

In July 1872, this "class of discontented, ignorant people," led by Patrick Devy, formed a bilingual, German-Irish and Democratic organization which continued to be active in the city until 1897. The league's secret Committee of Safety agitated against all bond payments, and threatened to burn the city down if creditors tried to collect the debt or seize private property to pay it. The Union League saw the debt as a plot of the wealthy against the workers. As G. Baumann told the league on September 14, in an address in both German and English, "a certain clique of cunning men . . . men who from the first setting of this place had subsisted on the sweat of the laboring class of Watertown" had foisted the debt on the town. Their plot was foiled and resisted by the "workingmen only who fight for Right and Home." The antirepudiation *Democrat* called their meetings a "hodge-podge mess of drivelling, drooling gibberish and contemptible bosh."[37]

The league's vigorously militant stance culminated by September in a unanimous resolution that gave a sense of the depth and passion of its members. "Resolved that the Union League of the City of Watertown will use all justifiable means to protect their property from legal robbers as they would from thieves and highway robbers."[38] The only opposition to the league, an ineffective Citizen's Association, worked to compromise the debt in some way. The league's power grew, as first Devy and then Hezekiah Flinn, both Leaguers, gained seats in the state legislature in the late 1870s, where they worked to keep the debt unpaid.

The Supreme Court, in *Almy v. City of Watertown* (130 U.S. 301, 1889), decided that the debt claims must be served on the mayor and that the state legislation prescribing this mode of service was proper. That the city had no mayor could not be brought into the argument, and the case effectively sealed Watertown's victory over the bondholders. The Milwaukee attorney who had represented the bondholders for twenty-five years, and perhaps held most of the bonds himself, later settled with the city, exchanging over $600,000 in bonds for a $15,000 settlement. In 1894 the city government began normal operations again, thus ending thirty-five years of turmoil.

There were five positions on the debt taken by different groups of townspeople. The handful of well-off local capitalists who also held city bonds wanted complete payment of the debt. The out-of-work railroad laborers first supported payment of the original debt, but whether they later joined the repudiation groups is not clear. The Union League—German, Irish, and Democratic, though not in tune with the town's democratic newspaper—advocated strict repudiation but also seemed to represent numerous small property holders as well as the propertyless. The Citizen's Association, apparently Republican, wanted to compromise the debt, a position comfortable to the smaller entrepreneurs and probably to all three town newspapers. And finally nonleague Democrats maintained an uneasy fifth position that skirted around favoring complete repudiation.

That property owners could have supported so militantly the antiestablishment Union League is no surprise, for as in most newly founded western cities, the acquisition of small real property holdings was possible for all but the totally destitute.[39] Economic class differences grew at the margins between three groups: these very small property owners, who could literally tear down their houses and move them to another town; the local entrepreneurs, who possessed a bit of capital and the spirit typified by the Duluthian who happily worked hard but "worked the other fellow at the same time"; and the handful of local capitalists, who invested heavily in city bonds and local economic activities in addition to their regional activities.[40] Ethnic splits, articulated through political parties, fractured these three economic classes, leaving a world of local politics which hotly contested the economic issues. These issues, which can often be subsumed under the concept of boosterism, directly but differently affected the fortunes and jobs of town dwellers.

Class differences usually accounted for various positions on debt. Small property holders willingly issued debt and willingly repudiated it, standing to gain from city debt that boosted economic and population growth but having little to lose. The petty capitalist also favored the issuance of debt that promised to make the city grow, having tied his or her economic future to the city.

For this reason, then, the petty capitalist stood for good credit, for debt payment when feasible and for readjustment when not. For them, local government's fiscal catastrophe spelled personal economic doom. The few wealthy resident bond holders and backers of larger local corporate enterprises favored debt for economic growth and payment at all costs. These basic positions became complex when overlaid by party and ethnic positions. The Democrats and the Irish tended to favor repudiation as in the post-Reconstruction South. And Republicans, "Americans of the New England Puritan type, men of refinement and culture,"[41] and the native-born and Germans, would in general work for the soundness of city credit and "reputation."

Fiscal Crises

Watertown used its debt-issuing abilities to foster economic growth. When the expectations of growth were not met, conflict occurred along class and political lines, and this conflict determined the outcome of the city's position regarding debt obligations. The city's internal conflict over finances directly tied local taxpayers of all classes to local politics and to the larger economy. Debt, the corporate privilege of the city, represented an opportunity and a risk, and the city's fate demonstrates its continuing boldness. Had the rail ventures originally underwritten by city debt succeeded, one imagines the city might have experienced somewhat more economic growth, growth that in retrospect would have been deemed natural.

Idiosyncratic or nonexistent data collection methods preclude any systematic time series analysis of total urban revenues and expenditures for the United States prior to the revision of census priorities in 1902.[42] However, an interrupted time series analysis of the annual number of defaults on municipal bonds from 1850 to the late 1940s confirms two aspects of debt financing. First, the number of defaults per year slowly drifted upward from 1850 on, although an adjustment for the number of urban dwellers suggests that the per capita number was more or less stable. Second, a statistical analysis of the depressions of 1873, 1893, and the 1930s confirms that only one, the Great Depression, had any unexpected impact. With the exception, therefore, of the Depression of the 1930s, we may conclude that defaults on municipal bonds stayed surprisingly stable.[43] Whatever other transitions came about in the urban budget, failures to honor debt have been relatively few. We should use them for the rare look they provide at the politics of the city budget, rather than as signs of imminent urban catastrophe.

Data reflecting the urban balance sheet from 1929 to 1982 cannot directly be compared with the default data even though the two overlap, but several implications can be drawn from them.[44] Most important is the long upward drift after the Depression, reflecting cautious but increasing use of state and local debt. Since 1968, this drift has approached debt payment proportions reminiscent of the early Depression. As case studies emphasize, and the experience of Watertown exemplifies, these fiscal positions constitute necessary but not sufficient conditions for default crises. The key to turning high debt payment ratios into default is most often found in popular politics, most likely local taxpayer action. And this in turn depends on local political allegiances and cleavages. Because of the overlay of special districts, increasing dependence of cities on intergovernmental transfers, and the rise of sophisticated urban services, the municipal budget has drifted far from the comprehension of most taxpayers. Operating costs and urban services are the only budgetary issues to have become the center of political attention in the twentieth century. Debt as an issue only comes to the fore in potential default crises, as that of New York City in the mid-1970s and Cleveland in the late 1970s. Only when the broad political issues centering on using the city as an economic machine can be articulated should we expect purposeful defaults by city governments.

The Watertown story illustrates the great difference between private corporate enterprise and the city. Although cities are public corporations whose legal status resembles private corporations, their essence does not derive solely from the charter.[45] Cities, in fact, are historical, social, geographic, economic, and cultural entities that exist prior to and independent of the enabling legislation that makes it possible for them to borrow and act in some ways like legal persons. If the legislation giving them corporation privileges were to be eliminated, cities would be seriously altered, many new cities of the nineteenth century might never have been built, and the remarkable growth of the American urban network would have been retarded. But cities would not disappear as a social form. This often overlooked, simple fact explains some of the anger and apparent irresponsibility of city officials and inhabitants of bankrupt cities, both in the nineteenth century and today. They perceive the city as a whole, and in a fiscal crisis value their indebtedness bonds, relative to the rest of the budget, much less than do the financiers, who would seem at these moments of crisis to control the city's fate.

When New York City's fiscal crisis became apparent in 1973, one commentator asserted that it was simply inconceivable that the city could fail. And in a sense this was a realistic observation, for cities are far more than legal fictions enabled by legislative fiat to act like persons. City officials differ from corporate officials, whose responsibility to the shareholders is to multiply capital. This is not to say that city officials have always done well in exercising their obligations. In fact, what becomes apparent in examining individual city stories is that there has been a deep and perhaps irremediable disjuncture between electoral and fiscal responsibility. Smart politicians spend the money of their constituents' grandchildren. Yet this disjuncture is older than the American urban network: in a mass demonstration in fourteenth-century Florence, some 5,000 residents demanded a ten-year moratorium on debt repayment.[46]

This gap between political responsibility and politically created public debt accounts for other invisible costs displaced by the urban present to the urban future. For instance, the economic advantages of central place locations appear to be persisting into the electronic age, in spite of dismal predictions to the contrary. These advantages accrue to the whole society. But the long-run costs of building and maintaining central places are high, and it is probable that these costs are not fairly allocated, over either space or time. Though this is a much-contested terrain in urban economics, the argument that the central cities do not bear excessive costs relative to prosperous suburbs and exurban areas has yet to be conclusively demonstrated.

Debt is the way in which capital costs are paid over time, while taxation allocates these costs over space. Yet the use of debt has been enlisted in support of economic growth as well as for urban services. While voters can approve or reject bond issues, it is not clear how wisely, creatively, or humanely debt has been used. In a sense, the proper use of debt has been conceived as a parallel to the debt usage of other corporate enterprises, even though few could argue that such principles would apply to the purpose and function of a city. When in the nineteenth century debt became an issue of public debate and discussion, as in Watertown, its complexities, if not possibilities, came to the fore. One cannot help but be impressed by the vigor and richness, as well as the irresponsibility, of the public argument surrounding debt.

Since the 1930s the issues surrounding local debt have become more complex, the arguments more abstract, and the conflict buried. And, for better or worse, it is almost impossible to imagine popular local action of the kind seen in the defaulting cities of the nineteenth century. A look at some aggregated data on municipal debt suggests that we are once again approaching a situation ripe for crisis, although the lack of political understanding of debt adds an unpredictable element to any potential crisis.

The Depression and Federal Finance of Local Government

Consistent annual data on local revenues prior to 1929 are not obtainable, but nearly comparable information can be found for 1902, 1913, 1922, and 1927. These data indicate that federal aid to state and local government varied between 0.6 percent and 2.2 percent prior to the Depression. From 1902 property tax had declined slightly in its contribution to local revenue, but remained within the 60 percent range. Given that these estimates may be slightly high owing to inconsistent data, we can nevertheless conclude with some confidence that the local finance mix from the beginning of the century until 1930 had exhibited stability, especially when compared with the dramatic effects of the Depression and World War II.[47]

For 1929 to the present, aggregated state and local government expenditure and receipt data for the United States are available annually. These data mark the shifting role of the federal government in state and local government. To an unknown extent they also hide the changing fiscal posture of the city by lumping urban affairs with state-level activities. Nevertheless, the patterns are instructive and set the context for understanding post-Depression urban finance. Nineteen-thirty marked the high point in local government property tax revenue, about 4.5 billion dollars, until well into World War II, 1944. The absolute bottom in receipts came in

1934 at under 4 billion dollars, but recovery did not really begin until the end of World War II, eleven years later. The proportion of total receipts accounted for by property tax, which began a decline in 1933 that has not yet ceased, does not clearly reflect the fifteen-year-long collapse in the urban economy from 1930 to 1945. In the early 1930s property tax accounted for 60 percent of all state and local revenues; by the 1970s this proportion had fallen to 20 percent. As discussed earlier, this reflects the dilution of the urban situation by the increase in state income tax revenues, but the trend if not the level is correct.

Both in absolute and proportional values, federal aid to local governments has increased since 1929, fluctuating widely during the 1930s, then beginning its long upward trend. From accounting for less than 2 percent of local governments' receipts in the late 1920s and early 1930s, the federal contribution increased to over 20 percent for the recent period 1972–1981.

The ratio of expenditures to receipts gives a simple index to the overall balance sheet of state and local governments, indicating if governments spent more than they took in. The last depression year with a positive balance was 1933, and the condition was not to be corrected until 1949. Then followed twenty years of alternating deficits and excesses, until 1968, when a long deficit pattern comparable only to the late Depression began. As of 1982, only seventeen of the fifty-five years since 1929 had positive balances.

Yet the specter of government budgets becoming more and more dedicated to debt service has not followed precisely the same pattern as have most indicators of state and local government finance. The percent of total expenditures dedicated to interest payments hit a peak in 1933 of 8 percent. The narrow range of this index, from a high of 8 percent to a low of 2.8 percent in 1950, suggests that as an aggregate it minimizes much more severe local imbalances, for instance Detroit's budget, with over half committed to fixed-debt service obligations. However, the interest peak accurately identifies 1933 as the most severe point in the Depression crisis. Moreover, it shows a steady climb back toward high interest to expenditure proportions after 1968. By 1982, interest payments consumed almost 7 percent of state and local government budgets, a very high figure matched only by the first three years of the Depression.[48]

The history of earlier defaults suggests that although the economic basis for a default crisis may be present, only local political action will cause default. If anything, the default history of Watertown, though exaggerated, accurately shows how default was a conscious political action. Of all depressions since 1850, only that of the 1930s can be shown to have had a meaningful impact on urban defaults. And though it is apparent that this depression did drive cities to default, many defaults during the 1930s were more specifically caused by the bank holiday, which deprived cities of local sources of cash, on which they were highly dependent.[49]

The Depression probably hit Detroit, fourth largest city during the period, most directly because of its large proportion of automobile workers. It is somewhat surprising, then, that Detroit struggled along, even managing to make local welfare contributions with no support from the federal government. The city did not default until the bank holiday of February 1933 simply and abruptly dried up its cash resources. Thus the local banking situation rather than the larger pressures of the Depression toppled the city into default. Had it not been for the closing of the banks, the city might have continued to get along, on a much reduced budget but without defaulting.[50] Cities may not be capable of controlling the larger economy, but Detroit's experience demonstrates that default crises are neither inevitable nor irreversible. Urban finance can be a field for creativity and a central arena for the democratic use of city government.

The expansion of the city budget over the nineteenth and twentieth centuries should be regarded neither as an intrusion of government into formerly communal affairs nor as an expansion of the role of government. Rather, it should be seen as an outcome of the transformed role of local government, a transformation from the regulation of the local economy to the promotion of the local economy. This promotion occurred both directly—as in granting of land and direct capital investment financed through the issuance of municipal debt—and indirectly—through the creation and implementation of the service city. City government had not merely grown, it had changed, and as it changed, it shaped the trajectory and consequences of growth. Its budget marked the front lines of that change.

7 ✩ Transportation: From Animal to Automobile

There are two different analyses of the relationship of urban transportation technology to cities. The first argues that new technologies changed the shape of cities. The second argues that the changing shape of cities encouraged new technologies, which in turn further facilitated the change. I wish to present a third: that city governments subsidized and in other ways encouraged new technologies, and these in turn interacted with differing combinations of the first two scenarios. The active role of city government paved the way—often quite literally—for the sprawling cities of the twentieth-century United States.[1] The role of locally promoted forms of transportation helped shape the cities to physically match their rough, aggressive, and boisterous political, social, and economic environment.

How Transportation Shapes Our Urban Views

Perceptions of the physical city have always been formulated through the medium of transportation. Transportation modes predetermine even our sense of the social and economic city. Approaches by water are visually thrilling, as the skyline creates an imposing sense of shape, while aerial approaches are all too often contradicted by the earthly experiences that follow. To enter any modern city by train guarantees the depressing sight of the backs of factories, the worst housing, and a view of the city's wasteland. Freeways edit our sense of space and often disguise what turn out to be pleasant residential neighborhoods. Bicyclists learn much about road surfaces, the efficiency of street sweeping, traffic patterns, and city smells.

The transportation mode also determines the significance of terrain. San Francisco's hilly vistas quickly lose their charm for the walker or bicyclist, while angled and narrow streets have little appeal for the delivery truck driver in Columbus, Ohio's German Town. The restored cobblestones in Philadelphia's Society Hill are beautiful to look at but terrible to clean; and the long-distance air commuter to Washington, D.C., curses the quiet that the building of Dulles Airport in the farthest outskirts of the city has brought.

A traveler's choice of transportation entails perceptions of transportation modes. Tramps know where trains slow down. Business travelers know a place by length of time from airport to hotel. Commercial pilots attach much significance to Grand Island, Nebraska, which marks from their perspective an important transcontinental route point. Californians, the most experienced freeway users in the world, personalize their routes, calling them not by number but by city names representing the freeway terminus, no matter whether one is leaving or arriving. Few users of the world's busiest freeway, the Ventura, know its official number; even fewer actually go to the city of Ventura. Half of the travelers drive away from Ventura when they get on the freeway; most use it to commute from various suburban locations to downtown Los Angeles.[2]

Because so much of our initial knowledge of a city derives from a transportation perspective, we often err in our analyses of the relationship between the two. Because automobiles, for instance, structure how we visualize mid-twentieth-century U.S. cities, we begin to think that the automobile has actually structured them. Consider, for instance, how urban observers have viewed the relationship of the automobile and the city. In the early twentieth century they saw the automobile as the solution to urban problems from slum housing to traffic congestion; by the 1960s it had become the cause of urban problems.[3] Both positions are wrong, but their wrongness suggests the power which we willingly attribute to transportation technology. Technology is far less significant in determining our urban history than most people allow.

Just as the popular symbol of the late nineteenth-century city was corruption, often involving bribes paid by street railroad "rings" to gain monopoly franchises, so the symbol of the twentieth-century city often is said to be the automobile. Virtually every textbook that discusses the late nineteenth-century city mentions corruption and franchises; similarly, most use a picture of a busy Los Angeles freeway as a metaphor for the postwar city. If the unsavory and tantalizing side of the street railway was corruption, the automobile has also been given a villain's role by twentieth-century urban analysts. Ironically, while popular historical thought considers the politics of the street railways to have been bad because they were corrupt, the automobile today is viewed as bad because it destroyed a mass transit system superior to that of many English cities, the same corrupt street railways. That the automobile also was the enemy of corruption and monopoly is all too often forgotten.[4] So today we see the story of the city and the car in technical terms, rather than political ones. And this inconsistency has obscured our analysis.

In addition, because what remains of the nineteenth century's public transit system—subways, fixed rail trolleys, and their descendants, motor buses—has become the major form of inner-city transit for the poor, it is easy to project this current state of ridership backward. The result then, is the notion that the public transit which automobiles replaced was somehow more accessible to the poor and therefore more democratic. The erroneous reasoning goes like this: when the cities only had trains, trolleys, and horse-drawn cars, then the more extensive public transit system was an inherently more equitable one than exists today, for today, one must be able to drive and have enough wealth to be able to buy an automobile, otherwise one is forced to take a much restricted public transit system. This would be a reasonable scenario were it not for the fact that prior to the automobile, public transit simply cost too much for the poor and often even for the working class. In Pittsburgh, for example, the automobile did not replace the trolley, it replaced walking. In Baltimore, however, only 10 percent of the population walked to work, so there the automobile allowed people to live in larger houses, to disperse farther from streetcar lines.[5] This complex relationship is important to remember. For anyone who has read Upton Sinclair's The Jungle, the message should be memorable enough: only now and then could one of the many working members of the family afford the cost of carfare home. Had they been able to ride regularly, the family would not have disintegrated, for the kids would have come home after work, and Una would not have contracted pneumonia and died. Thus in some cities the streetcar was a luxury available only to the middle classes and white-collar workers, while other cities, like Baltimore, were better served, in a way more consistent with our imagined view of the past.[6] And more important, the fixed rail system was a mode of transportation that almost everyone was willing to eliminate. For transportation monopoly was considered by reformers to be a major turn-of-the-century urban problem, and the fixed rail transport system epitomized that problem.

The twentieth-century urban ridership despised fixed rail transit. Its proponents were far more successful in promoting their franchises as a means of suburban growth than as a means of mass transit. The use of street railways to promote middle-class suburban real estate development was quite explicit. One late nineteenth-century Milwaukee newspaper supported extending franchises for street railways because, "Milwaukee is in the business of growing." In 1912 the socialist government of Milwaukee saw suburbanization as a solution to central city housing congestion. And control of fixed rail transit fare did not concern working-class politicians very much: at their lowest, the fares were still beyond the budgets of the mass of workers.[7]

Intensive research on the journeys made to work by Philadelphians between 1850 and 1880 confirms that walking was the principal mode of transportation for over 80 percent of all the city's residents. It is interesting, however, that between 1850 and 1880, the average journey to work of industrial workers doubled, from about a half mile to about a mile. This increase, the researchers conclude, came about because of expanding housing opportunities and shorter working days, not because of the replacement of horse-drawn omnibuses with street railways. If technological innovation had anything to do with transport for the urban masses, it was the technology of mass housing construction on inexpensive land that mattered.[8]

Americans have become accustomed to thinking about cities and transportation in a purely passive vein. Technological change, so this thinking goes, brings with it inevitable social, economic, geographical, and political consequences. This implicitly passive model masquerades as one showing active causality. But really it conceptualizes historical change as human response rather than action—people and societies respond to the inherent utility and functionality of inventions; along comes a clever and persistent inventor, and the course of history changes. In fact, inventions and technical innovation only have meaning in an aggressively sup-

portive social, political, and economic environment: without a social and political system willing to make the appropriate innovations, no technology has inherent utility.

The Deterministic Vision

For those who study the city and its transportation technology,
the temptation to succumb to technological determinism has
proved too great to resist. Geographers have built an especially se-
ductive case for such determinism in accounting for the spatial
relationship of cities in the United States to one another as well
as within themselves. Starting in the 1960s, geographers have
claimed that the history of transportation has been the backbone
of the American city's history.[9] This deterministic view has per-
meated the major syntheses of U.S. urban history: Sam B. Warner
built his narrative scenario of American urban change on this technologically determined model.[10]

This model of change envisions four technologically different
modes and hence eras of transport: wagon and sail, steam and iron
rail, the steel rail, and most recently, the automobile and aircraft.
The transportation narrative can be summarized as follows: first
came the era of sails and, to a lesser extent wagons, and in the
1820s, canals. They were succeeded in the 1840s by steam driven
trains running on iron rails and steam driven boats, which were in
turn followed by trains running on steel rails. In the early twentieth
century, hard surfaced roads and the internal combustion engine
once again began to reshape the urban landscape; in the post–World
War II era, air transport had its impact. Cities changed both internally and externally in parallel and in response to these changes.
Canal transportation opened up the Midwest, and rails quickly followed suit, opening the western edge of the Midwest and Far West.
Hard surfaced roads created such cities as Las Vegas and Phoenix,
while air transport accelerated the boom of the southwestern cities
in general. Internal changes saw a gradual growth of cities, each
transport technology breaking old barriers of size: in general most
cities have been limited in spread by a commute of one-half to one
hour, and feet, rails, and roads each expanded the commuting per-
ipheries of cities.

The argument has intuitive appeal: Warner developed it in his
text to help account for today's differences between major metrop-

olises. New York represents a city whose compact internal shape and economic prosperity was initially determined in the first era when its harbor made it the major North American entrepôt, a position that was strengthened by the Erie Canal and early rail developments. Mainly a walking city because of the era in which it grew, subsequent transportation changes never really eradicated New York's essence. Chicago typifies the second and perhaps third eras, growing at a hub of lake and rail shipping, with fixed rail transport allowing it to spread itself across the flat Illinois terrain. Its lesser density came from a prototypical fixed rail transit system, culminating in the El. Los Angeles exemplifies the third and fourth eras, its initial sprawl made possible by fixed rail transit which the automobile accelerated, boulevards and freeways literally replacing the tracks of the famous Red Cars. And Phoenix represents a city of the fourth era, a city that without automobiles, trucks, and air transport would probably return to its ashes.

This model offers very persuasive descriptions, but descriptive power is not necessarily analytic power. For the description is only partial, and its inferences incorrect. It lulls us into thinking that the technology of each age *caused* changes in urban growth. Such causal thinking is often done in the case of Los Angeles, a city with a transportation system that has collected more than its fair share of pejorative attention. For Los Angeles is often seen as the city of the automobile, a city whose spread was caused by the availability of a new technology. Los Angeles today is indeed a city dependent on the automobile, but its basic shape, including the greater metropolitan area and suburbs, came in the preautomobile era of fixed rail transit, when Huntington's Red Cars carried riders across the whole basin for distances of up to forty, even sixty miles.[11] And the city's peculiar shape, with a long narrow tentacle of land stretching some twenty miles southwest from city center to the port at San Pedro, exemplifies the political move that annexed a railroad right-of-way to the sea. This port did not merit being called a port when visited by Richard Henry Dana in 1835— it was little more than a muddy beach. But the same political aggression that annexed the potential port to Los Angeles also created from unpromising beginnings the biggest commercial harbor on the West Coast. Not only did the automobile and aircraft merely reinforce and amplify Los Angeles' shape but Angelenos consciously chose to abandon the Red Cars for the automobile.[12] Thus

/ 163

the arguments made by the technological determinists are not entirely wrong, for each transport technology has indeed had profound consequences for the shaping of our cities. Rather, the determinists forget that political action was the necessary prior step for technological change. The financial success of the Red Cars depended on a monopoly franchise and intense land speculation by the railroad owners; the acquisition of rail access to a potential port was a conscious political and economic move by the city; the conversion of dirt tracks into modern city streets came as the result of political action. Of far greater historical and contemporary importance than the shaping power of transportation technology have been the enormous political, social, and economic efforts by governments—local, state, and federal—to promote them and make them functional. In fact, very little urban history has unfolded in the purely rational way that the technological determinist model implies.

Politics Causes Technological Change

In the case of transportation, cities have not been passive recipients of a technologically determined imperative. Local political action profoundly mediated the relationship between transportation and urban geography. Aggressive, highly conscious local action created the economic and legal environment that fostered the new technologies and their subsequent adoptions. Ports, railroad rights-of-way, roads, and finance—all had to be effectively implemented before any technology could be invested in and perfected. And these changes occurred at the local level in the United States, bringing the role of local government rather than that of technology to the fore. The technological determinism that pervades our assumptions about transportation and the city affects most of all our attitude toward the automobile. When we examine railroads or water transport, the role of nature—in obstructing progress with mountains and cold weather or in providing natural harbors and waterways—has introduced its powerful, if sometimes subtle, hand. Similarly, the government has played a prominent role in our thinking about these technologies, from the building of harbors and canals and the suppression of pirates to the massive, nineteenth-century subsidization of the railroads. But the automobile does not seem to fit so easily into this category; surely here is a case where technology—the light, inexpensive, mass-produced vehicle—led the way.

Before confronting this notion directly, let us consider why we think that the automobile precipitated a "natural" technological revolution. Partly we have this notion because of the hobbyist enthusiasm generated for automobiles. Unlike trains and steamships, automobiles and their technologically important predecessors, bicycles, were far more easily affordable and therefore dispersed. All other forms of mass transit took massive corporate investment, both private and public: the automobile required a third partner, the individual consumer. And the consumers directly owned a substantial share of the capital in the new transit system. Very quickly they provided another mode for the ancient competitive sport of racing. Americans are still familiar with the names of early automobile racing heroes, including two brothers carried on in at least one automobile brand name, Louis and Gaston Chevrolet. Even before they gained widespread practicality, both bicycles and automobiles were fun.

Moreover, in their very early decades, bicycles and automobiles, because of their relatively low individual capital costs, were almost impossible to monopolize. Hundreds of bicycle manufacturers existed in the 1890s. Similarly, with automobiles, the big three oligopolies of the post–World War II era did not exist prior to the Depression, when over fifty viable manufacturers in a dozen states competed for customers. In the antimonopolist political atmosphere of the late nineteenth and early twentieth century, any innovation that promised to break the hold of monopoly capital—including that of the street railways—was bound to have enthusiastic adherents. Such especially was the case with the automobile.[13]

Transport technologies have always captured the cultural imagination. In the Roman world, charioteers, like Porphyrius of Constantinople, became great popular heroes. Americans raced horses and the horses themselves became great popular heroes and heroines (Lexington in the mid-nineteenth century). In the mid-nineteenth century trains were celebrated in poetry (Emily Dickinson wrote, "I like to see it lap the miles and lick the valleys up") while individual engines ("Tom Thumb," 1830, to "999," 1893) became the focus of folk ballads. Although train races were not feasible, state fairs often had steam engine crashes, an attraction that lasted into the 1930s. Following the train, the bicycle became the symbol of progress: Mark Twain's Connecticut Yankee re-shaped the Middle Ages by mounting knights on bicycles.[14] Bicy-cles, automobiles, and airplanes have served for the past century as the image with which to convey the notion of progress. As with the microcomputer in the 1980s, these machines stood for the per-ceived new age; the new age was real and palpable because a central feature of these machines was, as it still is, their accessibility. The poor and the rich alike can own and shape their automobiles. Prior even to World War II the mass produced automobile became the raw material for working class artistic expression. In the post–World War II era, probably the ultimate form of automobile art is the low-rider, a Mexican-American custom car so refined as an art form that it is nearly nonfunctional, either as transportation or as cultural expression, outside of its specialized southwestern urban environment.[15]

The central argument of this book is that our understanding of U.S. cities must consider two histories simultaneously: the his-tory of outside factors that shaped the growth of cities, and the history of their own self-determination. We can gain some insight into the spread of the automobile as a major form of transportation if we first test the commonsense, determinist hypothesis that con-ceives the technology itself as promoting change. The familiar ar-gument is this: from the 1890s to the eve of World War I the au-tomobile was an expensive and impractical toy for elite consumption.[16] Then Henry Ford began mass production of the Model T, a car so cheap and reliable that it was seized upon by millions as a form of transportation. The diffusion of this new tech-nology forced governments to begin investing in more reasonable roads, so that up to the very present, traffic congestion and con-tinued spread of the technology has spurred public investment in roads. Only the oil crisis of 1973 has caused the government to pause in its headlong race to accommodate the revolutionary automobile.

Actually, the spread of the automobile is in many ways anal-ogous to the current microcomputer revolution. Hobbyist had for several years been building their own toy computers prior to the massive diffusion of the microcomputer, and it was only the in-vention of new uses—game playing, word processing, database management, and spreadsheets—that suddenly fostered the expansion of the microcomputer industry. It is still uncertain if enough use will be made of these tools to continue their potentially dramatic impact. For a tool without a function is not even a toy; it is just a curious piece of machinery, with an aesthetic appeal similar to that of an old mill. Automobiles and their immediate cultural and technical predecessors, bicycles, did not have any obvious utility when they were first experimented with. Both required good roads to work. For the hobbyists, small racetracks would have done quite well, but for extensive diffusion, both bicycles and automobiles had to have a utility. This utility, transportation, could only be achieved through good roads. With this model, then, we might guess that the adoption of the automobile as privately owned transportation on a mass scale had to have been *preceded* by good roads. And good roads are purely political creations.[17]

The Politics of Good Roads

Although American cities had notoriously poor-quality streets, particularly in comparison to those in Europe, the rural roads and highways were even worse. The good roads movement in the United States began as a peculiar coalition of urban bicyclists and farmer reformers, who took the initiative with the publication of the League of American Wheelmen's reform journal, *Good Roads*, in 1892. The first volume unintentionally highlighted the contrast between urban and rural interests. Of the nearly 240 contracts for surfacing announced by the journal, fewer than ten were for rural areas. Moreover, most of the articles, which were intended to persuade readers of the benefits of hard surfacing, also showed how it improved the profitability of farming by increasing the pulling capacity of horses. Most of the rural photos showed mud roads; urban ones were usually before and after paving. Farmers refused to support road paving for fear of higher taxes and because of the free rider problem, or the thought that one county might pay for paving used by outsiders. In Wisconsin, 70 percent of the urban voters supported good roads in 1908, while the opposite pattern held true for rural areas. The federal government explicitly recognized the problem of rural resistance and urban action, and the federal Office of Public Road Inquiries and its agents toured the country with demonstrations designed to convince farmers of the benefits of road surfacing. Special Agent and Road Expert E. G. Harrison, in a turn-of-the-century lecture and surfacing demonstration, told a rural Michigan audience, "We are not here to build city streets, nor boulevards. Cities are able to pay for their expensive streets and know how to build them. . . . Here we have not even built the best kind of macadam road. For that you must go to your cities and look at the boulevards."[18]

The earliest history of bicycles, automobiles, and airplanes indicates that in their first two decades, these machines were not practical forms of transportation but fancy toys. Until the end of the nineteenth century the elite found the bicycle an exciting substitute for the horse, only to be replaced around the turn of the century by even more exciting machines, the automobile and, somewhat later, the airplane. Bicycles were too costly and roads were too poor for them to become a useful mode of transportation at first. By the time road quality had been improved, especially in the United States, the cost of automobiles had dropped to where ordinary people could buy them, and the advent of the closed, reliable automobile made its relative utility exceed that of the bicycle. The scenario with aircraft has been similar: that the land for an automobile racetrack passed over to a small group of businessmen who enjoyed airplanes for what became Minneapolis' first airport should therefore not be surprising. City support of the airport followed six years later, in 1926, when the city gave the Park Board responsibility for its management, as befitted a recreational resource. Ultimately, these actions forged the way for commercial air travel, just as city street surfacing had forged the way for automobile travel.[19]

Those familiar with contemporary urban mass transportation arguments may wonder why the emphasis here is on personal rather than mass transportation, on cities as positive actors rather than losers in the struggle to keep their mass transit systems. While the need for and convenience of fixed rail transit should not be minimized, it is important to keep in mind that deliberate urban policy, in the form of street surfacing, encouraged automobile and truck traffic. The grim picture of decline usually painted is only a small portion of the story of urban transportation. Cities and the people in them to a large extent chose their forms of transportation.[20]

Prior to World War II, roads, streets, and highways were primarily the responsibility of state and local governments. Federal interest was at a level too modest to be considered meaningful. The commonsense and critically unexamined hypothesis that these governments responded to the new requirements introduced by automobile technology might be simply, if crudely, tested by comparing the annual change in miles of hard surfaced roads to the annual change in numbers of automobiles registered in the previous year.[21] Unfortunately, the collection of relevant data for the local level is as difficult as the national level is easy. Two inferences may be drawn from this problem: that collecting data was easier then, so much so that only the federal government bothered to collect it from localities and publish it; or that possibly the federally collected data are in fact crude estimates. The data problem itself reflects the evolving political status of the automobile. The measurement of the first critical variable, the number of registered automobiles, assumes some system of consistent registration. Yet statewide registration came only in the second decade of the twentieth century: Minnesota, for instance, had local registration by the police until 1909. And no local registration data for Minnesota have been recorded except by unsystematic sources: by local police departments for the pre-1909 period, and for the 1920s by the National Automobile Chamber of Commerce. Thus for the crucially important pre–World War I period, we must use highly limited and only sketchy sources.

A careful examination of the potential sources for one city, Minneapolis, shows that all of the data relevant to an empirical study of the expansion of the automobile and cities simply is not accessible in reasonable quality for statistical tests. Basically, one cannot find data on hard surfaced roads and automobile registrations for the same times and places. This suggests that the relationship between the two may be less obvious than we expect. The Annual Reports of the City Engineer for Minneapolis illustrate extremely detailed monitoring of surfaced road expansion conducted regularly on the local level. For each year through the 1920s, not only are data available for the miles of surfaced and graded (dirt) streets but also detailed color maps list the kinds of surfacing for all city streets. The total length of streets varied little through the early decades of the century; most streets were graded dirt or gravel, sprinkled with oil by horse-drawn wagons in the summer to reduce dust. The city worked hard at surfacing its streets, prodded in the nineteenth century by bicyclists, and in the twentieth

Columbus, Ohio, circa 1870,

Muddy City Streets:

Each of these three pictures gives a different view of city streets, prior to paving. Dirt dominates the street scape of central Columbus, in a picture representing the monumental best of the Ohio's state capital. The grain elevators of Defiance, Ohio, are nearly inaccessible to wheeled traffic. This photograph appeared in *Good Roads* magazine, a national reformist journal dedicated to improving road surfaces. Its intent was to convince farmers that investment in hard surfacing meant economic good sense for everybody, city folk and country folk alike. The rails of the streetcar in the lower picture are barely visible over the street slop: note how plank footpaths get pedestrians from place to place. Note also the man with the broom just to the left of the streetcar; presumably he kept the street filth off the plank walks. Until local governments invested in extensive paving, there was little point in developing or buying automobiles or motor trucks.

Source: Ohio Historical Society; *Good Roads*, 1 (1892), 239; Minneapolis History Collection, Minneapolis Public Library.

Defiance, Ohio, circa 1890,
and
Excelsior, Minnesota, circa 1900.

by wagon users, automobilists, and most of all by the city engineers, who simply wanted longer-wearing surfaces. The expansion
rate of hard surfaced streets increased from about 1902 to 1911,
well before the automobile became widespread. Then the expansion rate for hard surfaced roads declined consistently after this
first decade. Thus the age of hard surfaced roads preceded the age
of the automobile.

Unfortunately, the exact number of automobiles in the city
cannot be measured with any consistency. But a remarkable series
of traffic surveys conducted by the city engineer's department
throughout 1906 suggests at least one reason why the collection of
accurate automobile registration data seemed irrelevant early in the
century.[22] From August through December the city surveyed ten
different twelve-hour samples of daytime, midweek downtown
traffic in order to determine the relationship of usage to street surface wear. Only one automobile chugged by for every fifteen horse-
drawn wagons and four bicycles. The average traffic for the period
tells much about the nature of transport within the city: the mean
daily figures were 2,722 horse-drawn vehicles (fully two-thirds trotting—the sign of a truly bustling city), less than 3 horse riders, 786
bicyclists, and only 183 automobiles (equivalent to about half of
the city's total). Thus, there was on average, winter and summer,
a horse-drawn vehicle every 16 seconds, a bicycle every 55 seconds,
and a car every 4 minutes.

The minute number of horses ridden by individuals may seem
surprising, but their high initial cost, even higher cost of stabling,
and the undesirable odors from nearby stables all precluded their
use as commuting transportation. One sees, in fact, from this survey that urban horses might be best compared to farm tractors or
semitrailer trucks today: utilitarian but expensive. For the tiny
number of horses trotting down the street with an individual rider
were more than offset by the daily average of 4,000 horses pulling
just under 3,000 carts and wagons. There would have been more
horses a decade and a half earlier, because as late as 1890, 60 percent of the street railway mileage in U.S. cities used animal power.
And as this usage ended in the first decade of the twentieth century, horses continued to be the major power for hauling bulky,
heavy loads. The progressive city engineer of Minneapolis included
photos of modern street machinery in his reports: the steam powered traction engine that pulled the grader had horse-drawn wagons

Street Scene, Cleveland, circa 1910
The hard surface streets of cities made everything move more smoothly.
Here, wheeled vehicles, both animal and internal combustion engine powered, do everything from moving households to carrying goods to competing with foot traffic. Contrast the utility of this street to those in the
preceding illustration.

Source: Keystone-Mast Collection, California Museum of Photography, University
of California, Riverside.

following. And in other construction photos of 1911 one spies almost as many horses as workers. It is no wonder that the bicycle and automobile seemed like sanitary improvements in urban transport.[23]

Considering that four of the ten survey days were in Minneapolis' cold November and December, the high ratio of bicycles to other modes of travel is almost astonishing. Only on a very rainy, cold (38 degrees) November Tuesday did automobile traffic exceed bicycles, and both were vastly exceeded by horse-drawn vehicles. And apparently only the slippery streets deterred the bicyclists. On a dry but below-freezing December first, 208 bicyclists rode by, outnumbering the 76 automobiles; maybe the cars would not start. One can only guess about snowy days; probably only horse-drawn vehicles moved about.

Pittsburgh conducted similar traffic surveys starting in 1917, counting full days in midsummer only. If we assume that Pittsburgh was not wildly different from Minneapolis, then we can compare the surveys in order to discover the obvious: during the years around World War I the internal combustion engine had begun to triumph over animal power. Two times as many gasoline powered vehicles as horse powered ones entered the city's downtown; the survey did not include bicycles. And a decade later, in 1927, the downtown had begun to look, sound, and smell like the downtown of today: almost fifty times as many gasoline powered as horse-drawn vehicles entered.[24]

The broadening scope of government data collection suggests the growing level of utility and range for the automobile. The Minneapolis city clerk registered but did not always report automobiles prior to 1909, when the state took over. The state, however, did not keep data on registration at the local level. In the 1920s the Chamber of Commerce apparently was able to obtain data to send to the National Automobile Chamber of Commerce. Consequently, there are only a handful of city-specific data on the number of automobiles. Prior to 1910, they were machines to be counted locally. During the World War I decade the automobile expanded its boundaries beyond the sphere of local governments to the state level, and in the World War II era, the federal government got into the act, not registering automobiles, but exerting a real data collection effort. Minneapolis, for example, had 533 automobiles in 1907 (apparently the first year it registered them), added

472 in 1908, and (perhaps) 142 in 1909 and 1910. Perhaps the market for such costly devices had been saturated. All these numbers are to be regarded with caution, but they give a rough idea. The survey in the 1920s showed far more automobiles—55,000 in 1924, zooming steadily up to just under 134,000 by 1929.[25]

The national evidence on the relationship of cities to cars bears out the suggestive examples drawn from these two cities. Two regressions, one for 1910 and the other for 1920, establish quite forcefully the early and quickly reversing relationship between cities and cars. For each decade, the regressions relate the number of cars to urban and rural populations, by state, controlling with a dummy variable for the wealthier and more industrially advanced North. The coefficients for 1910 show that the urban population was at least four times as likely to have cars as the rural population. Henry Ford was quick to realize that the rural deficiency represented a market, and his famous Model T was designed in part to overcome the rural road problem with its very high ground clearance and a simple, high-torque engine. Only as states surfaced more rural roads and highways, did the Model T lose its appeal. By 1920 the urban-rural automobile relationship had reversed: the total number of automobiles per capita had increased in both, but rural populations now had more cars than did urban ones.[26] The automobile had become ubiquitous, no longer to be an urban phenomenon.

Were further urban data available, one could demonstrate that statewide data on improved roads concealed the urban dominance in road surfacing until the eve of World War I. Minnesota, for instance, had virtually 90 percent of its surfaced roads in Minneapolis and St. Paul. With proper data sources, no doubt the various timing, local variation, and demographic characteristics affecting the hard surfaced road transformation could be precisely isolated.

The foregoing analysis helps established the causal priorities of one major part of the twentieth-century urban transportation revolution. To reiterate, automobiles did not cause this revolution; the expansion of a high-quality road system did. Roads made the automobile a revolutionary form of mass transportation—no road, no cars. A 1924, survey of automobile owners tersely summarized a doctor's comments: "efficiency of cars increases in direct proportion to road improvement." The city of Houston, desperately grasping for the key to prosperity, assumed that "street paving means growth," equating, "paving and progress."[27] And because roads were in the critical early decades of the century a local government service, the automobile revolution represents the efforts of local government. These efforts, furthermore, were not directly caused by the automobile, but rather because pavement was seen as having varied public utilities, most particularly in increasing the carrying capacity of horse-drawn vehicles.

This was not a new departure for American cities. So ordinary had this role of government become by the twentieth century that city council minutes and engineers' reports simply list expansions. No controversy existed, for after all, hard surfaced roads lasted longer than graded ones. To engineers it seems the major question was what kind of surfacing would best withstand the rubber and steel tires used on horse-drawn wagons.

If local governments had not singlemindedly or even consciously promoted the automobile in their paving of streets, their next step was indeed oriented toward the automobile. They granted political permanence to the automobile after they paved its routes by requiring home builders to provide off-street parking and garages.

The Impact of Technological Change

Tracing the spatial impact of these city-subsidized forms of transportation can be quickly accomplished. Most people seem to be willing to commute for a half-hour to a full hour each way to work, whether in the Middle Ages or today. In order to understand internal city shapes, we can estimate the maximum distance from the center as around one-half hour's travel, leaving one hour to completely traverse the city. By calculating the relative speed of different transportation modes, the city can be outlined. If we add to these estimates the relative user costs of new transport technologies, we can construct an urban map that includes income differences. Finally, this mental picture can be modified by other factors—e.g., closeness to fixed employment points like ports, waterfalls, and wealthy service employers; malodorous plants and prevailing wind and smoke patterns; terrain that precludes comfortable housing such as rock outcroppings and swamps—and one can quickly account for the residential map of most American cities. Of course, this image has changed over time. Until the era of streetcars and fixed rail transit, wealthy urban dwellers had to walk, but rail transit allowed them to move away from urban congestion starting in about 1840 and continuing to around 1920, when the much more accessible automobile began to fill in and expand beyond rail lines.[28] With the automobile, suburbs became accessible to families of modest means, families without servants, and by the end of World War II, working-class suburbs had leap-frogged across the elegant streetcar suburbs of the 1920s.

Such housing and journey-to-work patterns are important to the visual world of every urban dweller today. Once the basic and easily grasped underlying patterns have been made explicit, the physical appearance of cities can be read quickly. This imaging process also allows appreciation of anomalies like ethnic pockets, residential remains, and demographic alterations to land use patterns. Figure 7 outlines an imaginary city, one without any unusual terrain characteristics, which would have been circular and compact during the "walking city" era, around 1800. With a diameter of about three miles, anyone could have walked across town in about an hour. By the mid-nineteenth century, the city would have begun to take on a star shape, extending its fingers out along rail lines, beyond the old, more compact city. Residents who could afford street railways would have to live nearer the rail lines the farther they were from city center, so that their total journey time would be the same whether far from the center or closer in. And the automobile, rather than extending these fingers farther, would have begun in the 1920s to fill in the gaps.

Consequently, as a whole, the automobile city became more rather than less dense, for although the individual houses of the walking city and street rail suburbs were more compactly situated, the cities had unsettled areas between the fingers of rail lines. Subjectively, for instance, Los Angeles seems to be thinly settled because of the automobile and is often considered to typify a "spread city," its sprawling shape determined by the automobile. Yet in many ways it typifies cities of the street rail era, lacking the compact center of waking cities, five of its seven major freeways following earlier street rail lines.[29] And because the automobile has allowed it to fill in evenly, Los Angeles became by 1980 the third densest metropolitan area in the United States, nearly as dense as New York and New Orleans and leading the seemingly dense places such as Chicago, Boston, and Philadelphia.[30]

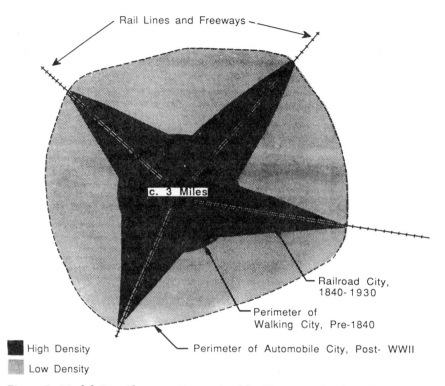

Figure 7. Model City Shape as Determined by Transport Mode and Journey to Work Time

This model should be modified a bit farther to bring the hypothetical city into the mid-twentieth century. Two economists have presented a persuasive argument that an analog of major significance to automobile residential mobility is truck mobility, and that the latter freed many economic activities from their downtown locations beginning in the World War I era. The consequence: while the automobile filled in the star-shaped pattern of residences inherited from the railroad, the truck moved many industries to the periphery in order to lessen rent and labor costs, and in the process formed the industrial basis of what we now call the doughnut city, with its economically active rim.[31]

The automotive transportation scenario, to summarize, followed the building of the streets and roadways of the United States.[32]

The transformation of land transportation of the nineteenth and twentieth centuries may be conceived as one involving a shift in public investment, from the subsidization of iron and steel rails laid on wooden ties to surfacing laid more directly in contact with the ground. Technological innovation and adoption of new forms of transportation quickly followed the changing surfacing materials. It is reasonable to speculate that had investment in hard surfaced roads begun earlier, automotive technology would have replaced animal power all that much more quickly.

Again, the contrast with English industrial cities is instructive. These cities saw a lag, first in building horse-drawn rail lines, and later with steam and electrification. New York had horse-drawn trams in 1832, nearly thirty years before such a form of transport in England. Intercity rail transport had a major impact in the removal of housing for rights of way, creating urban areas isolated by the barrier of the rails. And because British transportation companies were forbidden to engage in real estate speculation, there was little or no building ahead of demand in order to profit from the sale of suburban real estate. Thus the law and preexisting housing made the urban rail transport business less profitable from the beginning. As a result, most English cities had to build their own rail lines, leasing them to contractors and often, by the end of the century, finding no contractors willing to bid, having to run the transport service themselves.[33] Entering the twentieth century, then, British urban transport had the potential of serving the working class, and of serving as an instrument of city planning and housing policy, for it was already a directly subsidized, city-run enterprise. Because the painful reality of direct subsidy had been present from the start, and because the huge profits from land speculation had been absent, mass transit in England was assumed to be a costly enterprise.

In the United States, however, the subsidies had been all indirect, usually in the form of appreciating land values that came as a consequence of the successful construction and utilization of the road, street, or railroad. This custom had been established for roads in the late eighteenth century, when Congress in 1796 authorized Colonel Ebenezer Zane to construct a trail which became known as Zane's Trace through the Northwest Territory. His aid consisted of land grants whose value would appreciate when he completed the road. Thus very early on, the granting of monopolies and speculation in real estate became the acceptable forms of state aid to private enterprise. Cities subsequently underwrote the building of street railroads to the new suburbs in exactly the same manner. In Los Angeles, for instance, in 1907, streetcar entrepreneur Moses Sherman wrote that the length of one route would depend on the amount of capital raised by landowners who would profit from increased property values; he raised capital directly from them.[34] Because this form of subsidization did not really appear to be subsidization, direct subsidy of fixed rail urban transit in the twentieth century still seemed wrong, although public responsibility for roads had been well accepted by the late nineteenth century. Using different mechanisms, then, Americans encouraged fixed rail transit and later hard surfaced road transit far earlier than their British counterparts. Given that from the early nineteenth century on, growth for American cities had meant expansion, and given that growth was a major concern to all, it is no wonder that they led in forms of city transportation. England was always influenced by the precedent of the classic walled city; indeed, the non-walled city, as in England's industrial midlands, was more often considered a problem created by the industrial revolution. Free of such precedents, American cities encouraged spread as a positive good.

Thus, from their origins in the early nineteenth century, modern American cities have continuously and aggressively changed their shape. Their edges continue to be a blur, the center continues to dominate as a reference point, as a point of maximum rent, but the centrifugal urge remains primary. Even the densest, least automobile-accessible American city, New York, is declining in population except at its far edges, where it is actually spreading, growing, and building.[35] Yet the New York of popular perception, the New York liked most by visitors, the "real" New York, is central Manhattan. No paradox, this, but instead the essence of the American city: without walled edges, the center must dominate as reference point, as the most accessible place; but without walls, the new growth, the least costly land, will continue to be on the outward fringes.

From places with filthy, muddy streets, and animal-powered transportation, with urban rail transit available only to a privileged handful, American cities have built themselves into quickly ac-

Road Work, Minneapolis, 1911.
This photograph, the original for which is lost, is one of many which the city engineer used in his annual reports. It shows the mixed nineteenth-century technologies used to construct the foundations of the twentieth-century city. Horse-drawn vehicles assist the steam powered traction engine. Municipal journals of the same period carried ads for specially engineered, horse-drawn, street-paving equipment. These publications supplied the information, even in the age of animal power, which brought on the age of the automobile.
Source: Minneapolis, City Engineer, *Annual Report* (1911-1913), 24 e.

cessible environments with paved, much cleaner, and more controlled surfaces. A much higher proportion of the population uses wheeled transport than could have been imagined at the beginning of the century, when most people only knew walking. Street signs now give clear directions to all. The evils of congestion, the central urban problem less than eighty years ago, are nearly forgotten. Suburban spread and decreased crowding have probably increased social tolerance. One analysis of mid-nineteenth century Detroit has shown that because residential patterns decreased contact among different ethnic and racial groups, the city had fewer riots than did, say, St. Louis, at the same time.[36] It may be no accident that popular white support of legislation against housing discrimination came in the 1950s, the consequence of suburbanization.

It remains to be seen if the cost of this transformation in toxic by-products will outweigh all of the gains in the end. Pollution continues to be a serious problem, but it is hardly a new one: urban residents of a hundred years ago inhaled dust composed of ground horse manure and coal dust, and walked across streets paved with cedar blocks, that oozed horse urine on summer days. Automobile pollution poses a chemical hazard of much larger dimensions, given the sheer success of the internal combustion engine. But at this point, and given the distance already traveled, the prognosis for urban transportation is surprisingly good.

8 ☆ Home Ownership and Mobility

As cities expanded in number, size, and kind across the United States, their populations also changed. Feet, wagons, handcarts, cars, trucks, and trains moved individuals and families from city to city, house to house, and apartment to apartment with a frequency that has almost defied measurement and analysis. Historians use words like "dizzying" and "churning" to describe this residential activity. To use an aquatic metaphor, urban societies were no longer made up of placid, deep pools, but tumbling rapids, swift currents and, on occasion, eddies. For every stable community, historians find dozens of uncharted rapids. For social historians in the 1980s, the fixed society of Thornton Wilder's *Our Town* had become the oddity: when Hal Barron's study of such a small town appeared recently, it almost struck a new chord in the profession, so rare have such places become.

Residence provides the basic element of an individual's relationship to a place. For a city or town dweller, residence may determine physical perception, political participation, monetary demands (through property tax), risk to health and well-being, and access to virtually all the services which cities supply. Throughout the nineteenth and twentieth centuries, a central image has served as the standard against which to judge social and economic change. The image: an owner-occupied, single family home inhabited by the same family for decades, though not for a whole lifetime. But this image is only a partially accurate reflection of reality. Home ownership in the United States, moreover, is deeply interrelated to economic attainment, residential mobility, and the nature of the developing American city; they can in fact be seen as aspects of the same central concern.

Three major issues dominate the history of urban housing: tenure, cost, and quality. Tenure centers on the question of how many people owned their own houses or dwellings and how many rented. Cost centers on the proportion of their incomes people paid for housing, and on who could choose to own or rent. And quality centers on exactly what people could get with their money. These three measurements are, of course, interrelated, and they must be considered together. For instance, a populace with complete home ownership costing only a tiny portion of its income might be living in huts, while a population with no home ownership and relatively high rental costs might all be living in palaces, their capital invested elsewhere. Housing tenure, real cost, and quality are tied together, and how they are tied becomes a major aspect of the social history of U.S. cities.

The Values of Home Ownership

Probably the best known portrayal of turn-of-the-century urban housing can be found in Upton Sinclair's *The Jungle*. In the novel, the Lithuanian family of Jurgis Rudkiss all pool their incomes to buy a new detached house in a Chicago suburb, but their happiness soon disappears as one disaster after another strikes. The house isn't new after all, for a succession of would-be owners has moved through, then lost possession, unable to keep up payments. Payments are much higher than the family can afford, because they did not take property taxes into account. The house has shiny new paint, but is in fact poorly built. The cost of public transport to work, the stockyards, turns out to be unaffordably high, so they walk long hours. Soon desperate, the family takes in boarders, sends the older kids to work, and becomes miserably tied to meeting payments. Their infant son drowns in the unpaved, unsewered, muddy street. Working far from home, the older kids stay out all night, falling into bad company. The family's income falters during hard times, and they fail to make payments, finally losing the house. A depressing story, and one that belies this chapter's cheerful statistics.

Not completely inaccurate, *The Jungle* illustrates how much our urban world has changed, often, if not always, for the better. First, the very premise that in the early twentieth century, barely literate, unskilled immigrant workers could even buy a house is quite amazing, suggesting that in spite of this particular story's outcome, housing opportunities were indeed comparatively good in the United States. Prior to World War I, less than 10 percent of British homes were owner-occupied, whereas in the United States, this figure stood at 37 percent in 1890, and had risen to 50 percent at the end of World War II.[1] If anything, Sinclair's novel may exaggerate the ease with which the family got into the housing market; no wonder the Rudkisses were happy. But the realtor cheated them: the "new" house has had other dwellers. In the novel this comes as a shock and bad omen, one which the family ignored. Others have not been able to make the payment schedule, either. Sinclair implies that this is a crooked scheme by the property owner, although how exactly it works remains unclear. Payments are higher than the family expects, as they had not considered property taxes.

This is one reason many working-class homeowners and politicians of all kinds were against high taxes, or any taxes, but this resistance to taxes in turn accounts for one reason the Rudkisses' son drowned—low taxes won't pave streets. No doubt the Rudkisses would have supported high city debt that promised to bring in more industry, more people, and increase property values, for then they would have profited. We see in one family's tragedy part of the city's fiscal dilemma: urban finances are highly democratic, but home owners have two conflicting desires. They want low taxes and high services; they also want high growth, which can be promoted by high debt. Only the latter seemed to offer a truly free lunch, or even a profit. And they usually voted for low taxes and low services.[2]

Even worse, perhaps, when the Rudkisses do fall behind in their payments, they are threatened, not with foreclosure, but with the loss of their house. This turn of events occurs because they do not have a mortgage but what we would call a contract for deed. Therefore, they have no equity and thus lose everything. Why? Here we must backstep and be reminded that mortgages are often good things, not bad ones. A mortgage is a loan for which a house provides collateral, but the borrower actually owns the house. However, most lenders prior to the 1940s were unwilling to risk home mortgages to ordinary people. So in the case of the Rudkisses, the lender and actual home owner was a speculator, functioning as a banker, taking only the risk that the family would damage his property, the house. Had the Rudkisses had a mortgage, they could have sold the house when they couldn't keep up payments, thus retaining their equity. It didn't help them any, but at this time, access to mortgage credit was on the rise, and had been since 1890, both in the percentage of home owners able to get mortgages and in the values of the houses financed. Cooperative savings and loan associations eased the entry of ordinary people into the mortgage market. Just over one-fourth of all houses were mortgaged in 1890, but by 1980 this had risen to 65 percent. Of the enormous increase in owned homes in the twentieth century, 64 percent was directly owing to increased mortgage availability. So the villain in this part of The Jungle's plot is not the evil of credit, but lack of access to it. The Rudkisses took a bigger gamble than they realized, perhaps than they should have, but had they managed to keep the house, they would have been wildly fortunate.[3]

Home ownership has long vexed the analysis of American social, political, and economic life. And from the time of the Constitution on, real property ownership has assumed much meaning. In the colonial period, home ownership meant land ownership, farming. Hector St. John de Crèvecoeur, the French writer and farmer, lived in America and analyzed the white American's character from this perspective. And it was the ownership and cultivation of land, he believed, that made the poor of Europe into virtuous Americans, "the useless become useful." Land ownership kept Americans from becoming wild hunters, as he imagined the Indians to be, for "it is the chase and the food it procures that have this strange effect." From the vantage point of the twentieth century, it seems evident that Crèvecoeur attached too much importance to property ownership: certainly other factors contributed to the American character. But what Crèvecoeur did not see at all was even more crucial for the centuries that followed—that property ownership directly affected local fiscal politics.[4]

For from the European perspective, property ownership implies an attachment to the land and the capital it represents, something of more importance in societies where fewer actually own property. In a society such as present-day America, where well over half of the families own property, and where a large proportion of those who do not have made their decision out of choice rather than necessity, the ownership of property is likely to have less important meaning—yet at the same time it is likely to have more widespread (though less visible) background importance. The widespread access to property, especially through home ownership, has made pervasive if not dramatic differences to the nature of American urban life, which we have been slow to recognize. The most significant of these differences has been to attach great passion and self-interest to local politics through the tax on real property.[5] Although the politics of "tax revolts" have emphasized this aspect of American urban home ownership, it must be stressed that this is not a new, but a very traditional aspect of American cities. And this should help remind us that home ownership has tied the fortunes of a broad cross section of Americans—one that excludes only the very rich and the very poor—to local politics and government in a very direct way. Even when he or she pays far more taxes indirectly to the federal government, most home owners experience the direct annual or semiannual payment of monies to a local government. And these payments link the individual to local government in a way both traditional and traditionally troubled, a way that has had and continues to have fundamental consequences for our cities.

This pervasiveness has confounded scholars of the left who have tried to conceive of home ownership in terms of theories developed for societies where property owning was not widespread. For the left, home ownership among the American working class continues to cause analytic conundrums, for how can an exploited working class slowly expand its already relatively high level of home ownership? The subtlest analysts have had to see working-class property owners as dupes, as mistaking their true class interests for those of the wealthy.[6]

The pro–home ownership position is an old as property qualifications for voting, which were based on the notion that property tied the owner's future to the locale in a deeper and more responsible way than did renting. The disappearance of property requirements for voting by the 1820s, except in Rhode Island and Virginia, did not indicate that the conceptual link of property and community membership had also disappeared. In fact, the requirements of property ownership, taxpaying, or militia membership persisted longer for local elections than for federal or state ones, specifically because local elections so often concerned fiscal matters that were thought to obligate freeholders more than renters. As one historian points out, "the last stand of the principle of 'no representation without taxation' " was in the sphere of local elections. Iowa recognized this local distinction to the point of having separate property qualifications for votes on local fiscal matters.[7] But one factor that weakened the tie between voting and property was simply the huge growth of urban property ownership, a growth that was not restricted to any one class, making property qualifications less discriminatory in nature.

This is not to say that the link between property ownership and political franchise had altogether disappeared. In the 1920s, eugenicists saw home ownership as a major factor in promoting the healthy growth of genetically sound children. In the introduction to *The Better Homes Manual,* the director of Better Homes in America wrote about the virtues of home ownership using the parable of the sower, modified in line with the eugenics movement. Admitting that any person "at birth is gifted with actual or potential qualities which can be traced to heredity," he pointed out that, like plants, even the most genetically favored would not prosper in a bad environment: "A wholesome development of even the best selected seed thus may be prevented by improper or unfortunate conditions of environment." Indeed, "the home is the environment in which the life and development of the child are determined." Thus, home quality supplied the "primary means of character" development. In fact, the control of home quality was thought to have great promise for improving a people "even in the absence of social control of heredity." This introduction was followed by a whole chapter on home ownership, where none other than President Herbert Hoover urged that "it behooves parents to achieve home ownership..." in order to properly raise children.[8]

Thus there developed two prongs to the virtue of the home ownership argument, one emphasizing the family environment and the other emphasizing the home owner's tie to the community. These two virtues, one family centered and intrinsic, the other community centered and extrinsic, continue to be seen as major benefits of home ownership. The two winners of a recent essay contest on home ownership sponsored by the Beverly Hills Board of Realtors neatly summed up these themes. One claimed that the purchase of a home changed an "outsider" to an insider: "that person is now a vibrant part of a coexisting group known as a community..." whose "voice would help steer the course of America." The other essayist developed the second, inner virtue of home ownership, explaining how the home owner "could produce a stable environment for his family and descendants." "Ownership of land," he concluded, "helps to develop America's most important future, her children."[9]

Housing Types

Our image of urban housing is probably dominated by the brilliant photographs of late nineteenth-century social reformers, whose pictures of tenements carried a sober and depressing message to their contemporaries and to us today. Our imaginations tell us that most nineteenth-century, and early twentieth-century, urban people lived in gloomy two-room apartments. Our imaginations are only partly correct, however, and we must put our ideas into a proper social context, reasoning first from our own experiences, then from historical research on both family life and residential mobility.

First, our own experiences. Probably very few readers of this book have lived in only a single residence during their lifetime. I am lucky enough to know two such remarkable people, both of whom live in houses most Americans would happily accept. One is the granddaughter of the Norwegian immigrant who built the house: she is the third generation to live in it. Contrary to popular folklore, such people have always been unusual in the United States. Most Americans have lived in housing circumstances very much contingent on their own career and family needs. Finally, no matter how constricted by the costly housing market, most of us can expect to live in different housing circumstances as we age and as our needs and resources fluctuate. I grew up in a turn-of-the-century suburb in a big house. During any college years, I lived in the bedroom of a boardinghouse. After I married, I lived in a small apartment, and moved to several different ones. Finally, I bought a house, the first of two, the location of each determined by work; residential amenities were determined first for a childless couple, and later for a family with children. Presumably, as I age my needs will change, and I fully expect to someday end up living and dying in a room the size of which I had when a child. At each stage of this very ordinary sequence of housing, I felt I had a form (if not quite substance) of housing superior to all others. As a child, I though apartments were dreadful; as a student, I thought suburban

Bandits' Roost, New York (Jacob Riis), 1885.
This famous posed picture is supposed to show an overcrowded, sinister slum. Alternatively, one could interpret it as showing a genuine community, where neighbors chat and visit, and where communal standards of cleanliness dictate that the laundry be done continuously.

Source: Museum of the City of New York.

Bohemian Flats (Minneapolis), 1895.
With the Mississippi River in background, this late nineteenth-century immigrant shantytown demonstrated the free standing single-family homes possible for urban immigrants. Deprived of most city services, the residents here still had a community church, gardens, access to the river for fish and for wood (which floated by from lumber mills upstream). Careful inspection shows that the unpainted houses had polished windows, neat curtains, and an air of tidiness achieved only through hard work.

Source: M. Eva McIntyre photograph, Minneapolis History Collection, Minneapolis Public Library.

Milwaukee Avenue, 1987.
These small, free-standing houses, built for railroad workers in the late
nineteenth century, were bypassed by urban development until recent,
very careful, restoration. Central air conditioning, a street turned into a
pedestrian mall, careful utilization of all existing interior space, and far
fewer persons per house turned housing for the working class into housing
for professionals. This successful conversion suggests how densely populated working class and ethnic neighborhoods, like Bohemian Flats (preceding illustration), were they still standing, might have fared as genteel
and prestigious housing developments.

Source: photo by author.

lawns and home ownership too oppressive for words; right now there is no house too big for my desires; presumably when I am old all of my former houses will seem too inconvenient and troublesome. The point to this narrative is that the perception of housing quality is highly subjective, variable, and often narrowly rigid.

There is no objectively "good" housing form. In the late nineteenth century reformers were concerned with creating airy and light places. Why? Because they were still influenced by miasmal theories of disease; because most people had strong body odor; because heating and lighting equipment polluted; because the feeble artificial lighting made the urban world dim if not dark. Electric lights, steam heat, daily bathing, easily laundered polyester clothes, lead-free interior finishes, and cleansers without toxic and nasty smelling oils have made these concerns now only aesthetic. In fact, the well-ventilated and airy places so desirable a century ago are now stigmatized as drafty, poorly insulated, and unevenly illuminated.

While big cities did have tenements of the kind made famous by Jacob Riis's ominous view of New York's "Bandits' Roost," photographed in the mid–1880s, such rental apartments were not the only type of working-class urban housing. Detached, wood frame houses characterized far more the American urban house.[10] While New York tenements suffered from lack of ventilation, dampness, and unlighted rooms, more typical houses were simple wooden affairs, drafty, with no running water and outhouses for toilets. (A century later, these toilet pits are a goldmine for antique bottle hunters, who excavate them with an enthusiasm which would have been inconceivable to their previous inhabitants.) Their small yards had room for gardens, for chickens, perhaps for a cow or a pig. Relatively few of these wood frame houses have lasted into the late twentieth century, but their brick counterparts, built as working-class housing, are enjoyed a renaissance as they are painstakingly restored by their latest round of owners.

Family historians have recently begun to use the concept of the life course, or family cycle, as a way of studying the family in the past.[11] They point out that needs, income, and expenditures vary as people move into different age-related roles, from children to single young adults, young married couples, families with growing and older children, families whose children have left, and older people. The old model of the nuclear family must be made more dynamic. Historically, the average ages during various parts of the life course have changed, and the family's mode of coping with different parts of the life course have also changed. Clearly housing needs change with the life course. But in times not long past, housing and the life course had a very different pattern, and the change is due principally to the decreased size of families today and the movement of women into the workforce outside the home.

Today, women typically have careers outside the home which differ from men's mainly in that they are more interrupted by family care. Occupational opportunities have combined with, or perhaps even been driven by, much smaller family sizes, which have in turn reduced the amount of time a woman devotes to child care. In 1840, a woman with six children could have expected to be tied to the home for a minimum of eighteen years, so if her first child was born when she was twenty-five, she would not have been eligible to enter the outside work force until she was forty-two. Instead, she supplemented the family income by working in her home, taking in lodgers. Lodging was an essential part of a nineteenth-century family's income, with working-class as well as relatively affluent families taking in boarders throughout their lives. Single adults and often young families could expect to board with other families until they moved out and in turn took in their own boarders. Boarding did not end as a widespread practice until the post–World War I era, when it fell victim to social reformers' concerns about the presence of strange men in the homes of women whose husbands were at work, as well as to decreasing family size and increasing opportunities for women to work outside of the home. Until its demise, boarding meant, for women, that the home was a place of heavy labor. Carrying water up and down stairs for laundry, cooking, and household cleaning entailed toil every bit as demanding for women as what their husbands found outside the home.[12] Distance from water was far more important to these women than the light and airy rooms that housing reformers so loved to discuss. Thus we must temper the significance that we attach to our own housing standards when we apply them to the past.

Around the 1920s, then, the family's economic mode changed. Women worked less in the home and more outside the home, while at the same time the size of the nuclear family continued to decline. The average household—meaning the number of people who occupied a housing unit, whether family, boarders, or others—was 5.8 in 1790, and has steadily dropped from 4.8 in 1900 to 2.8 in the 1980s. Perhaps more dramatic, 50 percent of households in 1790 numbered over 6; by 1950 only about 10 percent were so large. However, the age at which family formation begins has also dropped considerably. The median age at first marriage in 1890 was 26 for men, 22 for women; in 1970 it had dropped to 23 and 21 respectively. Probably one reason that the marriage age has dropped is the increased access to housing, both rental and owned, and the increased ease of acquiring mortgages. The long-term historical trend, then, is one toward shrinking yet also younger families, who are more able to obtain housing.[13]

The Myth of Residential Stability

The family's changing strengths and needs over a lifetime have combined with another social factor, residential mobility, to challenge our view of urban housing. Folk wisdom has it that since World War II, Americans have become a rootless, mobile people, breaking ranks with our more rooted, small-town past. It has often been speculated that people who clearly had not shared these deep roots, such as foreign immigrants or rural blacks moving to northern cities, suffered psychologically and culturally precisely because their cultural roots had been destroyed. In the late nineteenth century, when tramps thronged throughout the land in search of work, observers often thought that a particular form of mental disorder— wanderlust—had caused them to roam. Oscar Handlin's appropriately titled *The Uprooted* captured some of this thinking as it focused on the debilitating cultural effects of migration on European immigrants to American cities.[14] Immigration historians now insist that no such cultural destruction occurred, but the issue has attracted attention because everyone assumed that the immigrant experience contrasted with a native-born ideal—a stable, settled, and rooted population. Obviously, as cities expanded so quickly, this could not have been the case, but the assumption still remained: the image—that a family moved to some new place and then stayed put—has shown far more stability than the families ever had.

It is no wonder that "success," whether economic or moral, has come to be associated with residential stability, while transiency has been associated with economic failure, psychological instability, and social deviance. The very notion of community has as its absolute precondition residential stability. When urban sociologists, from Georg Simmel in the nineteenth century to Louis Wirth in the twentieth, wrote of the disintegrative and alienating features of urban society—features which inexorably pushed urban dwellers to anomie, repressed anxiety, and deviance—they assumed that only in a residentially stable community could a society maintain its proper organic life.

Urban historians have learned a good deal about residential mobility for accidental reasons. When in the 1960s the new urban historians began to study the question of occupational mobility for people of ordinary means, one obstacle persistently hampered their research: attrition made it almost impossible to gather a large enough sample to follow occupational changes through the lives of men and their sons. Researchers would begin their studies with seemingly robust samples of some 2,000 people, only to find that they disappeared rapidly from decade to decade; to make statements about the relationship of sons' careers to fathers' careers, historians often had to generalize from a handful of cases. This unforeseen discovery set research back considerably: almost by definition, that handful of ordinary families who stayed in any one place long enough to be studied were statistical freaks. Instead of describing the nature of occupational mobility, historians uncovered a social world of astonishing residential fluidity.

This fundamental discovery about mobility should be kept in mind. Persistence of residence in one city for more than a decade never rose to much greater than 70 percent and very often hovered around 35 percent. That is, every city lost about half of its inhabitants every decade. Actually, even this figure understates the case, since many residents stayed only six months or a year, so a city might have experienced the turnover or renewal of its total population three or four times in a decade. For instance, Stephan Thernstrom estimated that in Boston in 1890, with a total population just under 450,000, at least 157,000 families, or more than 600,000 persons, had entered the city in the preceding decade, while 138,000 families had moved out. And Boston was unusual in its high degree of residential persistence! These figures were even higher from a neighborhood perspective, as residential movement within the city was even greater than movement into and out of the city. People who stayed in the same house, apartment, or room were the exception, not the rule. The scope of residential mobility suggests that, like the growth of cities themselves, residential relocation has been the norm in U.S. cities. The question to be asked, rather than why people moved, is why they did not move. We often associate the idea of social stability with residential permanence, but we might just as easily look at permanence as stagnation from another perspective.

The technical difficulties encountered in following a sample of ordinary people *including* those who departed are daunting, but one historian, Peter Knights, has actually traced the paths of a very high proportion of a sample of some 2,000 men (men only are used, to avoid the difficulties arising from women's name changes when marrying) residing in late nineteenth-century Boston. His evidence demonstrates some not-too-surprising features: suburbanization, highly volatile movement within neighborhoods, movement undertaken in order to follow specific lines of work. But most clearly, residential mobility had none of the pathological connotations urbanists have often given it. One study of nineteenth-century Buffalo and the surrounding region showed that for a wide range of occupations, including the professions, local ties made little difference in rootedness until people had reached the age of 55. While early Buffalo may have been atypical, this research hints that one of the primary economic reasons to stay in any place, a network of local economic contacts, had had little influence on the younger working population. Additional evidence from a quite different context, the city of Leicester, England, indicates that renters, at least, when given the opportunity, moved rather than stayed: the suggestion again is that we must consider residential mobility the norm rather than a response to some problem or crisis. And finally, if we consider the act of registering to vote as a sign of community attachment and participation, Howard P. Chudacoff has made the startling discovery that in early twentieth-century Omaha, those who were more mobile were also more likely to register to vote. Again, the evidence indicates that mobility is ordinary and even socially positive. Residential movement may or may not have been a sign of opportunity, but there is no evidence that portrays it as something negative.[15]

High rates of residential movement, which we can no longer necessarily construe as negative or even undesired by the people who moved, seem inconsistent with the relatively high rates of single family housing and home ownership. But we must consider first that neither the rate of ownership nor that of residential departures was so high as to cancel out the other. That is, 50 percent of the adult population could have left every five years and the remainder could still have been home owners. In fact, some research has shown that cities with high rates of residential persistence were no more likely to have high home ownership than those with low persistence rates. Many cities, such as Boston, had high persistence and low home ownership rates, while others, such as Indianapolis, had high persistence and high ownership. There is some slight evidence to show that home owners in early Buffalo were less likely to depart than were nonowners, but the relationship is so slight as to be difficult to interpret. Thus it is possible that a high degree of access to housing encouraged persistence, although the converse did not hold true: a low degree of access did not in itself deter persistence.[16] Thus far, the precise relationship of high mobility to other social features is unclear, and it must therefore remain as a background feature of American society, one to always be remembered when examining other aspects of the city.

Trends in Home Ownership

Certainly one feature of increasing home ownership and continued residential fluidity might be indexed by the real estate industry. If nothing else, a society with high home ownership and mobility must have supported a vigorous business in real estate transactions. And if combined ownership and mobility increased or decreased, then the industry most directly affected should have been real estate. Data are available on the number of people employed in real estate sales since 1900, and these may be examined either as a percentage of employed persons or as realtors per thousand owned homes. As one study of a Hamilton, Ontario, realty firm indicates, much activity was concerned with rental rather than sales, so one must exercise caution in tying home ownership to the realty business. Even though the percentage of persons engaged in the real estate business has increased in the last century, it declined for the period between 1930 and 1970. The data are too inconclusive to deserve much emphasis, but a regression equation predicting the number of realtors by owned homes *and* older persons suggests that the decrease in realtors between 1930 and 1970 may have been due to the increasingly older and presumably less mobile population. In this regression, an increase in home ownership does seem to produce an increase in realtors, though at a decreasing rate.[17]

Home ownership in the United States has always been high relative to Europe, and it has been on the rise since at least 1890, probably since much earlier. For the era prior to 1890, we have only scattered data that do not accurately index the United States as a whole. Colonial cities may well have had very high ownership rates. Data show over 50 percent home ownership in the poorest ward of New York City in 1703, with the other four wards ranging up to 90 percent, giving an estimated rate for the whole city of 72 percent. The high ownership rate (among taxpayers) continued until 1730, but dropped steadily thereafter until the end of the century. Boston ownership declined to 60 percent by the beginning of the eighteenth century. Rather than seeing these apparently high rates as indicators of a prosperous past, it is probably more accurate to regard them as demonstrating the relative wealth and privilege that accrued to most colonial city dwellers, as well as the lack of rental property, and the difficulty of establishing a separate household for anyone but a potential owner. In Germantown, a suburban village five miles from the center of Philadelphia, by the final years of the eighteenth century, over 50 percent of the homes were owner-occupied. In addition, renters tended to live in inferior quality homes. Unfortunately, these data, drawn from the 1798 Federal Direct Tax list, do not indicate age, so they do not reveal whether the renters were also the young.[18] These scattered data all hint that colonial city life was in all probability much more privileged than city life by 1830, and that home ownership declined until the mid-nineteenth century.

Data relevant to the nineteenth century prior to 1890 are suggestive, but equally unsystematic. For Hamilton, Ontario, home ownership for all heads of household dropped from 35 percent in 1851 to 30 percent in 1861 (due, the study's authors suggest, to the depression of the mid–1850s), then rose to 33 percent in 1871. For nearby Buffalo, the figure stood at 37 percent in 1855. In the whole state of Massachusetts, 23 percent of all manual laborers owned their homes in the early 1870s, more than the 20 percent of all salaried employees who owned. In Richmond, Virginia, 30 percent of all white householders owned their homes. In San Francisco, among all men over forty, about 30 percent owned homes, the Irish owning more (32 percent) than the Germans (30 percent), who in turn owned more than native-born whites (28 percent). This ranking is reversed, in a sense, when considering the value of the property owned: Irish-owned properties values were valued at less than half of those owned by the native-born. The crude consistency of these mid-nineteenth century rates suggests that the midcentury era may have had the lowest urban home owning proportions in U.S. history, perhaps because better investment opportunities existed for those with enough money and information, perhaps because of a decline in real wages, perhaps because of a lag in housing construction. It is highly possible, therefore, that the pattern in home ownership was very high in the eighteenth century, declined to a low in the mid-nineteenth century, and has slowly risen since then.[19]

The 1890 census enumerated home ownership for the whole nation. As table 5 shows, overall rates of nonfarm home ownership stayed stable at 37 percent from 1890 to 1900, then rose to 46 percent in 1930 and to 61 percent in 1975. These percentages do not simply index middle-class access to housing; most homes were owned by blue-collar workers or immigrants.

And in an absolute sense, these figures are too low, for they mask the effects of changes over the life course. That is, recently married families were far less likely to own homes than were older ones. In 1983, for instance, 85 percent of all two-person households between the ages of forty-five and sixty-five owned their homes, whereas far fewer married couples between twenty-five and twenty-nine (about 25 percent) owned their own homes. (Rural families are more likely than urban ones to own their homes: the figure in the twentieth century has consistently run about 20 percent more for farm families.) The population of the United States has consistently become older, so we should not be too surprised that home ownership has increased. But could all the increase be because of aging? It is almost impossible to estimate the proportion of households which "should" have been able to own houses compared to that which actually owned their houses. But a crude correction of the figures for 1890 and 1970, by estimating the proportion of urban dwellers over thirty-five years old and using this as the denominator for the number of owned urban houses shows that there were

TABLE 5

HOUSING OWNERSHIP AND MORTGAGES, 1890–1978

Year	% owned	% mortgaged	Mortgage Sources[a]		
			% individuals	% S & L	% banks
1850	26[b]				
1860	–				
1870	38[b]				
1880	–				
1890	36.9	27.7			
1900	36.5	32.0	53.9	34.4	11.7
1910	38.4	33.3	40.1	40.7	19.2
1920	40.9	39.8	45.2	39.9	14.9
1930	46.0	–	41.2	38.1	20.7
1940	41.1	45.3	32.8	33.5	24.7
1945	50.8	–	33.3	34.7	28.5
1950	53.4	44.0	21.0	37.1	39.5
1960	61.0	56.8	15.1	50.7	30.3
1970	62.0	60.6	13.4	55.8	23.2
1975	64.0	63.0	18.0	55.4	19.2
1978	64.6	63.9	21.3	54.3	18.5
1979	–	64.0	23.8	51.6	18.6
1980	–	64.6	26.3	49.4	18.0
1981	–	64.5	29.0	47.0	17.6
1982	–	–	34.2	41.6	17.1
1983	–	63.8	36.5	40.0	16.2
1984	–	–	36.7	39.8	16.1

[a]These proportions are on total amount loaned, not on individual mortgages. Individual is noninstitutional debt; S&L, is savings and loan and mutual savings groups; Banks includes banks and other financial intermediaries. These percentages do not add up to 100% because I have excluded federal mortgages.

[b]Lee Soltow, *Men and Wealth in the United States, 1850–1870* (New Haven: Yale University Press, 1975). These are not exactly comparable to the other figures, with the exception of the 1870 value, for they are not by unit of housing but by adult male.

NOTE: Owned and Rented are for nonfarm; Realtors is as percent of all employed persons, Realtors/Owners is number of realtors per thousand owned homes.

SOURCE: Data from Bureau of the Census, *Historical Statistics of the United States, Colonial Times to 1970 (Washington, D.C.: Government Printing Office, 1975)*, 646–648, updated for post–1970, slight differences from 1970 and earlier from Bureau of the Census, *Statistical Abstract of the United States, 1982–1983* (Washington, D.C.: Government Printing Office, 1982), 501; nonfarm tenure, Bureau of the Census, *Statistical Abstract of the United States, 1982–1983* (Washington, D.C.: Government Printing Office, 1982), 757; Bureau of the Census, *Statistical Abstract of the United States, 1985* (Washington, D.C.: Government Printing Office, 1984), 731; mortgages, 1940–1983, Bureau of the Census, *Statistical Abstract of the United States, 1985* (Washington, D.C.: Government Printing Office, 1984), 741.

forty-seven owner-occupied homes for every 100 older persons in 1890, rising to sixty in 1970. The implication: that rising home ownership is only partially tied to the aging population and that age-adjusted rates still show nearly a century of gradual increase.[20]

Ideally one would like to tie all the demographic factors together to see what the net increase in ownership is after adjusting for all demographic changes. Using highly aggregated data for the whole United States, we might estimate this net increase with the following equation:

URBAN HOMES OWNED = (POPULATION AGED 0–14) + (POPULATION AGED 15–34) + (POPULATION AGED 35+) + (MORTGAGE DEBT) + (YEAR).

The variable *YEAR* captures the actual change in home ownership trends; the other variables account for demographic effects and mortgage availability. If we use this formula, the variable *YEAR* proves to be computationally insignificant. In other words, the year has no effect on the increase in ownership, which comes entirely as a consequence of demographic effects and increasing access to mortgages. Indeed, the population over thirty-four and the amount of mortgage debt are the two positive factors in ownership growth, accounting almost completely for the changing proportion of homes owned.[21]

Various sources suggest that the rise in home ownership from the middle of the nineteenth century was seen as a socially desirable goal, one which access to credit had fostered. Cooperative banks, or Building Associations, or People's Banks, may have been one of the prime reasons for this rise or return to high home ownership. Social reformers certainly hoped so, for they saw these sources of debt as gathering "little rivulets of money" and sending them "forth in well-directed channels to build homes and do this and that and the other thing for the amelioration of society." Home building and ownership, reformers thought, would do more "to upbuild the country, to make men and women uphold the institutions of the land, than anything else." Thus access to borrowing appears to underlie the access of so many city dwellers to ownership. And Sinclair's gloomy picture in *The Jungle* of the evils of borrowing must stand revised. Notwithstanding our image of nasty tenements produced by nineteenth-century urban photographers, more privately owned homes, not fewer, have accompanied the growth of American cities.[22]

A valuable survey conducted by the Bureau of Labor Statistics in the 1880s helps confirm and refine this larger view. The survey asked workers in Grand Rapids furniture factories, Detroit iron foundries, and a cross section of industries in Maine for information on their incomes as well as ethnicity, age, home ownership, and borrowing. These data show a strong correlation of age with home ownership, the percentage of those owning homes rising steadily from 25 percent at age twenty-five to 70 percent at age fifty-five. As these surveys queried relatively well-paid industrial workers, the absolute levels of home ownership are not as meaningful as the clear relationship to age, which does support the view that age must be considered a major factor in home owning proportions.[23]

Deliberate Housing Discrimination

The overall trend in increasing home ownership hides individual catastrophes such as befell the Rudkiss family, fictional but certainly representative of a large minority. So also the positive trend masks the effects of deliberate urban racial and ethnic discrimination. Until the Supreme Court decision of 1948 (*Shelley v. Kramer*, 334 U.S. 1), most states allowed cities to discriminate against blacks, Jews, and Asians through the use of restrictive housing covenants, legal documents that bind land owners to racially discriminatory sales or rentals. It is interesting that the neighborhood in St. Louis out of which this case arose had been racially integrated for over sixty years. The court ruled that it was the state enforcement of such private covenants which violated the Fourteenth Amendment. The effect of these covenants was to restrict potential housing for minorities and to create large urban areas that were "lily white" or, even more exclusively, white Anglo-Saxon Protestant.

Data on Chicago show with stark clarity the economic consequences of housing discrimination for blacks, who by the turn of the century had to pay 10 percent to 15 percent more than whites for comparable housing. Data for Los Angeles display the same results: blacks up to the 1950s paid more for comparable housing than whites. In addition, in Los Angeles, housing discrimination kept blacks from moving near employment, so that during World War II, blacks working in the aircraft industry faced long and very difficult commutes. In any place that restrictive racial covenants forced people to compete for artificially limited housing stocks, the net consequences were to raise rents for them and lower rents for whites. Thus whites directly benefited from racial exclusion any time it forced blacks into denser housing. Because the minorities were in fact minorities, the negative effects of such discrimination on individuals were larger than the positive effects for individual whites. For instance, in a city that had a 9 percent black population paying 30 percent more for comparable housing, the benefits to whites in lowered costs would be diluted, simply because there were so many more of them. Thus on an individual basis, black losses might have been ten times greater than white gains: while a black family could expect to spend 30 percent more on rent, whites on average could expect only a 3 percent savings in rent.[24] If guilt and anger paralleled costs and benefits, whites would have felt only one tenth as guilty as blacks felt angry. Returns to white people for rental and housing discrimination would only have begun to be large when the black minority became a majority.

In spite of racial discrimination, black home ownership, although consistently lower than white, has also increased substantially since it has been measured separately, starting in 1920. Just under one-fourth of all black homes, urban and rural, were owned by their occupiers in 1920; by 1980 this had increased to just under 45 percent. Although such figures say nothing about the quality of homes owned, the figure is nearly as high as that for overall home ownership in Britain, for instance.[25]

When the enforcement of racially restrictive covenants became illegal, discrimination in housing did not end, but continued in a less visible, still costly form: that of redlining and discriminatory lending, the latter promoted by the federal government through the Federal Housing Administration (FHA). These various practices emphasize the critical importance of access to mortgages in housing, for all work to exclude some from the credit apparatus. Redlining is the practice, now illegal, of lenders drawing boundaries around neighborhoods where they will not extend mortgages. These areas usually contain older housing stock, poor people, and racial minorities. The net effect of redlining on the neighborhood is to increase credit costs and therefore housing costs at the same time that it ensures a neighborhood's decline in value. Similar practices by major federal credit insurers, the FHA and the Veterans

Administration, which subsidizes loans to military veterans, have lowered the price of credit by defining acceptable kinds of housing and neighborhoods. Acceptable looked exactly like white middle-class suburbs; unacceptable meant racial integration, condominium housing, mixed land use—that is, houses and shops on the same street. The effect of such lending is to drive down the value of the redlined neighborhoods and drive up the value of the approved ones. This insures that approved neighborhoods are indeed less risky investments, and thus a vicious cycle of high credit costs, increased housing costs relative to size and quality, greater crowding, less desirable tenants, vice, and the like, drives the neighborhood perceived by lenders as risky to in fact become risky, while those perceived as solid become even more solid. Recent detailed work by Kenneth Jackson shows how discriminatory lending has had an unsavory, federally sanctioned history until very recently.[26]

The history of bigotry in housing illustrates the larger problem of access to credit and housing. If lenders agree that any one group, population, or residential neighborhood is not likely to maintain or increase its value over the long term of the loan, then in all probability their prediction will become correct, a truly self-fulfilling prophecy. When in the nineteenth century the notion of long-term home mortgages was almost unknown, their very rarity meant that their risk was indeed high. A century later, mortgages had become a secure form of investment because the urban world had successfully been divided into the predictable and the unpredictable. The increase of home ownership has resulted from two immediate causes that cannot be disentangled: the rising real income of most Americans and the rising access to credit. One can argue that rising real income and mortgage-based residential segregation provided the driving force, with access to credit following safely behind. But clearly, once they have secured credit, whole neighborhoods and formerly proscribed groups can become owners.

Racial discrimination has been only one of several factors shaping ethnic and racial residential clustering. For over two decades, historians of ethnicity have demonstrated how new immigrants deliberately settled in ethnically distinct neighborhoods. Every city has had its Little Italy or Poletown just as today some have Koreatowns or Little Saigons. And most have had far more geographically and ethnically distinct "urban villages." Minneapolis, for instance, had an almost inaccessible neighborhood of East

European immigrants on the bank of the Mississippi River called Bohemian Flats. Neighborhoods often specialized to the point of housing mainly immigrants from a single village in Europe. Within these neighborhoods, regional and village ties were quite often preserved. What was simply German to English ears might have been Bavarian or Westphalian to its inhabitants. In the most detailed analysis of neighborhood settlement patterns yet done, Olivier Zunz has shown how immigrants in late nineteenth-century Detroit chose ethnic neighborhoods over all other factors in locating housing. The logic of ethnicity overrode employment location and class considerations when people decided where to live. Zunz argues that by 1920 this had begun to change, however, with employment-related "mill villages" emerging, multi-ethnic and defined predominantly by occupation. One enormous exception occurred for the growing number of black Detroiters, who were segregated into racially distinct ghettoes. In other words, as most ethnic neighborhoods lost their linguistic and cultural distinctiveness, black neighborhoods gained theirs. Race and class, more than ethnicity, began to define city neighborhoods after 1920.[27]

American cities have always been places with flexible boundaries whose economic interest was in growth, and where land speculators realized their profits through the extension of credit to many small buyers. Since entrenched economic interests did not have an established city shape to preserve in order to maintain power, widespread home ownership became a reality very early. Given the relative youthfulness of the population, which contributed to its residential volatility, this high percentage of home ownership is even more surprising. In many ways the early nineteenth-century vision of an America unrestrained by ancient European fetters has proved to be correct. That mortgages were the tools that facilitated a move toward residential ownership is a somewhat less romantic feature of our cityscape, yet this aspect of urban housing shares a common feature with the increasing access both to private transportation and to corporate borrowing by cities. What have often been cast as urban evils are proving to have been linchpins in the development of the American city.

9 ☆ The Active City, 1870–1980

At the beginning of the twentieth century, well-off American intellectuals worried constantly about the potential for chaos, for violent class conflict, in the city. Adna F. Weber wrote in 1899: "The danger of class antagonism is particularly grave in the cities. Dives and Lazarus become figures too familiar to let us rest in peace. The chasm created by the industrial system yawns widest in cities; and the means of bridging it will require careful consideration." He knew he directed his observations to relatively prosperous social thinkers, for his book, *The Growth of Cities*, which contained this observation, cost $4—well over the daily wage of a skilled urban laborer and more than twice that of an unskilled laborer. The message of the parable Weber evoked bluntly confronted the wealthy. The rich man, Dives, who allowed the beggar, Lazarus, to die at his door, went to hell; Lazarus to heaven. Weber reminded his readers of this pungent message in a hardheaded, data-filled, and generally optimistic scholarly tome intended to comprehend the modern urban world.

The social consequences of urban rationality, anonymity, and individualism were also central concerns of European sociologists Georg Simmel and Max Weber. Simmel attended to the dangers of excessive individualism, which he attributed to the scale and anonymity of metropolitan life. Max Weber, however, envisioned the causality as running the other way. The spirit of individualism had been the engine which drove the transformation of corporate medieval society and its highly ordered cities. In Weber's view, once individualism had replaced the values of feudal, corporate society, modern urban capitalism could arise. Urban institutions accommodated this new individualist outlook. Thus while Weber, in

America, worried about how "exaggerated individualism" and related class antagonisms threatened social solidarity, the European Weber saw individualism as the force underlying liberation and urban bureaucratization.[1]

Urban intellectuals were articulating these concerns during the period when the transition from a responsive, regulatory, city to an active, service providing city culminated, between 1870 and 1920. By 1915, Frederick C. Howe could write with apparent confidence about "the elementary services of the city. Their necessity," he observed, "is recognized by all." The local manifestations of this new kind of city have been difficult to recognize as anything special, because from our late twentieth-century viewpoint the "new" mode of government seems so reasonable, so unexciting, and so mundane. Even when historians have been careful to not prejudge the transition as one conforming to "common sense," they have had difficulty constructing a causal analysis. Jonathan Prude's description of the era prior to this transition in three western Massachusetts towns—Dudley, Webster, and Oxford—details the remarkable local resistance to the public funding of roads. He places the issue in the context of an expanding conception of public good, demonstrating most intriguingly how this conception came about almost in spite of the industrial expansion of Samuel Slater's mills in Webster. The towns did not merely respond passively to the wishes of industrial capitalists but developed their new orientation independently. Of course, they did not become by any means the active service cities of the twentieth century, but they did begin to change.[2]

The major changes of the modern world—population growth, the expansion of the urban network, industrial growth, and the rise of industrial capitalism—all occurred in roughly the same time frame. It is tempting, therefore, to deem them "natural." But natural they were not. Nor were their specific urban manifestations. Some came inadvertently—the broad social services of the uniformed police, for example. The uniform made the police officer the first visible, regular, public, around-the-clock, and authoritative representative of the city government, a significant advance. The uniformed police found themselves supplying services unheard of before. Parents asked police to help them find lost children, and the police soon found it necessary to find special rooms to hold the lost children and to hire a matron to watch them. Travelers learned to ask police officers for directions. Indigents—tramps, newly arrived immigrants, and the homeless—asked the police to house them in the jails or special lodging rooms. The city asked them to inspect boilers, report open sewers, suppress strikes, to do the odd jobs which there had never been anyone to handle before.

Urban services included a wide array of social welfare provisions, which have too often been attributed to electoral politics and to the political machine, in particular. For the past thirty years many historians have interrupted political machines like Tammany Hall in New York as the forerunners of modern social services. The argument is that in order to retain power, the machines had to ensure voting allegiance of poor immigrants. This they did through personal assistance in times of financial need, through jobs for the jobless, through a general attention to private events like funerals and weddings, as well as through the more blatant buying of votes. The machines provided, it has often been described, a personalized relationship to government for city dwellers. To compete at the polls with these machines, the reformers had to fight their corruption but also to substitute formalized city assistance—urban welfare services—for personal assistance. This argument wraps up a neat causal model, but one that does not adequately describe the actual scenario.

In reality, cities had provided welfare to the poor prior to the rise of political machines. Their service providing, active mode of governance developed independently. The one significant change was that the earlier city government responded to individual requests for aid; the new form systematized welfare and sought to attack the very causes of need. In the new model of welfare, individual assistance became nothing more than a temporary expedient in service of the larger good. Cities had tried, for instance, to reform individual paupers before (witness Philadelphia's Bettering House and others like it), but the end of the nineteenth and beginning of the twentieth century saw urban reformers struggling to understand poverty's roots and transform society itself. Urban social reformers changed their focus from the individual to the group. The welfare principle then, like the underlying principle of the new kind of city, became one of active, systematic intervention rather than response to individual problems. The city still responded to individuals asking for aid, but it also created new organizations which no paupers had requested, from municipal lodging houses to employment agencies, attempting to systemically change the conditions that caused individual impoverishment.[3] Max Weber would have called it the process of rationalization and subsequent bureaucratization.

Politics in the Progressive Era

Two sociologists, M. Craig Brown and Charles N. Halaby, have recently begun to publish the results of the first systematic and comprehensive research on urban political machines. Their results overturn many historical generalizations about machine politics, most of which derived from a highly influential article published in 1948 by another sociologist, Robert Merton. Brown and Halaby's research first establishes that the era between the 1880s and World War I was indeed the heyday of the machine, with almost 80 percent of the thirty largest cities experiencing, for at least short periods of time, governance by machine. However, they go on to show that most of these machines neither established nor long enjoyed their legendary hegemony; in fact, most machines retained power for only two or three elections. Brown and Halaby conclude from this finding that particularly in the complex and competitive environment of large and diverse cities, a typical "factional" machine simply could not maintain organizational power.[4]

Their research further shows that those political machines that actually enjoyed the staying power and dominance of legend grew slowly from the post–Civil War era to the 1930s, when ten of the thirty largest cities were under machine control. These successful machines controlled election after election, dispensing patronage through jobs and contracts over periods stretching up to twenty-five years. Brown and Halaby's somewhat surprising conclusion is that machines actually thrived in smaller places, preferably those politically unified by progressive reforms. Two of the longest-lived machines were in the medium sized cities of Omaha and Rochester. Only for a few decades in the late nineteenth century did machines enjoy the big-city power with which we have long associated them.

Brown and Halaby sum up their survey of urban political machines by redefining them as "organizations operating in environments of varying complexity and diversity" which temper the actual history of the machines. This definition steers the concept of machines away from an exclusive focus on immigrants, on individualized and personalized neighborhood politics, and away from Merton's older notion that the machines unified otherwise fragmented modern cities. Instead, it stresses that the machine was neither invincible nor inevitable, that in fact it worked best in a stable political environment, and that the modern city often fragmented the machine.

Historians enjoy reading and repeating the quips and cynical philosophy allegedly propounded by Boss Plunkitt of Tammany Hall from his "office," a bootblack stand in front of the courthouse. Thus Plunkitt's infamous distinction between "honest boodle" and "graft": the first is a monetary advantage gained by inside knowledge of city government actions (for instance, buying land speculatively in an area about to get urban services), while the second, graft, is profit made by bribing or controlling a politician.[5] Plunkitt's utterances have often been used to exemplify the high degree to which machines had polished their techniques and their own accounts for their actions. Yet the bosses who ruled best did not always need the high media profile that the better known had achieved. And much of our evidence on machines comes from the progressive journalists who sought to discredit them; though perhaps reluctantly, we must at least partly discount their legendary prevalence and cynicism as reform rhetoric.

Machine politicians broke tradition with their elite political predecessors in a significant way by introducing the concept of the career or professional politician. The machine politicians profited directly from their political work, rather than profiting indirectly as had the "patrician elite." As Samuel H. Ashbridge, who became mayor of Philadelphia in 1899, allegedly stated, "I mean to get everything out of this office there is in it for Samuel H. Ashbridge."[6] This statement, quoted by muckraker Lincoln Steffens to establish Ashbridge's criminal rapaciousness, may be interpreted as an example of political greed, but it should also serve as a reminder that many machine politicians had no other means of support— their political activities had to support them, since they could not live off their private wealth. Machine politicians were the shock troops who professionalized local politics. Without doubt, the initial impact of any professional politician would have seemed unsavory as jobs that had once been voluntary and honorific became closely contested and careerist.

Another source of the negative reaction that immigrant politicians elicited in print must be regarded as springing from deep biases within the journalists who wrote for the respectable classes. These biases arose both from ethnic hostility and resentment at a newly professional local politics that mocked the grander issues and rhetoric of national politics. From Plunkitt's bad grammar in the 1890s to the malapropisms of Chicago's Mayor Richard Daley in the 1960s and 1970s, the local machine politician has been a portrayed as a professional without class.[7] Patrician newspaper editors could wink at other forms of social, political, and economic injustice and corruption when supported by men well born and well spoken. But they winced when the Plunkitts opened their mouths. To say this is not to make the exaggerated claim occasionally introduced into the historiography that we must therefore regard bosses as democratizing city politics, as introducing compassion to the organization of the city, or as creating modern welfare services.[8] But it does give a historical explanation for the curious origins of the image of political machines as creatures purely at home in the fragmented, industrial, and polyglot metropolis. The most outrageous political machines offended because of their style; not their substance.

Many historians have claimed that commission government represented the triumph of the business community over ward-based, working-class politics. In an article analyzing who voted for the commission form of government in New Brunswick, New Jersey, Seth Scheiner has gathered data that show that substantive issues, like political corruption, sometimes had more meaning than did the voters' social and economic characteristics. He argues that most voters did not like the corrupt Democrats and that class did not make a difference in who supported the reform government in 1915. A reanalysis of his data supports this point, showing that when simultaneously adjusting for occupation and ethnicity, a majority of those who voted for commission government were professionals and Republicans. The local Democrats' changing position on commission government, as Scheiner claimed, determined the victory and across-the-board support of commission support of commission government. New Brunswick, was of course only one small city of the early twentieth century, but it exemplifies the point that there was more to city government than simple demographics.[9]

Financing the Service City

The transition to the service oriented city happened partly through local intention and partly as an unintended consequence of other actions. Certain important features, such as police welfare service, were unintended. But city budgets were too visible and too hotly contested to allow any inadvertent change. The individual histories of urban schooling, fire departments, streets, sanitation, water, and welfare all trace the innovative struggles of engineers, doctors, entrepreneurs, politicians, and citizens through the nineteenth century. Clearly some aspects of this sudden explosion of aggressive urban services are located in the larger history of the nineteenth century. Some of these more global changes have been discussed in earlier chapters: population growth, the expansion of the urban network, the extension of the franchise, technological change. And some will not be discussed here: industrial growth, the sophistication of the capitalist system, the revolutionary increase of agricultural output, and national political unification. Which were the relevant causal mechanisms? In which direction did the causality run? Was urban change merely froth on the waves, buffeted by more profound ground swells? How often did changes at the city level affect the larger system?

Let us first return to the business corporation that developed in the United States in the early nineteenth century. As legal entities, corporations had traditionally functioned at the whim of government to "facilitate the growth, prosperity, and welfare of the community." During the first decades of the nineteenth century, the public purpose of the corporation had been subsumed by private motives. Protecting and multiplying capital, these legal structures "released" (as J. Willard Hurst proclaimed) the energies of thousands of entrepreneurs.[10] U.S. cities participated vigorously in this aspect of development, becoming public, political engines for economic action. By about 1840, the modern corporate legal machinery had been created, partly by legislation and partly by the Supreme Court, using curious legal theories derived from the behavior of nation states.[11] Although city corporations were considered to be different from private, profit-making corporations, cities participated, to a limited but very significant extent, in the corporate revolution. In the process they changed themselves from passive regulators to actors.

Colonial and early nineteenth-century cities had covered their expenditures directly from their current revenues—property taxes, fines, and fees. Cities balanced their account books annually, ending each fiscal year with their budgets neatly balanced. Most local governments operated in the black, and debt service figured largely in their budgets only because they spent so little. In 1798, for example, New York City spent 60 percent of its budget on the night watch, poorhouse, and prison; less than 2 percent on schools; about 10 percent on lighting; and the remainder, less than 30 percent on miscellaneous services.[12] Capital expenditures were limited to amounts that could be covered by annual tax levies. Indirect beneficiaries of the capital expenditures, those people who did not directly use the new road or school or sewers, resented large lump sum payments to cover capital investments. Debt, the critical feature of the modern corporation, allowed the costs to be distributed over time and space. Additionally, the long-range positive economic consequences of the debt, growth and increased property values, occurred as the debt was paid off, rather than far in the future. The population, economic, and property value growth eased the burden of debt payments. In the spirit that had expected all corporate borrowing privileges to be limited to works benefiting the whole community, early nineteenth-century cities slowly began to finance major projects by selling bonds, via their privileged status as corporations.[13] Bond repayment was relatively secure, depending as it did on property taxes rather than business success. Thus from the beginning, municipal bonds constituted a stable investment in an unstable world. They were as "safe as houses."

The ability to finance large capital outlays through municipal debt ensured that the initiative for large capital projects remained at the local level.[14] This proved both a limitation and a boon. A limitation, for the state legislature or constitution often limited the amount of debt to a proportion of a city's total property value. In addition, bond issues had to be approved by voters who were usually reluctant either to spend or to undertake projects that reshaped or in any way threatened established property interests. In contrast, Baron Haussmann's massive destruction and rebuilding of Paris in the late nineteenth century could never have been financed by local resources. Funded at the national level, his project stretched the finances, credulity, and patience of the whole French government.[15] But the very local orientation of governmental structure in the United States also proved a boon, because any village, town, or city could have access to capital, with which it could create and expand its infrastructure—its streets, sewers, water supplies, schools, and public buildings.

Thus a uniquely powerful local ability to raise capital, combined with a highly limited ability to contravene established property interests, provided the financial basis for the transition from the responsive city to the service city. Cities could finance their own expansion and building far more easily than they could change or challenge what existed; they had comparatively greater power to build than they did to regulate. And because what they built had to be construed in the broad public interest, city governments slowly began to shift their daily activities away from regulating access to their unique privileges and toward acting in a positive, nonregulatory manner. Debt financing depended on future property values and taxes and therefore on economic growth. This encouraged debt for purposes that enhanced economic activities, population growth, and property values. From setting the price of bread in the marketplace, local governments moved slowly toward serving the infrastructural needs of the breadsellers and bakers.

This shift in the nature of governmental initiative had a parallel on the level of state government. There the legislative character of incorporation changed over the second half of the nineteenth century, from individually granted charters with express limitations and no implied powers to general incorporation laws, where limitations had to be directly stated and where other, vaguer powers were implied. Once this step had been taken, the legislative initiative shifted from actively creating a particular corporation, stipulating its rights and privileges, and assuming that all things unstated were forbidden to broad, general legislation. Legal historians refer to this as the change from positive to negative regulation, highlighting the difference between a state that expressly granted the right to specific activities and a state that acted as a guard.[16] By the late nineteenth century, when the federal government began attempting to regulate monopolies, the shift had been completed. Now government had to become constantly vigilant in its monitoring broad sectors of the national economy. The creation of the Interstate Commerce Commission in the late 1880s is often taken as the beginning of the form of federal regulation that proliferated in the twentieth century: an organized regulatory bureaucracy.[17]

When, toward the end of the nineteenth century, a resurgent elite interest in local government manifested itself in the Progressive movement, local government had become firmly action oriented. Local officials spent long hours making detailed daily decisions about streets, sewer, and water supplies. The age of the political dabbler had passed. That so many of the Progressive reformers stuck with the chore is a tribute to their dedication and professionalism. The Progressive movement and the professional literature that it produced, though it may not have created the new model of the service city, certainly helped legitimize and rationalize it. The Progressive movement did not, however, create a permanent, elite civil service as in Europe and Britain. Continued dedication to a demanding yet low-profile and low-paying job by a wealthy upper-middle class would have required that municipal affairs become far more respectable, selective, and well paid than they ever have. Progressivism never developed the institutional or organizational support necessary to make local government a viable elite calling. That later in the twentieth century politics became a career simply accentuates the dedication and professional skill required by the active governmental system.

Directing City Policy

David C. Hammack's history of the actual decision-making process in late nineteenth-century New York demonstrates that neither government by the elite nor political machines could implement policy directly or clearly. Hammack contends that New York City's wealthy elite was by the end of the nineteenth century a group so diversified by ethnic, religious, and philosophical differences that it could neither project nor implement a coherent vision of city policy. Political machines managed existing diversity and fragmentation rather than trying to articulate general planning goals. Consequently, in several critical decisions—the creation of greater New York, the unification of the schools, and the creation of the subway system—neither the economic elite nor the political machines could establish a detailed plan of what they wanted, nor could either act decisively toward prescribing policy goals for these major local issues.

Hammack argues that New York's pluralistic elite made it different from, and in a sense a forerunner of, places like Stamford, Connecticut, or Birmingham, Alabama, where unitary elites or political machines could still effect a policy control in the late nineteenth century, though they slowly lost their power by the late twentieth century. Yet it is more likely that different historical methods used by those who have analyzed these three cities have magnified the differences between cities, and obscured the substantial similarities. Hammack's findings on New York City, for instance, resemble those of Harold Platt, whose book on Houston, Texas, during the same period appeared a year after Hammack's. In size and political composition Houston contrasted wildly with New York. Yet Platt, like Hammack, examined for Houston the actual content of and process involved in making local policy decisions, rather than focusing solely on the reputations or backgrounds of the elite. Consequently, a story of local conflict within the elite also emerges from Houston. Unlike Hammack, Platt does not interpret this conflict as proof of a pluralist power structure, where competing elites vie for the political support of the nonelites. Rather, he emphasizes the complexity of the issues involved, the lack of a clear direction in building a new urban world.[18]

Hammack shows how the substance of actual decisions cannot be neatly determined by examining the kinds of people who made them. The social origins of mayors or other officeholders help us to identify who governed a city, "but the decision-making evidence suggests that its significance was limited." This observation leads Hammack to conclude that power was becoming more dispersed in American cities. Thus he challenges those who claim that the concentration of wealth is followed by the concentration of power. Wealth did not in itself create a single elite, but rather many competing ones. The debate, as Hammack asserts, must revolve on the issue of how power worked, rather than who had access to power.[19]

As the specific services supplied by cities have expanded, the larger objects of urban policy have become more dispersed, hindering the formation of any clear issues around which the elite might organize. Even the concept of city-provided services as being special has disappeared. For instance, for over a decade Los Angeles has debated whether or not to begin a subway system. But the debate is not over the exact nature of city services, nor is it over the practical provision of transportation. Instead, it is about the potential for billions of dollars of federal aid. Theoretically a local issue, its cost is in Washington, while its benefits are in Los Angeles. The meaning and impact of the actual mass transit project is so unclear that the debate has lacked energy except on the ideological issue of controlling federal expenditures.

The modern form of American city which emerged late in the nineteenth century could not have been steered by a powerful elite, because no one could yet articulate a clear vision of how the city worked, much less a direction in which to steer. Would the wealth represented by New York's richest man, J. P. Morgan, have been augmented more by a centralized subway, a dispersed school system and city government? Neither he nor his advisors could tell for sure. And until such a vision had been articulated, there was little incentive to form strong positions related to social or economic class. Hammack observes that "the political factionalism of the economic elites during the 1880s and 1890s defies brief summary, and that factionalism reflected fundamental disagreements about policy." And these disagreements came within a supposedly unified elite.[20]

Thus the description of the power elite must not pretend to be an adequate analysis of how decisions were made or whom they benefited. Nor should the absence of a clear elite position in New York City's decision-making process serve as a validation of the claim that the modern city disperses power. The absence of an elite determination of political decisions can mean either that there was no single elite position to be taken or that there was no single elite to define the correct position. One of the central arguments of this book is that our form of city is too new to sustain an analysis of any clear set of policy decisions: thus the issues posed by pluralist political theories cannot yet be resolved. Because the new city's form and function are in flux, no class or interest group can yet attain the high ground in directing urban policy, because no one knows where the high ground is. It is important to remember that by 1920, local debates focused on modes of implementation, or on the specific service levels, not on fundamentals. No one proposed to return to the purely regulatory city. Virtually no one even remembered it.

City Services

Cities' services show us much about their underlying goals.[21] By the last two decades of the nineteenth century the city's goals look both familiar and banal. Generally they included protecting private property (fire fighting); suppressing crime; controlling behavior in public areas; building and maintaining streets and sewerage systems; aiding the poor; schooling children and sometimes adults; funding public libraries; providing recreation and entertainment; supporting a minimal level of health; temporarily assisting all persons incapable of caring for themselves, from lost children to tramps to the insane; enforcing public morality; expending direct financial aid to private capital, a rather ambiguous and highly flexible category; and constructing not-for-profit public buildings in which to house these activities.

Railroads exemplify the specific impact of those technological changes which city governments serviced. To make the railroads effective economic agents, they had to first be brought into the cities, towns, and villages. Local governments encouraged these decisions by supplying a complex package of costly services that included rights of way, crossing protection, station and rights of way policing, fire protection of railside houses, control of buildings and streets near rail facilities, and infrastructural expansion into computer suburbs. Consequently, by 1890, 46 percent of all rail passengers entering towns and cities over 10,000 were commuters traveling less than twenty miles.[22] Similar forms of encouragement persisted into the auto and air age.

Other mechanical innovations of the nineteenth century, such as elevators, boilers, gas, electricity, and new building methods, also depended on city inspectors to standardize and regulate them. Safety standards were implemented by local government. In order to regulate the laying of pipes and wires, cities had to plan for streets. Sometimes, they still looked like a chaotic mess, an explosion in a spaghetti factory, but for positive, not negative reasons. By the end of the nineteenth century, New York and Brooklyn had more telegraph and phone wires than all of Britain. Planning and control only seemed to be absent because so much innovation was rapidly occurring. By the early twentieth century, private regulation started, as real estate developers began to gain expertise in planning infrastructural expansion for subdivisions, and urged their new standards on city governments.[23]

Schooling, although not solely the province of urban government, has had an urban locus because of the city's unique central place advantages. Schooling has almost always occupied a major portion of the city budget, a portion that has diminished only because so many other items have grown. Educational historians argue over the intentions of school reformers in the nineteenth century, debating whether schools were established to create a docile working class or as a democratic attempt to spread learning through a whole society. But they do agree that rural resistance to school reform was not unlike rural resistance to road surfacing, a fear of high taxes compounded by a narrow conception of the public good and worries about the potential for free riders. In 1860 and 1880, for instance, places in rural Massachusetts spent at least fifty percent less per capita on schools than did small cities, a concrete instance of how they "belligerently resisted educational innovation."[24] The creation of the publicly supported school system as we now know it was a late nineteenth- and early twentieth-century innovation. Principally urban in origin, it was certainly one of the premier urban services. Universal schooling eased and promoted technological as well as social change. Urbanist Roger Lane concludes that one of the accomplishments of increased schooling in late nineteenth-century Philadelphia was to reduce substantially the number of accidental deaths. The city, he argues, educated its inhabitants to deal with the new technologies that transformed its kitchens (gas ovens), buildings (elevators), and streets (wheeled vehicles of all kinds) into sometimes lethal environments.[25] The most familiar educational counterpart in today's city is automobile driver education. Thus the transformation of the United States in the late nineteenth and early twentieth century into a schooled society may be considered both as a part of the expansion of urban services and as an urban service that actually facilitated technological change.

The thousands of small towns and villages that promoted themselves by using their real property tax potential as collateral also provided a service, albeit indirectly: they promoted agriculture, befitting their functions as agricultural entrepôts. These urban places all served an agricultural hinterland, enabling farmers to take advantage of new agricultural machinery, from steel plows with interchangeable parts to harvesting machines. The farmers bought from the traveling salesmen of McCormick, Harvester, and Deering, who moved from tiny town to tiny town on the rails, carrying with them information about new equipment. The dense network with its quick access to large cities such as Chicago or Omaha enabled both wealthy and poor farmers to dispense with year-round laborers, by providing a temporary labor pool of hoboes from the towns and cities. These migrant workers traveled to and from major cities on the urban rail networks, their theft of rides tolerated by the railroad companies as long as their labor filled the boxcars with agricultural produce. Tramps rode the rails and stayed overnight in small-town jails for free. They traveled back to larger cities to find news of agricultural jobs, and they increased the agricultural output and ultimately the vitality of the urban network itself.[26] The seemingly tenuous connection between town boosting, the railroads, and farming all fed directly into the role of local government as service provider.

Legitimizing the Service City

In the twentieth century local practice became national expectation. First the Progressive movement, later federal assistance during the Depression and World War II, and finally the postwar boom in federal expenditures and programs all subsumed these locally developed services, though piecemeal and patchy, preserving them in a tangle of red tape. Locally administered programs got vital shots of federal economic aid during the Depression, while the federal government began to initiate its own new programs. This intervention standardized the quality and eliminated inconsistencies in local programs from region to region. The very novelty of the twentieth-century welfare state has distracted attention from the transition from regulation to service city, but at the same time, federal aid has made the new kind of city a permanent institution.

The Progressive movement formally legitimized the service city, with organizational reforms solidifying the century-long shift from regulation to service. Considered from this perspective, the Progressives simply capped an urban revolution that had been a century in the making. But their unique contribution was to bring these government activities to a new level of consciousness, intentionality, and purpose. By starting "good government clubs" throughout the country and writing prolifically in a great many forums, the Progressives ensured a critical and detailed examination of the workings of cities, the likes of which had never been seen before.

Perhaps most reflective of their intellectual effort was the spate of serious journals which they started, all devoted to a systematic examination and reform of city life. These ranged from the explicitly reform oriented *Forum* (1886) to the much more mundane *Plumber and Sanitary Engineer* (1877), *Municipal Affairs* (1897), and *The Municipal Review* (1911). A dip into any one of these is still rewarding, for they were in fact forums for a broad range of people and ideas, from good-hearted amateurs to experts on street lighting. Using argumentation, experimentation, statistics, and photographs, they exposed and attacked particular problems in particular cities, proposing solutions that might also be usable elsewhere. From ill health and slum housing to budgeting and zoning, their attention to the service city never wavered. It is difficult today to imagine so many interested nonprofessionals discussing with technicians the building of urban parks, the width of streets, or the advantages of municipal electric systems. Individual state journals devoted their pages to problems unique to their smaller cities, from legislation to weather. And all functioned (as most still do) as how-to manuals: how to select shade trees, design street lighting, and buy supplies—consumer magazines for cities. One journal promised its subscribers that it would cover "health and sanitation, street pavement, water supply, garbage and sewage disposal, public markets, municipal ownership, franchise control, city planning, charities and corrections, taxation and assessment, finance, accounting methods, home rule, and many other subjects." Another claimed it did not "attempt to reform but to inform." For "being born of the need for efficiency and consecrated at the altar of information," it pronounced, "we worship facts."[27]

In cities of all sizes and types local Progressive reformers introduced city health clinics, school hot lunch programs, dental clinics and eyeglass dispensaries, employment centers, zoning, building and boiler inspection, civil service, carefully rationalized welfare services, commission and city manager forms of government. These numerous reforms made the mechanics of city living ordinary and invisible: that is their true success story.

By the 1920s, urban progressivism had become less visible and more mundane, its very success leading to a kind of professional culture that no longer could include amateurs.[28] The dull routines of businesslike city managers replaced the intrinsically dramatic and sensational boss-baiting of the previous century. City experts, city libraries, and specialized professional conferences signaled the bureaucratization and continuation of city services. The oral and individual culture of running cities gave way to one of written rules, of guidelines, of technical manuals. To make a broad range of services ordinary and expected had been the ultimate Progressive goal: its achievement would of necessity be met by silence.

The Depression and Its Effect on City Services

In the 1930s, the crisis of the Depression rigorously tested the organizational permanence of the service city. It challenged urban service as a mode of government. The crisis had two aspects. The first, of course, was the economic suffering, unemployment, business failure, and bank closures. The second, more subtle and perhaps more damaging, probably came as a consequence of the first: the reversal of migration into cities, which ended the population growth that had been expanding cities for more than 200 years. Depopulation or even population stability meant that property values plummeted, suddenly paralyzing a whole fiscal system structured on the theretofore not unreasonable expectations of steady growth.

As a result, in the 1930s most cities had great difficulties maintaining some of these services, even at greatly reduced levels, particularly as unprecedented demands for welfare caused by unemployment reached crisis proportions. City budgets had been shaped with the assumption of fiscal predictability. City finances had, since the mid-nineteenth century, depended on the unarticulated but powerful policy of "incrementalism," planning expenditures almost completely on the basis of the previous year's revenues and expenditures, in spite of any political rhetoric to the contrary.[29] The shock of the Depression penetrated far deeper than any incremental tradition could have predicted. Detroit, for instance, had over 25 percent unemployment, as the automobile industry both inside and outside the city had massive layoffs. The city's mayor, Frank Murphy, angrily confronted those like Henry Ford whose suburban factories paid no city taxes but whose workers relied on city relief. The city tried valiantly to assist the unemployed with its own resources, paring down but not eliminating its other services. With federal government assistance not forthcoming for three years, the city's efforts were not entirely effective, and thousands of families left for other cities or returned to their rural homes. The rural South, for instance, which had been sending migrants north for three decades, suddenly became a destination for many of the unemployed. But 1933 finally saw a federal underwriting and occasionally a complete takeover of many welfare services formerly administered on a local level. Some federal relief funds, jobs for the unemployed, and capital for some businesses, while not dramatic in impact, did partially alleviate city burdens. Federal intervention did not end the city government's role as an active provider, but it did obscure this remarkable urban orientation historically by stepping to the center stage of public perception and remaining there.[30]

Local Government and the Detectives

A similar instance is the highly visible federal effort at crime control, which has upstaged what continues to be a major local, urban service. In its reliance on local crime control, the United States is unique among modern industrial nations. Although the uniformed modern police were a significant urban innovation, it is not the police officer but the private detective whom we most associate with the city.[31] Yet the actual relationship between the detective and the city is a far less interesting and informative one than that between police and the city. The detective profession grew from the mid-nineteenth century on, pioneered by the famous and sometimes infamous Pinkerton National Detective Agency, "The Eye That Never Sleeps." Private detectives prospered because police were creatures of local government, limiting them to the pursuit of specific tasks within municipal boundaries. Many economic and some criminal activities expanded well beyond the boundaries of any one city, and private police were in a unique position to intervene in these. Detectives had to locate their headquarters in major cities, though, to take advantage of the central communications advantages they offered. Thus although detectives have a big-city image of urban mystery and intrigue, this was fos-

/ 223

tered by the unique geographical limitations of police in the United States and their essentially municipal allegiances.

Detective agencies developed two special roles that ensured their survival, working first for railroads and a little later for large antiunion employers. The railroads' far-flung operational networks had generated a uniquely modern managerial problem: decision-making ability had to be delegated, and lower level employees trusted by distant supervisors.[32] Spies, hired from the Pinkerton agency or dozens of similar agencies scattered around the country, could pose as passengers and "test" the honesty of employees, for example by trying to bribe conductors for train rides without tickets. Detectives operated on principles in some ways the opposite of city police. Detectives depended on secrecy and duplicity for their work, while the uniformed police had to emphasize their visibility and openness. Like independent and secret auditors, private detectives could report back to management without going through the normal avenues of corporate communication. When large industrial concerns had different kinds of employee problems—whether of mistrust or of union organization or of potential strikes—detective agencies supplied the independent, secret, and often illegal private armies they needed.

Police could not always easily side with employers, precisely because city police had to maintain political legitimacy. Because of the city government's electoral vulnerability, this legitimacy had to be perceived as fair. Often the local pressure was for the police to side with strikers, particularly when the employers were either unpopular or nonlocal. The translocal origins of the Pinkertons reduced their political vulnerability. Although they needed the urban economy and its disjuncture of political and economic boundaries, they could not have existed if constrained by those political and legal forces exerted on city government and its uniformed police.

As a private enterprise, the detective agency's main responsibility was to itself, although the federal government began to concern itself, though somewhat timidly, with detective agencies after the Pinkertons were disgraced by the Homestead massacre of 1892. The Homestead massacre has come to epitomize the relationship of the detective agency to organized labor. During a strike and lockout at Andrew Carnegie's Homestead, Pennsylvania, steel plant, two barges full of quickly hired and deputized Pinkerton agents sailed up the Monongahela River and unsuccessfully attacked the strikers. Gunfire from the shore killed several Pinkerton agents, emphasizing the violence of the confrontation. The single most spectacular of many such incidents involving dozens of less well-known detective companies, the Homestead massacre made perfectly clear to the nation at large that whatever their nominal role, detective agencies constituted private armies in the hire of capital. It has taken a century of detective novels to make the public forget about the reality of these industrial mercenaries. The independent, fictional detective so popular with modern readers resembles his or her real-life counterpart about as much as Moby Dick resembles most whales.

The Modern City and Crime

The dangers posed by crime and fire have probably always concerned city dwellers. Historians have attempted with only qualified success to estimate levels of intentional and nonintentional violence and property damage over time, but the measurement problems are formidable. Survey data on rates of criminal victimization began to be gathered in the United States only recently, in 1973. By the second half of the twentieth century, police had begun to keep fairly accurate counts of all offenses reported to them, and coroners had begun to preserve their records with some care. The FBI started in 1930 to aggregate and report major offense categories in their Uniform Crime Reports, although these probably contain unknown biases and reporting errors, for they depend on the accuracy and consistency of local police record keeping. From the mid-nineteenth century until about World War I, individual city police departments kept and published detailed records of their own activities, including arrests, but usually not on criminal offenses merely reported or known to them. The concept of offenses known to the police gained currency in the United States only after the widespread use of telephones. Felony court and penitentiary data are available from much earlier periods, but these are as distant from arrests as arrests are from actual criminal offenses. Thus, the farther back we go in time, the less distinct become the indicators of crime and violence.[33]

The best evidence suggests that actual rates of violent crime and perhaps property crimes have been declining for centuries. There is evidence, albeit scattered and somewhat contradictory, of significant shifts in the kinds as well as amounts of urban offenses in the United States. The colonial era seemed preoccupied with crimes against religion and morality, offenses we would call victimless today. By the end of the eighteenth century, a more modern mix of offenses, principally assaults and thefts, seemed to predominate. During the course of the nineteenth century, at least one study found a rise in crimes of theft by deception and illicit business practices. Another study has shown that there may have been a decline in public disorder from 1850 to the present. And a study of violent crimes in Philadelphia has found an intriguing decline in urban homicide and accidental death up to the Depression, with a parallel rise in suicide.[34]

European historians, looking at whole nations rather than cities, have emphasized the relationship between violence and property crimes, finding an increase in property crimes with the coming of industrial capitalism and urbanization.[35] There is a good deal of debate on this topic, but it does not seem to have drawn in historians of American urban crime, who instead focus on the changing prosecution patterns and levels of minor public order offenses. The most persuasive position in this debate is that since the middle of the nineteenth century, the actual level of public order offenses, disorderly conduct, and drunkenness, has declined. Cities have grown more orderly, and the decorum so much on the minds of our Victorian predecessors has become today's reality.[36]

Because American cities grew so rapidly until the post–World War II era, all these declining rates of crime may have been invisible to urban inhabitants, including the police. The total number of offenses increased as cities grew, even though the rates fell. As a result, those most aware of city affairs—the police, politicians, newspaper reporters and editors—would have been more likely to register increases in total criminal offenses rather than decreases in per capita crime or subtle shifts from one kind of offense to another. Even though homicide rates in Philadelphia declined in the late nineteenth and early twentieth century, the chances of being killed by a stranger or by a gun increased.[37] Again, this raised the level of fear of crime even though the rate of violence was declining.

Even when actual change may be established by the historian, it is difficult to tell how the various segments of the city perceived this slowly changing statistic. Customarily, nineteenth-century newspaper editors and crime reporters displayed cynical attitudes toward most crimes and even their victims. This condescension distanced readers from the reports of offenses; it also distanced editors and reporters from a world with which very few wished to be associated. Police reporters used the lowest courts as sources for amusing stories, for a theater of the lower class. Because most crimes of violence took place between persons known to one another and because the victims of many thefts were the poor or those knowingly at risk (men visiting prostitutes at night, for instance), the psychological distancing may be have reflected the actual distance of most people from crime.

In the nineteenth century most observers of city life believed in the existence of a "dangerous class," a group of people responsible for but also suffering most from crime and disorder. This group was similar to but not the same as the working class: it corresponded more to Marx's *lumpenproletariat*. The notion of a "dangerous class" was not uniquely American, the phrase originally having appeared almost simultaneously in Britain and France. The phrase and concept does seem to have been almost exclusively urban, however. The dangerous class or classes were feared as internal enemies, enemies that changed the nature of the city from a civilized place into a wilderness. "The dangerous classes are in a state of war with social interests; our freedom allows them to come and go, and a town has its hiding places almost as inaccessible as a wilderness of woods."[38] Crimes most likely to generate public passion and fear were those that most obviously threatened the innocent, not assaults or even homicides within the "dangerous class." These more socially threatening crimes could range from public rowdiness in respectable sections of a city to offenses against middle-class victims chosen for their innocence and weakness. By the first decades of the twentieth century the phrase fell out of use, partly no doubt because of its pejorative nature, but partly also because social scientists had begun to ask more precise questions about the identity of the poor and the criminal.

Extortion plots and kidnapping by the notorious Black Hand organization probably aroused the most public sentiment in the final decades of the nineteenth century, even though the victims were mostly poor Italian immigrants. Perhaps most disturbing was that these crimes highlighted the inability of the state or city to protect some of its poorest constituents. The Black Hand, almost exclusively made up of Sicilian immigrants in New Orleans, Chicago, and New York, provoked a good deal of public sympathy for its victims.[39] In one form of extortion, the criminal demanded a sum of money with a written note signed with a crudely drawn black hand; the implied threat was either kidnapping or maiming. Terrified victims often complied. Major cities developed Black Hand specialists within their police departments, so that when the police did find out about such threats, the offenders were often arrested, with deportation the usual punishment. Because of the symbolic power of the Black Hand notes, the police received a good deal of positive notoriety when they intervened successfully. Whether the crimes promoted fear outside the Sicilian community is somewhat doubtful, although it does seem that the fear of kidnapping, of foreign criminals, and of the loss of children without any hope of recovery aroused a good deal of empathetic public reaction.

As the sensational example of the Black Hand suggests, publicity generates much of the public feeling about crime. By the end of the nineteenth century, popular writers often stressed the degeneration of the human species under metropolitan conditions. Henry George claimed, "this life of the great cities is not the natural life of man. He must under such conditions deteriorate physically, mentally, morally." Adna F. Weber stood apart from more popular writers, refusing to subscribe to such glib generalizations, instead devoting a whole chapter to systematically analyzing "the physical and moral conditions" of large cities. After examining all the contemporary data he could, he concluded that "the amount of viciousness and criminality in cities is probably exaggerated in popular estimation from the fact that the cities have long been under the blaze of an Argus-eyed press, so that the worst is known about them. They have hitherto overshadowed the evils in the moral life of villages." Weber noted, with obvious satisfaction, that the number of bars per capita sufficed "as a rough index of a town's morality," and there were more in New York's smaller towns than in its large cities, suggesting that *they* had the laxer moral standards![40]

Probably very few Americans today can understand or justify the relative neglect of crime victims compared with the money, attention, and effort spent on criminal offenders. Some states have established victim's bills of rights, but it is widely known and resented that the public cost of prosecuting and incarcerating offenders far exceeds anything spent on victims. The high visibility of such legislation helps obscure the local nature of crime control. Like so many of the new city services, relatively recent in historical terms, crime control has already become so mundane, so banal as to be invisible. The widespread anger over "coddled" criminals and their uncompensated and suffering victims is the consequence of almost a century and a half of building crime control organizations at the local level. Two centuries ago, the victim of a crime could expect nothing to happen unless he or she initiated some activity and paid the accompanying fees. With the reforms creating a uniformed police came free prosecution, and the principle, if not the reality, of a police-initiated discovery of crime and apprehension of criminals. For the first time in history, a formal, tax-supported organization took systematic responsibility for the control and prevention of crime and the active protection of the public.

And it was a process repeated over and over, for in many city agencies a small service quickly became a necessity of civilization. Once the barest outline of a service structure had been created, demand soared, both in amount and in range, so that within ten years of their creation, urban police departments found themselves providing a broad range of services. Police may not yet be terribly successful at achieving their goal of active crime deterrence rather than passive reaction to complaints. But the principle that has been used to justify their existence is very important and has become a concrete part of modern life. This is the principle of an active state, a state systematically intervening in its society and economy rather than solely exercising and protecting its sovereignty. In the context of American urban history, the service city encompassed and implemented this principle. The service city provided this new active principle with a local context and a real implementation. Cities and towns implemented their active governments, but at least as much of the impetus came from the beneficiaries of the service as from the providers. By the mid-twentieth century, the best departments consciously fashioned themselves in this "service style."[41] In the nineteenth century, almost as quickly as they had hit the pavements in their controversial new uniforms, the police had directed strangers, untangled traffic jams, helped accident victims, and performed dozens of other non-crime-related chores that neither they nor their creators had anticipated. Their modest range of catchall services served as precedents for a whole range of now-customary city services.

Pluralism and the Local State

These services are important in their very banality, in their ordinary and now predictable qualities, and in their representing the mundane side of urban life. From rubbish collection to traffic control, it is these that form the central elements of the local state.[42] If the essence of feudalism was the surrender of individual liberty for protection, then the essence of the modern individual to state relationship, while still incorporating the expectation of military protection, has now penetrated to the level of buffering the day-to-day hassles of ordinary life.[43] Michel Foucault portrays this subtle working of state power as invidious, gathering into its ambit ever more of the individual's life from cradle to grave.[44] But this penetration is not necessarily as repugnant as Foucault implies. It clearly can be invidious in fascist regimes, yet it also can be positive, humane, and supportive. The fact of this new relationship between state and individual is relatively neutral; its larger context determines whether it is good or bad.

But the relatively recent penetration of the state into the mundane, which began in the 1840s, should make us rethink the shock we feel when we read about the seventeenth-century state's policing of religious beliefs and sexual morality, as so bitterly and vividly portrayed by Nathaniel Hawthorne in *The Scarlet Letter*. Historians now know that Dimsdale and Hester Prynne's "crime" drew heavy punishment not because of sexual morality so much as stinginess. Local governments feared that they might have to provide support for poor single women with children. Towns "warned out" paupers for similar reasons. Welfare provisions that have become a regular if begrudged part of nineteenth- and twentieth-century governments drove seventeenth- and eighteenth-century governments to almost paranoid fears that paupers might become dependent on local welfare.[45] The town in which a pauper or poor woman and her illegitimate child resided bore the responsibility for their support. The pre-nineteenth-century state thus prosecuted individual morality only because of its concern with costly consequences: children in need.

The modern state treats our own lives in much finer detail, if

Traffic Control, Cadillac Square (Detroit), circa 1920.
Detroit must have been very proud of its traffic control boxes. A similar
picture adorned the front cover of the municipal reform magazine, *New
Jersey Municipalities* for June 1918. Neither photo shows an animal powered vehicle, but the Pittsburgh traffic survey of 1917, told a different story.
In hilly Pittsburgh, there was still one horse-pulled vehicle for every two
gasoline-powered ones. Did the Detroit photographers wait until only gasoline-powered vehicles were in view?

Source: Burton Historical Collection: Detroit Public Library.

with less moral concern. Few of us would consider this more in-trusive than the moral surveillance in the New England colonies, but only because it is now customary, unexamined. In the twen-tieth century poor and single mothers receive support, but only after the government probes and documents their lives in intimate detail. That this seems so ordinary, so unexceptionable, and so per-fectly reasonable indicates how much more tolerant we have be-come of state intervention and its fiscal consequences than our colonial predecessors.

State intervention has made our lives easier, at least in a sig-nificant material sense. It also has had complex social conse-quences. It has made our lives more separate, for forced cultural sharing and mutuality is no longer necessary in order to catch crim-inals, support the destitute, or fight fires. Richard Sennett, in his book, *The Uses of Disorder*, makes the bold if unconvincing ar-gument that street confrontations are a good thing, for they educate various cultural groups about one another.[46] But the growth of the local service sector of government occurred just as cultural hom-ogeneity declined in the mid-nineteenth century. U.S. cities be-came a welter of national and local immigrant cultures, and their organizational service structure became less dependent on volun-teers, on shared values and goals. (Today, many smaller cities and towns depend on volunteer fire departments. Were the data avail-able, one might suspect that the presence of volunteer fire depart-ments would correlate highly with demographic homogeneity.) In this way we have gained a tolerant system without requiring in-dividual or group tolerance. It is a system that in fact protects the intolerant from one another. That individual police officers do not tolerate cultures outside of the mainstream has been a truism from the time of their creation, yet they make possible the latitudinarian urban milieu. Law, not social pressure, forces their grudging tolerance.

Would our tolerance for ethnic and racial differences be as great if cities still depended on forced cooperation for fire fighting and policing? Undoubtedly it would not. The history of urban riot-ing and violence supports this position. From the colonial period up to the 1830s, most urban riots reflected cultural homogeneity. The riots centered on class or economic issues. The New York City flour riot of 1837, for instance, sent a clear message to merchants and the city government that flour prices were too high. The mayor responded to the attack on a flour warehouse by forcing merchants to lower prices. With the heavy influx of Irish immigrants which began in the 1830s in Boston, the nature of urban riots began to shift from violence aimed at a specific goal to violence articulating ethnic hostility. The attack on the Ursuline convent in Boston in 1834, for instance, clearly demonstrated an early outbreak of hostility toward Irish Catholic immigrants. By the mid-nineteenth century, even riots over concrete issues took on ethnic or racial overtones. The Draft Riots of 1863 in New York, for example, while expressing the resentment of poor, newly arrived Irish laborers toward the draft, also conflated this issue with Irish resentment of blacks.

Riots by whites targeting racial minorities—anti-black, anti-Chinese, and anti-Hispanic—continued in American cities from the Civil War era through World War II. Most of these riots were over urban turf or expressed resentment over jobs. Anti-Chinese riots from Oregon to Southern California expressed white working-class hostility at Chinese laborers, and the Chicago race riots of 1919 reflected housing competition between poor blacks and whites, while the anti-Hispanic Zoot Suit riots during World War II in Los Angeles focused on the new jobs Hispanics had found during the war.[47]

Rather than wonder at the numerous riots between ethnic and racial groups in U.S. cities, we might better wonder at cities which did not have riots. John C. Schneider has explored this question for mid-nineteenth-century Detroit. He argues that most cities had had Irish-German riots, but that in midcentury Detroit residential segregation produced different, noncontiguous paths between home and work. As a consequence, the city's geography forestalled ethnic riots like the four that erupted in St. Louis between 1844 and 1854.[48] That there were no more riots in the potentially turbulent nineteenth century can be attributed to the stable bureaucracies that had supplanted voluntary organizations and begun to supply urban services. In spite of the antagonism that individual police officers felt, for instance, they were more rule-bound in their social control efforts than their predecessors, particularly the night watch. Similarly, all the evidence on volunteer fire departments prior to their bureaucratization around midcentury suggests that they galvanized ethnic rivalry and violence.[49] One can only guess that as cities grew more ethnically and racially heterogenous, volunteer fire departments and night watch forces would have created and exacerbated intergroup hatred and combat.

But the means with which these potentially conflicting groups tolerated one another lay not in increased cultural tolerance but in the new formal structures, service organizations that automatically put out fires and arrested criminal offenders, with relatively little regard to race or ethnicity. It was no longer necessary, as it had been in the eighteenth century, for citizens to share ideas about the community or about the mundane tasks of city housekeeping. The abstract tool of city services, funded by a general property tax, accomplished these chores without requiring specific consent or even much consideration. By the early twentieth century, issues of public safety no longer centered on whether or not the city could do anything more than depend on volunteers. Instead of asking to provide safety, urbanites asked how much safety could they get. To walk the street unmolested, to not worry about burglary, to expect fire fighters to be paramedics, had become a universal desire, an expectation, and a right, one never imagined by our founding fathers.

The Sunbelt: Something Completely Different

In order to stress what is unique about American cities, this book's themes have been addressed at a high level of generalization. But no one concerned with the U.S. city in the last quarter of the twentieth century can ignore the phenomenal urban transformation of the South, virtually a totally post–1950 phenomenon. When I moved to Charlotte, North Carolina, in 1973, I found a South with cities so new, so spread out, so oriented toward shopping centers and commercial strip development, that finding old things became a personal obsession. In contrast with the new urban South, Los Angeles seems old and compact. For the new urban South is far more new and urban than it is South.

Southern cities have historically been the bailiwick of elites, usually commercial ones. To ensure their dominance in the early twentieth century, the elite diluted political opposition by instituting at-large, nonpartisan elections. Residentially segregated minorities lost their ward-based political representatives, and the at-large elections effectively stopped the formation of neighborhood or even bipartisan city councils. Later, the expansion of city boundaries and even the merging of city and county governments continued to weaken the impact of any dissident votes, so that the commercial elite continued until very recent times to dominate city governments. Federal enforcement of the 1964 Voting Rights Act and busing to achieve school desegregation had the sudden effect of turning these strategies for political domination on their head. Fragmented school district boundaries limited the busing of students in northern cities, where districts often coincided with municipalities, so that within each political unit, no meaningful integration could take place. But the large consolidated districts of the South, created as a by-product of the enlarged city boundaries, made busing work very effectively. When in 1974, parents and students at South Boston High School began to resist busing with increasing violence, a small delegation of students visited southern cities to learn how to integrate schools peacefully. Thus ended two centuries of northern lead in social progress.[50]

In the 1970s southern cities often found themselves catapulted into national prominence as genuine political contests began to end the white hegemony. Governments headed by blacks (Atlanta, 1973), Hispanics (San Antonio, 1982), or women (Houston, 1982) helped moderate the image of an oppressive, reactionary culture.[51] Thus southern cities skipped much of the historical political development of the North, leaping from their anachronistic eighteenth-century governments right into the late twentieth century.

They gained more than political attention. Air conditioning, inexpensive housing, and nonunion labor attracted newer industries to the South. The national media permanently linked sunbelt cities and an urban avant-garde with advanced technology, postindustrial economic progress, and amenities unavailable in the frost belt. Kirkpatrick Sale's influential 1975 book, *Power Shift: The Rise of the Southern Rim and Its Challenge to the Eastern Establishment*, described the economic and demographic growth of southern cities and reflected the ambiguity, admiration, and concerns of the northeastern urbanites as they watched the South eclipse them.[52] During the civil rights movement of the 1960s, national media had shown the nation a South of cruel white Neanderthals, an image confirmed in films like *Deliverance*, which portrayed a brutal rural culture, half-human and half-monster. Quite remarkably, this popular image has reversed in less than two decades. The most economically, socially, and culturally backward region of the country appears to have become its hope for a prosperous and progressive future.

It had been a long wait, for southern urban leaders and promoters had been trying to achieve this urban transformation for a century. The rise of a new South with a scrubbed-clean, high-technology image must have fulfilled the dreams of promoters like Henry Grady. Grady, an Atlanta journalist, urged southerners in the 1880s to diversify, industrialize, modernize, and urbanize; he sold a "new South" to northern investors and entrepreneurs. The "new South" movement failed to do much more than create a few expositions, even though Grady's suggestions were modest enough: emulate Grand Rapids, Michigan, he had told a Texas audience in 1887. Ironically, it may have been the very failure of the movement, the continued dependence on staple crop agriculture, the low level of technological change in agriculture, and low investment in railroads and other heavy industry that created the conditions that a century later fostered economic and urban growth. In the post–World War II era, the urban South had no aging industrial plants, no collapsing sewers and bridges. It was ready to be built anew with transportation connections based on hard surface roads, deep water ports and air travel, urban governments with broad geographical spread, and governments desperately anxious to subsidize new industry.[53]

Vast bureaucracies, labyrinthian services, professional lobbyists pressuring state and federal governments, and aggressive city trade missions that visit other states and nations, all reflect the complex and aggressive creature which urban government has become. This government, by becoming professionally competent, has also at times become invisible by virtue of its efficiency. Yet its subtlety and importance have not been forgotten by those in a position to compare service benefits. In the 1980s local governments around the country have found themselves engaged in bidding competitions with one another for various high-technology industries, most prominently computer-related ones.[54] The improbability of the competitors and the winners suggests just how widespread the net of services has become. For instance, in the competition for the newly formed consortium called the Microelectronics and Computer Technology Corporation, fifty-seven cities bid, including San Diego, Austin, Atlanta, and the urban region between Raleigh, Durham and Chapel Hill, North Carolina called Research Triangle Park.

The winning city, Austin, and its local businesses, offered a package of monetary subsidies through nontaxation clauses, land, and buildings. But more important, Austin offered a combination of educational, cultural, and intellectual resources and services which the other cities could not match. The insight to be gained from this is that city services can be made visible when necessary. In this case virtually the whole bundle of services had to be presented by competing cities in order to appeal to the life-style demands of a highly educated workforce in a position to make a collective locational choice. They consciously evaluated city services as an integral feature of modern city life just as they did other more obvious amenities like weather and cost of living. That such a cautious decision-making process resulted in four sunbelt cities competing with one another demonstrates how far things have come in the urban South, how virtually all the reasons for aggressive economic interests to stay in the North in 1883 would a century later attract them to the South. Henry Grady would have been proud. Thomas Jefferson would have been shocked.

Epilogue:

How Do We "Watch" Our Cities?

The complexity of a city government, the multifariousness of its duties, make it the most difficult kind of government to watch. Even the national government does not undertake to regulate so many details, and the general supervision to which it is limited can be more easily watched.   —Adna F. Weber

Even the evils of the city are not necessarily inherent in urban life.

The American city collects its revenues more justly than do any of the cities of Europe.

—Frederick C. Howe

What we can determine in the future and what has already been determined about cities is important, but not always obvious. How we structure our way of looking at cities determines what we see. If we are careless, what we see can be a biased guide to both the present and the past, for buildings and streets conceal as well as reveal the meanings they may have contained. Our understanding of cities and their history will always be a mix of the visual with other forms of knowledge. In the first epigraph above, Adna F. Weber, the prime exponent of a statistical approach to the city, uses visual verbs. Comprehension of the city, even to him, included seeing. We interpret what we see in buildings, their meaning, through the actions of those who currently use them. Sometimes what can be seen today is a good metaphor for the past; too often it is not. Only a historically informed vision can tell.

We often see our cities in terms of problems, and the city's success or failure in coping with them. And American cities are far more successful than we sometimes realize. This does not imply that a whole range of deep problems do not yet plague them. Cities may not have achieved all that they should have, but it is remarkable to consider the accomplishments represented by police and fire departments, public health departments, schools and libraries, bridges, sewers, and hard surfaced streets. Virtually all came about as the result of local political initiatives within the past 150 years.

Frederick C. Howe, a Progressive urban reformer, realized that seemingly urban problems were not always the consequence of some essential evil of the city. This is a lesson we easily forget. For if the city itself causes urban problems—crime, poverty, indifference—then the obvious solution is to get rid of the city. This is why Howe made it very clear that urban problems, enormous as they were and are, stem largely from nonurban causes, even though they require urban solutions. The success of our cities is in constant jeopardy because, like their physical infrastructures, urban organizations require constant maintenance. City schools, public safety organizations, the taxing apparatus, and other organizations were all built with a tremendous expense of energy at a time when self-interest and public virtue were not incompatible. The very success of these organizations, however, has destroyed the visible link between self-interest and public virtue. Consequently, the postwar era has seen cities begin to drift, unaware that the world they now inhabit is not automatically self-renewing.[1]

The fiscal, criminal, infrastructural, and educational crises facing American cities today are not nearly as bad, objectively, as those cities faced earlier, except in one very important respect. In earlier crises, citizens knew that no outside force would save them, that they themselves had to make everything happen. We have had the cushion of post–World War II prosperity and growth, the cushion of relatively newly built infrastructures, the cushion of newly completed and still evolving educational systems. All these tend to obscure the fragility and impermanence inherent in such organizations.[2]

The essence of cities is not material accretion, but human action, human institutions, human organizations. When human actions change, the cities change. Without action, cities can disappear. Because today's important city organizations are labor-intensive service providers, variations in labor input can rapidly damage the essence of city life so invisibly provided by these organizations. Organizations that took a century to build can be wiped out very quickly. Ironically, when they work well, we do not have to know about them, so that their very success can lead to forgetfulness, neglect, and potential disaster.

The Pied Piper of Hamelin should be the quintessential urban myth. It is most visibly appropriate when applied to schooling, for the generations who have had good schooling often wish to quit paying the piper. But the same story obtains for the rest of the city. We do not want to pay for public safety either. For this, we have given the piper a promissory note to be paid off by our children, the same ones we are too stingy to educate. That is, by allowing enormous future benefits for police and fire pensions, cities have managed to forestall potential labor problems over current wages with promises of future payments.[3]

Urban crises are not just the objective problems of a handful of cities failing to meet their debt obligations; they are more severe. Urban crises are bred by the very ignorance of how cities work, of how we got to where we are in less than two centuries. These seemingly solid, permanent structures are youthful and fragile when measured in generations. My own great-grandparents were born when American cities did not have paid, regular police, when children attended public school irregularly and only until their early teens, when fire departments were run by amateurs, when home ownership came only through extraordinary efforts, when all but the rich walked to work, when the destitute slept under bridges, when the unemployed had no welfare, when nine-year-old orphans supported themselves and slept in castaway boxes. About the time of birth of my grandparents, cities—local governments—began to formally run organizations obligated to seek out and aid the poor, seek out and stop crime, enforce fire codes. Such "services" finally became regularized only about when my parents were born. Thus, the urban organizations that now regularly provide such services have been created in just three generations.

They could disappear in fewer than three generations. We do not have to have schools, police, public health officers, metropolitan water districts, planning rules, or any of the customary urban services we now have. They can deteriorate and go away more easily than they were created. This may happen. Abandoned cities, some great, most anonymous, fill the archaeological record. We may leave to future generations the hulls of cities created by our predecessors and used up by us, at once ignorant children and profligate parents.

In 1899, Adna F. Weber concluded his great *Growth of Cities* by urging continued reform for cities. He cited Charles H. Cooley's call, "Humanity demands that men should have sunlight, fresh air, the sight of grass and trees. It demands these things for the man himself, and it demands them still more urgently for his wife and

children." Weber's major basis for hope was "the 'rise of the suburbs' . . . which furnishes the solid basis of a hope that the evils of
city life, so far as they result from overcrowding, may be in large
part removed." Ironically, until very recently, postwar urban analysts have supported the confused viewpoint that suburbs were not
cities, and that they were somehow to blame for social problems
located in cities. Moreover, this thesis was complicated by the difficulty of seeing how very local city history and power still is, in
spite of the increased role of federal government. Recent historical
and political analysis promises to change these misperceptions.
Kenneth Fox, for instance, has reconsidered the role of suburbs,
accepting their ascendance since the 1940s and showing how they
play a critical and positive role in the future of cities. Thus, we
may see our concept of the city itself finally begin a difficult readjustment, to that of an unprecedented urban form: a decentralized
and complex world that is neither village nor central city, a city
form that represents a genuinely new settlement pattern in
history.[4]

My hope is that historians can do their share of helping us
rethink our cities. Historically centered self-understanding can remind us to take care of our new urban world, for it has been only
recently constructed and may be more fragile than we realize. Historical understanding can also tell us not to reject what we have
built so recently, but to keep building it, to make it better by realizing what an adventure it truly is.

This epilogue and indeed much of this book has a tone cheer-
ier and more optimistic than many urban histories. Even a hint of
optimism about cities may come as a surprise to some. It came as
a surprise to me, for the very researching and writing of this book
has changed my mind about U.S. cities. After all, central cities are
collecting pools for our society's human wastage, and visual and
chemical pollutants abound, while political and planning misman-
agement stun any newspaper reader. Consequently, it is difficult
not to see recent urban history as the history of social problems.
However, we must be just as cautious in attributing the decrease
of urban problems to urban actions. For instance, I have not made
the entirely plausible claim that improved city services, water supplies, and sewerage are responsible for improved urban life expect-
ancy. These things probably helped, but specialists have not been
able to identify with precision the causes of the decline in mor-

tality which occurred in the nineteenth and early twentieth century. Nor does the historical scenario of our cities portend an entirely rosy future. Again, the contemporary problems are too obvious and enormous. And it may be that for all their potential and flexibility, cities in the future will be unable to properly identify or handle the problems thrust upon them. So far, the evidence is that they can, and that is a good sign indeed.

The woe of municipal fragmentation can also be thought of as the promise of variety. This variety in multiple governments gives people the chance, for instance, to move to a dry suburb, where the sale of liquor is prohibited, yet still live in a large metropolis—Oak Park, Illinois, or Edina, Minnesota, for example. Fragmentation does hinder the coordination of large governmental projects, but metropolitan governance commissions have begun to be built. A more serious difficulty is that municipal fragmentation allows the creation of wealthy enclaves, municipalities where only the rich can dwell. This means that some of their tax potential is lost from other cities, but the benefit may be that their elitist values are isolated from the rest of society. Similarly, small municipal enclaves may be ethnically or racially exclusive—Dearborn, Michigan, for example, is a nearly all-white town, while Compton, California, is nearly all black. Such exclusion denies others their chances to participate fully in a society, exclusion that is clearly wrong. But the error would be to throw out the good with the bad, losing the benefits of small governmental units and local options to combat serious social wrongs. The United States introduced the reality of a pluralistic society to the world, and the patchwork quilt of local government may be its modern contribution.

A fundamental problem arising from the accumulation of small municipalities into great metropolises is that the costs incurred by one place may fall on its neighbor. The development of high-rise office structures in one municipality, for instance, raises the congestion and pollution while robbing sunlight from nearby places, without bringing any tax benefits. This is a modern version of the same structural flaw that affected Homestead, Pennsylvania, where Carnegie's steel mill just outside town contributed nothing to the tax coffers. Equitable solutions to this type of problem will probably be found only via state-level adjudication.

Current urban transformations may lead us to a new understanding of American urban life. A recent, highly perceptive article in *The New York Times* by John Herbers, "Now Even the Suburbs Have Suburbs," discusses the fascinating growth of the ten leading nonurban, urban counties (that is, places with many people but no city governments) in the United States. Calling them "exurban counties," Herber expresses a proper concern that these centerless places have no clear sense of local government or of place. Polls have revealed that nearly 50 percent of urban Americans would prefer living in small cities, under 10,000, which suggests that the search for the suburban ideal will continue, that urban places will continue to shift and leapfrog over one another. This has been going on for a century and a half, and perhaps the major shift is in how local governments promote the new towns. In the nineteenth century, growth was the goal; now growth is for new places the reality, and there may even be no one local government to articulate that as policy. Is this bad? Our own history must make us cautious, for it may be that as we continue to work out new kinds of cities, we will work out new kinds of polity. The fragmentation of living without a mayor, but with school boards, county commissioners, and flood control districts may be more in the eyes of the beholder than in the experience of the users. American urban forms have never been as anarchic as they seemed to outsiders, so we must remember that flexibility, change, and intense localism may have benefits we have yet to appreciate.[5]

The history of American cities should do far more than make us rethink current problems. It should make us think about how our contemporary life is historical in its very essence, from our personality characteristics to the bureaucracies and institutions that we live in and sometimes fight against. When Emerson said, "The past has baked our loaf," he was referring to this fundamental aspect of our existence. The difficulty in thinking about the present as a part of the past is that, because we cannot change the past, it seems fruitless. But it can be liberating, for by learning what we have made and have changed, we learn what we can change. We also learn our limits, what we cannot alter. We learn that we in cities are fundamentally different from our medieval predecessors, that a vision based on a partial understanding of them does not provide us with an adequate goal for the future. We learn that our cities are highly flexible, that they have never experienced stasis, that diffuse sprawl and blurred boundaries are their heritages, that a hustling support of private enterprise is a long tradition, and that numerous multiple and small governments have been with us from the start. We also learn that American taxpayers have always been stingy as we tried to pass on the costs of services to the future through growth, but that we have historically been willing to create the service providing city and to indebt ourselves for infrastructural expansion, which in turn has promoted technological change. It is a complex legacy, one without easily identified heroes and villains. But the promise is there of an adaptive and potentially humane future.

Notes

Introduction

1. James Bryce, *The American Commonwealth* (London: Macmillan, 1891, 3d ed., 1917), II, 660–661, 666.
2. Surveys include Howard P. Chudacoff, *The Evolution of American Urban Society* (Englewood Cliffs, N.J.: Prentice-Hall, 1981), and Sam Bass Warner, Jr. *The Urban Wilderness: A History of the American City* (New York: Harper and Row, 1972). More topically specialized surveys include Kenneth T. Jackson, *Crabgrass Frontier: The Suburbanization of the United States* (New York: Oxford University Press, 1985); David R. Goldfield and Blaine A. Brownell, *Urban America: From Downtown to No Town* (Boston: Houghton Mifflin, 1979); Carl Abbott, *The New Urban America: Growth and Politics in Sunbelt Cities* (Chapel Hill: University of North Carolina Press, 1981); and Zane L. Miller, *The Urbanization of Modern America: A Brief History* (New York: Harcourt, Brace, Jovanovich, 1973). For bibliography, see Doyce B. Nunis, Jr., ed., *Los Angeles and Its Environs in the Twentieth Century: A Bibliography of a Metropolis*, compiled under the auspices of the Los Angeles Metropolitan History Project (Los Angeles: Ward Ritchie Press, 1973).
3. Frederick H. Wines, *Punishment and Reform* (New York, 1895), cited by William R. Brock, *Investigation and Responsibility: Public Responsibility in the United States, 1865–1900* (New York: Cambridge University Press, 1984), 102.
4. I try in this book to avoid the pitfalls of two competing intellectual paradigms that have come to characterize much historical writing about the city. Often interesting history has come from both perspectives, but neither has been able to build a truly city-focused urban history. Neither has been able to stress the developing relationship between formal organizations and social change, and their city-based interaction. These two dominant and mutually exclusive paradigms have fragmented urban history, fragmented the history of government from the history of various city institutions like schools and police,

and from the social history of the city. They have led to an impasse in the field itself, producing more and more research but fewer and fewer central questions. And as the history of cities is itself a relatively narrow aspect of American history, we are too often left with a rich landscape of research ignored by its own producers. One of these models conceptualizes the history of the city within the context of social control. Essentially this position assumes that urban and industrial growth have bred misery and potential rebellion and that dozens of urban institutions, from political machines to welfare systems and schools, have all worked deliberately to prevent city dwellers from rebelling. Although this book does not disagree that many city organizations did indeed control the behavior of their citizens, it argues that this is a meaningless point, that all societies have controlling organizations and enforced behaviors. If anything, the degree of control in nineteenth-century U.S. cities was remarkable in its latitude, not its restrictiveness. The other historical model is functionalism, its central and unstated argument contrasting with the social control position. The functionalist perspective sees urban history as an unproblematic and natural sequence of causes and consequences: first a problem appears, e.g., poverty; then a solution, e.g., welfare agencies. While the social control analysis sees hidden motives behind every urban innovator, the functionalist approach is to pick an agency, and then show how it responded to a "problem." The elemental dynamics of stories cast in such molds show the struggle of the forces of reform against the forces of conservatism.

5. Richard Hofstadter, *America at 1750: A Social Portrait* (London: Jonathan Cape, 1972), xii.

6. Quotation in Clay McShane, *Technology and Reform: Street Railways and the Growth of Milwaukee, 1887–1900* (Madison: State Historical Society of Wisconsin, 1974), 67.

7. For notable exceptions, see J. Rogers Hollingsworth and Ellen Jane Hollingsworth, *Dimensions in Urban History: History and Social Science Perspectives on Middle-Size American Cities* (Madison: University of Wisconsin Press, 1979), and Daniel J. Elazar et al., *Cities of the Prairie Revisited: The Closing of the Metropolitan Frontier* (Lincoln: University of Nebraska Press, 1986), and *Cities of the Prairie: The Metropolitan Frontier and American Politics* (New York: Basic Books, 1970). For the postwar city, see Kenneth Fox, *Metropolitan America* (London: Macmillan, 1985).

8. Cited in Douglas E. Booth, "Transportation, City Building, and Financial Crisis: Milwaukee, 1852–1868," *Journal of Urban History* 9 (May 1983), 347, from Bayrd Still, *Milwaukee: The History of a City* (Madison: State Historical Society of Wisconsin, 1965), 174–175.

1 Writing About Cities

1. Lewis Mumford, *The Culture of Cities* (New York: Harcourt, 1938), 346, 495–496, 551.

2. Ibid., 548, 543.
3. Ibid., 201, 519, figure 28; Arthur M. Schlesinger, *The Rise of The American City: 1878–1898* (New York: Macmillan, 1933); Reyner Banham, *Los Angeles: The Architecture of the Four Ecologies* (New York: Harper and Row, 1971); Robert Venturi, Denise Scott Brown, and Steven Izenour, *Learning From Las Vegas* (Cambridge, Mass.: MIT Press, 1972).
4. Mumford, *The Culture of Cities*, 166–167.
5. Ibid., 58, figure 30, 72.
6. Daniel Schaffer, *Garden Cities for America: The Radburn Experience* (Philadelphia: Temple University Press, 1982), 11, 169. Schaffer, in a remarkably even-handed assessment, points out that Radburn achieved its social harmony by using realtors who "discouraged" Jews and blacks, and that the town itself had no government, that it was run by the company that developed it.
7. Lewis Mumford, *The Highway and the City* (London: Secker & Warburg, 1963), 9.
8. Mumford, *The Culture of Cities*, 165, figure 21.
9. Mumford, "Megalopolis as Anti-City," in *The Urban Prospect* (London: Secker & Warburg, 1968), 138–140.
10. Jane Jacobs, *The Death and Life of Great American Cities: The Failure of Town Planning* (New York: Random House, 1961), 9.
11. Ibid., 15.
12. Ibid., 105.
13. T. J. Jackson Lears, "The Two Richard Sennetts," *Journal of American Studies* 19 (Fall 1985), 81–94; Richard Sennett, *Families Against the City: Middle Class Homes of Industrial Chicago, 1872–1890* (Cambridge, Mass.: Harvard University Press, 1970).
14. Thomas L. Haskell, *The Emergence of Professional Social Science: The American Social Science Association and the Nineteenth-Century Crisis of Authority* (Urbana: University of Illinois Press, 1977).
15. James Leiby, *Carroll Wright and Labor Reform: The Origins of Labor Statistics* (Cambridge, Mass.: Harvard University Press, 1960) describes Wright's career as an enlightened missionary of the movement to gather data that made an enormous impact, perhaps *the* impact, on late nineteenth- and early twentieth-century census data collection. See especially the bibliography of Wright's publications (222–234). The career of his more visible predecessor, Francis A. Walker, director of the 1870 and 1880 census, president of MIT and early activist in the founding of the American Economic Association, is described in James P. Munroe, *A Life of Francis Amasa Walker* (New York: Holt, 1922). Bureau of the Census, *Historical Statistics of the United States, Colonial Times to 1970, Bicentennial Edition* (Washington, D.C.: Government Printing Office, 1975).

16.   RESIDUAL PLOT OF ALL DATA SERIES ADDED (NATURAL LOGS), 1790–1960

Year	Observed	Predicted	Residual	Standardized Residuals		
				−2.0	0	2.0
1790	5.7	4.9	0.87			*
1800	4.7	5.0	−0.31		*	
1810	4.7	5.1	−0.46	*		
1820	4.9	5.3	−0.35	*		
1830	4.9	5.4	−0.46	*		
1840	5.2	5.6	−0.31		*	
1850	5.3	5.7	−0.40	*		
1860	6.0	5.8	0.23		*	
1870	6.0	6.0	0.06		*	
1880	5.8	6.1	−0.31	*		
1890	6.5	6.3	0.28		*	
1900	7.4	6.4	1.00			*
1910	7.0	6.5	0.52		*	
1920	7.5	6.6	0.82			*
1930	7.3	6.8	0.49		*	
1940	7.7	6.9	0.76			*
1950	5.9	7.1	−1.13	*		
1960	5.9	7.2	−1.29	*		

Variable	Coefficient	Std. Error	T(DF = 16)	Prob.
Year	0.0137	0.0031	4.388	0.0005
Constant −19.7				

R^2 = 0.546   R = 0.739   F Ratio 19.25   Prob. 0.0005

SOURCE: Calculated from Bureau of the Census, *Historical Statistics of the United States, Colonial Times to 1970* (Washington, D.C.: Government Printing Office, 1975), A-4–A-9.

17.   Adna F. Weber, *The Growth of Cities in the Nineteenth Century: A Study in Statistics* (New York: Macmillan, 1899); Katharine L. Bradbury, Anthony Downs, and Kenneth A. Small, *Urban Decline and the Future of American Cities* (Washington, D.C.: The Brookings Institution, 1982), 172–173: the authors look at the relationship of urban poverty to other problems, such as crime, and conclude that perhaps eliminating or at least moving the poor, "deconcentrating the poor," might not be a "long-term remed[y]," but it is "probably a prerequisite" for such long-term remedies. A quick glance at historical and comparative information contradicts their policy recommendation, yet they do not even pursue this intriguing avenue.

18.   Robert M. Fogelson, *The Fragmented Metropolis: Los Angeles, 1850–1930* (Cambridge, Mass.: Harvard University Press, 1967) best exemplifies this perception of a fragmented reality. For my discussion of synthesis, see Eric H. Monkkonen, "The Dangers of Synthesis," *American Historical Review* 91 (December 1986), 1146–1157.

19.   Some of the better-known city biographies include Bessie L. Pierce, *A History of Chicago*, 3 vols. (New York: Alfred A. Knopf, 1937–57);

Bayrd Still, *Milwaukee: The History of a City* (Madison: State Historical Society of Wisconsin, 1965); Blake McKelvey, *Rochester*, 4 vols. (Cambridge, Mass.: Harvard University Press, and Rochester: Christopher Press, 1945–61); and Constance M. Green, *Holyoke, Massachusetts: A Case History of the Industrial Revolution in America* (New Haven: Yale University Press, 1939). Recent examples of this important genre include Don H. Doyle, *Nashville in the New South: 1880–1930* (Knoxville: University of Tennessee Press, 1985); and Don H. Doyle, *Nashville since the 1920s* (Knoxville: University of Tennessee Press, 1985). A recent specialized study is Gary R. Mormino and George E. Pozzetta, *The Immigrant World of Ybor City: Italians and Their Latin Neighbors in Tampa, 1885–1985* (Urbana: University of Illinois Press, 1987).

20. Eric H. Monkkonen, *The Dangerous Class: Crime and Poverty in Columbus, Ohio, 1860–1885* (Cambridge, Mass.: Harvard University Press, 1975).

21. The "old" urban history is wonderfully summarized in Charles N. Glaab, "The Historian and the American City: A Bibliographic Survey," in Philip M. Hauser and Leo F. Schnore, eds., *The Study of Urbanization* (New York: John Wiley, 1965), 53–80. He presciently observes that a "rather dramatic academic breakthrough seems imminent" (72). He cites fourteen essays on historiography, including three in the 1940s; four in the 1950s; and four in the 1960s. For some examples of the new urban history, see Stephan Thernstrom, *Poverty and Progress: Social Mobility in a Nineteenth Century City* (Cambridge, Mass.: Harvard University Press, 1964); idem, *The Other Bostonians: Poverty and Progress in the American Metropolis, 1880–1970* (Cambridge, Mass.: Harvard University Press, 1973); Stephan Thernstrom and Richard Sennett, eds., *Nineteenth-Century Cities: Essays in the New Urban History*, Yale Conference on the Nineteenth-Century Industrial City, 1968 (New Haven: Yale University Press, 1969); Thernstrom, "Reflections on the New Urban History," *Daedalus* C (Spring 1971), 359–375; idem, "The New Urban History," in Charles F. Delzell, ed., *The Future of History: Essays in the Vanderbilt University Centennial Symposium* (Nashville: Vanderbilt University Press, 1877), 43–52; Kathleen N. Conzen, *Immigrant Milwaukee, 1836–1860: Accommodation and Community in a Frontier City* (Cambridge, Mass.: Harvard University Press, 1976); Clyde Griffen and Sally Griffen, *Natives and Newcomers: The Ordering of Opportunity in Mid-Nineteenth Century Poughkeepsie* (Cambridge, Mass.: Harvard University Press, 1978); Sam Bass Warner, Jr., *Streetcar Suburbs: The Process of Growth in Boston, 1870–1900* (Cambridge, Mass.: Harvard University Press, 1962); idem, *The Urban Wilderness: A History of the American City* (New York: Harper & Row, 1972); Olivier Zunz, *The Changing Face of Inequality: Urbanization, Industrial Development, and Immigrants in Detroit, 1880–1920* (Chicago: University of Chicago Press, 1982).

22. Robert Sweirenga, "Towards the 'The New Rural History': A Review

Essay," *Historical Methods* 6 (1972), 111–122; Hal S. Barron, "Rediscovering the Majority: The New Rural History of the Nineteenth-Century North," *Historical Methods* 19 (Fall 1986), 141–152.

23. Richard Jensen, "Found: Fifty Million Missing Americans," paper presented at the annual meeting of the Social Science History Association (Rochester, November 1980).

24. Gary W. Cox, David Galenson, and J. Morgan Kousser, "The Log-Linear Analysis of Contingency Tables: An Introduction for Historians," *Historical Methods* 15 (1982), 152–169; Patrick M. Horan, "Occupational Mobility and Historical Social Structure," *Social Science History* 9 (1985), 25–48.

25. Michael B. Katz, Michael J. Doucet, and Mark J. Stern, *The Social Organization of Early Industrial Capitalism* (Cambridge, Mass.: Harvard University Press, 1982).

26. Monkkonen, "Residential Mobility in England and the United States, 1850–1900," in *Themes in British and American History: A Comparative Approach, c.1760–1970,* (Milton Keynes, England: Open University Press, 1985), 77–83.

27. Michael Frisch, "American Urban History as an Example of Recent Historiography," *History and Theory* 18 (1979), 350–377; idem, "Ladders, Forests, and Racing Trails," *Labor History* 15 (1973), 461–466; James Henretta, "Social History as Lived and Written," *American Historical Review* 84 (December 1979), 1293–1322; James Henretta, "The Study of Social Mobility: Ideological Assumptions and Conceptual Bias," *Labor History* XVIII (1977), 165–178; John E. Bodnar, *Immigration and Industrialization: Ethnicity in an American Mill Town, 1870–1940* (Pittsburgh: University of Pittsburgh Press, 1977).
The radical relativist critique of history is particularly vulnerable. It claims that we must take the past on its own terms, just as some anthropologists claim to do with other cultures. But this assumes that we can know the culturally different and very distant past, a nonrelativist assumption. Thus, we come to the crux of the relativist dilemma: the assumption that other cultures have other mentalities leads to the corollary that they cannot properly be understood from the outside. It may be cultural imperialism to see the past with our modes of analysis, but to do otherwise is an epistemological impossibility, by definition. How could one, for instance, write a properly cultural relativistic history of a group that had as a fundamental belief that there was no such thing as history, only an eternal present? Or could there be a properly appreciative understanding of a group that did not share the modern belief in culture?

28. Some of the new urban historians continue to be optimistic about mobility research; see Howard P. Chudacoff, "Success and Security: The Meaning of Social Mobility in America," *Reviews in American History* 10 (December 1982), 101–112. The two reanalyses of Thernstrom's data include Gary W. Cox, David Galenson, and J. Morgan Kousser, "The Log-Linear Analysis of Contingency Tables: An Introduction for Historians," *Historical Methods* 15 (Fall 1982), 152–169,

and Patrick M. Horan, "Occupational Mobility and Historical Social Structure," *Social Science History* 9 (Winter 1985), 25–48.

29. Susanne Lebsock, *The Free Women of Petersburg: Status and Culture in a Southern Town, 1784–1860* (New York: W. W. Norton, 1984); Zunz, *Changing Face of Inequality.*

2 The Premodern Heritage

1. Giorgio Buccelatti, "The 'Urban Revolution' in a Socio-Historical Perspective," *Mesopotamia* XII (1977), 19–39; see also his "The Origin of Writing and the Beginning of History," in Giorgio Buccelatti and Charles Speroni, eds., *The Shape of the Past: Studies in Honor of Franklin D. Murphy* (Los Angeles: Institute of Archeology, 1981). Ira M. Lapidus, "Cities and Societies: A Comparative Study of the Emergence of Urban Civilization in Mesopotamia and Greece," *Journal of Urban History* 12 (May 1986), 257–292. Raymond Williams, *The Country and the City* (New York: Oxford University Press, 1973).

2. There is an extensive anthropological literature about "lazy hunters and gatherers," arguing that the invention of agriculture actually *reduced* the amount of leisure time. See, for instance, Marshall Sahlins, *Stone Age Economics* (Chicago: Aldine, 1972). Peter Just, "Time and Leisure in the Elaboration of Culture," *Journal of Anthropological Research* 36 (1980), 105–115, argues that only when leisure time became scarce could it become valuable and therefore worth rationalizing.

3. Peter Hall's justly renowned *The World Cities*, 3d ed. (London: Weidenfeld and Nicolson, 1984), 246, typifies the easy association of the industrial revolution and the modern city; he characterizes that period important to cities as beginning with this revolution.

4. Larry Long and Diana DeAre, "The Slowing of Urbanization in the U.S.," *Scientific American* 249 (July 1983), 33–41; Peter Laslett, *The World We Have Lost* (New York: Charles Scribner, 1966), 9, points out that for most people in premodern England, the parish church was the "single group activity which they ordinarily shared with others outside their own families"; E. A. Wrigley and Roger Schofield, *The Population History of England, 1541 to 1871* (Cambridge, Mass.: Harvard University Press, 1981).

5. Robert Higgs, "Cities and Yankee Ingenuity, 1870–1920," in Kenneth T. Jackson and Stanley K. Schultz, eds., *Cities in American History* (New York: Alfred A. Knopf, 1972), 16–22. The contribution of smaller cities to entrepreneurship is suggested also by the conclusions of John N. Ingham, "Rags to Riches Revisited: The Effect of City Size and Related Factors on the Recruitment of Business Leaders," *Journal of American History* 63 (1976), 615–637, who found that in smaller, newer cities, manufacturers were from nonelite backgrounds, contrary to larger and older cities.

6. Gunter Barth, *Instant Cities: Urbanization and the Rise of San Francisco and Denver* (New York: Oxford University Press, 1975).

7. For instance, Cotton Mather spoke as though Boston were a walled city in 1693: "But as a proof that Contempt which this Unbelief has cast upon these proffers, I would seriously ask of the so many Hundreds above a Thousand People within these Walls: which of you all, O how few of you, can indeed say, *Christ is mine, and I am his, and he is the Beloved of my Soul!*" *The Wonders of the Invisible World* (London, 1862; orig. pub. Boston, 1693); citation supplied by Jon Butler.

8. On militias, see Lawrence D. Cress, *Citizens in Arms: The Army and the Militia in American Society to the War of 1812* (Chapel Hill: University of North Carolina Press, 1982); John K. Mahon, *History of the Militia and the National Guard* (New York: Macmillan, 1983). Quotation on Boston from John F. Sly, *Town Government in Massachusetts (1620–1930)* (Cambridge, Mass.: Harvard University Press, 1930), 41.

    For walls in St. Louis, see James B. Musick, *St. Louis as a Fortified Town* (St. Louis: R. F. Miller, 1941). Musick says that after 1812 the towers were dismantled so that the stones might be used for other construction, though one tower served as a jail until 1819 (112–114), both fates commonly met by the walls and entry gates of British and European cities. Howard J. Nelson, "Walled Cities of the United States," *Annals of the Association of American Geographers* 51 (March 1961), 1. It is interesting that Latin American cities often seem to have been planned as unwalled, grid pattern cities, influenced by some very small cities in Southern France, perhaps; see George Kubler, "Open-Grid Towns in Europe and America," in Richard P. Schaedel, Jorge E. Hardoy, and Nora Scott Kinzer, eds., *Urbanization in the Americas from its Beginnings to the Present* (The Hague: Mouton Publishers, 1978), 327–342.

    In Canada, Louisburg seems to have been much like a fortified European town although it was functionally a fort. The English tore down its walls in 1758 and the town disappeared; John W. Reps, *Town Planning in Frontier America* (Princeton: Princeton University Press, 1971), 78–80.

9. Max Weber, *The City*, trans. and ed. Don Martindale and Gertrud Neuwirth (New York: The Free Press, 1958).

10. Sam B. Warner, Jr., *The Urban Wilderness: A History of the American City* (New York: Harper & Row, 1972).

11. Carl Bridenbaugh, *Cities in the Wilderness: Urban Life in America, 1625–1742* (New York: Capricorn, 1955), 154–155, 325. Pigs, for instance, were a visible feature of American cities through the first half of the nineteenth century. They lived on garbage and human and animal excrement in the city streets and underneath stables. As late as 1865 the Superintendent of Health in Providence had to make arguments in favor of ridding the city of pigs, estimating that there were 400 hogs in Providence: Edwin M. Snow, "Report on Swine," *Providence City Documents* (Providence, 1865). Michael H. Frisch, *Town into City: Springfield, Massachusetts, and the Meaning of*

Community, 1840–1880 (Cambridge, Mass.: Harvard University Press, 1972), 159, reports that in 1865 Springfield similarly tried to ban pigs. For additional evidence on pigs, see Bettina Bradbury, "Pigs, Cows, and Boarders: Non-Wage Forms of Survival among Montreal Families, 1861–1891," *Labour/le Travail* 14 (Fall 1984), 9–46; Richard L. Bushman, "Family Security in the Transition from Farm to City, 1750–1850," *Journal of Family History* 6 (Fall 1981), 238–256; Constance M. Green, *The Secret City: A History of Race Relations in the Nation's Capital* (Princeton: Princeton University Press, 1967), 78; Harold L. Peterson, *Americans at Home: From Colonists to Late Victorians* (New York: Charles Scribner, 1971), plate 103, cartoon; Hendrik Hartog, *Public Property and Private Property: The Corporation of the City of New York in American Law, 1730–1870* (Chapel Hill: University of North Carolina Press, 1983), 139–142, 151, 201; idem, "Pigs and Positivism," *Wisconsin Law Review* no. 4 (1985), 899 – 935.

12. John R. Stilgoe, *Common Landscape of America, 1580 to 1845* (New Haven: Yale University Press, 1982), 99.
13. Bridenbaugh, *Cities in the Wilderness*, 155.
14. Darrett B. Rutman, *Winthrop's Boston: A Portrait of a Puritan Town, 1630–1649* (New York: W. W. Norton, 1972), 41–67.
15. For a careful study that shows the low degree of urban networks, see Carville V. Earle, *The Evolution of a Tidewater Settlement System: All Hallow's Parish, Maryland, 1650–1783* (Research Paper no. 10, Department of Geography, University of Chicago, 1975), who calculates "urban potentials of an agricultural parish": these show a continuous increase (with only one deviant year) from 1680 to 1789 (table 20). These potentials contrast with the actual development of urban nodes. In figures 9–16 Earle maps the location of occupational specialists, like merchants, ministers, and millwrights, in order to look at the clustering characteristics of urban or potentially urban sites. With the exception of London Town and its court house, there is surprising flux and no clear pattern of urban hierarchy. Richard Wade, *The Urban Frontier: The Rise of Western Cities, 1790–1830* (Cambridge, Mass.: Harvard University Press, 1959). For an example of how a nearby big city pulled away urban functions, see Stephanie G. Wolf, *Urban Village: Family, Community, and Family Structure in Germantown, Pennsylvania, 1683–1800* (Princeton: Princeton University Press, 1976). Quotation from James T. Lemon, "The Urbanization and Development of Eighteenth Century South East Pennsylvania and Adjacent Delaware," *William and Mary Quarterly* 24 (October 1967), 508, 510–511.
16. Walter Christaller, *Central Places of Southern Germany* (Englewood Cliffs, N.J.: Prentice-Hall, 1966); August Losch, *The Economies of Location* (New Haven: Yale University Press, 1954). For a discussion of Philadelphia's economic ties to its hinterland towns and farms, see Diane Lindstrom, *Economic Development in the Philadelphia Region, 1810–1850* (New York: Columbia University Press, 1978).
17. Brian J. L. Berry, "Cities as Systems within Systems of Cities," *Papers*

and Proceedings of the Regional Science Association 13 (1964), 147–163, quotation on 161. This article contains the classic statement of the systems theory view. Berry saw cities as a part of a system that could be studied scientifically by regional science. For the historical application of a looser concept of urban systems, see: Michael P. Conzen, "The Maturing Urban System in the United States, 1840–1910," *Annals of the Association of American Geographers* 67 (March 1977), 88–108; Michael P. Conzen, "A Transport Interpretation of the Growth of Urban Regions: An American Example," *Journal of Historical Geography* 1 (October 1975), 361–382; Allan R. Pred, *Urban Growth and the Circulation of Information: The United States System of Cities, 1790–1840* (Cambridge, Mass.: Harvard University Press, 1973); Allan R. Pred, *Urban Growth and City-Systems in the United States, 1840–1860* (Cambridge, Mass.: Harvard University Press, 1980); Jeffrey Williamson and Joseph Swanson, "The Growth of Cities in the American Northeast, 1820–1870," *Explorations in Entrepreneurial History* IV (Fall 1966) Supplement, 1–101; Eric E. Lampard, "The Evolving System of Cities in the United States: Urbanization and Economic Development," in Harvey S. Perloff and Lowdon Wingo, Jr., eds., *Issues in Urban Economics* (Baltimore: Johns Hopkins University Press, 1968), 81–139.

18. Wyatt W. Belcher, *The Economic Rivalry Between St. Louis and Chicago, 1850–1880* (New York: Columbia University Studies in History, Economics, and Public Law, 1947); James W. Livingood, *The Philadelphia-Baltimore Trade Rivalry, 1780–1860* (Harrisburg: Pennsylvania Historical and Museum Commission, 1947); Jeffrey S. Adler, "Vagging the Demons and Scoundrels: Vagrancy and the Growth of St. Louis, 1830–1861," *Journal of Urban History* 13 (November 1986), 3–30, shows how this rivalry affected even the crime control policy of St. Louis. Michael P. Conzen, *Farming in an Urban Shadow: The Influence of Madison's Proximity on the Agricultural Development of Blooming Grove, Wisconsin* (Madison: State Historical Society of Wisconsin, 1971).

19. For an excellent introduction, see Leslie J. King, *Central Place Theory* (Beverly Hills, Cal.: Sage Press, 1984); Christaller, *Central Places of Southern Germany*; Losch, *Economies of Location*.

20. B. R. Mitchell, *European Historical Statistics, 1750–1970* (New York: Columbia University Press, 1978), 13–14; Department of International Economic and Social Affairs, *Demographic Yearbook* (New York: United Nations, 1983), 268; *Los Angeles Times* (8 April 1984), 11. Geographers debate the relationship of primacy and distributed urban networks to economic development or dependency, political dominance, and other issues: for a succinct summary with bibliography, see Nancy Ettlinger, "A Note on Rank-Size and Primacy: In Pursuit of a Parsimonious Explanation," *Urban Studies* 21 (May 1984), 195–197. For Paris, see Edward Berenson, *Populist Religion and Left-Wing Politics in France, 1830–1852* (Princeton: Princeton University Press, 1984).

21. Pred, *Urban Growth and the Circulation of Information*, 14–15.
22. On coffee house functions see, for instance, Robert G. Albion, *The Rise of New York Port, 1815–1860* (New York: Charles Scribner, 1939), 260–286, where he places them in a larger description of New York City's commercial world.
23. James H. Johnson, *Urban Geography: An Introductory Analysis* (New York: Pergamon Press, 1967), discusses the rank size rule, 99–103; see also, King, *Central Place Theory*.
24. Bridenbaugh, *Cities in the Wilderness*, 109. Bernard Bailyn, *The New England Merchants in the Seventeenth Century* (Cambridge, Mass.: Harvard University Press, 1955), 82, shows how seventeenth-century New England merchants maintained "without exception, close ties—usually kinship relations—with merchants in England"; Albion, *The Rise of New York Port*, 230–241; and Christine L. Heyrman, *Commerce and Culture: The Maritime Communities of Colonial Massachusetts, 1690–1730* (New York: W. W. Norton, 1984).
25. Pred, *Urban Growth and the Circulation of Information*.
26. Gary B. Nash, *The Urban Crucible: Social Change, Political Consciousness, and the Origins of the American Revolution* (Cambridge, Mass.: Harvard University Press, 1979) shows the power of mass politics in the colonial cities and in turn the importance of these cities in the American Revolution.
27. Ken Young and Patricia L. Garside, *Metropolitan London: Politics and Urban Change, 1837–1981* (London: Arnold, 1982), 22–23.
28. Derek Fraser, *Power and Authority in the Victorian City* (Oxford: Blackwell, 1979); D. B. White, *A History of the Corporation of Liverpool, 1835–1914* (Liverpool: Liverpool University Press, 1961); Clive Emsley, *Policing and Its Context, 1750–1870* (London: Macmillan, 1983), 68.
29. Bernard Bailyn, *The Ordeal of Thomas Hutchinson* (Cambridge, Mass.: Harvard University Press, 1974), 12, discusses the prosperous Royalist merchant's extensive property holdings in Boston, his suburban country house, and hundred of acres of farm land. In *The New England Merchants*, Bailyn shows how for merchants "real property was the most secure, if not the only secure, form of investment" (99). As a result, "one commodity absorbed the intense interest of every merchant without exception—land" (101). For a brief exposition of the consuming drive for land as wealth in the sixteenth and seventeenth centuries, see G. R. Elton, "Contentment and Discontent on the Eve of Colonization," in David B. Quinn, ed., *Early Maryland in a Wider World* (Detroit: Wayne State University Press, 1982), 114–118.
30. Peter Clark and Paul Slack, *English Towns in Transition, 1500–1700* (Oxford: Oxford University Press, 1976), 46–61.
31. Albion, *The Rise of New York Port*. The importance of initial advantages in determining city growth relative to other factors, from changing technology of transportation to specialization to size, has generated considerable debate among economists and geographers who

are interested in building general models of growth. For a summary of this literature with extensive bibliographic notes, see Edward K. Muller, "Regional Urbanization and the Selective Growth of Towns in North American Regions," *Journal of Historical Geography* 3 (January 1977), 21–39. Carville V. Earle, "The First English Towns of North America," *Geographical Review* 67 (January 1977), 34–50, argues that the English conceived of the settlements as towns with monopolies, thus deliberately creating small primate towns. Natural advantages favored some over others, but only after the initial settlement decisions had been reached. Thus the process was political. Elsewhere, Earle and Ronald Hoffman, "Urban Development in the Eighteenth-Century South," *Perspectives in American History* X (1976), 7–80, make a different argument, claiming that the nature of the region's staple crops determines the nature of urbanization, in particular of networks; cotton and tobacco needing only minimal port towns, wheat supporting a more developed urban network. Hence the differences between Maryland and the colonies further to the south.

Joseph A. Ernst and H. Roy Merrens, " 'Camden's Turrets Pierce the Skies!' The Urban Process in the Southern Colonies in the Eighteenth Century," *William and Mary Quarterly* 30 (October 1973), 555, make the bizarre argument that size is unimportant relative to economic function: thus tiny southern colonial hamlets that performed vital economic functions constituted cities. Presumably then, a tiny inn or gas station in the middle of the desert or even a turnpike toll booth could be a city, if not a metropolis!

32. Peter N. Carroll, *Puritanism and the Wilderness: The Intellectual Significance of the New England Frontier* (New York: Columbia University Press, 1969), argues that the "idea of a collective society" was contradicted by "endorsement of the subjugation of wild lands" (3). The Puritans' "inability to produce a suitable theory of society . . . reveals the importance of the wilderness" (4). Stilgoe, *Common Landscape*, 52–54, emphasizes the New Englanders' consciousness of a dichotomy between the town *and* its cultivated fields and cleared meadows versus the uncontrolled and feared wilderness. Even the woodlots were often considered wilderness.

33. Louis Hartz, *The Founding of New Societies: Studies in the History of the United States, Latin America, South Africa, Canada, and Australia* (New York: Harcourt, 1964), 1–6, has developed the notion of a "fragment culture." Hartz draws certain conclusions for this concept which I do not intend to invoke here, in particular the notion that the "fragments" of European culture in the new world ceased their evolution but continued to progress in Europe. The founding fathers saw the Constitution as documenting the United States's escape from feudal ties.

34. Gideon Sjoberg, *The Preindustrial City: Past and Present* (New York: Free Press, 1960), 91–92. For a summary of the declining utility of walls see Josef W. Konvitz, *The Urban Millennium: The City-Build-*

ing Process from the Early Middle Ages to the Present (Carbondale: Southern Illinois University Press, 1985), 47–53.

35. John Borchert, "American Metropolitan Evolution," *American Geographical Review* 57 (July 1967), 301–332; note that Warner, *Urban Wilderness*, acknowledges his periodization scheme to Borchert, 60.

36. Johnson, *Urban Geography*, discusses density gradients, 52–57, 172–173; see also, Werner Z. Hirsch, *Urban Economics* (New York: Macmillan, 1984), 60–67, 72, 76.

37. Kenneth A. Lockridge, "Land, Population, and the Evolution of New England Society, 1630–1790," *Past & Present* 39 (April 1968), 62–80; Kenneth T. Jackson, "Urban Deconcentration in the Nineteenth Century: A Statistical Inquiry," in Leo F. Schnore, ed., *The New Urban History: Quantitative Explorations by American Historians* (Princeton, N.J.: Princeton University Press, 1975), 110–142; John W. Reps, *Town Planning in Frontier America* (Princeton: Princeton University Press, 1971), quotation from 428. Reps cites the authorities Alberti and Thomas More, who in the fifteenth and sixteenth centuries had advocated moving noisy or smelly industry outside of the city (7, 12). In addition he cites a 1695 law in Annapolis, which required that all trades that "annoy, or disquiet the neighbors or inhabitants of the town" must be located outside of its boundaries (135).

38. Richard R. Beeman, "The New Social History and the Search for 'Community' in Colonial America," *American Quarterly* 29 (Fall 1977), 422–443.

39. Albion, *New York Port*, 373–386, describes the early nineteenth-century competition of New York City with Boston, Philadelphia, and Baltimore for the "Western front," the opening up of cities and the agricultural west through rail and canal trade.

40. Henry C. Binford, *The First Suburbs: Residential Communities on the Boston Periphery, 1815-1860* (Chicago: University of Chicago Press, 1985). Binford establishes that the suburban communities of Boston preceded commuting, that they were independent political and cultural communities, "trying to exploit opportunities available at the city's edge" (2). Thus he makes clear that even for suburbs, politics determined transportation shape, the antitechnological determinist position this book develops. Bridenbaugh, *Cities in the Wilderness* (306), notes "the unique development . . . the appearance of suburbs" with mansions for the wealthy in the 1740s. Boston and New York, he says, remained compact, but the wealthy there may simply have maintained two places of residence, thus avoiding the appearance of suburban development. And the very wealthiest Bostonians, like John Winthrop, from the outset, granted themselves huge country estates to provide incomes (Rutman, *Winthrop's Boston*, 45).

41. The work on individual New England towns has been systematically tested for New Hampshire and confirms the finding that when towns reached an optimal density, out-migration began to occur. Darrett B. Rutman, "People in Process: The New Hampshire Towns of the Eigh-

teenth Century," *Journal of Urban History* 1 (1975), 268–292; see also, Charles Wetherell, "A Note on Hierarchical Clustering," *Historical Methods* 10 (Summer 1977), 109–116.

42. Jon A. Peterson, "The City Beautiful Movement: Forgotten Origins and Lost Meanings," *Journal of Urban History* 2 (August 1976), 415–434.

43. Population pressure and the resolution of selective out-migration functioned in small towns from the colonial era onward. Philip J. Greven, Jr., *Four Generations: Population, Land, and Family in Colonial Andover, Massachusetts* (Ithaca: Cornell University Press, 1970) established the pattern of family control over population relative to the increasingly scarce agricultural resources for seventeenth-century New England towns. John P. Demos, *A Little Commonwealth: Family Life in Plymouth Colony* (New York: Oxford University Press, 1970), 136, 499, argues for social tension brought on by community. Douglas L. Jones, "The Strolling Poor: Transiency in Eighteenth Century Massachusetts," *Journal of Social History* 3 (January 1975), 28–54. Daniel S. Smith, "The Estimates of Early American Historical Demographers: Two Steps Forward, One Step Back, What Steps in the Future?" *Historical Methods* 12 (Winter 1979), 24–38, has shown how colonial towns with limited growth possibilities used migration as a "safety-valve." Hal S. Barron, *Those Who Stayed Behind: Rural Society in Nineteenth-Century New England* (New York: Cambridge University Press, 1985) shows how Chelsea, New Hampshire, handled limited opportunities for growth and kept a stable community through the last half of the nineteenth century through no in-migration and the out-migration of older children.

44. Nash, *The Urban Crucible*, 126–127, 172, 179.

45. At least through the first half of the nineteenth century, cities constructed public market buildings. See Don H. Doyle, *The Social Order of a Frontier Community: Jacksonville, Illinois, 1825–1870* (Urbana: University of Illinois Press, 1978), 195, for a discussion of a small city's market built in 1834.

46. James Stirling Young, *The Washington Community, 1800–28* (New York: Columbia University Press, 1966).

47. Ibid., 19–20.

48. Michel Foucault, *Discipline and Punish: The Birth of the Prison*, trans., Alan Sheridan (New York: Pantheon Books, 1977); Michel Foucault, *The History of Sexuality*, trans. Robert Hurley (New York: Pantheon Books, 1978).

49. See Jon C. Teaford, *The Municipal Revolution in America: Origins of Modern Urban Government, 1650–1825* (Chicago: University of Chicago Press, 1975), 39–43, which discusses Boston's refusal to license a market, casting an interesting light upon the benefits and costs of city market control.

50. Ibid.,

51. Ibid., 97, 99, 106, 115. Teaford argues that economic ideologies of unrestricted trade and freedom from governmental interference mo-

tivated the sweeping away of the city's regulatory power. But the early nineteenth-century belief was that the "power to tax involves the power to destroy," which suggests that postrevolutionary city charters were not actually designed to facilitate Adam Smith's principles of free trade. This famous view on tax as a power to destroy was expressed in 1819 by Chief Justice John Marshall in *McCulloch* v. *Maryland*.

3 Growth Begins

1. During the Revolution, the British occupation of the city sent the population over 30,000, according to Oscar T. Barck, Jr., *New York During the War for Independence* (New York: Columbia University Press, 1981), 215. Ira Rosenwaike, *Population History of New York City* (Syracuse: Syracuse University Press, 1972), 8, reports from Evarts B. Greene and Virginia D. Harrington, *American Population Before the Federal Census of 1790* (New York, 1932), a population of 21,863 for the whole of the island of Manhattan in 1771, 13,046 for 1756. Of course, there was no federal census prior to 1790. By using the log of the city's population from 1790 to 1870, which is a virtual straight line, one can estimate the previous two decade's populations without the mid-1770s wartime bulges. These give population estimates of 14,762 for 1770 and 22,971 for 1780, considerably less than those in the colonial censuses.
Constant = 4.36, coefficient = 0.192, R = 0.9978, R^2 = 0.996. Source: *1970 Census of Population: Characteristics of the Population*, vol. 1, Pt 1., Sect. 1, (Washington, D.C.: Government Printing Office, June 1973) 116–119. England, of course, did see some enormous new cities constructed in the nineteenth century in the industrial midlands. Nevertheless, most of its cities built upon the legal precedents of ancient charters and corporate privileges.
2. Jan de Vries, *European Urbanization, 1500–1800* (London: Methuen, 1984), 21–22, 53–54, deals deftly with this problem, the "tar baby of urban studies."
3. Standard Metropolitan Statistical Areas, or SMSAs, introduced as an urban accounting measure in 1950, are designed to capture the "natural" boundaries of cities, many of which are now composed of dozens of smaller political entities but whose population merges across boundaries to make up one large urban area. These measures have been improved by a newer measure, the Standard Consolidated Statistical Area, which ignores the county boundaries used in the SMSA measure. See Bureau of the Census, *Standard Consolidated Statistical Areas and Standard Metropolitan Statistical Areas; Defined by the Office of Management and Budget, January 1981* (Washington, D.C.: Government Printing Office, 1981), and Ira Rosenwaike, "A Critical Examination of the Designation of Standard Metropolitan Statistical Areas," *Social Forces* 48 (March 1970), 322–333. About three-fourths of the U.S. population lived in SMSAs in 1980. *Statis-*

*tical Abstract of the United States: National Data Book and Guide
to Sources, 1982–83* (Washington, D.C.: Government Printing Office,
1982), 649.
4. Brian J. L. Berry, "The Counterurbanization Process: America since
1970," in Berry, ed., *Urbanization and Counterurbanization* (Beverly
Hills: Sage Press, 1976). *Statistical Abstract, 1982–1983*, 15.
5. de Vries, *European Urbanization*, 45, 74, 146.
6. The relative growth rates of cities under 10,000 compared to those
larger may be estimated by regression, using the numbers in each
category by decade.

CITIES OVER 10,000 POPULATION PREDICTED BY CITIES UNDER
10,000 POPULATION, 1790–1970

Dependent Variable: Cities Under 10,000[a]

Variable	Coefficient	(SEE)	T(DF = 17)	Prob.
Cities Over 10,000[a]	1.226	(0.095)	12.85	0.00000
Constant	66.96			

R^2 = 0.907; Prob. = 0.00000; Durbin-Watson Test = 1.143

[a]First differences.
SOURCE: Data calculated from Bureau of the Census, *Historical Statistics of the United States, Colonial Times to 1970* (Washington, D.C.: Government Printing Office, 1975), 11.

7. James W. Vance, *The Merchant's World: The Geography of Whole-
saling* (Englewood Cliffs, N.J.: Prentice-Hall, 1970). De Vries, *European Urbanization*, 159–161, citing and adding to Fernand Braudel's
Afterthoughts on Capitalism and Material Civilization (Baltimore:
Johns Hopkins University Press, 1977), 85–86, traces as the metropolitan centers of the European and world economy, Venice (fourteenth century), Antwerp, Genoa, Amsterdam (seventeenth and early
eighteenth century), and London up to 1929, "until the mantle
crossed the Atlantic Ocean to New York" (deVries, 160). In 1888,
Mayor Abram S. Hewitt analyzed the city's prospects, charting how
"its imperial destiny as the greatest city in the world is assured by
natural causes, which cannot be thwarted except by the folly and
neglect of its inhabitants." In particular he emphasized the need to
maintain or improve the city's harbor and docks, its streets (which
needed paving), rapid transit, parks, and to keep taxes light. Cited by
David C. Hammack, *Power and Society: Greater New York at the
Turn of the Century* (New York: Russell Sage Foundation, 1981), 192–
193.
For a discussion of probable sizes and numbers of British cities
and towns, see Peter Clark and Paul Slack, eds., *English Towns in
Transition, 1500–1700* (New York: Oxford University Press, 1976),
8–9 and maps 1 and 2.

8. English statistics calculated from data in C. M. Law, "The Growth of the Urban Population in England and Wales, 1801–1911," *Transactions of the Institute of British Geographers* 41 (June 1967) 125–143. U.S. statistics from Rosenwaike, *Population History*, 58, and the Bureau of the Census, *Historical Statistics of the United States, Colonial Times to 1970* (Washington, D. C.: Government Printing Office, 1975). Note that Pred, *Urban Growth and the Circulation of Information: The United States System of Cities, 1790–1840* (Cambridge, Mass.: Harvard University Press, 1973) has emphasized New York's dominance by showing how it has remained the primary metropolis. The point I wish to make here is comparative; that while number one, the city most emphatically was not the only metropolis.

9. George Rogers Taylor, *The Transportation Revolution, 1815–1860* (New York: Rinehart, 1951); Edward K. Muller, "Selective Urban Growth in the Middle Ohio Valley, 1800–1860," *Geographical Review* 66 (April 1976), 199.

10. Robert W. Fogel, *Railroads and American Economic Growth: Essays in Econometric History* (Baltimore: Johns Hopkins University Press, 1964) and Albert Fishlow, *American Railroads and the Transformation of the Antebellum Economy* (Cambridge, Mass.: Harvard University Press, 1965).

11. John Borchert, "American Metropolitan Evolution," *American Geographical Review* 57 (July 1967), 301–332. In some places, North Dakota, for instance, railroad companies did determine both location and forms of small towns, see John C. Hudson, *Plains Country Towns* (Minneapolis: University of Minnesota Press, 1985). For a general discussion, see Michael Conzen, "The American Urban System in the Nineteenth Century," in David T. Herbert and Ronald J. Johnston, eds., *Geography and the Urban Environment: Progress in Research and Applications* (London, 1981), IV, 295–347.

12. Herbert W. Rice, "Early Rivalry among Wisconsin Cities for Railroads," *Wisconsin Magazine of History* 35 (Autumn 1951), 15, shows that between 1836 and 1859, 125 Wisconsin cities and towns were granted charters for railroad corporations: of these only fourteen built any railroad at all.

13. See the summary of the federal support of roads in Department of Transportation, Federal Highway Administration, *America's Highways, 1776–1976: A History of the Federal-Aid Program* (Washington, D.C.: Government Printing Office, 1977), 16–27. Carter Goodrich, "National Planning of Internal Improvements," *Political Science Quarterly* LXIII (March 1948), 16–44, provides a classic summary and critique of early federal transportation aid: although the focus of his article is federal, it is clear that local transportation seemed far less important that did national. One can only surmise that the historian's interest in national underwriting of long transport routes came as a consequence of local, urban successes, and the unexamined assumption that national transportation was somehow more important to economic growth than local.

14. Roberta B. Miller, *City and Hinterland: A Case Study of Urban Regional Growth and Regional Development* (Westport, Conn.: Greenwood Press, 1979); Hal S. Barron, *Those Who Stayed Behind: Rural Society in Nineteenth-Century New England* (New York: Cambridge University Press, 1984); Hal S. Barron, "Rediscovering the Majority: The New Rural History of the Nineteenth-Century North," *Historical Methods* 19 (Fall 1986), 141–152. Robert Doherty, *Society and Power: Five New England Towns, 1800–1860* (Amherst: University of Massachusetts Press, 1977) examines the mobility patterns of five small towns, including a declining one, in a regional network. Stephanie Graumman Wolf, *Urban Village: Population, Community, and Family Structure in Germantown, Pennsylvania 1683–1800* (Princeton: Princeton University Press, 1976); John C. Hudson, *Plains Country Towns* (Minneapolis: University of Minnesota Press, 1985). Edward K. Muller, "Selective Urban Growth," and also "Regional Urbanization and the Selective Urban Growth of Towns in the North American Regions," *Journal of Historical Geography* 3 (January 1977), 21–39.

15. On entrepreneurial rivalry, see Harry N. Scheiber, "Urban Rivalry and Internal Improvements in the Old Northwest, 1820–1860," *Ohio History* 71 (October 1962), 227–239, or the classic, James W. Livingood, *The Philadelphia-Baltimore Trade Rivalry, 1780–1860* (Harrisburg: Pennsylvania Historical and Museum Commission, 1947). See Harold L. Platt, *City Building in the New South: The Growth of Public Services in Houston, Texas, 1830–1915* (Philadelphia: Temple University Press, 1983), Chapter 1, and 175–176, for a sensitive analysis of one side of a local rivalry, its entrepreneurial, environmental, and to a lesser extent systematic facets. H. T. Johns, *Duluth*, (Duluth: n.p., c.1873), 1.

16. Earl Pomeroy, *The Pacific Slope: A History of California, Oregon, Washington, Idaho, Utah and Nevada* (New York: Alfred A. Knopf, 1965); Lyle Dorsett, *The Queen City: A History of Denver* (Denver: Pruett, 1977); *1970 Census of Population: Characteristics of the Population*, vol. 1, Pt. 1, Sect. 1, (Washington, D.C.: Government Printing Office, June 1973), 116–119.

17. Ellen Liebman, *California Farmland: A History of Large Agricultural Landholdings* (Totowa, N.J.: Rowman & Allanheld, 1983) analyzes the historical growth of California's large land holdings, identifying quite different reasons and usages for such parcels over the past two centuries. Essential to her explanation is the role of government—in the Spanish period, the explicit policy of nonprivate land holding and urban-oriented settlement patterns; and in the second half of the nineteenth century, the creation of parcels and private sales schemes of state and federal governments, both facilitating large-scale land accumulation patterns.

18. Jane M. Pederson, "The Country Visitor: Patterns of Hospitality in Rural Wisconsin, 1880–1925," *Agricultural History* 58 (July 1984), 347–364.

19. *Statistical Abstract, 1982–1983,* 16, 20.
20. David Clark, *Urban Geography* (London: Croom Helm, 1982), 49, cited in deVries, *European Urbanization,* 6.

4 The Emerging Service City

1. See Jon C. Teaford, *The Municipal Revolution in America: Origins of Modern Urban Government, 1650-1825* (Chicago: University of Chicago Press, 1975), 3–34. Teaford emphasizes the reforming zeal of the Massachusetts Bay colonists, without pointing out their caution in reminding England of the precarious state of their charter. One wonders how much this resulted from reforming zeal and how much from a rural power bias created in the fifty years prior to the revocation. Nathan Mathews, Jr., *The City Government of Boston* (Boston: Rockwell and Churchill, 1895), 164, discusses Boston's first charter of 1822.
2. Marc A. Weiss, *The Rise of the Community Builders: American Real Estate Developers, Urban Planners, and the Creation of Modern Residential Subdivisions* (New York: Columbia University Press, 1987).
3. Bayrd Still characterizes the growth of formal, bureaucratized city services in Milwaukee as "inevitable," even though his own detailed research shows nothing of the kind. Quoted by David B. Tyack, *The One Best System: A History of American Urban Education* (Cambridge, Mass.: Harvard University Press, 1974), 31.

   For a general discussion of resistance to roads in the late eighteenth and early nineteenth centuries see John R. Stilgoe, *Common Landscape of America, 1580 to 1845* (New Haven: Yale University Press, 1982), 128–132. For the specific local instance of resistance to Slater, see Jonathan Prude, *The Coming of Industrial Order: Town and Factory Life in Rural Massachusetts, 1810–1860* (New York: Cambridge University Press, 1983), 170–173.
4. See Teaford, *The Municipal Revolution,* 18, 52.
5. Sidney L. Harring, *Policing a Class Society: The Experience of American Cities, 1865–1915* (New Brunswick, N.J.: Rutgers University Press, 1983); Anthony M. Platt, *The Child Savers: The Invention of Juvenile Delinquency* (Chicago: University of Chicago Press, 1969). See Michael B. Katz, *Poverty and Policy in American History* (New York: Academic Press, 1983) for an empirical analysis of poor relief systems in New York from the social control perspective. See also Andrew Scull and Stanley Cohen, eds., *Social Control and the State: Comparative and Historical Essays* (Oxford: Martin Robertson, 1983). For critiques of the social control thesis as it relates to social welfare, see Walter I. Trattner, ed., *Social Welfare or Social Control? Some Historical Reflections on Regulating the Poor* (Knoxville: University of Tennessee Press, 1983); Eric H. Monkkonen, *Police in Urban America, 1860–1920* (New York: Cambridge University Press, 1981).
6. Racist utterances, ethnic hostility, and class bias have only become unfashionable and in bad taste in the past thirty years or so. Virtually

any nineteenth- or early twentieth-century newspaper contains statements outrageous enough to offend the sensibilities of any contemporary reader. When in the post–World War II era scholars began to become more sensitive to such explicit biases, they began to question the benign motives of earlier social activists. The contemporary historian should feel obligated to point out racism, sexism, and class bias, but must be equally cautious in making such negative social attitudes or actions the sole explanation for past behavior. It is important and appropriate to be aware of the unfair aspects of crime control, but one must not let these aspects become the central focus of analysis. In letting them dominate, far more significant underlying dynamics can disappear. For a sustained critique of the erroneous thinking that the social control approach has fostered, see Thomas L. Haskell, "Capitalism and the Origins of the Humanitarian Sensibility, Part I," *American Historical Review* 90 (April 1985), 339–361.

A major conceptual complexity in the broad history of crime and its control in the United States emerges from the disparity between the levels of government involved in defining and enforcing the criminal law. While the definition of criminal behavior has always been predominantly at the level of the colonial or state government, certain offenses have been reserved for higher sovereignty. However, the government level which assumes the greatest obligation for crime control has changed considerably from the seventeenth century, reflecting in part the changing nature of the state itself. The publicly imputed sense of obligation first grew from its traditional level with the adoption of city- and state-run penitentiaries in the late eighteenth and early nineteenth century, then escalated with urban policing through the second half of the nineteenth century. Finally the federal government assumed new responsibilities in the early twentieth century with the newly designated federal crimes of kidnapping and bank robbery and the creation of the FBI. See Ernest K. Alix, *Ransom Kidnapping in America, 1874–1974: The Creation of a Capital Crime* (Carbondale: Southern Illinois University Press, 1978); David K. Watson, "Growth of the Criminal Law of the United States," *Congressional Serial Set*, 57th Congress, 1st Session, Doc. 362 (1902).

7. For a classic early empirical analysis purporting to show how urbanization causes crime, see Marshall B. Clinard, "The Process of Urbanization and Criminal Behavior," *American Journal of Sociology* 48 (September 1942), 202–213. Monkkonen, *The Dangerous Class: Crime and Poverty in Columbus, Ohio, 1860–1885* (Cambridge, Mass.: Harvard University Press, 1975) builds a criticism of the hypothesis that urbanization causes crime.

8. Roger Lane, *Violent Death in the City: Suicide, Accident and Murder in Nineteenth-Century Philadelphia* (Cambridge, Mass.: Harvard University Press, 1979).

9. Ted R. Gurr, "Historical Trends in Violent Crime: A Critical Review of the Evidence," in Norval Morris and Michael Tonry, eds., *Crime and Justice: An Annual Review of Research*, vol. 3 (Chicago: Uni-

versity of Chicago Press, 1981), 295–353; for England and Wales, see V. A. C. Gatrell, "The Decline of Theft and Violence in Victorian and Edwardian England," in Gatrell, B. P. Lenman, and G. Parker, eds., *Crime and the Law: The Social History of Crime in Western Europe since 1850* (London: Europa, 1980), 238–370.

10. Richard Block, ed., *Victimization and Fear of Crime: World Perspectives* (Washington, D.C.: Bureau of Justice Statistics, 1984); Dan A. Lewis and Greta Salem, *Fear of Crime: Incivility and the Production of a Social Problem* (New Brunswick, N.J.: Transaction Books, 1986). For a brief summary of the relationship of reporting to crime, see Herbert Jacob and Robert L. Lineberry, "Governmental Responses to Crime," Executive Summary (Evanston, Ill.: Northwestern University, 1981), 12–14.

11. Arthur P. Scott, *Criminal Law in Colonial Virginia* (Chicago: University of Chicago Press, 1930), 218–219, cites the example of Williamsburg, where four night watchmen were voted annual salaries in 1722; the continuity of this arrangement is doubtful. Philadelphia's first night watch was not created until 1702, and existed as a voluntary watch until 1751, when a paid watch was created. All persons chosen by the council had to serve on the voluntary force or were fined. Howard O. Sproggle, *The Philadelphia Police, Past and Present* (Philadelphia, 1887), 39–44; Theodore N. Ferdinand, "Criminality, the Courts, and the Constabulary in Boston: 1702–1967," *Journal of Research in Crime and Delinquency* 17 (July 1980), 193.

12. Harring, *Policing a Class Society*, 33–34, claims that there was a "direct link" between riots like the Chicago lager beer riots and the creation of the police. I fundamentally disagree, see Monkkonen, *Police in Urban America*, 49–58. Wilbur R. Miller, *Cops and Bobbies: Police Authority in New York and London, 1830–1870* (Chicago: University of Chicago Press, 1976).

13. For resistance to uniforms, see Monkkonen, *Police in Urban America*, 44–46.

14. Gustave Beaumont and Alexis de Tocqueville, *On the Penitentiary System in the United States and Its Application in France* (Carbondale: Southern Illinois University Press, 1979, 1st American edition, 1833), 55.

15. Pieter Spierenburg, ed., *The Emergence of Carceral Institutions: Prisons, Galleys and Lunatic Asylums, 1550–1900*, Centrum voor Maatschappijgeschiedenis, 12 (Rotterdam: Erasmus University, 1984), 22–24; Gary B. Nash, "Poverty and Poor Relief in Pre-Revolutionary Philadelphia," *William and Mary Quarterly* 33 (January 1976), 3–30. Reflecting their medieval perspective, the early English colonizers of Virginia saw cities and towns as institutions of social control, since their inhabitants could be under surveillance. See Sylvia D. Fries, *The Urban Idea in Colonial America* (Philadelphia: Temple University Press, 1977), 110–111; Stephen S. Webb, "Army and Empire: English Garrison Government in Britain and America, 1569 to 1763," *William and Mary Quarterly*, 3d ser., 34 (January 1977), 1–31.

16. Nicole H. Rafter, *Partial Justice: Women in State Prisons, 1800–1935* (Boston: Northeastern University Press, 1984), 35. Don H. Doyle, *The Social Order of a Frontier Community: Jacksonville, Illinois, 1825–1870* (Urbana: University of Illinois Press, 1978), 62–91, devotes a chapter to Jacksonville's institution and railroad hunting: it succeeded in getting some state institutions, like the deaf and dumb asylum, but failed to get the penitentiary. See W. David Lewis, *From Newgate to Dannemora: The Rise of the Penitentiary in New York, 1796–1848* (Ithaca: Cornell University Press, 1965); Negley K. Teeters, *The Origins of the Penitentiary: The Walnut Street Jail at Philadelphia, 1773–1835* (Philadelphia: Pennsylvania Prison Society, 1955).

17. Roger Lane, *Policing the City: Boston, 1822–1885* (Cambridge, Mass.: Harvard University Press, 1967); James F. Richardson, *The New York Police, Colonial Times to 1901* (New York: Oxford University Press, 1970); Lowell M. Limpus, *History of the New York Fire Department* (New York: Dutton, 1940), 243, quoting an 1864 report by the volunteers which made a last ditch attempt at self-reform. For a different interpretation, see Richard B. Calhoun, "New York Fire Department Modernization, 1865–1870: A Civil War Legacy," *New-York Historical Society Quarterly* (January/April 1976), 7–34.

18. Bruce Laurie, "Fire Companies and Gangs in Southwark: The 1840s," 71–87, and David R. Johnson, "Crime Patterns in Philadelphia, 1840–1870," 103, both in Allan F. Davis and Mark Haller, eds., *The Peoples of Philadelphia: A History of Ethnic Groups and Lower-Class Life, 1790–1840* (Philadelphia: Temple University Press, 1973); *New York Times* (3 January 1853), p. 6, col. 1.

19. Limpus, *History of the New York Fire Department*, 187–188, 196–198, 210–211, 241–242. Letty Anderson, "Hard Choices: Supplying Water to New England Towns," *Journal of Interdisciplinary History* XV (Autumn 1984), 216–217, discusses fire insurance in relation to water supply, an essential element of the changing fire fighting technology. In the 1880s, lower fire insurance rates for cities with water systems were assured, and by 1888, she notes, the American Water Works Association claimed insurance rate reductions of 20% to 50% in towns with adequate water supply. Essentially, one may argue, the insurance industry rationalized and distributed the risks of fire so that it made economic sense for property owners to opt for higher taxes imposed by municipal water and fire fighting. Prior to such cost sharing, property owners would be willing to take the risk that *their* property would not be destroyed by fire.

20. Judith W. Leavitt, *The Healthiest City: Milwaukee and the Politics of Health Reform* (Princeton: Princeton University Press, 1982), 42, dates the creation of the Milwaukee Board of Health to 1867: the police, created in 1874, provided the city with regular, if low-level, health control in parallel with the Board's more direct and medically oriented work. While one attended to basic sanitation problems— open sewers, improper disposal of slaughterhouse offal—the other worked on more specific diseases.

21. For my discussion of the many activities of the police, see Monkkonen, *Police in Urban America*, 86–128. T. D. Woolsey, "Nature and Sphere of Police Power," *Journal of Social Science* (1871), 97–114: this article comes at what may be an important transitional point in the concept of the police power of the state. Originally it was considered, as a legal concept, to express the power of any state entity to control the order and housekeeping, in a behavioral sense, of its inhabitants and visitors. Woolsey's article uses the concept of a dangerous class to reorient the term toward the exclusive control of criminal behavior. Twenty-five years later, authors writing on police power did not even mention earlier and broader concepts: by the end of the nineteenth century the term applied specifically to the duties and obligations of the city police departments in the very narrowest sense. See for the latter, H. C. Kudlich, "The Abuse of Police Power," *The Forum* (1897–98), 487–500.
22. Seymour J. Mandelbaum, *Boss Tweed's New York* (New York: John Wiley, 1966).

5 From Closed Corporation to Electoral Democracy

1. Judith M. Diamondstone, "Philadelphia's Municipal Corporation, 1701–1776," *Pennsylvania Magazine of History* XC (April 1966), 183–201.
2. Chilton Williamson, *American Suffrage: From Property to Democracy, 1760–1860* (Princeton: Princeton University Press, 1960).
3. Jon C. Teaford, *The Municipal Revolution in America: Origins of Modern Urban Government, 1650–1825* (Chicago: University of Chicago Press, 1975), 68–90, provides the details of the charter challenges and revisions. Amy Bridges, *A City in the Republic: Antebellum New York and the Origins of Machine Politics* (New York: Cambridge University Press, 1984).
4. Edward M. Cook, Jr., *The Fathers of the Towns: Leadership and Community Structure in Eighteenth-Century New England* (Baltimore: Johns Hopkins University Press, 1976), 98, 111–112.
5. Lee Benson introduced this concept in his analysis of voter support for Andrew Jackson, *The Concept of Jacksonian Democracy: New York as a Test Case* (Princeton: Princeton University Press, 1961); see also the review article by Richard L. McCormick, "Ethno-Cultural Interpretations of Nineteenth-Century American Voting Behavior," *Political Science Quarterly* 89 (June 1974), 351–377.
6. Alexander Keyssar, *Out of Work: The First Century of Unemployment in Massachusetts* (New York: Cambridge University Press, 1986), 262.
7. Terrence McDonald, *The Parameters of Urban Fiscal Policy: Socioeconomic Change, Political Culture and Fiscal Policy in San Francisco, 1850–1906* (Berkeley, Los Angeles, London: University of California Press, 1986), 240, states that "the public sector was bound by

chains that the policymakers themselves had formed." McDonald also shows how pluralistic reform came from the elite boss, with James Phelan's explicit electoral strategy to woo voters to a new, positive conception of the state. "Reform in San Francisco, therefore, was forced, because of its politically insurgent status, to be pluralistic in its class and ethnic bases" (260). Burton W. Folsom, Jr., *Urban Capitalists: Entrepreneurs and City Growth in Pennsylvania's Lackawanna and Lehigh Regions, 1800–1920* (Baltimore: Johns Hopkins University Press, 1981), 76, quotes from the Scranton *Republican* (18, 25 May and 8 June 1866).

8. Robert A. Dahl, *Who Governs? Democracy and Power in an American City* (New Haven: Yale University Press, 1961) developed this scenario based upon a prosopographical analysis of the elected officials of New Haven. For an application of Dahl's typology to the mayors of Chicago, see Donald S. Bradley and Mayer N. Zald, "From Commercial Elite to Political Administrators: The Recruitment of the Mayors of Chicago," *American Journal of Sociology* 71 (September 1965), 153–167. Michael H. Frisch, *Town into City: Springfield, Massachusetts, and the Meaning of Community, 1840–1880* (Cambridge, Mass.: Harvard University Press, 1972), 243–244, shows that Dahl's model obscures at least at much as it illuminates about Springfield between 1840 and 1880. Working-class aldermen actually decreased in proportional representation by 1880, although Frisch's narrative suggests that they regained power in the next two decades.

9. For a book that clears up much Tweed apocrypha, see Leo Hershkowitz, *Tweed's New York: Another Look* (Garden City, N.Y.: Anchor Press, 1977).

10. The four biographies here are based on articles in Melvin G. Holli and Peter d'A. Jones, eds., *Biographical Dictionary of American Mayors, 1820–1980: Big City Mayors, Baltimore, Boston, Buffalo, Chicago, Cincinnati, Cleveland, Detroit, Los Angeles, Milwaukee, New Orleans, New York, Philadelphia, Pittsburgh, San Francisco, St. Louis* (Westport, Conn.: Greenwood Press, 1981). These are: (Lawrence) Jacob Judd, 211–212; (Coman) Leo Hershkowitz, 75; (Low) W. Roger Biles, 221–222; (Wagner) Lurton W. Blasingame, 377–378.

11. David M. Tucker, *Memphis Since Crump: Bossism, Blacks, and Civic Reformers, 1948–1968* (Knoxville: University of Tennessee Press, 1980), 17–39.

12. Blaine A. Brownell, "The Urban South Comes of Age, 1900–1940," in Brownell and David R. Goldfield, *The City in Southern History: The Growth of Urban Civilization in the South* (Port Washington, N.Y.: Kennikat, 1977), 142–143.

William H. Pease and Jane H. Pease, *The Web of Progress: Private Values and Public Styles in Boston and Charleston, 1828–1843* (New York: Oxford University Press, 1985), 224. The Peases argue that Boston's entrepreneurs operated in a friendly political milieu, but that they did not use it or expect it to supply them capital or decrease risk (39). Charleston's entrepreneurs, on the other hand, acted only when the government would support their activities (52). This limited their scope of activity and contributed to a less aggressive entrepreneurial community. The Pease's argument depends on an analysis of a large sample of elites, economic and political. They present the results of their careful collective biographies in table A-4 (236). A reanalysis of the tables shows that while their assertions are statistically significant, the size of the differences is not substantively large. For instance, for the two cities' economic elites to have had exactly the same levels of political participation, 18 of 1,000 in Boston's economic elite would have to have been more active, and 17 of 424 in Charleston's would have to have been less active. These are quite small differences, some of which may be due to Boston's much greater size. For a social analysis of the backgrounds of Atlanta office holders, see Eugene J. Watts, *The Social Bases of City Politics: Atlanta, 1865–1903* (Westport, Conn.: Greenwood Press, 1978).

13. Folsom, *Urban Capitalists*, 76.
14. See McDonald, *The Parameters of Urban Fiscal Policy.*
15. Note that because smaller cities displayed more of the booster spirit, the older eastern cities seemed to be less self-promoting, but this was simply a matter of size, rather than any inherent difference. Carl Abbott, *Boosters and Businessmen: Popular Economic Thought and Urban Growth in the Antebellum Middle West* (Westport, Conn.: Greenwood Press, 1981), 206, contrasts the East with the rest of the United States, ignoring smaller eastern towns, and focusing on the historical literature of antiurbanism which came from reformers. For a discussion of eastern boosterism in a small city, see Carl Abbott, "Norfolk in the New Century: The Jamestown Exposition and Urban Boosterism," *Virginia Magazine of History and Biography* 85 (1977), 86–96; for the South, see Justin Fuller, "Boom Towns and Blast Furnaces: Town Promotion in Alabama, 1885–1893," *Alabama Review* 29 (1976), 37–48. Robert Higgs, "Cities and Yankee Ingenuity, 1870–1914," in Kenneth T. Jackson and Stanley K. Schultz, eds., *Cities in American History* (New York: Alfred A. Knopf, 1972), 16–22. Holli and Jones, *Biographical Dictionary of American Mayors, 1820–1980.*
16. Don H. Doyle, *The Social Order of a Frontier Community: Jacksonville, Illinois, 1825–1870* (Urbana: University of Illinois Press, 1978). For local government in Jacksonville, see Don H. Doyle, "Chaos and Community in a Frontier Town: Jacksonville, Illinois, 1825–1860" (Ph. D. diss., Northwestern University, 1973), 266–280. For a systematic and rich study that intentionally avoids a focus on large cities, see J. Rogers Hollingsworth and Ellen Jane Hollingsworth, *Dimensions in Urban History: Historical and Social Science Perspectives on Middle-Size American Cities* (Madison: University of Wisconsin Press, 1979). Henry Binford, *The First Suburbs: Residential Communities on the Boston Periphery, 1815–1860* (Chicago: University of Chicago Press, 1985), 154.
17. Michael H. Frisch, *Town into City: Springfield, Massachusetts, and the Meaning of Community, 1840–1880* (Cambridge, Mass.: Harvard

University Press, 1972); Stuart M. Blumin, *The Urban Threshold: Growth and Change in a Nineteenth-Century American Community* (Chicago: University of Chicago Press, 1976); Lewis Atherton, *Main Street on the Middle Border* (Bloomington: Indiana University Press, 1954); Robert Dykstra, *The Cattle Towns* (New York: Alfred A. Knopf, 1968).

18. Michael Conzen, "The Maturing Urban System in the United States, 1840–1910," *Annals of the Association of American Geographers* 67 (1977), 88–108.

19. Sinclair Lewis, *Babbitt* (New York: Harcourt, 1922). *Chicago Press and Tribune*, 4 January 1859, quoted by Abbott, *Boosters and Businessmen*, 128. See Abbott, 227–258, for an extensive and valuable bibliography of materials on boosterism, government, and economic growth.

20. Folsom, *Urban Capitalists*; Daniel J. Walkowitz, *Worker City, Company Town: Iron and Cotton-Worker Protest in Troy and Cohoes, New York, 1855–84* (Urbana: University of Illinois Press, 1978); Margaret F. Byington, *Homestead: The Households of a Mill Town* (Pittsburgh: University of Pittsburgh Press, 1974).

21. On boosterism generally, see Daniel J. Boorstin, *The Americans: The National Experience* (New York: Random House, 1965), 113–168; Allan Bogue, "Social Theory and the Pioneer," *Agricultural History* 34 (January 1960), 21–34; Dykstra, *The Cattle Towns*; and Doyle, *The Social Order of a Frontier Community*, especially 62–91.

22. Doyle, *The Social Order of a Frontier Community*, 62.

23. Blaine A. Brownell, *The Urban Ethos in the New South, 1920–1930* (Baton Rouge: Louisiana State University Press, 1976).

24. Laura A. Brockington, "Redeeming North Carolina: The Wilmington Race Riot of November 1898" (Honors Thesis, Department of History, University of California, Los Angeles, 1983) shows how Democrats promoted a "race riot" to expel the Republican and Populist government of the city.

25. Richard L. Ransom and Richard Sutch, *One Kind of Freedom: The Economic Consequences of Emancipation* (New York: Cambridge University Press, 1977); see also the debate stimulated by this book, Gary M. Walton and James F. Sheperd, eds., *Market Institutions and Economic Progress in the New South, 1865–1900* (New York: Academic Press, 1981).

26. Daniel J. Elazar, *The American Partnership: Intergovernmental Cooperation in the Nineteenth-Century United States* (Chicago: University of Chicago Press, 1962), 42, 61, 171, 265, 266–277.

27. Jon C. Teaford, *The Unheralded Triumph: City Government in America, 1870–1900* (Baltimore: Johns Hopkins University Press, 1984), 83–102; Hendrik Hartog, *Public Property and Private Power: The Corporation of the City of New York in American Law, 1730–1870* (Chapel Hill: University of North Carolina Press, 1983); Elazar, *The American Partnership*, 208–209.

28. Samuel Kernell, "The Early Nationalization of Political News in

America," *Studies in American Political Development: An Annual* 1 (1986), 255–278, and Monkkonen, "Comment on Kernell," *Studies in American Political Development: An Annual* 2 (1987), 337–340.

For a study that analyzes the notion of community, public and private, as envisioned by newspapers, see David P. Nord, "The Public Community: The Urbanization of Journalism in Chicago," *Journal of Urban History* 11 (August 1985), 411–442. Although Nord is concerned with the issue of community, his article also provides an illuminating contrast between the relatively backward looking *Times* in a full-fledged, antigovernment stance, contrasted with the probusiness, proservice stance of the city's two other leading newspapers, the *Tribune* and the *Daily News*. The latter two papers fully supported the emerging service city, even though one was "conservative" and the other pro-working class. The difference exemplifies the transition from a regulatory to a service city.

6 Paying for the Service City

Some of the details in this chapter have been drawn from my research presented in "The Politics of Municipal Indebtedness and Default, 1850–1936," in Terrence J. McDonald and Sally Ward, eds., *The Politics of Urban Fiscal Policy* (Beverly Hills: Sage Press, 1984), 125–159. I wish to thank Pat Thane for sharing her insights and bibliographic knowledge of British public policy with me.

1. Terrence J. McDonald, *The Parameters of Urban Fiscal Policy: Socioeconomic Change, Political Culture and Fiscal Policy in San Francisco, 1860–1906* (Berkeley, Los Angeles, London: University of California Press, 1987), 158–261, shows how politically sensitive *all* politicians were in making the annual budget. He argues that because of this delicacy, incrementalism rather than any more dramatic actions surrounded the urban budget: see also McDonald and Ward, eds., *The Politics of Urban Fiscal Policy*, 13–37. Michael H. Frisch, *Town into City: Springfield, Massachusetts, and the Meaning of Community, 1840–1880* (Cambridge, Mass.: Harvard University Press, 1972), 174, provides evidence for a similar view, although he also argues that the impact of local wartime expenditures, in particular for hiring draft substitutes during the Civil War, changed and enlarged the sense of the city budget (66). Leon Fink, *Workingmen's Democracy* (Urbana: University of Illinois Press, 1983), 34, makes a similar argument for those particular cases where explicitly labor-oriented parties won local elections, claiming that the Knights of Labor had a more limited conception of the role of the state than did industrial leaders. However, at least some of his evidence shows that local Knights candidates did actually increase local expenditures (58).

For a useful summary of the structure of local government as created by the Northwest Ordinance in the late eighteenth century, see Edward W. Bemis, "Local Government in Michigan and the

Northwest," *John Hopkins University Studies in Historical and Political Science* 5 (March 1883).

2. Mancur Olson, *The Logic of Collective Action* (Cambridge, Mass.: Harvard University Press, 1964). For a historical discussion of public goods, the free rider problem, and governmental expenditures, see Roger L. Ransom, "In Search of Security: The Growth of Government in the United States, 1902–1970," in Ransom, Richard Sutch, and Gary M. Walton, eds., *Explorations in the New Economic History: Essays in Honor of Douglass C. North* (New York: Academic Press, 1982), 131–136 and n. 11. For a background theory of local government see Charles M. Tiebout, "A Pure Theory of Local Expenditures," *The Journal of Political Economy* LXIV (October 1956), 416–424.

3. Joseph Schumpeter, "The Crisis of the Tax State," *International Economic Papers* 4 (1954, first published in 1918), 5–38. Aaron Wildavsky, *Budgeting: A Comparative Theory of the Budget Process* (Boston: Little, Brown, 1975). For background on tax, see Sumner Benson, "A History of the General Property Tax," in G. C. S. Benson, S. Benson, H. McClelland, and P. Thompson, eds., *The American Property Tax: Its History, Administration, and Economic Impact* (Claremont, Cal.: College Press, 1965), 11–81; and Richard T. Ely, *Taxation in American States and Cities* (New York: Crowell, 1888), especially on tax history (25–54), and his reform proposals (251–263), which he makes in the context of a sophisticated analysis of the role of local government. In fact, Ely took the strength and taxing ability of local government as the main index of social and economic development, arguing that "as the South develops, local government must become more important" (261). H. Secrist, "An Economic Analysis of the Constitutional Restrictions on Public Indebtedness in the United States," *Bulletin of the University of Wisconsin* 637, Economic and Political Sciences, 8, 1 (Madison, 1914); E. R. A. Seligman, *Essays in Taxation* (New York: Macmillan, 1923).

4. See, for instance, Paul V. Betters, *Recent Federal City Relations* (Washington, D.C.: U.S. Conference of Mayors, 1936), for the range of federal programs with urban impact; Clarence E. Ridley and Orin F. Nolting, eds., *What the Depression Has Done to Cities* (Chicago: International City Managers' Association, 1935).

5. Paul V. Betters, *Municipal Finance Problems and Proposals for Federal Legislation* (Chicago: American Municipal Association, n.d.), and *Cities and the 1936 Congress* (Washington, D.C.: U.S. Conference of Mayors, 1936).

6. *The National Income and Product Accounts of the United States, 1929–76: A Supplement to the Survey of Current Business* (Washington, D.C.: Department of Commerce, Bureau of Economic Analysis, 1981), table 3.3, 128–129.

7. Glenn W. Fisher and Robert P. Fairbanks, *Illinois Municipal Finance: A Financial and Economic Analysis* (Urbana: University of Illinois Press, 1968), table 35, 160–161.

8. For Illinois proportions of total local government revenues by tax sources, see Bureau of the Census, *Census of Governments* 5, 6 (Washington, D.C.: Government Printing Office, 1967), Bureau of the Census, *Historical Statistics on Governmental Finances and Employment* (Washington, D.C.: Government Printing Office, 1977), 86. For 1962, Fisher and Fairbanks, *Illinois Municipal Finance*, 161; for 1977, Bureau of the Census, *City and County Data Book, 1983* (Washington, D.C.: Government Printing Office, 1983), table A, 11.

9. Terry Schwadron, ed., *California and the American Tax Revolt: Proposition 13 Five Year Later* (Berkeley, Los Angeles, London: University of California Press, 1984).

10. Ransom, "In Search of Security," 127.

11. Eric H. Monkkonen, "*Bank of Augusta v. Earle*: Corporate Growth v. States' Rights," *The Alabama Historical Quarterly* 34 (Summer 1972), 113–130.

12. New York City met its last draft call in cooperation with the county: the county board of supervisors authorized individual bounties of up to $1,000 to be paid to the men after they had volunteered and mustered. The money came from a county bonded debt of $4,000,000. The stipulation that the bonds be countersigned by the mayor and that he be responsible for actually finding the volunteers makes clear the joint city-county responsibility. *New York Times* (2 January 1865), p. 8, col. 4.

Dollars

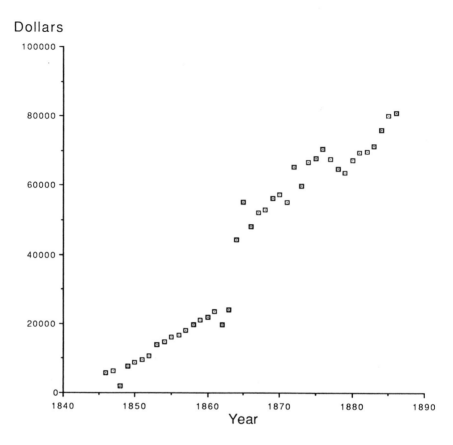

Year

13. Henry Binford, *The First Suburbs: Residential Communities on the Boston Periphery, 1815–1860* (Chicago: University of Chicago Press, 1985), 222–225; Frisch, *Town into City*, 53–113; Ely, *Taxation in American States and Cities*, 456–457; Richard Sylla, "The Economics of State and Local Government Sources and Uses of Funds in North Carolina, 1800–1977" (paper presented at National Bureau of Economic Research Conference on Research in Income and Wealth, Williamsburg, Virginia, March 22–24, 1984).

LOCAL DEBT AS DETERMINED BY LOCAL POPULATION, AGE OF STATE, AND CIVIL WAR STATUS

Dependent Variable: Total Debt[a]

Variable	Coefficient	(SEE)	F	Sig.
Rebel = 1[b]	0.9436	(0.2115)	19.910	0.00001
LPW70[c]	1.2231	(0.0741)	272.608	0.00000

Constant = 0.7448; Adj. R^2 = 0.4888

[a]Log of total, bonded and unbonded, local debt in county, 1870.
[b]Dummy variable, with 1 indicating Confederate membership.
[c]Log of white population in cities over 4,000 in the county.
NOTE: Cases include 284 counties with recorded debt for local governments; because missing data and zero debt could not be distinguished, all zero value counties were excluded. A regression with bonded debt gives virtually the same results. LPB70, the log of black population in cities over 4,000 in the county, and STATEAGE, the number of years between entry to union and 1870, did not enter in a stepwise regression.
SOURCE: Debt: Bureau of the Census, *Ninth Census of the United States: The Statistics of the Wealth and Industry of the United States* (Washington, D.C.: Government Printing Office, 1872), 15–68; population data from Bureau of the Census, *Compendium of the Tenth Census, Part I* (Washington, D.C.: Government Printing Office, 1883), 380–405.

14. Frisch, *Town into City*, shows how in the decade of the 1860s, city growth and rising property values allowed a reduction of property taxes and simultaneous expansion of the city budget. Doyle, *The Social Order of a Frontier Community*, for instance, shows how Illinois College barely managed to raise $800 by subscription in 1828 and little more in 1853, even though the college was considered an important asset to Jacksonville (23, 77). Bayrd Still, "Patterns of Mid-Nineteenth Century Urbanization in the Middle West," *Mississippi Valley Historical Review* 28 (1941), 200–206, has dubbed the mid-nineteenth century the "subscription period" of midwestern city growth, but by this he seems to refer to the era when a fee or labor were substitutable for city dwellers, suggesting the degree of cash shortage or lack of civic enthusiasm in the very early years of most new cities. See Edward C. Kirkland, *Men, Cities and Transportation: A Study in New England History, 1820–1900*, (Cambridge, Mass.: Harvard University Press, 1948), 309–322, for a discussion of governmental finance of railroads which includes city government. Frisch, *Town into City*, discusses local railroad politics, 180–191.

15. Alberta Sbragia, "Cities, Capital, and Banks: The Politics of Debt in the United States, United Kingdom, and France," in Kenneth Newton, ed., *Urban Political Economy* (New York: St. Martin's Press, 1981), cited by John Modell, "Afterword," in McDonald and Ward, eds., *The Politics of Urban Fiscal Policy*, 161–174. For an excellent discussion of the local role of bonds in Houston, see Harold L. Platt, *City Building in the New South: The Growth of Public Services in Houston, Texas, 1830–1915* (Philadelphia: Temple University Press, 1983), 37–39.

16. Henry Roseveare, *The Treasury* (London: Allen Lane, 1969); J. Roland Phillips, "Local Taxation in England and Wales," in J. W. Probyn, ed., *Local Government and Taxation in the United Kingdom* (London: Cassell, Petter, Galpin, 1882), 471–472; J. Thackeray Bunch, "Municipal Boroughs and Urban Districts," in Probyn, *Local Government*, 291.

   Bureau of the Census, *Report on Valuation, Taxation and Public Indebtedness in the United States* (Washington, D.C.: Government Printing Office, 1884), table XXI, 882. Pages 649–672 summarize state constitutional debt restrictions and ceilings. By 1881, fifteen of thirty-eight states had set ceilings, and three had authorized legislatures to set ceilings, most at 5%. Twenty-four had restricted the right of cities to invest in railways and twenty-five the right to own stocks of private corporations. And one, Massachusetts, began to legislate limits in 1875; Royal S. Van de Woestyne, *State Control of Local Finance in Massachusetts* (Cambridge, Mass.: Harvard University Press, 1935), 10.

   To estimate crudely the comparative debt ceilings, assume a real property tax of 1%. Two year's collection of this tax would equal approximately 2% of the property's value, the British ceiling. This contrasts to a ceiling in the United States of 5% to 25% of the property value! For a discussion of debt ceilings, see Arthur M. Hillhouse, *Defaulted Municipal Bonds, 1830–1930* (Chicago: Municipal Finance Officers' Association, 1935). A modern manual on debt concludes that "debt restrictions have not significantly restrained the total volume of state-local borrowing. To avoid these limits, special districts have often been created . . . [resulting in] an increase in the cost of borrowing." J. Richard Aronson and Eli Schwartz, eds., *Management Policies in Local Government Finance* (Washington, D.C.: International City Management Association, 1975), 234.

   For a useful analysis of the experience of Massachusetts, see Van de Woestyne, *State Control of Local Finance in Massachusetts*. He concludes variously that debt ceilings were "effective" (32) and that they gave cities an upward goal, thereby increasing local debt (71). More to the point, he shows how between 1875 and 1911 Massachusetts granted over 1,500 exceptions to its own legislated debt and taxation limits (34): the state collection and publication of statistics was partially mandated to keep such exemptions down (55). He also cites a Fall River tax strike in 1930 (136–137) and gives sources for was partially mandated to keep such exemptions down (55). He also cites a Fall River tax strike in 1930 (136–137) and gives sources for annual data: 1871–1910, State Tax Commissioner; 1906–1935, Statistics of Municipal Finance.

For a survey of debt restriction, see *State Constitutional and Statutory Restrictions on Local Government Debt* (n.p.: Advisory Commission on Intergovernmental Relations, September 1961) and *State Constitutional and Statutory Restrictions on Local Taxing Powers* (n.p.: Advisory Commission on Intergovernmental Relations, October 1962). That a tax rate estimate of one percent is reasonable, consider the estimated national capital of Britain in buildings and farm capital, about 2.3 billion pounds in 1885: Phyllis Deane and W. A. Cole, *British Economic Growth, 1688–1959: Trends and Structure* (Cambridge: Cambridge University Press, 1967), table 71, 274.

17.   Quotation from Platt, *City Building in the New South*, 179. Source for U.S. debt for 1880, Bureau of the Census, *Report on Valuation, Taxation and Public Indebtedness in the United States* (Washington, D.C.: Government Printing Office, 1884), table XXI, 882. Pages 649–672, state constitutional debt restrictions and ceilings.

The equation, based on thirty-five States, as the cases, excluding the city of Washington, D.C., Maine (with very little debt), Maryland (with the greatest per capita debt) as outliers:

Dependent Variable: Net Debt per Capita[a]

Variable	Coefficient	(SEE)	T(DF = 32)	Sig.
Age (years since 1790)	−.429	(0.093)	−4.627	000
Region[b]	−15.632	(4.980)	−3.139	004
Cities[c] per 100,000	−3.283	(1.038)	−3.165	003

Constant = 76.561; Adj. R^2 = 0.616

[a]For all cities in states over 7,500 per capita urban.
[b]1 for South; 2 for North.
[c]Over 7,500 per capita urban.
NOTE: A dummy variable for limit and one for number of cities were not included in a stepwise regression, where their probability would have been 0.896 and 0.510 respectively. All but three debt ceilings were established prior to 1877. States with ceilings (as percent of taxable real estate) and dates include: Maine, 5% (1877); Pennsylvania, 7% (1873); West Virginia, 5% (1872); Georgia, 7% (1877); Alabama, 0.5% (1875); Louisiana, 1% (1879); Texas, 2.5% (1876); Arkansas, 0.5% (1874); Illinois, 5% (1870); Indiana, 2% (1881); Wisconsin, 5% (1874); Minnesota, 5% (1879); Missouri, 1% (1875); Nebraska, 15% (1875); Colorado, 3% (1876); California, 7% (1879).
SOURCE: Bureau of the Census, *Report on Valuation, Taxation and Public Indebtedness in the United States* (10th Census, VIII) (Washington, D.C.: Government Printing Office, 1884), table XXI, 882. For limit provisions, 649–672.

A similar regression may be estimated as an alternative test. This equation uses the per capita local debt in 1880 as the dependent variable, a similar value for 1870 (prior to the debt limits in all states) as an independent variable which captures the effect of all forces affecting debt such as region, age of state, and other unknown ecological factors. To this is added a single additional independent variable, whether or not the state had debt limitation. Again, the states of Maryland and Maine have been excluded as outliers, although the equation estimates are similar with them included. The two per capita debt figures may have some slight differences, as that for 1870 is per capitized on all cities over 4,000, as opposed to 7,500.

The estimate results confirm the test above. Limitation had no effect on per capita local debt.

Dependent Variable: Net Debt per Capita, 1880[a]

Variable	Coefficient	(SEE)	T	Sig.
Limit	−0.404	(6.313)	−0.064	0.949
Debt PC 1870[b]	0.393	(0.083)	4.75	0.00004

Constant = 25.41; Adj. R^2 = 0.377

[a]For all cities in state over 7,500 per capita urban.
[b]Debt for all city and town government; population for all places over 4,000.
Source: For 1880: Bureau of the Census, *Report on Valuation, Taxation and Public Indebtedness in the United States* (10th Census, VIII) (Washington, D.C.: Government Printing Office, 1884), table XXI, 882. For limit provisions, 649–672. For 1870 debt: Bureau of the Census, *The Statistics of the Wealth and Industry of the United States* (9th Census) (Washington, D.C.: Government Printing Office, 1872), table I, 11; population data calculated from Bureau of the Census, *The Compendium of the Tenth Census*, Part I (Washington, D.C.: Government Printing Office, 1883), table XXIV, 380–405.

Finally, a stepwise regression can be estimated, allowing the limitation variable to drop out and considering several 1870 variables. Here, once again, the number of cities per capita in 1870 has a significant and negative effect on local debt a decade later.

Dependent Variable: Net Debt per Capita, 1880

Variable	Coefficient	(SEE)	T(DF = 32)	Sig.
Debt PC 1870	0.361	(0.070)	5.145	0.000
Cities PC 1880	−3.763	(1.05)	−3.596	0.001

Constant = 43.77; Adj. R^2 = 0.556

Although this state-by-state test may be the best way to see if debt limitation movements had any measurable impact, it should be noted here that this may not be the best level at which to capture the impact of local debt for individual cities.

18. In the same year rates, that is real property taxes, brought local gov-

ernment an income of 25.7 million pounds, B. R. Mitchell and Phyllis Deane, *Abstract of British Historical Statistics* (Cambridge: Cambridge University Press, 1962), table 9, 414. These estimates must be seen as crude and suggestive only, for differences in taxation, forms of land tenure, and the like make clear comparisons difficult. See David Cannadine, "Urban Development in England and America in the Nineteenth Century: Some Comparisons and Contrasts," *The Economic History Review* XXXIII (August 1980), 309–325. The tax rate of 1.1% on total value conforms with the twentieth century expectation that a 1% tax on property is about "right." For example, in the long struggle to simplify and rationalize British tenure and taxation, the bill coming closest to passing advocated a 1% tax on the capital value of the land, Avner Offer, *Property and Politics, 1870–1914* (Cambridge: Cambridge University Press, 1981), 247.

Population base for these estimates from P. J. Waller, *Town, City and Nation: England, 1850–1914* (Oxford: Oxford University Press, 1983), 7.

The range of projects in England and Wales for which the Treasury's Board of Public Works Loan Commissioners had outstanding local government indebtedness in 1880 included: public housing, baths, bridges, burial grounds, canals, cattle disease prevention, churches, harbors, parks, local government buildings, asylums, prisons, public works, schools, workhouses, and one railway (Portpatrick); Phillips, "Local Taxation," 485–486.

19. Phillips, "Local Taxation," 481. Each department of Glasgow's government borrowed independently until the 1883 Glasgow Corporation Loans Act. See Tom Hart, "Urban Growth and Municipal Government: Glasgow in a Comparative Context, 1846–1914," in Anthony Slaven and Derek H. Aldcroft, eds. *Business, Banking and Urban History; Essays in Honor of S. G. Checkland* (Edinburgh: John Donald, 1982), 202. See also his table 2, 202, reproduced below.

CITY AND PORT INCOME, 1846–1914 (IN THOUSANDS OF POUNDS)

Year	Total income	From rates (%)	Other	From port
1846/47	80	35 (44)	45	55
1850/51	120	70 (41)	50	66
1860/61	270	170 (63)	100	101
1870/71	850	270 (32)	580	164
1880/81	1000	380 (38)	620	236
1890/91	1260	400 (32)	860	355
1900/01	2740	769 (28)	1971	443
1910/11	3768	1067 (28)	2701	566
1913/14	4589	1402 (30)	3187	630

SOURCE FOR ILLINOIS DEBT: *Journal of the Constitutional Convention of the State of Illinois* (Springfield: State Journal Printing Office, 1870), 99–105.

Note: "Other" includes city "trading" as profit made by its gas companies and municipal transportation.

For the building of the Leeds city hall, see Asa Briggs, *Victorian Cities* (Harmondsworth: Pelican, 1982), 139–183; for a detailed discussion of the controversy over the funding of the city hall, see Derek Fraser, "Politics in Leeds, 1830–1852" (Ph.D. diss., University of Leeds, 1969), 459–466, 504–505, 517. Water profits paid for the town hall in twelve years according to one source: Brian Barber, "Municipal Government in Leeds, 1835–1914," in Derek Fraser, ed., *Municipal Reform and the Industrial City* (Leicester: Leicester University Press, 1982), 106. Barber shows how for Leeds the national government subsidized local government, beginning with a 25% police supplement in 1856. He estimates a total subsidy of city income which rose from 8% in 1895 to 21% by 1905 and 22% by 1910 (107).

20. City count from United States Postal Service, *National Zipcode and Post Office Directory* (Washington, D.C.: U.S. Postal Service, 1981). For an account of railroad-directed town building, see John C. Hudson, *Plains Country Towns* (Minneapolis: University of Minnesota Press, 1985).

21. James Willard Hurst, *Law and the Conditions of Freedom in the Nineteenth-Century United States* (Madison: University of Wisconsin Press, 1956); Robert A. Lively, "The American System: A Review Article," *Business History Review* XXIX (March 1955), 81–96.

22. Literature on incorporation is extensive, but the studies of Oscar Handlin and Mary Handlin, *Commonwealth, A Study of the Role of Government in the American Economy: Massachusetts, 1774–1861* (Cambridge, Mass.: Harvard University Press, 1947), and Louis Hartz, *Economic Policy and Democratic Thought: Pennsylvania, 1776–1800* (Cambridge, Mass.: Harvard University Press, 1948), remain classics. Bayrd Still, "Patterns of Mid-Nineteenth Century Urbanization in the Middle West," *Mississippi Valley Historical Review* 28 (1941), 187–206, shows how the first charters of Buffalo (1832), Chicago (1837), and Cleveland (1836) "were strikingly similar in form" (190), Chicago's differing from Buffalo's in only a dozen trivial instances. See Binford, *The First Suburbs*, "The Community as Business Corporation," 118–124, for an excellent discussion of the incorporation of Cambridge, Mass., in the 1840s.

23. This argument deliberately paraphrases Georg Simmel, "The Metropolis and Mental Life," in Kurt H. Wolff, ed., *The Sociology of Georg Simmel* (London: Free Press of Glencoe, 1950), 409–424.

24. Ransom, "In Search of Security," 125–148; and Lance Davis and John Legler, "The Government in the American Economy, 1815–1902: A Quantitative Study," *Journal of Economic History* 26 (December 1966), 514–552, estimate nonfederal spending in lieu of aggregated, published data.

25. These values calculated from Bureau of the Census, *The Statistics of the Wealth and Industry of the United States* (Ninth Census, vol. III) (Washington, D.C.: Government Printing Office, 1872), 11; *Report*

on Wealth, Debt, and Taxation; Part I. Public Debt (Eleventh Census) (Washington, D.C.: Government Printing Office, 1892), 57. The per capita figures are approximately $23.80 for 1880 and $21.90 for 1890: it is impossible to per capitize this figure correctly, for there is no way to know the base population. The two values reported above for 1870 and 1880 are more reasonably accurate, for the Census Bureau reported the population base of the cities reporting their debts. There is no doubt that these comparative figures for 1880 and 1890 are deflated, but they have been deflated by the same unknown amount, so are comparable to each other.

The 1880 census contains a table summarizing indebtedness for places over 7,500 people and per capitizes by state with the population base representing only that of reporting cities. Here the average net debt per capita is $51.09, but the range by state is large, from $2.62 in Colorado to $127.66 for Washington, D.C. Bureau of the Census, *Report on Valuation, Taxation and Public Indebtedness in the United States* (Tenth Census, vol. VIII) (Washington, D.C.: Government Printing Office, 1884), table XXI, p. 882.

Post-1902 data from U.S. Department of Commerce, Bureau of the Census, *Census of Governments, 1962,* VI, no. 4, *Historical Statistics on Government Finances and Employment,* tables 3, 5, 6.

26. See Hendrik Hartog, "Because All the World Was Not New York City: Governance, Property Rights, and the State in the Changing Definition of a Corporation, 1730–1860," *Buffalo Law Review* 28 (1979), 91–109, and Hendrik Hartog, "Property as Government in Eighteenth-Century America," *The Journal of Legal Studies* 10 (June 1981), 305–348, especially 344.

27. This scenario diverts considerably from that so subtly presented by Hartog, "Because All the World Was Not New York City," and "Property as Government in Eighteenth-Century America." Hartog's concern is with establishing the origins of the modern distinction between public and private corporations. He shows how in the eighteenth century the notion of municipality referred to any local delegation of state power, and how the city was best considered as its corporation. In the mid-nineteenth century, the separation between public corporations, such as the city, and ones for private gain became articulated. In the eighteenth century, he argues, no such separate conception was possible because each corporation, by its very nature, was based on a singular and unique charter.

28. Hartog, "Because All the World Was Not New York City," 92–100.

29. Clyde F. Steiner, Gilbert Y. Steiner, and Lois Langdon, *Local Taxing Units: The Illinois Experience* (Urbana: The Institute of Government and Public Affairs, 1954); Glenn W. Fisher and Robert P. Fairbanks, *Illinois Municipal Finance: A Financial and Economic Analysis* (Urbana: University of Illinois Press, 1968), table 35, 160–161.

30. Bureau of the Census, *Historical Statistics of the United States: Colonial Times To 1970* (Washington, D.C.: Government Printing Office, 1975), 368, 1086; Bureau of the Census, *Statistical Abstract of*

the United States, 105th ed., (Washington, D.C.: Government Printing Office, 1984), 283.

31. On the school centralization movement, see David B. Tyack, *The One Best System: A History of American Urban Education* (Cambridge, Mass.: Harvard University Press, 1974), 129–147; Bureau of the Census, *Census of Governments: 1962*, vol. I, 29, 66; Fisher and Fairbanks, *Illinois Municipal Finance*, 95–96.

32. William F. Whyte, "The Watertown Railway Bond Fight," *Proceedings of the Wisconsin State Historical Society* (1916), 273.

33. Ibid., 277, 278.

34. Ibid., 281.

35. *Watertown Democrat* (10 September 1874 and 9 March 1876).

36. Eric Hobsbawm and George Rude, *Captain Swing: A Social History of the Great English Agricultural Uprising of 1830* (New York: W. W. Norton, 1975); Watertown *Republican* (26 June 1872).

37. Cited in Whyte, "The Watertown Railway Bond Fight," 297; 2 January 1873.

38. Watertown *Republican* (4 September 1872).

39. Kathleen H. Underwood, "Town Building on the Frontier: Grand Junction, Colorado, 1880–1900" (Ph. D. diss., University of California, Los Angeles, 1982). Home ownership was so accessible in late nineteenth-century Detroit that Oliver Zunz sees it as an ethnic choice that reflected neither occupational status nor wealth; *The Changing Face of Inequality: Urbanization, Industrial Development, and Immigrants in Detroit, 1880–1920* (Chicago: University of Chicago Press, 1982). He states, "owning one's own home was more an ethnocultural phenomenon than one of class" (153). California's four major cities had 37% home ownership in 1900 as compared to a national average of 26%. Calculated from Bureau of the Census, *Abstract of the Twelfth Census, 1900* 3d ed. (Washington, D.C.: Government Printing Office, 1904), table 90, 133–135.

40. James E. Cooley, *Recollections of Early Days in Duluth* (Duluth: by the author, 1925), 19. Jonathan Prude, *The Coming of Industrial Order: Town and Factory Life in Rural Massachusetts, 1810–1860* (New York: Cambridge University Press, 1983) shows how the wooing of industry in the case of Samuel Slater's mills did not mean blind acceptance of factory political power. Thus, the mill owners and the town fought over power (168).

41. Whyte, "The Watertown Railway Bond Fight," 285.

42. Kenneth Fox, *Better City Government: Innovation in American Urban Politics, 1850–1937* (Philadelphia: Temple University Press, 1977).

43. This analysis is developed in greater detail in Monkkonen, "Politics of Municipal Indebtedness."

44. These remarks and the data discussion for 1929–1982 are based on detailed information presented in Eric H. Monkkonen, "What Urban Crisis? A Historian's Point of View," *Urban Affairs Quarterly* 20 (June 1985), 429–448.

45. See Gerald E. Frug, "The City as a Legal Concept," *Harvard Law Review* 93 (April 1980), 1059–1154, for a discussion of the city as a corporation.

46. George C. Daly, "The Burden of Debt and Future Generations in Local Finance," *Southern Economic Journal* 36 (July 1969), 44–51, summarizes the logical arguments over the bearers of debt burden. A recent book on the fiscal crisis of New York State lays much of the blame for the current state and city fiscal crisis at the feet of Nelson Rockefeller. Although the book greatly exaggerates his culpability, there is an underlying and insightful premise—the debts that politicians accrue can come due well after their deaths. Peter D. McClelland and Alan L. Magdovitz, *Crisis in the Making: The Political Economy of New York State Since 1945* (New York: Cambridge University Press, 1981). Lauro Martines, *Power and Imagination: City-States in Renaissance Italy* (New York: Alfred A. Knopf, 1979), 136.

47. *Historical Statistics of the United States*, 1126–1127. For the years 1902, 1913, 1922, and 1927, the following values may be estimated. Revenue from the federal government: 0.7%, 0.6%, 2.1%, 1.5%. Revenue from property taxes: 67%, 66%, 64%, 60%. Expenditure on debt interest: 7.2%, 7.7%, 7.6%, 8.5%. These are not directly comparable to the data presented in note 48.

48.

PERCENT OF EXPENDITURES IN INTEREST ON DEBT, LOCAL AND STATE GOVERNMENT, 1929–1982

Year	%	Year	%	Year	%	Year	%
1929	5.10	1943	4.11	1957	3.51	1971	4.35
1930	5.41	1944	3.61	1958	3.53	1972	4.57
1931	7.38	1945	2.92	1959	3.80	1973	4.66
1932	7.38	1946	5.01	1960	4.12	1974	4.70
1933	8.01	1947	3.81	1961	4.13	1975	4.76
1934	6.77	1948	3.12	1962	4.25	1976	4.98
1935	6 04	1949	2.87	1963	4.26	1977	5.07
1936	6.32	1950	2.77	1964	4.26	1978	4.99
1937	5.70	1951	2.83	1965	4.18	1979	5.03
1938	5.26	1952	2.88	1966	4.08	1980	5.67
1939	4.78	1953	2.97	1967	3.96	1981	6.16
1940	5.06	1954	3.13	1968	3.92	1982	6.91
1941	4.58	1955	3.30	1969	4.08		
1942	4.30	1956	3.46	1970	4.21		

SOURCE: *The National Income and Product Accounts of the United States, 1929–76: A Supplement to the Survey of Current Business* (Washington, D.C.: Dept. of Commerce, Bureau of Economic Analysis, 1981), table 3.3, 128–129; *National Income and Product Accounts, 1976–1979: Special Supplement to the Survey of Current Business* (Washington, D.C.: Dept. of Commerce, Bureau of Economic Analysis, 1981), table 3.3, 25; *Survey of Current Business* 62 (August 1982), table 3.3, 7; *Survey of Current Business* 63 (February 1983), table 3.3, 5.

49. For a subtle analysis of New York City which explicates just this perspective on the past decade of the city's finances and which criticizes the incrementalist view, see Charles Brecher and Raymond D.

icizes the incrementalist view, see Charles Brecher and Raymond D. Horton, "Retrenchment and Recovery: American Cities and the New York Experience," *Public Administration Review* 45 (March/April 1985), 267–274.

50. Monkkonen, "Politics of Municipal Indebtedness."

7 Transportation: From Animal to Automobile

I am indebted to the work of Scott L. Bottles, which challenged me to rethink many traditional notions about urban transit. By showing the positive role of the automobile in Los Angeles, he has made the most difficult case the most convincing: see *Los Angeles and the Automobile: The Making of the Modern City* (Berkeley, Los Angeles, and London: University of California Press, 1987). See also Martin Wachs, "Automobiles, Transport, and the Sprawl of Los Angeles: The 1920s," *Journal of the American Planning Association* 50 (1984), 297–310, and Carlos A. Schwantes, "The West Adopts the Automobile: Technology, Unemployment, and the Jitney Phenomenon of 1914–1917," *Western Historical Quarterly* 16 (July 1985), 307–326. For an excellent overall coverage of land transportation, see Richard Bessel, "Transport," in *Science, Technology, and Everyday Life* (Milton Keynes, England: Open University Press, 1988).

1. Thus U.S. cities are less dense than Canadian cities, see Barry Edmonston, Michael A. Goldberg, and John Mercer, "Urban Form in Canada and the United States: An Examination of Urban Density Gradients," *Urban Studies* 22 (1985), 209–217.

2. Ray Hebert, "Ventura Freeway—It's Now No. 1," *Los Angeles Times* (10 March 1985), II, 1, 5.

3. Mark S. Foster, *From Streetcar to Superhighway: American City Planners and Urban Transportation, 1900–1940* (Philadelphia: Temple University press, 1981), 3–24.

4. David Ward, "A Comparative Historical Geography of Streetcar Suburbs in Boston, Massachusetts and Leeds, England, 1850–1920," *Annals of the Association of American Geographers* 54 (1964), 477–489, shows that the system in Boston truly was superior to that of Leeds. Scott L. Bottles,"The Making of the Modern City: Los Angeles and the Automobile, 1900–1950" (Ph. D. diss., University of California, Los Angeles, 1984).

5. The auto replaced walking as much as it did public transit in Pittsburgh. Joel A. Tarr, *Transportation Innovation and Changing Spatial Patterns in Pittsburgh, 1850–1934*, Essays in Public Works History, no. 6 (Chicago: Public Works Historical Society, 1978), 38. David O. Wise and Marguerite Dupree, "The Choice of the Automobile for Urban Passenger Transportation: Baltimore in the 1920s," *South Atlantic Urban Studies* II (1978), 153–179, show how the main advantage of the automobile in Baltimore was more housing for the dollar, as the city had a dense streetcar network.

6. Upton Sinclair, *The Jungle* (New York: Penguin, 1979; 1st ed. 1906).

For a clear demonstration of the relationship between high costs of fixed rail urban transport and suburban homes, see Gary R. Hovinen, "Suburbanization in Greater Philadelphia, 1880–1941," *Journal of Historical Geography* 11 (April 1985), 174–195. Joel A. Tarr, "From City to Suburb: The 'Moral' Influence of Transportation Technology," in Alexander B. Callow, Jr., ed., *American Urban History: An Interpretive Reader with Commentaries* 2d ed. (New York: Oxford University Press, 1973), 202–212, and Tarr, *Transportation Innovation and Changing Spatial Patterns*, 5, 6, 11, 14, 20–21, details the inaccessibility of fixed rail transit for most urban workers, for whom a round trip would cost between 15% and 20% of their daily wage.

7. Gary A. Tobin, "Suburbanization and the Development of Motor Transportation: Transportation Technology and the Suburbanization Process," in Barry Schwartz, ed., *The Changing Face of the Suburbs* (Chicago: University of Chicago Press, 1976), 101. Tobin's essay provides a subtle analysis of suburban expansion. The socialist government of Milwaukee argued that accessible suburbs would solve the "problem of congestion"; *Milwaukee Municipal Campaign Book, 1912* (Milwaukee: Social Democratic Party, 1912), 12. Quotation from Clay McShane, *Technology and Reform: Street Railways and the Growth of Milwaukee, 1887–1900* (Madison: State Historical Society of Wisconsin, 1974), 67; on working-class political attitudes, see his chapters 7 and 8.

8. Theodore Hershberg, Harold E. Cox, Dale B. Light, Jr., and Richard R. Greenfield, "The 'Journey-to-Work': An Empirical Investigation of Work, Residence, and Transportation, Philadelphia, 1850 and 1880," in Hershberg, ed., *Philadelphia: Work, Space, Family, and Group Experience in the 19th Century* (New York: Oxford University Press, 1981), 128–173.

9. John R. Borchert, "American Metropolitan Evolution," *The Geographical Review* (July 1967), 301–332; for a more precise analysis within one of Borchert's grander periods, see Michael P. Conzen, "A Transport Interpretation of the Growth of Urban Regions: An American Example," *Journal of Historical Geography* I (October 1975), 361–382.

10. Sam B. Warner, Jr., *The Urban Wilderness: A History of the American City* (New York: Harper & Row, 1972). Or see James J. Flink, "The Metropolis in the Horseless Age," in Margaret Latimer, Brooke Hindle, and Melvin Kranzberg, eds., "Bridge to the Future: A Centennial Celebration of the Brooklyn Bridge," *Annals of the New York Academy of Sciences* 424 (May 1984), 289. Flink asserts that "the settlement patterns and lifeways of contemporary metropolitan America, however, have been most of all shaped by the motor vehicle." The construction of this sentence exemplifies technological determinism: the car shapes the city. Such a causal construction is true only in the same trivial sense as, "chunks of hot metal cause death by bleeding," substitutes for, "thousands of Americans deliberately kill one another each year."

11. Fred Viehe, "Black Gold Suburbs: The Influence of the Extractive Industry on the Suburbanization of Los Angeles, 1890–1930," *Journal of Urban History* 8 (November 1981), 3–26; Spencer A. Crump, *Ride the Big Red Cars: How Trolleys Helped Build Southern California* (Los Angeles: Crest Publications, 1962).

12. Kevin Starr, *Inventing the Dream: California through the Progressive Era* (New York: Oxford University Press, 1985); Richard Henry Dana, Jr., *Two Years Before the Mast* (New York: Penguin, 1981), 146–147; Bottles, "The Making of the Modern City"; Martin J. Schiesl, "Airplanes to Aerospace: Defense Spending and Economic Growth in the Los Angeles Region, 1945–60," in Roger W. Lotchin, ed., *The Martial Metropolis: U.S. Cities in War and Peace* (New York: Praeger, 1984), 135–150.

13. Compiled from list of members, National Automobile Chamber of Commerce, *Facts and Figures of the Automobile Industry, 1926* (New York: National Automobile Chamber of Commerce, 1926); Bottles, "The Making of the Modern City."

14. For charioteers, see Alan Cameron, *Porphyrius—The Charioteer* (Oxford: Clarendon Press, 1973), 136–149, and idem, *Circus Factions: Blues and Greens at Rome and Byzantium* (Oxford: Clarendon Press, 1976). For locomotive names, see Freeman H. Hubbard, *Encyclopedia of North American Railroading: 150 Years of Railroading in the United States and Canada* (New York: McGraw-Hill, 1981), 306, and Benjamin A. Botkin and Alvin F. Harlow, eds., *A Treasury of Railroad Folklore: The Stories, Tall Tales, Traditions, Ballads, and Songs of the American Railroad Man* (New York: Crown, 1953), 382–383. For a discussion of Lexington and an exquisitely reproduced picture, see Roy King and Burke Davis, *The World of Currier and Ives* (New York: Random House, 1968), 78–79. According to King and Davis, Lexington sired 236 champions. They quote the poet Huder All's verse: "Whispers fly about the race-tracks when some mighty deed is done; 'Tis no more than we expected from the blood of Lexington!"

  Twain example cited by Frederick Alderson, *Bicycling: A History* (New York: Praeger, 1972), 104.

15. Gerald Silk, *Automobiles and Culture* (New York: Museum of Contemporary Art and Harry N. Abrams, 1984); Janicemarie A. Holty, "The 'Low Riders': Portrait of a Youth Subculture," *Youth and Society* 6 (1975), 495–512; Tom Wolfe, *The Kandy-Kolored Tangerine-Flake Streamline Baby* (New York: Farrar, 1965).

16. During the last decade of the nineteenth century, the bicycle was the mode of high fashion promenade in Paris: *Vanity Fair*, 1897, cited by Alderson, *Bicycling: A History*, 87. The automobile supplanted the bicycle as the mode of promenade during the first decade of the twentieth century, as is perhaps best exemplified in Lartigue's photos of the rich in the Bois de Boulogne. See Fred C. Kelly, "The Great Bicycle Craze," *American Heritage* 8 (December 1956), 69–73; Sidney H. Aronson, "The Sociology of the Bicycle (1879–1900)," *Social Forces* 30 (March 1952), 311.

17. This contradicts the analysis of James J. Flink, *America Adopts the Automobile, 1895–1910* (Cambridge, Mass.: MIT Press, 1970), 210–213, which merits some detailed attention. Flink first cites contemporary literature, 1899–1909, as evidence "that the development of adequate automobile roads lagged well behind the diffusion of the motor vehicle ... and that the automobile was widely adopted here [the United States] despite a relative scarcity of suitable roads ..." (211). As a further empirical test of this plausible argument, he correlates states by their rank ordering on three different variables—automobiles per capita, roads per square mile and percent of all roads that were improved, the latter two for 1904 and 1914, the former for 1910. The relationship with the earlier variables and the number of automobiles was modest, for the later period even slighter. From this he concludes that the number of automobiles had a "short-range deleterious effect ... on roads" (212).

The two models he tests may be written like this:

I. NUMBER OF AUTOMOBILES / POPULATION OVER 18 = MILES OF ROADS / SURFACE AREA OF STATE and,

II. NUMBER OF AUTOMOBILES / POPULATION OVER 18 = MILES OF IMPROVED ROADS / TOTAL ROAD MILES

(Both equations use rankings of states and both use lagged or led time periods. Flink does not explain why he ranks rather than uses actual values.)

Equation I as tested by Flink makes no sense: presumably the greater the population of a state, the more the miles of roads; yet a greater number of square miles only occasionally meant lesser population, considering the large, sparsely populated western states at the turn of the century. Thus as it stands his results for Equation I test nothing. To capture the relationship Flink intended to, the equation should have been constructed thus:

Ia. NUMBER OF AUTOMOBILES = POPULATION + MILES OF ROADS + MILES OF SURFACE AREA

Equation II examines the relationship between automobiles per capita and the proportion of all roads which was improved. Presumably, some states could have had very limited yet highly improved mileage, hardly an advantage for automobile owners. Again, to capture the relationship Flink wanted to, the equation might be rephrased as follows:

IIa. NUMBER OF AUTOMOBILES = POPULATION + MILES OF ROADS + MILES OF IMPROVED ROADS

This would capture the sense he intended, that automobiles had some relationship with improved rather than merely all roads.

As Flink's conclusions stand, then, they cannot be justified, for the empirical analysis captures neither the claimed relationship nor any other. Flink does not state his data sources; probably they were from the Department of Commerce, *Highway Statistics, Summary to 1955* (Washington, D.C.: Government Printing Office, 1957), cited in his bibliography.

Paul Barrett, *The Automobile and Urban Transit: The Formation of Public Policy in Chicago, 1900–1930* (Philadelphia: Temple University Press, 1983), 69–70, 139–153. The only theoretically informed history of roads is Hillaire Belloc's prescient *The Road* (London: Unwin, 1924). For an engineering history of American nonurban roads, see Department of Transportation, Federal Highway Administration, *America's Highways, 1776–1976: A History of the Federal-Aid Program* (Washington, D.C.: Government Printing Office, 1977), and Thomas H. MacDonald, "The History and Development of Road Building in the United States," *Transactions of the American Society of Civil Engineers* 92 (1928), 1181–1206. Edward C. Kirkland, *Men, Cities and Transportation: A Study in New England History, 1820–1900*, (Cambridge, Mass.: Harvard University Press, 1948), analyzes transportation only between cities.

18. Calculated from *Good Roads* I (January-June 1892), "Contract Notes," 171, 233, 291, 351. Philip P. Mason, "The League of American Wheelmen and the Good Roads Movement, 1890–1905" (Ph.D. diss., University of Michigan, 1958). Ballard C. Campbell, "The Good Roads Movement in Wisconsin, 1890–1911," *Wisconsin Magazine of History* 49 (Summer 1966), 276, 289–290. Quotation: E. G. Harrison from, "Gen. Harrison Tells How the Road was Built," *The Road Maker*, 1, 3 (Port Huron, Mich., c. 1900), 6, cited in Department of Transportation, Federal Highway Administration, *America's Highways, 1776–1976*, 47–48.

Interest in high-quality paving came as an early recognition that paving facilitated the movement of commercial freight. In New York in 1887, the issue of annexing surrounding cities such as Brooklyn was partly motivated by the poor quality of its streets, which directly lowered the efficiency of docks and wharfs in the city's harbor. In importance for facilitating commerce, streets—their paving and decongestion—were equal to docks and street railways. See Mayor Abram S. Hewitt, cited in David C. Hammack, *Power and Society: Greater New York at the Turn of the Century* (New York: Russell Sage Foundation, 1981), 192, 193, 233.

19. Alderson, *Bicycling: A History*, 85–106; Jerry Sandvick, "Early Airport Development and the Emergence of the Metropolitan Airport Commission," *Hennepin County History* 43 (Fall 1984), 3–17, describes how a group of Minneapolis businessmen purchased the defunct auto racetrack for airport land by subscription in 1920, not all that different from the funding for mid-nineteenth-century urban projects in England.

20. Glenn Yago, *The Decline of Transit: Urban Transportation in German and United States Cities, 1900–1970* (New York: Cambridge University Press, 1984) perpetuates the argument that mass transit did pose a viable alternative to the automobile early in the twentieth century. Few of the historians who study urban technology agree: the main reason for the perpetuation of the myth seems to be ignorance about fixed rail transit as it did exist and experience with successful

Technology and Reform, 38–39, for a summary of the reasons the automobile proved to be superior to fixed rail.

21. Of necessity, the uncertain quality of early automobile data render such tests crude and suggestive. On the one hand, if road building represented a passive local response to the new technological imperative introduced by the automobile, then new roads should have *followed* increases in automobile registration; on the other hand, should people have purchased automobiles following the expansion of the road system, then we can interpret the automobile transport revolution as technology following essential political decisions. The first hypothesis represents a technological determinist argument, the second a nondeterminist historical argument. Unfortunately, neither hypothesis can be clearly evaluated. If people in fact purchased cars in response to the opportunity to drive them, i.e., in response to more roads, and if they also purchased them on the basis of "neighborhood" or "contagion" effects, having observed the utility of their neighbors' cars, the model for change would look like this: INCREASE IN CARS = UTILITY + CONTAGION. This can be operationalized as: CARS ADDED = ROADS ADDED + CARS ADDED (For previous year) or, $c = r + c$ (t-1), but, because, by definition, c (t-1) $= r$ (t-2) + c (t-2), etc., the model has circular causation and therefore cannot accurately be tested except in the form, $c = r$ (t-1), or, in the obverse, $r = c$ (t-1).

The following correlation matrix presents a simple test of these two hypotheses. Notice that the variable for cars added is a cumulative one in that it represents change in annual registrations, not simply new cars purchased. The results are ambiguous: both road and automobile expansion seem to account for each other.

	Road	Cars	Roads, T-1	Cars, T-1
Roads	1.00000			
Cars	0.77166	1.00000		
Roads, T-1	0.83296	0.74704	1.00000	
Cars, T-1	0.81458	0.88187	0.77496	1.00000

Critical value (1-tail, 0.05) = +/– 0.35214
Critical value (2-tail, 0.05) = +/– 0.41228
N = 23

These hypotheses may be expressed in a somewhat more complex regression model. The functionalist model that local governments built more roads in response to "need" may be expressed as miles of hard surfaced roads being driven by the automobile registration in the previous year, the expansion of miles of hard surfaced roads in the previous year (as a public spending trend proxy), and the population over eighteen years old in the previous year, all for the period prior to 1930. This model is estimated below, using data for the whole United States.

Similarly, the hypothesis that the diffusion of the automobile

Similarly, the hypothesis that the diffusion of the automobile technology responded to increased utility may also be tested. Here a slightly more complex test must be used, for the idea is more subtle. Let us hypothesize that the annual change in the number of automobiles registered results from a combination of two major factors: first, the contagion effect of a spreading consumption item—"everyone else is getting one"; and second, the expanding hard surfaced road network which continuously increased the automobile's utility. Again, the micro-computer is a clarifying analog: purchases result from a combination of the contagion effect and the actual utility, the latter of which is driven by software (like roads for cars). For the automobile, these two factors can be specified as independent variables measured by, respectively, the change in total automobile registration in the previous year, and hard surfaced miles added each year, again including changes in the over-eighteen population in the previous year and again for the period prior to 1930. The second part of the figure reports the estimated regression for this model.

Several suggestive insights emerge from these regression estimates. First, roads did respond to cars and population the previous year, but the previous addition of roads was far more important. Holding all else constant, each added mile of hard surfaced road required only 1.4 miles of road the previous year, while requiring 286 cars or 322 additional people.

For automobiles, the regression must be estimated on annual changes, rather than the actual values of the variables. Contagion best explains the increase in automobiles (this emerged from the correlations, but the regression is much stronger). The number of roads added has virtually no effect, forcing us to strongly question if not simply reject the notion that more places to drive meant more car registrations. On the other hand, it is possible that the all-powerful variable, car registrations in the previous year, cumulatively captures both contagion and utility, for when estimated for hard surfaced roads in the previous year, the results show a positive relationship.

It is likely that these estimated relationships mask more significant urban relationships which conformed more closely to the earlier predictions made in this chapter. The specific urban cases may have been asked by national trends which aggregate city and county, state and local.

U.S. ROADS, AUTOMOBILES, AND POPULATION, 1906–1929

Dependent Variable: Roads

Variable	Coefficient	(SEE)	T(DF = 20)	Prob.
Roads, T-1	0.701	(0.084)	8.32	0.0000
Population, T-1	0.003	(0.001)	4.31	0.0003
Cars, T-1	0.004	(0.001)	4.04	0.0006

Adj. R^2 = 0.999; Durbin-Watson = 2.4568

Dependent Variable: Cars

Variable	Coefficient	(SEE)	T(DF = 20)	Prob.
Cars, T-1	0.754	(0.180)	4.182	0.0005
Roads	10.889	(14.314)	0.761	0.4562
Population	0.123	(0.225)	0.549	0.5894

Adj. R^2 = 0.7562; Durbin-Watson = 1.6299

Dependent Variable: Cars

Variable	Coefficient	(SEE)	T(DF = 20)	Prob.
Roads, T-1	58.377	(11.336)	5.15	0.00004

Adj. R^2 = 0.5581

NOTE: Roads are hard surfaced roads, Population is that over eighteen years old, and Cars is the annual change in registrations for previous year. All variables in this equation are first differences in order to eliminate serial correlation. The results are not substantively different from the regression on actual values.

SOURCE: Bureau of the Census, *Historical Statistics of the United States, Colonial Times to 1970* (Washington, D.C.: Government Printing Office, 1977), series A-40, p. 10; Q-56, p. 710; Q-152, p. 716.

22. *Annual Report of the City Engineer of the City of Minneapolis* (Minneapolis, 1906), 16–17. For pictures with horses in the background, see the *Report* of 1911–13, 25e, 123a. Such traffic surveys for earlier periods are rare. One, taken on the occasion of a great horse race in Brooklyn in the spring of 1823, recorded traffic passing through

Brooklyn after the race, and counted 13,048 persons, of whom fewer than one-fourth were on horses or in wheeled vehicles. Survey citations in Ralph F. Weld, *Brooklyn Village, 1816–1834* (New York: AMS Press, 1938), 278–279.

23. For a summary of the urban problems associated with horses, see Flink, "The Metropolis in the Horseless Age," 289–290. Tobin, "Suburbanization and the Development of Motor Transportation," 99, cites the horse-drawn rail statistics. On the horse manure problem, see Joel A. Tarr, "Urban Pollution Many Long Years Ago," *American Heritage* 22 (October 1971), 65–70. Ironically, in the early nineteenth century, horse manure had been much less of a problem, for the poor kept pigs which roamed the streets, eating manure and other organic waste. Social reformers outlawed pigs in the mid-nineteenth century, creating new waste problems that necessitated the hiring of street cleaners.

24. State of Minnesota, *Biennial Report of the Secretary of State, 1907–08 and 1909–10* (Minneapolis, 1908, 1910), 4, 6. Tarr, *Transportation Innovation*, 26–28, cites the Pittsburgh survey information.

25. National Automobile Chamber of Commerce, *Facts and Figures of the Automobile Industry, 1921–29* (New York: National Automobile Chamber of Commerce, 1921–29). In fact, some states did not achieve systematic registration until 1921; *Historical Statistics*, 730.

26. For a discussion of the Model T Ford and rural road conditions, see Peter J. Hugill, "Good Roads and the Automobile in the United States, 1880–1929," *The Geographical Review* 72 (July 1982), 327–349, esp. 336–337. This is a useful and comprehensive summary article. J. Interrante, "The Road to Autopia: The Automobile and the Transformation of American Culture," in David L. Lewis, ed., *The Automobile in American Culture: Michigan Quarterly Review* 19 and 20 (1980/1981), 502–517, argues that the car was more important for rural people—based on proportionally higher ownership by the 1920s.

NUMBER OF CARS IN 1910 AND 1920, AS PREDICTED BY
URBAN AND RURAL POPULATIONS

Dependent Variable: Number of Cars, 1910

Variable	Coefficient	(SEE)	T(DF = 43)	Sig.	Partial R^2
Region	5293.194	(1119.374)	4.73	0.0000	0.342
Urban	8.056	(0.393)	20.51	0.0000	0.907
Rural	1.914	(0.752)	2.55	0.0146	0.131

Std. Error of Est. = 2562.8; Adj. R^2 = 0.957

Dependent Variable: Number of Cars, 1920

Variable	Coefficient	(SEE)	T(DF = 43)	Sig.	Partial R^2
Region	158602.424	(26641.148)	5.95	0.00000	0.452
Urban	47.329	(7.398)	6.40	0.00000	0.488
Rural	146.503	(17.712)	8.27	0.00000	0.614

Std. Error of Est. = 59903.2; Adj. R^2 = 0.880

NOTE: Data for all states, excluding the District of Columbia and California, an outlier which far exceeded other states in number of cars, even in 1910. REGION is a dummy for the north, URBAN is the actual urban population, in thousands, as is RURAL the rural population.

SOURCE: Number of automobiles, *Highway Statistics: Summary to 1975* (Washington, D.C.: Dept. of Transportation, 1977), table MV 213; urban and rural population, Bureau of the Census, *Historical Statistics of the United States, Colonial Times to 1970* (Washington, D.C.: Government Printing Office, 1975), Series A195–209, 24–37.

For a discussion of the Model T Ford and rural road conditions, see Peter J. Hugill, "Good Roads and the Automobile in the United States, 1880–1929," *The Geographical Review* 72 (July 1982), 327–349, esp. 336–337. This is a useful and comprehensive summary article.

27. National Automobile Chamber of Commerce, *Facts and Figures of the Automobile Industry, 1924* (New York: National Automobile Chamber of Commerce, 1924), 20. Harold L. Platt, *City Building in the New South: The Growth of Public Services in Houston, Texas, 1830–1915* (Philadelphia: Temple University Press, 1983), 149; *Houston Daily Post* (15 September 1895), cited by Platt, 149.

28. McShane, *Technology and Reform*, 67, cites a newspaper mention in the 1890s of the "half hour limit." The first commuter train appeared in New York City in 1837, carrying riders up to Harlem; in less than ten years service extended to Westchester County: Kenneth T. Jackson, "Technology and the City: Transportation and Social Form in New York," in Latimer, Hindle, and Kranzberg, eds., "Bridge to the Future," 284. The foremost expert on urban rail transit contrasts rail and auto transit as point-to-point and lateral travel mechanisms: see

George W. Hilton, "Rail Transit and the Pattern of Modern Cities: The California Case," *Traffic Quarterly* 21 (July 1967), 379–393.

29. Compare the major freeways and urban rail lines in Reyner Banham, *Los Angeles, Architecture of the Four Ecologies* (New York: Harper & Row, 1972), 32, 92.

30. Larry Long and Diana DeAre, "The Slowing of Urbanization in the U.S.," *Scientific American* 249 (July 1983), 39. Specifically, they report densities of twenty-five "supercities," those over one million, in 1980.

31. Leon Moses and Harold F. Williamson, "The Location of Economic Activity in Cities," *American Economic Review* LVII (May 1967), 211–222.

32. See Clay McShane, "Transforming the Use of Urban Space: A Look at the Revolution in Street Pavements, 1880–1924," *Journal of Urban History* 5 (May 1979), 279–307. "These changes in streets literally paved the way for the automobile . . ." (300). McShane develops a convincing argument for the prior causality of the paving revolution, mixing two strands: one, the lobbying efforts of the good roads movement and engineers and two, somewhat less convincing to me, a changed attitude toward streets, which no longer regards them as play areas and undifferentiated public, social space. Pavement innovation came, McShane concludes, for "shifts in the cultural and political climate of nineteenth century cities" (302). Campbell, "The Good Roads Movement in Wisconsin," 290–291, develops convincing evidence based on voting patterns and numbers of automobiles that support for good roads developed independent of and prior to the diffusion of the automobile in Wisconsin.

33. Federal Highway Administration, *America's Highways, 1776–1976*, 16. Richard Dennis, *English Industrial Cities of the Nineteenth Century: A Social Geography* (Cambridge: Cambridge University Press, 1984), 110–140, provides a useful summary and analysis of the role of nineteenth-century urban transport in England; for the generally disputed argument that in Britain demand led transport, see P. W. Daniels and A. M. Warnes, *Movement in Cities: Spatial Perspectives on Urban Transport and Travel* (London: Methuen, 1980), 2–3.

34. William Fulton, "Those Were the Best Days: The Streetcar and the Development of Hollywood before 1910," *Southern California Quarterly* 66 (Fall 1984), 235–256: Sherman quoted on 238.

35. Peter Hall, *The World Cities*, 3d ed. (London: Weidenfeld & Nicolson, 1984), 150, map 6.3b.

36. John C. Schneider, *Detroit and the Problem of Order, 1830–1880: A Geography of Crime, Riot, and Policing* (Lincoln: University of Nebraska Press, 1980).

8 Home Ownership and Mobility

1. Hal S. Barron, *Those Who Stayed Behind: Rural Society in Nineteenth-Century New England* (New York: Cambridge University

Press, 1984). Upton Sinclair, *The Jungle* (New York: The Jungle Publishing Co., 1906). Probably, the Rudkisses moved to a "working man's reward," an inexpensive suburban development as pictured in Clifford E. Clark, Jr., *The American Family Home, 1800–1960* (Chapel Hill: University of North Carolina Press, 1986), 98. John Burnett, *A Social History of Housing, 1815–1970* (London: Methuen, 1980), 295; *Historical Statistics of the United States: Colonial Times to 1970* (Washington, D.C.: Government Printing Office, 1975), 646.

2. This formula, DEBT causes GROWTH which lower TAXES, was an explicit strategy of nineteenth-century city dwellers. In 1888 New York Mayor Abram S. Hewitt advocated funding new transit to the upper end of Manhattan, for the good of all city property owners: "Our rate of taxation depends upon the growth of the unoccupied portion of the city." He proposed that the city borrow the money, and then in turn contract to a private developer for new rail lines. Three years later, Hewitt said in specific reference to mass transit, "Our object should be to develop as much of the annexed district as possible, in order to get the benefit of taxation upon the increased value of the property." Cited by David C. Hammack, *Power and Society: Greater New York at the Turn of the Century* (New York: Russell Sage Foundation, 1981), 233, 237.

3. For examples of borrowing procedures, see Clark, *The American Family Home*, 87, 96–97. Bureau of the Census, *Statistical Abstract of the United States: National Data Book and Guide to Sources, 1982–83* (Washington, D.C.: Government Printing Office, 1982), 762; *Historical Statistics*, 651. For a recent discussion of the nature of mortgages and the rental industry in general, see Michael Doucet and John Weaver, "The North American Shelter Business, 1860–1920: A Study of a Canadian Real Estate and Property Management Agency," *Business History Review* 58 (Summer 1984), 234–262.

Helena Flam, "Democracy in Debt: Credit and Politics in Paterson, N.J., 1890–1930," *Journal of Social History* 18 (Spring 1985), 439–462, has analyzed the occupations of some mortgage holders in the 1893–95 and 1925–27 periods, and claims to find "trends" toward increased class differences, more rich getting bigger mortgages on bigger houses and fewer poor getting smaller mortgages on smaller houses, a practice which "reinforced" or "sustained" class differences (449–450, and especially the table on 449). The table below reproduces the data given by Flam to support her claim of "trends." She failed to analyze the data with even a Chi-square test: the test shows that there was no meaningful change in the distribution over time. In addition, it shows that the Rudkisses were not alone in having access to housing, that 20% of the Flam sample of mortgages went to unskilled workers.

NUMBER OF MORTGAGE HOLDERS

Occupation	1893–95	1925–27	Total
Business & prof.	114	161	275
Skilled	119	128	247
Unskilled & misc.	62	69	131
Total	295	358	653

Chi-Square = 2.682; D.F. = 2; Prob. = 0.2616

According to Kenneth T. Jackson, *Crabgrass Frontier: The Sub-urbanization of the United States* (New York: Oxford University Press, 1985), 196, the self-amortizing mortgage we now know was perfected in 1933 by the Federal Home Owner's Loan Corporation, a New Deal program.

4. J. Hector St. John de Crèvecoeur, *Letters from an American Farmer* (New York: Dutton, 1957), 52, 215. See also Sharon Salinger and Charles Wetherell, "Wealth and Renting in Prerevolutionary Philadelphia," *Journal of American History* 71 (March 1985), 826–840, esp. 836–837, which in a detailed exploration of rent and real property shows how real property ownership may have been quite fluid and have had little of the meaning which we, or Crèvecoeur, attach to it.

5. Morris Janowitz, *The Last Half Century: Societal Change and Politics in America* (Chicago: University of Chicago Press, 1978), 269–270, on politics of residence, which he claims has grown; contrast with Mark Gottdiener, *The Decline of Urban Politics: Political Theory and the Crisis of the Local State* (Beverly Hills: Sage Press, 1987). For one of the few books that recognizes the political and economic importance of home ownership, see David Halle, *America's Working Man: Work, Home, and Politics among Blue-Collar Property Owners* (Chicago: University of Chicago Press, 1984), 42–44, 115–118, 302; appropriately, Halle is English.

6. David Cannadine, "Urban Development in England and America in the Nineteenth Century: Some Comparisons and Contrasts," *The Economic History Review* XXXIII (August 1980), 309–325, shows how land tenure has incorrectly been used to explain urban housing and planning differences. Gwendolyn Wright, *Building the Dream: A Social History of Housing in America* (Cambridge, Mass.: MIT Press, 1981), 269, notes about recent neighborhood politics that "labels of 'right' and 'left' do not easily apply." See Matthew Edel, Elliot D. Sclar, and Daniel Luria, *Shaky Palaces: Homeownership and Social Mobility in Boston's Suburbanization* (New York: Columbia University Press, 1984), 297–302, for a subtle discussion of Marx. For the dupes argument, see Stanley Aronowitz, *False Promises: The Shaping of American Working Class Consciousness* (New York: McGraw-Hill, 1973); for a brief summary of the mobility argument see Edel, Sclar, and Luria, 134–135, who reexamine the notion that property provided

an avenue of wealth mobility for working-class Bostonians at the end of the nineteenth century, an argument developed by Stephan Thernstrom in *The Other Bostonians: Poverty and Progress in the American Metropolis, 1880–1970* (Cambridge, Mass.: Harvard University Press, 1973). To do so they reanalyze Thernstrom's data, claiming to show that a father's home ownership decreased a son's chances of upward occupational or other mobility. If the question of ownership is wrongly cast as one of wealth, it has also wrongly been reflected in the debate over freehold and leasehold land.

This conclusion certainly seems counterintuitive, and a reexamination of their statistics shows that the home ownership probably is associated with upward mobility. The critical issue is the coefficient sign of home ownership in regression equation 2, table 5.11, p. 148. The sign is negative, which they mistakenly interpret as meaning that home ownership associates negatively with sons' occupational positions. Yet a careful examination of their regression analysis table and its notes shows that the variable Home Ownership is actually the ratio between the estimated value of a home and the total nonhome wealth of a father. If a millionaire father had a home worth $100,000 his ratio would be 0.1; a father with smaller resources other than his home would have a high, positive ratio. Consider some hypothetical cases, estimated with their equation: Son's 1910 Occupation = 2.966 + 0.32 (Father's Occupation) + 0.0089 (Father's Wealth) − 0.958 (Father's Home Ownership: Ratio).

RATIO OF HOME VALUE TO NONHOME WEALTH

Value of home (in dollars)	Value of nonhome wealth (in dollars)	Ratio
0	0	0.00
0	100	0.00
100	20	5.00
100	100	1.00
150	200	0.75
200	300	0.66
250	400	0.625
300	800	0.375
10,000	1,000,000	0.01

These calculations suggest that the ratio variable that Edel, Sclar, and Luria estimated probably varies inversely to a family's wealth, assuming that the fathers in the analysis all owned homes. Therefore the negative sign of the coefficient shows that the father's home ownership/wealth ratio contributes in a substantively *positive* sense to the son's success. Wealthier families have children who are ultimately wealthier, including in real property, than do poorer ones. The rich, in other words, get richer. This is not terribly surprising, but considerably weakens the argument pursued so avidly by Edel, Sclar, and Luria, that home ownership neither reflects nor contributes to wealth accumulation. However, as the present chapter argues, even the relationship of home ownership is not as important as the notion that through real property taxes, home ownership ties ordinary citizens to their local government in a direct and significant way.

7. Chilton Williamson, *American Suffrage: From Property to Democracy, 1760–1860* (Princeton: Princeton University Press, 1960), esp. 219–221.

8. James Ford, "Introduction," in Blanche Halbert, ed., *The Better Homes Manual* (Chicago: University of Chicago Press, 1931), ix-x; Herbert Hoover, "Home Ownership," in Halbert, *The Better Homes Manual*, 6–7.

9. "Beverly High Juniors Win Bonds for Property Essays," *Los Angeles Times* (12 May 1985), Part VIII, 18.

10. For an important analysis of the urban house, see Robert G. Barrows, "Beyond the Tenement: Patterns of American Urban Housing, 1870–1930," *Journal of Urban History* 9 (1983), 395–420. Jules Tygiel, "Housing in Late Nineteenth Century America: Suggestions for Research," *Historical Methods* 12 (Spring 1979), 84–97. Sam B. Warner, Jr., *Streetcar Suburbs: The Process of Growth in Boston* (Cambridge, Mass.: MIT Press, 1962); Carolyn T. Kirk and Gordon W. Kirk, "The Impact of the City on Home Ownership: A Comparison of Immigrants and Native Whites at the Turn of the Century," *Journal of Urban History* VII (August 1981), 471–498, all provide an excellent introduction to urban housing. For a detailed discussion of home ownership mechanisms, see Howard P. Chudacoff, *Mobile Americans: Residential and Social Mobility in Omaha, 1880–1920* (New York: Oxford University Press, 1972), 111–129; and on Hamilton, Ontario and Buffalo, New York, see Michael B. Katz, Michael J. Doucet, and Mark J. Stern, *The Social Organization of Early Industrial Capitalism* (Cambridge, Mass.: Harvard University Press, 1982), 131–157.

11. For the life course perspective, see John Demos and Sarane S. Boocock, eds., *Turning Points, Historical and Sociological Essays on the Family* (Chicago: University of Chicago Press, 1978). In the sociological literature, the word has become one: "lifecourse." For an example of this concept applied to the analysis of black suburbanization prospects, see William H. Frey, "Lifecourse Migration of Metropolitan Whites and Blacks and the Strength of Demographic Change in Large Central Cities," *American Sociological Review* 49 (December 1984), 803–827: white suburbs of the post–World War II era absorbed a demographic cohort which has caused them in the 1980s to become filled with an aging population, while forced black migration has kept central cities more demographically mixed. A reduction in legal discrimination will not bring about quick changes, because of the relationship of migration to life course for the two demographically and geographically different groups.

12. John Modell and Tamara Haraven, "Urbanization and the Malleable

Household: An Examination of Boarding and Lodging in American Families," in Haraven, ed., *Family and Kin in Urban Communities, 1700–1930* (New York: New Viewpoints, 1977), 163–186. S. J. Kleinberg, "The Systematic Study of Urban Women," *Historical Methods* 9 (December 1975), 14–25, and Kleinberg, "Technology's Stepdaughters: The Impact of Industrialization Upon Working Class Women, Pittsburgh, 1865–1890" (Ph. D. diss., University of Pittsburgh, 1973), 94–103.

13. *Statistical Abstract of the United States; Historical Statistics 1982–1983*, 19, 43.
14. Oscar Handlin, *The Uprooted* (Boston: Little, Brown, 1952).
15. Thernstrom, *The Other Bostonians*, 15–16. Peter R. Knights, "The Contours of Nineteenth Century Lives: Lessons from a Study of Internal Migration Based on Boston" (paper presented at the Social Science History Association, Nashville, Tenn., 24 October 1981); R. M. Pritchard, *Housing and the Spatial Structure of the City* (Cambridge: Cambridge University Press, 1976). See also Charles Stephenson, "Tracing Those Who Left: Mobility Studies and the Soundex Indexes to the U.S. Census," *Journal of Urban History* I (1974), 73–84. On Omaha voting and mobility, see Chudacoff, *Mobile Americans*, 111–129.
16. Robert G. Barrows, " 'Hurrying Hoosiers' and the American Pattern: Geographic Mobility in Urban North America," *Social Science History* 5 (Spring 1981), 197–222; Michael Katz, Michael Doucet, and Mark Stern, "Migration and Social Order in Erie County, New York: 1855," *Journal of Interdisciplinary History* VIII (1978), 669–701, and Katz, Doucet, and Stern, "Population Persistence and Early Industrialization in a Canadian City: Hamilton, Ontario, 1851–1871," *Social Science History* II (1978), 208–229; and Michael Katz, "Social Class in North American Urban History," *Journal of Interdisciplinary History* XI (Spring 1981), 579–605. For the most extensive consideration of mobility, see Katz, Doucet, and Stern, *The Social Organization*, 102–130. For England, the evidence is that home owners stayed put; of course, they were a tiny fraction of the population. See Richard Dennis, *English Industrial Cities of the Nineteenth Century: A Social Geography* (Cambridge: Cambridge University Press, 1984), 260.
17. Doucet and Weaver, "The North American Shelter Business."

NUMBER OF REALTORS, 1900–1983

Year	Realtors (as percentage of employed persons)	Realtors (per 1000 owned homes)
1900	0.12	10
1910	0.21	15
1920	0.21	21
1930	0.31	14
1940	0.23	10
1950	0.24	7
1960	0.29	7
1970	0.33	7
1972	0.43	10.3[a]
1981	0.56	13.0
1983	0.56	13.1

[a]Number of owned homes interpolated.
SOURCE: Realtors: Bureau of the Census, *Historical Statistics of the United States, Colonial Times to 1970* (Washington, D.C.: Government Printing Office, 1975), 140, 142; Bureau of the Census, *Statistical Abstract of the United States, 1982–1983* (Washington, D.C.: Government Printing Office, 1982), 388; Bureau of the Census, *Statistical Abstract of the United States, 1985* (Washington, D.C.: Government Printing Office, 1984), 402. Homes owned: Bureau of the Census, *Historical Statistics of the United States, Colonial Times to 1970* (Washington, D.C.: Government Printing Office, 1975), 646–648; Bureau of the Census, *Statistical Abstract of the United States, 1982–1983* (Washington, D.C.: Government Printing Office, 1982), 757; Bureau of the Census, *Statistical Abstract of the United States, 1985* (Washington, D.C.: Government Printing Office, 1984), 731.

The regression relating owners to realtors is limited by a small period of observations: 1900 to 1975.

Dependent Variable: Realtors

Variable	Coefficient	(SEE)	$T(DF = 5)$	Prob.	Partial R^2
Owners	0.0191	(0.0044)	4.336	0.00746	0.7899
Urban old	−0.0154	(0.0050)	−3.067	0.02788	0.6529
Constant	59.1326				

Adj. R^2 = 0.7060; R^2 = 0.7900; F Ratio = 9.405; Prob. = 0.0202

SOURCE: See note 19. Realtors, *Historical Statistics*, 140, 142; *Statistical Abstract of the United States*, 388.

18. See Thomas J. Archdeacon, *New York City, 1664–1710: Conquest and Change* (Ithaca, N.Y.: Cornell University Press, 1976), my figures estimated from the data on 44, 94; Gary B. Nash, *The Urban Crucible: Social Change, Political Consciousness, and the Origins of the American Revolution* (Cambridge, Mass.: Harvard University Press, 1979), 62; G. B. Warden, "The Distribution of Property in Boston, 1692–1775," *Perspectives in American History* 10 (1976), 81–130;

Stephanie G. Wolf, *Urban Village: Population, Community, and Family Structure in Germantown, Pennsylvania, 1683–1800* (Princeton: Princeton University Press, 1976), 86–87. Bruce Wilkenfield, "The Social and Economic Structure of New York City, 1695–1795" (Ph. D. diss., Columbia University, 1973) has data on ownership among taxpayers which establishes a declining proportion of ownership throughout the eighteenth century; these are suggestive but not definitive. See Betsy Blackmar, "Re-walking the 'Walking City': Housing and Property Relations in New York City, 1780–1840," *Radical History Review* 21 (Fall 1979), 131–148, for further speculations on housing and the meaning of ownership.

19. The scattered mid-nineteenth-century data come from Katz, Doucet, and Stern, *The Social Organization*, 131–157; Massachusetts Bureau of Labor Statistics, *Seventh Annual Report*, Public Document 31 (Boston, 1876), xii, cited by Katz, Doucet, and Stern, 133; David Goldfield, *Urban Growth in the Age of Sectionalism: Virginia, 1847–1861* (Baton Rouge: Louisiana State University Press, 1977), 62–63; Robert A. Burchell, *The San Francisco Irish, 1848–1880* (Berkeley, Los Angeles, London: University of California Press, 1980), 62. Katz, Doucet, and Stern, and Edel, Sclar, and Luria, all try to account for the mid-nineteenth-century phenomenon of relatively well-off middle-class people renting while manual laborers owned. It may be that home owning has had very different economic implications in different eras.

Other nonfarm home ownership rates include: Robert Doherty, *Society and Power: Five New England Towns, 1800–1860* (Amherst: University of Massachusetts Press, 1977), 28: Worcester, 1850, from 16% poorest ward to 32% "some other parts"; Lee Soltow, *Men and Wealth in the United States, 1850–1870* (New Haven: Yale University Press, 1975): free adult males owning real property, all of the U.S., nonfarm = 26%, 1850 (p. 41). Adult white males owning real property, 1860, 43%. Nonfarm units occupied by owners, 1870, 38% (p. 50).

PERCENT OWNING HOMES (FARM AND NONFARM)

Age	1860	1870
under 35	27%	22%
35–44	53%	47%
45–54	64%	56%
55–64	68%	62%
65 +	61%	60%

In regressions based on percent owning homes and age as well as the log of age, the following coefficients are obtained. The furniture workers sample reported in Roger L. Ransom and Richard Sutch, "The Life-Cycle Transition: A Preliminary Report on Wealth-Holding in America," paper presented at California Conference on Economic

History, Laguna Beach, Cal., May 2–4, 1986, is twice as steep as that of the Soltow estimates, reflecting the relatively high income of the skilled workers. But the important thing is that both give nineteenth-century evidence on age and home owning: the range suggested is that for every year added, between 0.6 and 1.6 percent more of all nonfarm wealth groups together owned homes.

COEFFICIENTS

	Soltow 1860	Soltow 1870	Ransom 1890
Raw	0.8 (ns)	0.6	1.7
Log	42.5	12.2	61.9

(all with probabilities of 0.05 or greater)

Another estimate of the relationship of the country's changing age to its number of home owners, is simply to regress percent of homes owned on median age, hardly a subtle technique, for it ignores the peculiar properties of a dependent variable that can only range from 0 to 100 and an independent variable with similar properties. However, the estimate at least allows us to see in a crude way which decades were high, which low in home ownership.

HOME OWNERSHIP AND MEDIAN AGE

Dependent Variable: % Owned

Variable	Coefficient	(SEE)	T(DF = 9)	Prob.
Med. age	2.3560	0.4498	5.237	0.00054
Constant	−17.1509			

R^2 = 0.7530; F Ratio = 27.431; Prob. = 0.00054

Year	Observed	Calculated	Residual	Standardized residuals		
				−2.0	0	2.0
1850	26.0	28.791	−2.7905	*		
1870	38.0	31.382	6.6179			*
1890	36.9	35.858	1.0416		*	
1900	36.5	37.979	−1.4788	*		
1910	38.4	40.570	−2.1704	*		
1920	40.9	43.162	−2.2619	*		
1930	46.0	46.225	−0.2247		*	
1940	41.1	52.350	−11.2502 *			
1950	53.4	55.413	−2.0130	*		
1960	61.0	54.235	6.7650		*	
1970	62.0	54.235	7.7650			*

The message: the Depression should have had 10% higher home ownership, while the 1870s seem a little prosperous.

.0. The 1890–1970 data are from *Historical Statistics*, 646. Post-1975 data, from *Statistical Abstract of the United States, 1982–1983*, 25, 757. For occupation, ethnicity, and home ownership see Katz, "Social Class," and Kirk and Kirk, "Impact of the City on Home Ownership." Katz speculates that the lack of middle-class home ownership shows a class interest in other forms of capital investment. The Kirks, on the other hand, show that age accounts for the apparently unusual high immigrant ownership levels, a result similar to mine.

The purpose of discussing home ownership in this chapter emphasizes its consequences for taxation and local expenditures. The relationship to overall wealth holding and well-being is a separate and quite different topic. The apparently high proportion of colonial home owning, its dip to maybe 30% in the mid-nineteenth century, and its rise to over 60% in the 1970s is not to be taken as a direct index to wealth.

21.   STEPWISE REGRESSION, WITH URBAN POPULATION INCLUDED AT
            FIRST STEP, REJECTED AT FOURTH

Dependent Variable: Owners

Variable	Coefficient	(SEE)	F(1,10)	Prob.	Partial R²
Debt	0.0211	0.0036	34.141	0.00016	0.7735
Old	0.7156	0.0885	65.451	0.00001	0.8675

Constant = −1381.6493; Adj. R^2 = 0.893; Durbin-Watson Test = 2.2995

Variables not in equation:

Name	Partial R²	Tolerance	F to enter	Prob.
Urpb pop	0.0024	0.0598	0.022	0.8866
Middle	0.1208	0.4818	1.237	0.2949
Young	0.0779	0.2678	0.760	0.4060

Full regression
Dependent Variable: Owned

Variable	Coefficient	(SEE)	T(DF=7)	Prob.	Partial R²
Year	−29.4761	19.4171	−1.518	0.17279	0.2477
Debt	0.0349	0.0081	4.289	0.00362	0.7243
Old	1.1765	0.1923	6.119	0.00048	0.8425
Middle	−0.4347	0.1738	−2.501	0.04094	0.4719
Young	−0.3404	0.1477	−2.305	0.05462	0.4314

Constant = 55340.5726; Adj. R^2 = 0.926; R^2 = 0.957;
Durbin-Watson Test = 2.3491; F Ratio = 31.230; Prob. = 0.00012

All variables in thousands, first differences, with untransformed numbers. Urban and rural populations (and for 1945, age groups) for 1975–1978 linearly interpolated. Age groupings: Young = 0–14; Middle = 15–34; Old = 35 +. Age groupings for urban population as used in regression estimated by multiplying the number in age group by the urban proportion of total population. Owned is owned homes in thousands; Debt is all borrowing for homes, in $ millions. Urb pop is population in cities, in thousands.

SOURCE: Pre-1975: Bureau of the Census, *Historical Statistics of the United States, Colonial Times to 1970* (Washington, D.C.: Government Printing Office, 1975), 646–648. Post-1975, *Statistical Abstract of the United States: National Data Book and Guide to Sources, 1982–83* (Washington, D.C.: Government Printing Office, 1982), 25, 388, 757.

22. Franklin Sanborn, "Cooperative Banking in the U.S. (1873–1898)," *Journal of Social Science* 36 (December 1898), 128–133, on the reformist movement to get the poor access to banks, appends a talk by a Mr. Haskins of Poughkeepsie, from which the quotations are taken.

For a suggestive use of housing information, see Richard K. Lieberman, "A Measure for the Quality of Life: Housing," *Historical Methods* 11 (Summer 1978), 129–134.

23. Ransom and Sutch, "The Life-Cycle Transition."

24. Allen H. Spear, *Black Chicago: The Making of a Negro Ghetto, 1890–1920* (Chicago: University of Chicago Press, 1967), reprinted in Richard J. Meister, *The Black Ghetto: Promised Land or Colony?* (Boston: Heath, 1972), 35. Lawrence B. De Graff, "The City of Black Angeles: Emergence of the Los Angeles Ghetto, 1890–1930," *Pacific Historical Review* XXXIX (August 1970), 323–352, esp. 351–352, shows that Los Angeles by the 1920s, in spite of racial discrimination, offered blacks a better chance at home ownership than other cities with large black populations. Over one-third owned homes, as opposed to 10% in Chicago and 15% in Detroit. For racial covenants, see Clement E. Vose, *Caucasians Only: The Supreme Court, the NAACP, and Restrictive Covenant Cases* (Berkeley: University of California Press, 1959). A comprehensive view of housing discrimination which places it in the larger and more complex topic of zoning and planning is in Marc A. Weiss, *The Rise of the Community Builders: American Real Estate Developers, Urban Planners, and the Creation of Modern Residential Subdivisions* (New York: Columbia University Press, 1987), esp. chap. 6.

25. *Statistical Abstract of the United States, 1982–1983*, 757. By 1980, the percentage of black households with both spouses present had declined to 38%, contrasted to 62% for whites (45). Whatever else this means, it suggests that relative earning power by family was substantially less for blacks.

26. Jackson, *Crabgrass Frontier*, esp. 190–218.

27. *The Bohemian Flats*, Compiled by the Workers of the Writer's Program of the Works Project Administration (St. Paul: Minnesota Historical Society Press, 1986); Olivier Zunz, *The Changing Face of Inequality: Urbanization, Industrial Development, and Immigrants in Detroit, 1880–1920* (Chicago: University of Chicago Press, 1982); Herbert J. Gans, *The Urban Villagers: Group and Class in the Life of Italian-Americans* (New York: Free Press, 1962); David Ward, *Cities and Immigrants: A Geography of Change in Nineteenth-Century America* (New York: Oxford University Press, 1971); David Ward and John P. Radford, *North American Cities in the Victorian Age: Two Essays* (Norwich, Conn.: Geo Books, 1983); Howard P. Chudacoff, *The Evolution of American Urban Society*, 2d ed. (Englewood Cliffs, N.J.: Prentice-Hall, 1981); Kathleen N. Conzen, *Immigrant Milwaukee, 1836–1860: Accommodation and Community in a Frontier City* (Cambridge, Mass.: Harvard University Press, 1976); John Bodnar, *The Transplanted: A History of Immigrants in Urban America* (Bloomington: Indiana University Press, 1985); Rudolph J. Vecoli, "The Contadini in Chicago," *Journal of American History* (December 1964), 404–417.

9 The Active City, 1870–1980

1. Adna F. Weber, *The Growth of Cities in the Nineteenth Century: A Study in Statistics*, Columbia University Studies in History, Economics, and Public Law (New York: Macmillan, 1899), 427, 432. Rhys Isaac, *The Transformation of Virginia, 1740–1790* (Chapel Hill: University of North Carolina Press, 1982), 346, suggests a similar notion might inform the whole history of Anglo-America in the "rise of impersonal contexts of interaction." Max Weber, *The City*, Don Martindale and Gertrud Neuwirth, trans. and eds. (New York: Free Press, 1966); Georg Simmel, *The Sociology of Georg Simmel*, Kurt H. Wolff, trans. and ed. (London: The Free Press of Glencoe, 1950).

2. Frederick C. Howe, *The Modern City and Its Problems* (New York: Charles Scribner, 1915), 252; Jonathan Prude, *The Coming of Industrial Order: Town and Factory Life in Rural Massachusetts, 1810–1860* (New York: Cambridge University Press, 1983), 241–244. Morton Keller, *Affairs of State: Public Life in Late Nineteenth Century America* (Cambridge, Mass.: Harvard University Press, 1977) develops the idea of increased rationalization, decreased individual responsiveness, on the national level. But see also the review of Keller by Rowland Berthoff, *Journal of American History* 64 (March 1978), 1140–1142.

3. There is an enormous and rich literature on the history of welfare for the poor. For an introduction see James Leiby, *A History of Social Welfare and Social Work in the United States* (New York: Columbia University Press, 1978); Michael B. Katz, *Poverty and Policy in American History* (New York: Academic Press, 1983) and Katz, *In the Shadow of the Poorhouse* (New York: Basic Books, 1986); Paul Boyer, *Urban Masses and Moral Order in America, 1820–1920* (Cambridge, Mass.: Harvard University Press, 1978), and the continuing bibliography in the Social Welfare History Group *Newsletter*.

4. M. Craig Brown and Charles N. Halaby, "Machine Politics in America, 1870–1945," *Journal of Interdisciplinary History* 17 (Winter 1987), 587–612, and Brown and Halaby, "Bosses, Reform, and the Socioeconomic Bases of Urban Expenditure, 1890–1940," in Terrence J. McDonald and Sally Ward, eds., *The Politics of Urban Fiscal Policy* (Beverly Hills: Sage Press, 1984), 69–100. Robert K. Merton, *Social Theory and Social Structure* (Glencoe, N.Y.: Free Press, 1949). Terrence J. McDonald, "Comment," *Journal of Urban History* 8 (August 1984), 454–462. Brown and Halaby point out that possibly the least-known bosses, Tom Dennison of Omaha (1906–1933) and George Alderidge of Rochester (1899–1921), had the longest-lived regimes. Both men and cities contradict the stereotypical urban boss's image.

5. William L. Riordan, *Plunkitt of Tammany Hall: A Series of Very Plain Talks on Very Practical Politics, Delivered by Ex-Senator George Washington Plunkitt, The Tammany Philosopher, From His Rostrum—The New York County Court-House Bootblack Strand—and Recorded by William L. Riordan* (New York: McClure, 1905).

This lively and fascinating book has been taken at face value by historians for decades; I am dubious about its authenticity, given its broad humor and the fact that it was published by a reformist publisher. See note 7 below.

6. Melvin G. Holli, "Samuel H. Ashbridge," in Holli and Peter d'A. Jones, eds., *Biographical Dictionary of American Mayors, 1820–1980: Big City Mayors* (Westport, Conn.: Greenwood Press, 1981), 10: from Lincoln Steffens, "Philadelphia: Corrupt and Contented," *McClure's Magazine* 21 (July 1903), reprinted in Steffens, *The Shame of the Cities* (New York: Hill and Wang, 1957), quotation on 153.

7. Richard J. Daley, *Quotations from Mayor Daley*, compiled by Peter Yessne (New York: G. P. Putnam, 1969); clearly modeled on Riordan, this book takes self-damning quotations attributed to Daley by the press and arranges them topically. Both preserve the speakers' bad grammar. Compared to Plunkitt, Daley was a model of caution in his public statements on graft.

8. John M. Alswang, *Bosses, Machines, and Urban Voters: An American Symbiosis* (Port Washington, N.Y.: Kennikat Press, 1977), 150, argues, with no evidence at all, that urban political machines from Tweed to Daley "existed because of the very large numbers of dependent or semidependent people who have been found in the modern American city, and because it has been better able to respond quickly and directly to their needs." Alswang implicitly claims that the efficient social welfare services of the political machine contrast with the inefficient welfare systems of nonmachine-governed cities.

9. Seth M. Scheiner, "Commission Government in the Progressive Era: The New Brunswick, New Jersey, Example," *Journal of Urban History* 12 (February 1986), 157–180. See also Bradley R. Rice, *Progressive Cities: The Commission Government Movement in America, 1901–1920* (Austin: University of Texas Press, 1977).

Scheiner's data are all in percentages, the basis and limitation of the following reanalysis. His sums indicate that the wards were relatively evenly divided in their voting populations, but it is impossible to derive the actual numbers to use. There are two pairs of highly intercorrelated variables, and I have used only one of each pair in the regressions. Thus Natives may be read as the reciprocal of Foreign, Professional as the reciprocal of Blue Collar. The dependent variables are two votes on whether or not to create a nonpartisan commission form of government in New Brunswick, one in 1913 and one in 1915. The cases are the nineteen wards. Independent variables are each ward's proportion of Democrats (the reciprocal of Republicans), Factory Workers, Retail Workers, Professionals, and Native Borns.

REGRESSION ANALYSIS

Dependent Variable: 1913 Vote

Variable	Coefficient	(SEE)	T(DF = 11)	Partial R²
Democrat	−0.7440	0.2401	−3.098	0.4660
Factory	0.0683	0.3101	0.220	0.0044
Blue Collar	−0.2721	0.4296	−0.633	0.0352
Retail	−0.1986	0.4444	−0.447	0.0178
Professional	0.5129	0.6647	0.772	0.0513
Natives	0.3718	1.0398	0.358	0.0115
Foreign	0.0090	1.0743	0.008	0.0000

Constant = 77.9970; Adj. R² = 0.7840

Dependent Variable: 1915 Vote

Variable	Coefficient	(SEE)	T(DF = 11)	Partial R²
Democrat	−0.0492	0.3284	−0.150	0.0020
Factory	0.5949	0.4240	1.403	0.1518
Blue Collar	−0.7282	0.5875	−1.239	0.1225
Retail	0.2633	0.6077	0.433	0.0168
Professional	0.4214	0.9090	0.464	0.0192
Natives	0.7563	1.4220	0.532	0.0251
Foreign	0.4142	1.4692	0.282	0.0072

Constant = 16.8456; Adj. R² = 0.4207

Dependent Variable: Change from 1913 to 1915 Vote

Variable	Coefficient	(SEE)	T(DF = 11)	Partial R²
Democrat	0.6948	0.3257	2.133	0.2926
Factory	0.5267	0.4205	1.252	0.1248
Blue Collar	−0.4561	0.5827	−0.783	0.0528
Retail	0.4619	0.6027	0.766	0.0507
Professional	−0.0916	0.9016	−0.102	0.0009
Natives	0.3845	1.4103	0.273	0.0067
Foreign	0.4052	1.4572	0.278	0.0070

Constant = −61.1514; Adj. R² = 0.4684

10. Quotation from James N. Primm, *Economic Policy in the Develop-*

ment of a Western State, Missouri, 1820–1860 (Cambridge, Mass.: Harvard University Press, 1954), 35. For the classic exposition of the law as an agent of economic change, see J. Willard Hurst, *Law and the Conditions of Freedom in the Nineteenth Century United States* (Madison: University of Wisconsin Press, 1956) and Hurst, *Law and Economic Growth: The Legal history of the Wisconsin Lumber Industry* (Cambridge, Mass.: Harvard University Press, 1964). John A. Fairlie, "Municipal Corporations in the Colonies," *Essays in Municipal Administration* (New York: Macmillan, 1910), 48–94. See the several works by Hendrik A. Hertog: *The Properties of the Corporation: New York City and its Law, 1730 to 1870* (Chapel Hill: University of North Carolina Press, 1983); "Property as Government in Eighteenth Century America: The Case of New York City," *Journal of Legal Studies* 10 (1981), 305–348; "Because All the World Was Not New York City: Governance, Property Rights, and the State in the Changing Definition of a Corporation, 1730–1860," *Buffalo Law Review* 29 (1979), 91–109; "The Public Law of a County Court: Judicial Government in Eighteenth Century Massachusetts," *American Journal of Legal History* 20 (1976), 282–329. For a history of city corporations which focuses on the issues of public v. private, see Gerald Frug, "The City as a Legal Concept," *Harvard Law Review* 99 (1980), 1059–1154. Morton J. Horowitz, "*Santa Clara* Revisited: The Development of Corporate Theory," *West Virginia Law Review* 88 (Winter 1985–1986), 173–224, argues for a late nineteenth-century redefinition of corporations as persons.

11. Eric H. Monkkonen, "*Bank of August v. Earle*: Corporate Growth v. States' Rights," *The Alabama Historical Quarterly* 34 (Summer 1972), 113–130. R. Kent Newmeyer, *The Supreme Court under Marshall and Taney* (New York: Crowell, 1968), 72–81. According to Newmeyer, through the early court decisions on corporations, "the legal foundation was being laid for the promotional, non-regulatory state of post-Civil War America" (81).

12. Paul Studenski and Herman E. Kroos, *Financial history of the United States: Fiscal, Monetary, Banking, and Tariff, Including Financial, Administrative, State, and Local Finance*, 2d ed., (New York: McGraw-Hill, 1963), 59–60. They cite Edward D. Durand, *The Finances of the City of New York* (New York: Macmillan, 1898), 30.

13. On the conservatism of local government, see Studenski and Kroos, *Financial History*, 131–132. Note that Prude, *Coming of Industrial Order*, 243, mentions parenthetically how as Oxford began to provide urban services within its "expanded conception of the public good," its also went into debt. I argue that it was precisely this ability and activity that made possible a new conception of public good, of the service city.

14. Seth Low, former mayor of Brooklyn, contributed a chapter to James Bryce's monumental study, *The American Commonwealth* (New York: Macmillan, 1891) rev. 3d ed., 1917, vol. 1, 624–625, where he stated that the "motive" to achieve incorporated city status has been

"to make available the credit of the community in order to provide adequately for its own growth."

15. David H. Pinckney, *Napoleon III and the Rebuilding of Paris* (Princeton: Princeton University Press, 1958).

16. On general incorporation, see Lawrence M. Friedman, *A History of American Law* (New York: Simon and Schuster, 1973), 447. See also, Thomas K. McCraw, ed., *Regulation in Perspective: Historical Essays* (Cambridge, Mass.: Harvard University Press, 1981), and idem, *Prophets of Regulation: Charles Francis Adams, Louis D. Brandeis, James M. Landis, Alfred E. Kahn* (Cambridge, Mass.: Harvard University Press, 1984).

17. Jerome M. Clubb and Howard W. Allen, "Collective Biography and the Progressive Movement: The 'Status Revolution' Revisited," *Social Science History* 1 (Summer 1977), 518–534.

18. David C. Hammack, *Power and Society: Greater New York at the Turn of the Century*, (New York: Russell Sage Foundation, 1982), 320–326; Estelle F. Feinstein, *Stamford in the Gilded Age: The Political Life of a Connecticut Town, 1868–1893* (Stamford, Conn.: Stamford Historical Society, 1973); Carl V. Harris, *Political Power in Birmingham, 1871–1921* (Knoxville: University of Tennessee Press, 1977); Harold L. Platt, *City Building in the New South: The Growth of Public Services in Houston, Texas, 1830–1915* (Philadelphia: Temple University Press, 1983). Hammack's book contains a fine-grained analysis of New York City politics and decision making, while his notes constitute an excellent bibliography of the sociological, historical, and political science literature constituting the pluralist school of political analysis.

19. Hammack, *Power and Society*, 320, 322, 323, 322–326.

20. Ibid., 309.

21. Paul F. Lazersfeld, "The Logical and Methodological Foundations of Latent Structure Analysis," in Samuel A. Stouffer, ed., *Measurement and Prediction* (Princeton: Princeton University Press, 1950). For an introduction to the complex ideas implied, see Herbert A. Simon, *Administrative Behavior: A Study of Decision-Making Processes in Administrative Organization* (New York: Free Press, 1976), "On the Concept of Organizational Goal," 257–278.

22. John R. Stilgoe, *Metropolitan Corridor: Railroads and the American Scene* (New Haven: Yale University Press, 1983). Data on railroads and towns greater than 10,000 calculated from Bureau of the Census Office, *Report on the Social Statistics of Cities . . . 1890* (Washington, D.C.: Government Printing Office, 1895), table 74, 133–137.

23. For the role of the private builder in forcing on cities planning codes and zoning, see Marc A. Weiss, *The Rise of the Community Builders: American Real Estate Developers, Urban Planners, and the Creation of Modern Residential Subdivisions* (New York: Columbia University Press, 1987). Weiss compares the real estate industry's creation of planning to the participation of other industries in the creation of regulatory law.

24. Maris A. Vinovskis, *The Origins of Public High Schools: A Reexamination of the Beverly High School Controversy* (Madison: University of Wisconsin Press, 1985) reanalyzes the thesis proposed by Michael B. Katz, *The Irony of Early School Reform: Educational Innovation in Mid-Nineteenth Century Massachusetts* (Cambridge, Mass.: Harvard University Press, 1968), who claimed that the working class of Beverly opposed high schools. Diane Ravitch, *The Revisionists Revisited: A Critique of the Radical Attack on the Schools* (New York: Basic Books, 1978), and Michael B. Katz, *Class, Bureaucracy, and Schools: The Illusion of Educational Change in America* (New York: Praeger, 1971); David B. Tyack, *The One Best System: A History of American Urban Education* (Cambridge, Mass.: Harvard University Press, 1974). Quotation from Carl F. Kaestle and Maris A. Vinovskis, *Education and Social Change in Nineteenth-Century Massachusetts* (New York: Cambridge University Press, 1980), 140. See their separate analysis of two places, which highlights the differences between an aggressive small city, lively Lynn, and a rural area, boring Boxford, 140–184.

25. Roger Lane, *Violent Death in the City: Suicide, Accident and Murder in Nineteenth-Century Philadelphia* (Cambridge, Mass.: Harvard University Press, 1979). Finally, when schooling is considered as investment in human capital, the urban contribution to the overall national investment far exceed the rural contribution, once again highlighting the urban promotion of the economic transformation of the nineteenth century. Kaestle and Vinovskis, *Education and Social Change*, 194, shows how rural per capita schooling expenditures were only about half those of small cities, one-fourth those of a metropolis, even though schooling expenditures took up a larger share of the rural budget.

26. For a detailed set of analyses of the relationship of tramping to economic growth, see the articles in Eric H. Monkkonen, ed., *Walking to Work: Tramps in America, 1790–1935* (Lincoln: University of Nebraska Press, 1984).

27. A list of pre-1935 urban technical and reform journals includes the following, listed by title, founding organization, date of journal's founding, and other titles:

   State organizations: *The Municipality: Devoted to the Interests of Local Government* (League of Wisconsin Municipalities, 1900); *Municipal Law Reporter* (1909) followed by *The Borough Bulletin* (1917) Penn.; followed by *Pennsylvanian: The Magazine of Local Governments, Incorporating The Authority, The Hub, The Township Commissioner, The Borough Bulletin, Pennsylvania League of Cities, Assessors' Newsletter, Horizons*); *Kansas Municipalities: A Monthly Review of Municipal Progress and Problems* (League of Kansas Municipalities, 1914); *American Municipalities* (Iowa and Nebraska, pre-1914); *Texas Municipalities* (League of Texas Municipalities, 1914); *Minnesota Municipalities* (League of Minnesota Municipalities, 1916); *New Jersey Municipalities* (New Jersey State League of Municipalities, 1917); *Nebraska Municipal Review* (League of Nebraska Municipalities, 1917); *Illinois Municipal Review* (The Illinois Municipal League, 1922); *Virginia Municipal Review* (League of Virginia Municipalities, 1924); *Colorado Municipalities: The City Officials Magazine* "A Review of Civic Progress: Official Organ of The Colorado Municipal League" (1925); *Oklahoma Municipal Review* (The Oklahoma Municipal League, 1926); *Michigan Municipal Review* (League of Michigan Municipalities, 1928); *The Kentucky City* (The Kentucky Municipal League, 1930).

National organizations: *National Municipal Review*, succeeding *Proceedings of The . . . Conference for Good City Government And the . . . Annual Meeting of The National Municipal League* (Title Varies: *Proceedings of The National Conference For Good City Government*, Philadelphia, 1894); *City Government: A Monthly Magazine Devoted to The Practical Affairs of Municipalities* (Related to American Society of Municipal Improvements (?), 1896; originally may have been *Municipal Journal*; changed name to *Public Works*); *Municipal Affairs: A Quarterly Magazine Devoted to The Consideration of City Problems from the Standpoint of the Taxpayer and Citizen* (New York Reform Club, Committee On Municipal Administration, 1897); *League of American Municipalities* (1898); *The American City* (1909); *City Manager Bulletin*, succeeded by *Public Management* (City Managers Association, 1933); *The United States Municipal News* (American Municipal Association, and U. S. Conference of Mayors, 1934); succeeded by *The Mayor*, 1934–71; *Local Government Administration: An International Quarterly Review* (1935); *Legal Notes on Local Government* (Section of Municipal Lawyers of American Bar Association, 1936).

City engineering journals: *Plumber & Sanitary Engineer* (December 1877–November 1880); *Sanitary Engineer* (December 1880–October 1886); *Sanitary Engineer And Construction Record* (November 1886–October, 1887); *Engineering & Building Record and The Sanitary Engineer* (October 8, 1887–November 1890); *The Engineering Record, Building Record and Sanitary Engineer* (1890–1902); *Engineering News* (1902–1917); *Engineering News-Record* (1917). *Transactions of the American Society of Civil Engineers* (American Society of Civil Engineers, 1867).

28. John D. Buenker and Nicholas C. Burckel, *Progressive Reform: A Guide to Information Sources* (Detroit: Gale Research Co., 1980); Judith W. Leavitt, *The Healthiest City: Milwaukee and the Politics of Health Reform* (Princeton: Princeton University Press, 1982); Judith Rosenberg Raftery, "The Invention of Modern Urban Schooling: Los Angeles, 1885–1941," (Ph. D. diss., University of California, Los Angeles, 1984). For the fascinating story of school dental clinics and the surprising illustration of how their half-century existence was forgotten in the 1960s, see Steven L. Schlossman, JoAnne Brown, and Michael Sedlak, *The Public School in American Dentistry* (Santa

Monica, Calif.: Rand, 1986). On the professionalization of progressives, see Clarke A. Chambers, *Seedtime of Reform: American Social Service and Social Action, 1918–1933* (Minneapolis: University of Minnesota Press, 1963), and Allen F. Davis, *Spearheads for Reform: The Social Settlements and the Progressive Movement, 1890–1914* (New York: Oxford University Press, 1967).

29. For a discussion of "incremental" fiscal history, see McDonald and Ward, "Introduction," *The Politics of Urban Fiscal Policy*, 13–38.

30. Mark I. Gelfand, *A Nation of Cities: The Federal Government and Urban America, 1933–1965* (New York: Oxford University Press, 1975).

31. Frank Morn, *The Eye That Never Sleeps: A History of the Pinkerton National Detective Agency* (Bloomington: Indiana University Press, 1982); Eric H. Monkkonen, review of Morn in *American Historical Review* 88 (April 1983), 488; Rhodri Jeffreys-Jones, "Review Essay on U.S. Detectives," in *Journal of American Studies* 17 (August 1983), 265–274.

32. Alfred D. Chandler, Jr., *The Visible Hand: The Managerial Revolution in American Business* (Cambridge, Mass.: Harvard University Press, 1977), esp. 94–108.

33. For a discussion of the complex issues surrounding historical indicators of crime, see Eric H. Monkkonen, "The Quantitative Historical Study of Crime and Criminal Justice in the United States," in James Inciardi and Charles Faupel, eds., *History and Crime: Implications for Contemporary Criminal Justice Policy* (Beverly Hills: Sage Press, 1980), 53–73; Monkkonen, "Municipal Reports as an Indicator Source: The Nineteenth Century Police," *Historical Methods* 12 (Spring 1979), 57–65; and V. A. C. Gatrell, "The Decline of Theft and Violence in Victorian and Edwardian England," in Gatrell, B. Lenman and G. Parker, eds., *Crime and the Law: The Social History of Crime in Western Europe since 1500* (London: Europa, 1980), 238–370.

34. Douglas Greenberg, *Crime and Law Enforcement in the Colony of New York, 1691–1776* (Ithaca, N.Y.: Cornell University Press, 1976), 216, finds a rise in crimes of violence in the eighteenth century. In "Crime, Law Enforcement, and Social Control in Colonial America," *American Journal of Legal History* 26 (October 1982), 304, Greenberg claims that colonial offenses against morality declined in the eighteenth century. William E. Nelson, "Emerging Notions of Criminal Law in the Revolutionary Era," *New York University Law Review* 42 (May 1967), 450–482; Theodore N. Ferdinand, "Criminality, the Courts, and the Constabulary in Boston: 1702–1967," *Journal of Research in Crime and Delinquency* 17 (July 1980), 198–199, table 3, has good evidence that the apparent concern with crimes against morality in the colonial era is to a certain extent an artifact of the way in which researchers, particularly Nelson, have analyzed the data. By looking at the proportion of offenses, rather than the per capita or even absolute rates, the low amounts of property crime and crimes of violence make crimes against morals seem high. For Boston, be-

tween the year 1702 and the nineteenth century, all offenses had actually increased, including those against morality, except that the latter had increased less than others.

For rise in thefts of deception, see Eric H. Monkkonen, *The Dangerous Class: Crime and Poverty in Columbus, Ohio, 1860–1885* (Cambridge, Mass.: Harvard University Press, 1975), 35–39. John D. Hewitt and Dwight W. Hoover, "Local Modernization and Crime: The Effects of Modernization on Crime in Middletown, 1845–1910," *Law and Human Behavior* 6 (1982), 313–325, find no rise in thefts by deception for the period they analyze in Muncie. Evidence for decline in public disorder is analyzed in Monkkonen, "A Disorderly People? Urban Order in Nineteenth and Twentieth Century America," *Journal of American History* 68 (December 1981), 539–559; for comparable data on homicide, see Lane, *Violent Death in the City*.

35. Howard Zehr, "The Modernization of Crime in Germany and France, 1830–1913," *Journal of Social History* 8 (Summer 1975), 117–141; idem, *Crime and the Development of Modern Society: Patterns of Criminality in Nineteenth Century Germany and France* (London: Croom Helm, 1976); Vincent McHale and Eric A. Johnson, "Urbanization, Industrialization and Crime in Imperial Germany," *Social Science History* 1 (Fall 1976/Winter 1977), 45–78, 210–247; Abdul Q. Lodhi and Charles Tily, "Urbanization, Crime and Collective Violence in 19th-century France," *American Sociological Review* 37 (October 1972), 520–532.

36. Monkkonen, "A Disorderly People?"; Monkkonen, "Toward an Understanding of Urbanization: Drunk Arrests in Los Angeles," *Pacific Historical Review* L (May 1981), 234–244. This pattern did not hold true for St. Louis: see Eugene J. Watts, "Police Response to Crime and Disorder in Twentieth-Century St. Louis," *Journal of American History* 70 (September 1983), 340–358. Norbert Elias, *The Civilizing Process*, Edmond Jephcatt, trans. (New York: Urizen, 1978).

37. Lane, *Violent Death in the City*, shows that even though homicide rates declined in the late nineteenth and early twentieth century, the chances of being killed by a stranger or by a gun increased. Christopher Stone, "Vandalism: Property, Gentility, and the Rhetoric of Crime in New York City, 1890–1920," *Radical History Review* 26 (October 1982), 13–36, shows how the consciousness or concern—it is not clear which—about public destructiveness increased in New York.

38. T. D. Woolsey, "Nature and Sphere of Police Power," *Journal of Social Science* (1871), 111. Monkkonen, *The Dangerous Class*. Earliest British source in Oxford English Dictionary, 1859, citing Arthur Helps, *Friends in Council: A Series of Readings and Discourses Thereon*, Ser. II, vol. I, ii (London, 1859), 131. Clive Emsley, *Policing and Its Context, 1750–1870* (New York: Schocken, 1983), 87, identifies the earliest usage of the phrase by Henri Fregier, in France, as 1840. Thomas Duesterberg, "The Origins of Criminology in France: Penal Reform and Scientific Criminology in the Age of Revolution, 1789–

1840," 11–12, in John A. Conley, ed., *Theory and Research in Criminal Justice: Current Perspectives* (n.p.: Anderson, 1979), argues that Fregier's *Des Classes Dangereuses de la Population dans les Grandes Villes* (Paris: Bailliere, 1840) represented the position of liberal social economists, put forward to counter those who explained crime by examining the individual.

39. Thomas M. Pitkin, *The Black Hand: A Chapter in Ethnic Crime* (Totowa, N.J.: Rowman and Littlefield, 1977).

40. Henry George, *Social Problems* (Chicago, 1883), 317, cited by Weber, *The Growth of Cities*, 368, 407.

41. Monkkonen, *Police in Urban America, 1860–1920* (New York: Cambridge University Press, 1981), 109–128. James Q. Wilson in *Varieties of Police Behavior: The Management of Law and Order in Eight Communities* (Cambridge, Mass.: Harvard University Press, 1968) shows how some police departments have made their "catch-all" function into the main orientation of the department, in what Wilson terms a "service style."

42. For studies on trash and traffic, see Martin V. Melosi, *Garbage in the Cities: Refuse, Reform, and the Environment, 1880–1980* (College Station: Texas A & M Press, 1981), and John A. Gardiner, *Traffic and the Police: Variations in Law-Enforcement Policy* (Cambridge, Mass.: Harvard University Press, 1969).

43. Philip Abrams, *Historical Sociology* (West Compton House, England: Open Books, 1981).

44. Michel Foucault, *Discipline and Punish: The Birth of the Prison* (New York: Random House, 1977).

45. Douglas L. Jones, "The Strolling Poor: Transiency in Eighteenth Century Massachusetts," *Journal of Social History* 8 (Spring 1975), 36.

46. Richard Sennett, *The Uses of Disorder: Personal Identity and City Life* (New York: Vintage, 1970).

47. Richard Hofstadter and Michael Wallace, eds., *American Violence: A Documentary History* (New York: Alfred A. Knopf, 1970); Adrian Cook, *The Armies of the Streets: The New York City Draft Riots of 1863* (Lexington: Kentucky University Press, 1974); William M. Tuttle, Jr., *Race Riot: Chicago in the Red Summer of 1919* (New York: Atheneum, 1970).

48. Wilbur R. Miller, *Cops and Bobbies: Police Authority in New York and London, 1830–1870* (Chicago: University of Chicago Press, 1976), 153–154, has shown that ethnicity of New York City officers had little measurable relationship to the ethnicity of those whom they arrested. John C. Schneider, *Detroit and the Problem of Order, 1830–1880: A Geography of Crime, Riots, and Policing* (Lincoln: University of Nebraska Press, 1980), 138, discusses the lack of ethnic riots.

49. Bruce Laurie,"Fire Companies and Gangs in Southwark: The 1840s," in Allan F. Davis and Mark Haller, eds., *The Peoples of Philadelphia: A History of Ethnic Groups and Lower-Class Life, 1790–1840* (Philadelphia: Temple University Press, 1973), 71–87.

50. Four South Boston high school students visited Charlotte, North Car-

olina, to observe in person an example of successful crosstown busing to achieve integration, *New York Times* (24, October 1974), 36. See Jone Malloy *Southie Won't Go: A Teacher's Diary of the Desegregation of South Boston High School* (Urbana: University of Illinois Press, 1986).

51. On black mayors in the South, see the discussion by Edward F. Haas, "The Southern Metropolis, 1940–1976," in Blaine A. Brownell and David R. Goldfield, *The City in Southern History: The Growth of Urban Civilization in the South* (Port Washington, N.Y.: Kennikat, 1977), 185.

52. See Carl Abbott, *The New Urban America: Growth and Politics in Sunbelt Cities* (Chapel Hill: University of North Carolina Press, 1981), 3–10, for a historiographical analysis of the media phenomenon of the "sunbelt" mystique. For an excellent survey of the literature in addition to the phenomenon itself, see the introduction to Richard M. Bernard and Bradley R. Rice, *Sunbelt Cities: Politics and Growth since World War II* (Austin: University of Texas Press, 1983), 1–30. Kirkpatrick Sale, *Power Shift: The Rise of the Southern Rim and its Challenge to the Eastern Establishment* (New York: Random House, 1975).

53. Edwin D. Shurter, ed., *The Complete Orations and Speeches of Henry W. Grady* ([Austin?] Tex.: South-West, 1910): Grady's constant refrain was for the South to diversify and industrialize, to become like the manufacturing belt. An audience at the Dallas State Fair in 1887 heard him use Grand Rapids, Michigan, as a model for the South. Grand Rapids specialized in manufacturing furniture from nearby forest products; Grady argued that forested parts of the South could do the same, ignoring the obvious problems of transportation, population, and competing manufacturing enterprises (51). Presumably he would have been pleased with the belt of furniture manufacturing cities stretching along Interstate 85 from High Point to Thomasville in North Carolina, but disappointed that this enterprise has not diversified the regional economy to the extent he desired. See Arthur M. Schlesinger, *The Rise of the City, 1878–1898* (New York: Macmillan, 1933), 1–21, for a discussion of the city in the South.

54. Keay Davidson, "San Diego Loses to Austin in Luring High-Tech Firm," *Los Angeles Times* (18 May 1983), 1, 18. Also, in the *San Diego Union*, Fred Muir, "Hopes Fade for Research Firm Here" (17 May 1983), A-1,9; and Fred Muir, "Three Factors Cited in Loss of Big Research Center" (18 May 1983), A-1, 5; and editorial, "Lessons of Defeat" (13 May 1986), B-6. Also, Lawrence Ingrassia, "Four Cities Vie for High-Tech Joint Venture," *The Wall Street Journal* (12 May 1983), 35, 39; Robert S. Jones, "City Rejected for Research Center," *Atlanta Constitution* (18 May 1983), C-1,3; John Walsh, "Texans Woo and Whelm MCC," *Science*, 220 (3, June 1983), 1025; Joseph P. Kahn, "The Isosceles of Texas is Upon Us," *Inc.* 5 (October 1983), 155–158. For an advice-giving analysis of city/business partnerships, see Rich-

ard Erickson, "Trends for Economic Development," *The American City & County* 100 (October 1985), 50–54.

Epilogue: How Do We "Watch" Our Cities?

1. Adna F. Weber, *The Growth of Cities in the Nineteenth Century: A Study in Statistics* (New York: Macmillan, 1899). Frederick C. Howe, *The Modern City and Its Problems* (New York: Scribners, 1915). Howe also lists libraries, schools, and playgrounds as U.S. city achievements.
2. Eric H. Monkkonen, "The Sense of Crisis: A Historian's Point of View," in Mark Gottdiener, ed., *Cities in Stress: A New Look at the Urban Crisis* (Beverly Hills: Sage Press, 1986), 20–38.
3. For the pension problem, see Robert M. Fogelson, *Pensions, The Hidden Costs of Public Safety* (New York: Columbia University Press, 1984).
4. Weber, *Growth of Cities*, 474, 475. Historians have only begun to analyze the growth of the national government and the lessened visibility of local government: for a recent summary, see John J. Wallis, "Why 1933? the Origins and Timing of National Government Growth, 1933–1940," *Research in Economic History*, Suppl. 4, (Greenwich, Conn.: JAI Press, 1985), 1–51. For recent works that offer promising avenues to urban analysis, see Carl Abbott, *Urban America in the Modern Age: 1920 to the Present* (Chicago: Harlan Davidson, 1987); Kenneth Fox, *Metropolitan America: Urban Life and Urban Policy in the United States, 1940–1980* (London: Macmillan, 1985); Jon C. Teaford, *The Twentieth Century American City* (Baltimore: Johns Hopkins University Press, 1986); John Moellenkopf, *The Contested City* (Princeton: Princeton University Press, 1983); Ira Katznelson, *Urban Trenches: Urban Politics and the Patterning of Class in the United States* (Chicago: University of Chicago Press, 1981); Royce Hanson, *The Evolution of National Urban Policy, 1970–1980: Lessons from the Past* (Washington, D.C.: National Academy Press, 1982); Christopher B. Leinberger and Charles Lockwood, "How Business is Reshaping America," *The Atlantic Monthly* (October 1986), 43–52.
5. John Herbers, "Now Even the Suburbs Have Suburbs," *New York Times* (5 May 1985), 6E; John Herbers, "Many in Poll Prefer Small Towns," *New York Times* (24 March 1985), 28L.

Index

Active state, defined, 229
Aesthetics: Banham on, 12–13; Mumford on, 11–12
Age, and home ownership, 202
Agricultural History (journal), 27
Agriculture: colonial towns and, 60, 62; in nation-state, 36; small towns and, 219–220; southern, 128; urban revolution and, 33. *See also* Farmers
Airports, 159; city support of, 168
Air transport, 162
Alabama. *See* Birmingham; Mobile
American Commonwealth, The (Bryce), 1
Amy v. City of Watertown, 150
Anomie, 96
Apartments, 14, 188, 192
Architectural fallacy, 14
Architecture, 11–12, 14, 16
Arizona, 85, 86. *See also* Phoenix
Arts and Crafts movement, 11
Ashbridge, Samuel H., 210
Ashville, N.C., 3
Assessors, city, 139
Austin, Tex., 237
Automobiles, 164–165; city shape and, 159, 178; enthusiasm for, 165; Los Angeles and, 14, 163; Model T Ford, 175; perception of cities and, 159; pollution and, 181; registration data, 169, 174–175; residential mobility and, 177–178; roads and, 159, 160, 167, 168–169, 172, 174–176; in rural versus urban areas, 175; suburbs and, 177; urban sprawl and, 177; as villain, 159–160

Babbitt, George, 125
Baltimore, Md., 160
Banham, Reyner, 12–13
Bank of Augusta v. Earle (1839), 112, 136–137
Baumann, G., 150
Bellamy, Edward, 86
Berry, Brian, 44, 73
Better Homes Manual, The, 187
Betters, Paul, 20
Bicycles, 158, 165, 166, 167, 168, 172
Binford, Henry, 123
Biographical Dictionary of American Mayors, 1820 to 1980 (Holli and Jones, eds.), 123
Birmingham, Ala., 120
Birmingham, England, 52
Black Hand, 227–228
Blacks, 120; discrimination against, 202–203
Bogue, Allan, 127
Bonds, municipal. *See* Municipal bonds
Boosterism, 125–128, 142, 144,

Designer:	David Lunn
Compositor:	Auto-Graphics, Inc.
Text:	10 / 12 Trump Mediaeval
Display:	Trump Mediaeval
Printer:	Maple-Vail Book Mfg. Group
Binder:	Maple-Vail Book Mfg. Group

Politics / Government

- elite
- city vs. State, Fed. Gov.
- police vs. Neighborhood
-